The Psychology of Judicial Decision Making

American Psychology-Law Society Series

Series Editor
Ronald Roesch

Editorial Board
Gail S. Goodman
Thomas Grisso
Craig Haney
Kirk Heilbrun
John Monahan
Marlene Moretti
Edward P. Mulvey
J. Don Read
N. Dickon Reppucci
Gary L. Wells
Lawrence S. Wrightsman
Patricia A. Zapf

The Psychology of Judicial Decision Making

Edited by

David Klein

Gregory Mitchell

2010

Oxford University Press, Inc., publishes works that further
Oxford University's objective of excellence
in research, scholarship, and education.

Oxford   New York
Auckland   Cape Town   Dar es Salaam   Hong Kong   Karachi
Kuala Lumpur   Madrid   Melbourne   Mexico City   Nairobi
New Delhi   Shanghai   Taipei   Toronto

With offices in
Argentina   Austria   Brazil   Chile   Czech Republic   France   Greece
Guatemala   Hungary   Italy   Japan   Poland   Portugal   Singapore
South Korea   Switzerland   Thailand   Turkey   Ukraine   Vietnam

Published by Oxford University Press, Inc.
198 Madison Avenue, New York, New York 10016

www.oup.com

Oxford is a registered trademark of Oxford University Press

Library of Congress Cataloging-in-Publication Data
The psychology of judicial decision making / edited by David Klein, Gregory Mitchell.
p.   cm. — (American Psychology-Law Society series)
Includes bibliographical references.
ISBN 978-0-19-536758-4
1. Judicial process—United States—Psychological aspects.   I. Klein, David E., 1970–
II. Mitchell, Gregory, J.D.
KF8775.P78 2010
347.73′14019—dc22

2009023896

9   8   7   6   5   4   3   2   1

Printed in the United States of America
on acid-free paper

Series Foreword

This book series is sponsored by the American Psychology-Law Society (APLS). APLS is an interdisciplinary organization devoted to scholarship, practice, and public service in psychology and law. Its goals include advancing the contributions of psychology to the understanding of law and legal institutions through basic and applied research; promoting the education of psychologists in matters of law and the education of legal personnel in matters of psychology; and informing the psychological and legal communities and the general public of current research, educational, and service activities in the field of psychology and law. APLS membership includes psychologists from the academic research and clinical practice communities as well as members of the legal community. Research and practice is represented in both the civil and criminal legal arenas. APLS has chosen Oxford University Press as a strategic partner because of its commitment to scholarship, quality, and the international dissemination of ideas. These strengths will help APLS reach our goal of educating the psychology and legal professions and the general public about important developments in psychology and law. The focus of the book series reflects the diversity of the field of psychology and law as we will publish books on a broad range of topics.

David Klein and Gregory Mitchell are the editors of the latest book in the series, *The Psychology of Judicial Decision Making*. The book is a perfect fit for this series, as its intended audience is students and scholars from psychology, law, and political science who are engaged—or may be encouraged to engage—in exploring the intersection of psychology and judicial behavior.

While the book is grounded in psychological theory and research, the editors recognize that the study of the behavior of judges is complex, so both theory and research would be enhanced through debate and discussion by contributors from many professional backgrounds. To accomplish their goal, Klein and Mitchell assembled an impressive interdisciplinary group representing law, political science, and, of course, psychology. This group first came together at a conference in Virginia, where the participants had an opportunity to share and critique each other's ideas. Klein and Mitchell had a forward-looking perspective, as they wanted the book to provide an agenda for future research rather than a review of prior studies of judicial decision making. The contributors were asked to identify theories, concepts, or findings from psychology that could usefully be incorporated into thinking about how judges make decisions, and describe new research questions and the accompanying methodology to test hypotheses generated from this process. Having worked in an interdisciplinary faculty for a few years early in my career, I appreciate that bringing together an interdisciplinary group does not easily result in increased collaborations. Each discipline has its own traditions and approaches to scholarship, and the interdisciplinary boundaries often seem insurmountable. As the editors note in their introduction, examples of other disciplines drawing on psychology to inform the study of judicial decision making are rare. That the participants in the Klein and Mitchell project were able to overcome these interdisciplinary barriers is an impressive achievement. Klein and Mitchell wanted a book that would encourage students of judicial behavior to incorporate psychology into their work and also persuade psychologists and other students of decision making to pay more attention to the decision-making process used by judges. This book serves this purpose well.

Ronald Roesch
Series Editor

Contents

Part II. Judging as Specialized Activity

Part III. Evaluating and Improving Judging

Contributors

Brandon L. Bartels
Assistant Professor of Political Science
George Washington University

Lawrence Baum
Professor of Political Science
The Ohio State University

Eileen Braman
Assistant Professor of Political Science
Indiana University

Len Dalgleish
Professor of Decision Making
University of Stirling, and
head of the Decision Making program of HealthQwest

John M. Darley
Warren Professor of Psychology
Princeton University

Neal Devins
Goodrich Professor of Law and Professor of Government
College of William and Mary

Daniel A. Farber
Sho Sato Professor of Law
Boalt Hall
UC-Berkeley

Will Federspiel
Associate at McGuireWoods

David Klein
Associate Professor of Politics
University of Virginia

Robert J. MacCoun
Professor of Law and Public Policy,
UC-Berkeley

Wendy L. Martinek
Associate Professor of Political Science
Binghamton University

Gregory Mitchell
Daniel Caplin Professor of Law
University of Virginia

April Park
Ph.D. Candidate in Psychology
Kansas State University

Jennifer K. Robbennolt
Professor of Law and Psychology
University of Illinois

C. K. Rowland
Professor Emeritus of Political Science at Kansas University and Founder
Litigation Insights

Frederick Schauer
David and Mary Harrison Distinguished Professor of Law
University of Virginia

James Shanteau
University Distinguished Professor
    of Psychology
Kansas State University

Suzanna Sherry
Herman O. Loewenstein Professor
    of Law
Vanderbilt University

Emily Sherwin
Professor of Law
Cornell Law School

Dan Simon
Professor of Law and
    Psychology
University of Southern California

Barbara A. Spellman
Professor of Law and Professor of
    Psychology
University of Virginia

Philip E. Tetlock
Professor of Organizational
    Behavior and Mitchell Chair in
    Leadership
UC-Berkeley

Tina Traficanti
Attorney at Litigation
    Insights

Erin Vernon
Law student at Duke
    University

Andrew J. Wistrich
United States Magistrate
    Judge
Central District of California

Lawrence S. Wrightsman
Professor Emeritus of Social
    Psychology
University of Kansas

Introduction

David Klein

Over the years, psychologists have devoted uncountable hours to learning how human beings make judgments and decisions. Legal scholars and political scientists have expended immeasurable intellectual energy trying to understand why those particular human beings who sit on courts act as they do in presiding over and deciding cases. It might seem obvious that fertile intellectual ground lies at the intersection of these disciplines, and certainly some scholars have seen it this way. As far back as 1930, Jerome Frank drew on contemporary psychology to explain judging in his *Law and the Modern Mind*. And yet, nearly eighty years on, the area under active cultivation is quite small. To be sure, psychological concepts crop up in studies of judicial behavior from time to time, but it would be difficult to name a score of published studies that have relied extensively on current ideas and evidence in psychology to generate major theoretical propositions about judging. This is partly because students of judicial behavior traditionally have not engaged deeply with scholarship in psychology, but only partly; it is also the case that psychologists have tended not to focus on the kinds of questions that would be most helpful for understanding what professional judges do. This volume of essays grows from a belief that students of both judges and psychology would benefit from a dramatic expansion of research into the psychology of judicial decision making and closely related behavior.

The study of judicial decision making has indisputably made great strides in recent years, through the labors of hundreds of scholars from political science, law, economics, and other disciplines. Nevertheless, one could argue that there remains a lack of both depth and breadth to our understanding of what judges do. Even where scholars can make consensual and successful predictions of a judge's behavior—for example, that Justice J will vote for the conservative position in case C—they will often disagree sharply about exactly what happens in the judge's mind to generate the predicted result. (Does Justice J vote conservatively in a conscious effort to further his policy preferences, in an unconscious effort to do so despite a sincere desire to be guided by legal texts, or as a result of a method of interpretation that is independent of his ideology?) And as soon as we move beyond ideology, we enter areas where good predictions are much harder to come by. How will a judge's decision on a motion, verdict, or appeal be affected by precedents, the presence of an amicus curiae brief from the federal government, the plaintiff's race, a particularly eloquent brief or oral argument by the defendant's attorney, the preferences and arguments of other panelists on a collegial court, the opinions of the local bar, the presentations of expert witnesses, other demands on the judges' time? Why will it be affected that way? Some of these questions have been the subject of excellent scholarly analysis, but none have received definitive answers.

Naturally, various methodological difficulties unrelated to psychology have hindered attempts to study judging, and as scholars devise creative new ways to measure previously intractable concepts, observe hidden behaviors and influences, and design studies so as to control for more confounding factors, our understanding of judging will continue to improve. Still, anyone who has ever tried to choose fairly between serious competing legal arguments must have been struck by the depth, complexity, and mysteriousness of the mental processes involved in the evaluation. It is hard to see how we can hope to achieve a profound understanding of the far more complex and difficult undertaking we call judicial decision making without a close analysis of these underlying mental processes.

Thinking about the intersection of psychology and judicial decision making can do more than help us answer questions that have long troubled scholars; it can also point us toward equally exciting but less explored questions. To give just a few examples: What does it mean to judge well? Are some circumstances, personalities, or cognitive styles more conducive to good judging than others? Do most judges possess special reasoning skills that other people lack? Do judges care what other people think about them, and, if so, how does this affect their decision making? When different motivations come into play at the same time, which have the most influence on judges' behavior, and why?

While students of judging may be the primary beneficiaries of an engagement with psychology, the topics covered in this book should also interest academics doing basic research in the psychology of expertise, analogical reasoning, judgment and decision-making, and the psychology of small group behavior, with applications to the real-world behavior of professional decision makers rather than ordinary people providing opportunities to test the limits of basic theories and experimental studies. Do professional judges think the same way as ordinary people? Is their behavior affected by the same forces that affect the behavior of other people? If not, in what ways do their thinking and behavior differ, and why? Confronting questions like these can only strengthen research in psychology.

The authors of the essays in this book do not always agree about exactly how we should blend the study of psychology and judging or what we can expect to learn from doing so. But all agree that more rigorous thinking about the nature of the mental processes involved in judges' work will lead to deeper understandings of professional judging and psychology generally. Their essays can best be understood as invitations to other scholars to join in this enterprise, offering suggestions for research and surveying the theoretical and methodological promise and problems of different approaches. The authors occasionally present original empirical evidence, but more often their emphases are theoretical. In fact, the authors were encouraged to engage in free speculation, with the intention that the book raise more questions than it answers.

The book is divided into three sections. Essays in the first two sections are concerned with the empirical investigation of decision making. The third part of the book raises questions about whether and how we can evaluate judicial performance, with implications for the possibility of improving judging through the selection and training of judges and structuring of judicial institutions.

What chiefly distinguishes the first set of essays from the second is the perspective from which each set approaches the incorporation of psychology into the study of judging. Essays in the first section take as their starting point the fact that judges are human beings. From this perspective, one asks, "Knowing what we do about people generally, what should we expect of people put in the positions that judges are and asked to do what they do?" For example, people generally tend to engage in certain suboptimal reasoning processes at times (see Guthrie, Rachlinski, & Wistrich, 2001). How often and under what circumstances does judicial reasoning fall short in these ways? Among the general population, people vary in their characteristic ways of thinking (Stanovich, 1999). What kind of variation in cognitive styles might we find among judges, and with what impact on their behavior and the outputs of the judicial system? Or, to take the most common theme in the first section's essays, human beings act on a wide range of motivations. Which of those motivations influence the work of judges, and how?

An alternative approach to the psychology of judicial decision making eschews this focus on what judges have in common with other people and instead begins with what makes, or is supposed to make, judges different from other people or the mental processes judges employ different from the thinking other people do. The second set of essays begins with Frederick Schauer's argument for this approach. The other essays either engage this argument directly or direct our attention to specific tasks judges are required to perform or particular modes of reasoning in which they are expected to engage.

The essays in the third part of the book turn from what we know and can learn about how judges make decisions to reflections on the assessment of judicial performance. Understanding judicial behavior is not, after all, simply an academic exercise. Judges wield substantial power, including the power to make policy, and we naturally want our judges to exercise that power as fairly, competently, and appropriately as possible. The ability to draw on research to improve judging, say by predicting which of two candidates was more likely to excel as a judge or how court practices could be changed to help sitting judges perform better, would provide important practical benefits to society. In the final essay of the book, Daniel Farber and Suzanna Sherry make the best of current knowledge to offer some prescriptions. But the dominant focus of the essays in this section, beginning with Gregory Mitchell's, is on the challenges posed by this project, on the theoretical side as we attempt to determine precisely what it means for judges to perform well, and on the methodological side as we seek to assess judges' performance.

The practical and technical difficulties involved in studying judges are daunting, to say the least. Psychological research most often entails conducting experiments with the subjects of interest, but this method can take us only so far in studying judges. Judges are far from the most accessible subjects and typically are considerably less willing than undergraduates to participate in experiments. Even when researchers can persuade judges to participate (e.g., Guthrie, Rachlinski, & Wistrich, 2001), the experiments must necessarily lack something of the complexity and unpredictability of real-world judging situations; more importantly, they lack the stakes. The challenges involved in analyzing judges' thinking occupy the attention of a number of the authors here.

Methodological challenges is just one of several themes running through the book. Two others are particularly important. One of these is skepticism about the theoretical approaches to judicial decision making that dominate the political science and legal literatures. Viewed through the lens of psychological research, these approaches (fully described in Lawrence Baum's chapter in this volume) can appear both overly simplistic and unrealistically demanding. The essays point to a number of ways in which the dominant theories seem psychologically implausible and in which we can improve our understanding of judging by going beyond them.

The other major theme is the importance of differences across individuals, tasks, and situations. To be sure, students of judging have not simply ignored such differences in the past. But it seems fair to say that—perhaps because of excessive attention to the U.S. Supreme Court—we have often given less attention than we should to variation in types of cases judges hear, the environments in which they operate, and the exact nature of the reasoning tasks they are asked to perform. Psychology teaches us that we should not expect the mental processes judges engage in to remain invariant across very different conditions. It also teaches us to expect variation across individual judges in what they want to accomplish and how they think, but this kind of variation in particular has been the subject of precious little analysis.

As noted, the essays in this volume raise more questions than they answer. Furthermore, they are naturally not comprehensive in their coverage, and there may be some topics discussed only briefly here that should be part of a full-fledged psychology of judging. For example, psychologists in recent years have devoted considerable attention to the role—both positive and negative—that emotion plays in people's thinking (Forgas, 2000; Thagard, 2006). This could be an important area of inquiry for students of judges (see Posner, 2008, pp. 105–107). But the aim of this volume is not to lay out a complete framework for the study of psychology in judicial decision making; rather it is meant to encourage more scholars to engage in that study and provide suggestions for where to begin. To the extent it convinces readers that doing so can be intellectually exciting and practically important, it will have succeeded in its task.

This volume grew out of a workshop held in Charlottesville, Virginia, in March, 2007. The editors and contributors are grateful to the National Science Foundation for support of the workshop and book.

Part I

JUDGES AND HUMAN BEHAVIOR

1

Motivation and Judicial Behavior: Expanding the Scope of Inquiry

Lawrence Baum

Students of judicial behavior have taken only limited steps to incorporate psychological theory into research on judicial decision making. In my view, this represents a missed opportunity. It is true that judges and judging differ in important ways from the people and activities that psychologists generally study, so it is uncertain how much of what they have learned can be applied to judges' choices as decision makers.[1] Yet even if we approach psychological research with some caution, we can gain considerable insight on judicial behavior from that research. In this essay I discuss the value of psychological theory for an understanding of judicial behavior, both in broad terms and in relation to one key issue in judicial behavior.

The first section of the essay provides a preface to this Part of the book by discussing the dominant theoretical models and perspectives in the study of judicial behavior. I describe the state of theory about judging and evaluate that body of work from a psychological perspective. This perspective, I argue, highlights some important limitations to the ways that scholars generally think about judicial behavior.

The second section considers the motivations on which judges act. The study of judicial behavior implicitly centers on motivation, in that legal scholars and political scientists explain judges' choices in terms of what they seek to accomplish with their decisions. I discuss ways that psychological theory can help scholars to dig more deeply into judges' motives and thus to gain a richer understanding of the motivational bases for judicial decisions.

The Study of Judicial Behavior

Explanation of judges' choices is an important issue in legal scholarship and the central concern of political scientists who study the courts. Of course, judicial behavior takes many forms and occurs in many settings. The aspect of judicial behavior on which theory and research concentrate is the decisions that appellate courts (and especially the Supreme Court) reach on the merits of the cases they consider.

Models of Judicial Behavior

Students of judicial behavior in law and political science do not always make their theoretical premises explicit. For this reason, it can be difficult to sort out how particular pieces of empirical scholarship relate to theoretical models. However, taken as a whole, the work that is currently being done in political science is considerably more explicit in this respect than the work of past eras.[2]

Legal and SemiLegal Models

A good deal of legal scholarship rests on the normative premise that judges should devote themselves to interpreting the law correctly by applying appropriate rules of interpretation such as adherence to the plain meaning of statutory language and to relevant precedents.[3] In some legal scholarship of the past, this normative ideal was translated into an explanation: in deciding cases, judges try only to make good law in this sense. This explanation was effectively debunked by the legal realism movement of the early twentieth century (Fisher, Horwitz, & Reed, 1993). Although something like a pure legal model is reflected in some law-school teaching and occasionally appears in legal scholarship (see Cross & Nelson, 2001, pp. 1439–1443), it has essentially been discarded.

For some legal scholars and political scientists, the lesson of legal realism is that legal considerations have no impact on judges' choices. For others, the lesson is more complex: the law does not determine what judges do, but judges' efforts to interpret the law well do much to influence their choices. This complex version of legal realism, though usually implicit, is probably the majority position in legal scholarship. It also has supporters in political science, though the most prominent theoretical conceptions of judicial behavior ascribe little or no impact to legal considerations. Indeed, Jeffrey Segal and Harold Spaeth (2002), the leading proponents of what is called the attitudinal model of decision making, treat the traditional legal model and what might be called semilegal models as a foil that they seek to refute.

The view that judges give some weight to legal considerations is incorporated into a theoretical approach to the study of politics that has been labeled historical institutionalism. Adherents to this school, such as Howard Gillman (2001), Mark Graber (2006), and Keith Whittington (2000), argue that judges care about making good law as well as good policy. They articulate that position primarily through qualitative analysis of the course of judicial doctrine.

There is also a growing body of quantitative research aimed at determining whether the law in its various forms affects judges' choices. Two books (Spaeth & Segal, 1999; Hansford & Spriggs, 2006) have probed the Supreme Court's treatment of its own precedents. Mark Richards and Herbert Kritzer (2002; Kritzer & Richards, 2003, 2005) have done a series of studies in which they conclude that new Supreme Court doctrines reshape the justices' approaches to the cases to which those doctrines apply. In a book that combined quantitative and qualitative analysis, David Klein (2002) argued that judges on the federal courts of appeals respond to the decisions of other courts largely on the basis of a commitment to interpret the law well.

Attitudinal Models

Legal realism was reflected in the quantitative studies of Supreme Court decision making that political scientists began to undertake in the 1940s. The premise of these studies was that the justices acted primarily on the basis of their conceptions of good public policy—their policy preferences. Efforts to follow relevant rules of legal interpretation might also influence their choices, but on the whole policy considerations outweighed legal considerations. These scholars chose as their main dependent variable a judge's vote on the outcome of a case (in other words, which party wins).

C. Herman Pritchett (1954), the leading early scholar, was largely implicit in sketching out a theory of judicial behavior. Later, Harold Spaeth (1979) and Glendon Schubert (1965) adopted more explicit theories that were based partly on attitude theory in psychology. In their theoretical and empirical work, Spaeth and Schubert took the position that attitudes toward alternative policy positions accounted for all or nearly all of what Supreme Court justices do. This conception is reflected in the label of the attitudinal model. Spaeth and his collaborators (Rohde & Spaeth, 1976; Segal & Spaeth, 1993, 2002) have applied the attitudinal model specifically to the Supreme Court, based in part on the Court's institutional attributes. But other scholars extended the model to lower courts, especially the federal courts of appeals and state supreme courts.

From the 1960s to the 1990s, most of the political science scholarship on judicial behavior followed the attitudinal model. One body of work probed the dimensionality of votes in judicial decisions, a dimensionality that was assumed to reflect the structure of judges' attitudes toward policy questions (e.g., Schubert, 1965). Another body of work analyzed the determinants of judges' votes under the assumption that the primary basis for those votes was personal policy preferences (e.g., Tate, 1981).

In its original form, the attitudinal model was not linked to judges' motivations: the linkage between attitudes and votes was treated as more or less reflexive. By the 1960s, however, both scholars who embraced the attitudinal model and other students of judicial behavior were doing research that assumed a conscious judicial goal of achieving good policy (e.g., Rohde, 1972). In stages of the decision process such as selection of cases to hear on the merits (Schubert, 1962), judges were depicted as making calculations based on their desire to advance the policies they favored. In other words, they were behaving strategically. The reflexive and conscious conceptions of the linkage between attitudes and behavior have continued to coexist uneasily. But in pure strategic models, considered next, the conscious conception is dominant.

Strategic Models

Students of judicial behavior use the term "strategic" in multiple ways. The most common usage relates to intent. In this usage, strategic judges seek to achieve a desirable outcome for their actions by taking into account the responses of other people to those actions. In the original form of the attitudinal model, judges are not strategic when they cast votes on case outcomes. Instead, they take the position that best reflects their policy preferences regardless of how others might react to what they do. In strategic models, in contrast, judges might deviate from their most preferred positions if doing so would achieve a better result. To take the most prosaic example, an appellate judge might take a less liberal doctrinal position in a case than she would prefer in order to secure a majority for a relatively liberal position. As this description indicates, strategic models shift the focus from votes on dichotomous case outcomes as the dependent variable to doctrinal positions on an ideological spectrum.

Interest in judicial strategy goes back a long time, and in 1964 Walter Murphy published an influential book in which he explored an array of strategies that policy-oriented Supreme Court justices might employ. But in the 1990s scholars began giving more attention to strategic behavior, primarily because of the influence of rational choice models imported from economics. Pulling together these developments, Lee Epstein and Jack Knight (1998) wrote a book advocating a strategic model of Supreme Court decision making. In depictions by them and by other scholars, strategic considerations might lead the justices to take into account the prospective reactions of their colleagues as well as a variety of groups outside the Court, including the other branches of government and the general public.

Within political science, strategic models are now quite popular. Scholars routinely consider the possibility of strategic behavior, and much of the research on judicial behavior posits or assumes that judges are strategic. One example is the book on Supreme Court decision making by Forrest Maltzman, James Spriggs, and Paul Wahlbeck (2000), which uses information in the justices' papers to analyze strategy at several stages of decision making (see also Hammond, Bonneau, & Sheehan, 2005). Like that book, a good deal of empirical analysis by other scholars is aimed at documenting strategic action by judges or at ascertaining the extent to which such action occurs. Just as the attitudinal model represented the standard way of thinking about judicial behavior for a long time, strategic models now occupy that position (Epstein & Knight, 2000).

Some scholars move back and forth between attitudinal and strategic models without reconciling the two. Segal and Spaeth (2002) have sketched out a reconciliation. They suggest that Supreme Court justices are strategic, and they argue that strategic considerations affect what the justices do in most stages of decision making. But in voting on the outcome of cases, they argue, justices have no strategic reasons to depart from their most preferred policy positions. In this view, the justices can be said to think strategically and act attitudinally when they vote to affirm or reverse.

The difference between intent and result comes into play in a different way in Epstein and Knight's strategic model. The justices in that model care only about making good policy. But because the justices are concerned with acceptance of their decisions as legitimate, they sometimes act on legal considerations—most important, adhering to precedents that are inconsistent with their policy preferences (Epstein & Knight, 1998, pp. 163–177). In this view, the justices are policy-oriented but act as if they gave some weight to making good law.

Thus far, I have described strategy as a means to advance judges' policy goals. Judges could act strategically in the service of other goals as well. A legally oriented judge could use strategy to advance the judge's conception of good law, and strategy plays a role of a sort even in pure legal models. If judges conceive of good law as encompassing coherent legal rules, then judges on an appellate court may compromise with each other as a means to achieve clear, consensual decisions (Edwards, 2003).

Judges might also act strategically to advance multiple goals, sometimes balancing them against each other: good law and good policy (Spiller & Tiller, 1996), good policy and continued tenure in office (M. Hall, 1992). The work of some historical institutionalists treats Supreme Court justices as people who use strategy on behalf of both legal and policy goals (e.g., Gillman, 1997). But by and large, analyses of judicial strategy have focused on policy-oriented strategy.

Probing the Models

As the summaries of their tenets make clear, the dominant models of judicial behavior differ in important respects. Those differences are reflected in debates among scholars about the relative importance of legal and policy considerations for judges and about the extent and impact of strategic behavior. But in any field of scholarship, disagreements typically occur within a limited range, and competing camps share basic assumptions that are largely unnoticed. That is certainly true of the several models of judicial behavior.

It is useful on occasion to step back to identify and consider the assumptions that serve as foundations for work in a field. From a psychological perspective, several key assumptions seem problematical in certain respects. First, each of the models of judicial behavior implicitly centers on motivation, in that judges' actions are treated as driven solely by their goals: legal and policy preferences turn directly into choices in cases. Scholars who utilize these models seldom mention cognition explicitly (but see Segal, 1986), but the implicit assumption is that the cognitive processes involved in judicial decision making are straightforward and unproblematic.

This assumption is questionable on its face. The processing of information, analysis of alternatives, and selection among those alternatives that culminate in judges' choices are hardly straightforward. Even if we conceive of judicial decision making primarily in motivational terms, cognitive processes surely intervene between goals and choices. In reality, motivation and cognition are closely intertwined (Kruglanski, 1996).

The value of incorporating cognition into the study of judicial behavior is underlined by the limited body of scholarship that has done so (Rowland & Carp, 1996; D. Simon, 1998, 2004; Guthrie, Rachlinski, & Wistrich, 2001; Braman, 2004; Braman & Nelson, 2007) and by several chapters in this book. One important issue, especially relevant to this essay's concern with motivation, is the issue of cognitive capacity. There is reason to question the implicit assumption that judges can easily identify the course of action that will best advance their goals.

The pure attitudinal model probably makes the most minimal cognitive demands on judges, but even the task of applying policy preferences to the alternatives in a case can be difficult. In the spatial metaphor that adherents to the attitudinal model have always used, judges must locate both their preferences and the alternatives in a case along an ideological dimension. The other models, in their simple and complex forms, require more from judges. This is especially true of strategic models in which judges consider the prospective responses of other policy makers to their court's decisions. Psychologists and behavioral economists have amply demonstrated people's cognitive limitations (Kahneman & Tversky, 2000; see Mitchell, 2002). Judges certainly are not immune to those limitations (Guthrie, Rachlinski, & Wistrich, 2001).

Students of decision making in some other arenas have grappled with the impact of human cognitive limitations. Behavioral economists, for instance, have raised fundamental questions about the cognitive assumptions that underlie orthodox models of economic behavior and probed the ways that economic actors might depart from the predictions of the orthodox models as a result (Thaler, 1991). Similar inquiries into the cognitive element in judicial behavior are both necessary and potentially quite fruitful.

Second, in their treatment of judges' motivations, the dominant models of judicial behavior focus on proximate goals—generally the goal of making good legal policy (a term that I use to encompass law, policy, or a combination of the two). The exponents of these models say little about the basic motives that underlie proximate goals. In this respect, the scholarship on judging is in sharp contrast with theory and empirical research in social psychology.

Even though it narrows the scope of inquiry, a lack of attention to basic motives is not inherently problematical. However, the judicial goal orientations posited by the dominant models can be contested on motivational grounds. For one thing, these orientations are strikingly narrow. In these models, among all the considerations that might influence judges' choices, only their interest in the substance of legal policy actually exerts much influence.[4] But without an inquiry into the motives that underlie judges' goals, it is difficult to establish why a wide range of other goals that judges can be expected to hold should play no meaningful role in judicial behavior.

Further, the motivational basis for a strong judicial interest in making good law and policy is not obvious. This is especially true in light of the economic orientation that underlies strategic models of judicial choice (see Schauer, 2000, pp. 620–621). Legal and policy goals do not serve judges' self-interest in any conventional sense, so why are these goals so important to judges? A satisfactory answer to that question is needed to provide a firmer theoretical foundation for the dominant models of judicial behavior.

Third, social psychologists treat motivation as two-dimensional: it "energizes behavior and sends the organism in a particular direction" (Pittman, 1998, p. 549; see Chen & Chaiken, 1999, p. 76). Arguably, the two dimensions are so different that different terms should be applied to them. But both capture important elements of human behavior and sources of variation in behavior.

The dominant models of judicial behavior focus on the directional dimension, leaving the energizing dimension aside. More precisely, they assume that judges will exert the maximum effort to advance their goals—to get decisions right, however they define "right." That assumption is especially clear in strategic models, in which judges engage in very time-consuming labor to calculate their optimal strategic choices. Even if the maximum effort were sufficient to overcome the cognitive limitations that beset judges and other people, expending that effort would exact enormous costs from judges.

The assumption of maximum effort is consistent with the premise that judges care only about achieving good legal policy, but it is highly unrealistic. It is true that judges have strong incentives to give time and effort to the task of decision making, much stronger incentives than those of participants in psychological experiments. Even so, judges have other things to do with their time, and most (though not all) share the general human preference to expend less effort rather than more.

Indeed, the anecdotal evidence that some judges make less than a full commitment to their judicial work, a common subject of newspaper stories, is compelling. A few legal scholars, including some who take an economic perspective on the courts, posit that judges have a preference for leisure (e.g., Posner, 1995, pp. 123–126; Bainbridge & Gulati, 2002). These scholars surely are right. In thinking about judges' choices, we need to recognize their interest in limiting the time and labor they devote to their jobs.

Finally, scholarship on judicial behavior generally treats that behavior as homogeneous in important respects. This scholarship does allow for situational variation in the determinants of judges' choices, primarily across courts whose institutional characteristics vary in important respects. Scholars frequently note another source of situational variation, the relative salience of cases, and they have provided persuasive evidence of its impact (e.g., Maltzman, Spriggs, & Wahlbeck, 2000; Bartels, 2005, 2006; Unah & Hancock, 2006; and McAtee & McGuire, 2007). But salience has not been directly incorporated into the models that dominate the field, models that typically treat every case as equal.

More striking is the implicit but deeply rooted assumption that, at least within a particular court level, all judges act in the same ways. In attitudinal and strategic models, every Supreme Court justice acts solely on personal policy preferences. Justices also act on their preferences in uniform ways, responding to cases in terms of the same ideological dimensions and (in strategic models) adopting the same strategies. In these models the justices differ in their behavior because their preferences differ, but in other respects they are alike.

There are good theoretical and empirical reasons to question the emphasis on homogeneity in the dominant models. First of all, the potential impact of situational variation on judging is greater than these models allow. Though students of judicial behavior are sensitive to the effects of courts' institutional characteristics, those effects are likely more fundamental than the scholarship recognizes. This is especially true of the differences between trial and appellate courts (Rowland & Carp, 1996, chs. 6–7). And for judges on a particular court, case salience is only one of the situational variables that could affect decision making. In particular, judges might well act on different bases in carrying out different tasks—case selection and opinion writing, for example.

Interpersonal differences are a more complicated matter. Research in social psychology makes it clear that the situations in which people find themselves play a powerful role in structuring their behavior. One effect is to reduce interpersonal differences in the behavior of people who share the same situations: inherent characteristics of individuals are less important than most people think (Ross & Nisbett, 1991). Still, there remains considerable room for differences in behavior within a particular setting. The role of appellate judge and the structure in which appellate judges do their work constrain variation across individuals, but they hardly eliminate the potential for variation.

Indeed, the evidence of differences among judges on the same court is enormous in volume. Even a moderately attentive observer of the Supreme Court can easily identify variation in the style of the justices' opinions and of their participation in oral argument. Journalistic and scholarly accounts of the Court point to differences in the ways that the justices approach the tasks of individual and collective decision making. To take one example, biographies of Harry Blackmun and Sandra Day O'Connor point to significant differences between the two long-time colleagues (Greenhouse, 2005; Biskupic, 2005). Such differences are an essential part of the behavior that scholars seek to understand.

This discussion of the homogeneity assumption underlines a theme that runs through my consideration of the dominant models of judicial behavior: our understanding of that behavior would benefit if we address complexities that these models do not yet incorporate. At a different level, my prescription is for greater attention to the insights that can be derived from psychological theory. Psychological perspectives have played a limited role in research on judging, and within political science that role has declined somewhat over time.[5] One effect of that trend has been to reduce attention to complexity.

Of course, there is a tradeoff involved in confronting complexities in human behavior. While economic perspectives are applied most explicitly in strategic models of judicial behavior, the other major models implicitly accept the emphasis in economic theory on the use of simplifying assumptions to make analysis more manageable (see Segal & Spaeth, 2002, pp. 44–46). The inherent value of such simplification is obvious. And in practice, simplification makes empirical research more manageable and (not incidentally) more publishable.

Even so, there are clear benefits to be gained from considering the implications of human complexity. Even if scholars retain their commitment to the current simplified models, recognition of the divergence between those models and reality helps in understanding and interpreting empirical findings. Further, at least some of the complexities left aside by the dominant models can be built into those models and into empirical research. Thus the complexities of human behavior that are identified by psychological theory can and should be incorporated into the study of judging.

The Psychology of Judicial Motivation

Because the scholarship on judicial behavior has focused so much on judges' goals, motivation is a good place to start in thinking about how psychological theory can inform our understanding of judges' choices. In this section I consider issues relating to each of the assumptions that I have identified as problematical. These issues overlap with each other, and in the final discussion (on motivation and cognition) I discuss one theoretical approach that addresses multiple issues.

Goals and Motives

The assumption that judges seek primarily (or solely) to make good policy, widely accepted in political science, has primarily an inductive basis. Unsystematic observation of judges' choices and systematic analysis of those choices suggest to scholars that judges are acting on their policy preferences. To take one example, the evidence of an ideological dimension in the votes of Supreme Court justices on case outcomes lends itself to the conclusion that the justices' choices are strongly policy-oriented.

The assumption that the goal of making good law is important to judges, accepted by most legal scholars and many political scientists, is more deeply rooted in theory. But the theory on which scholars rely is primarily normative: trying to interpret the law accurately and well is a role prescription for judges. Here too, little is done to connect the goals that scholars posit and the motivations that must underlie these goals.

Some political scientists have developed a rationale for judges' concentration on legal policy, one that sidesteps the question of motivation. This rationale rests on the exclusion of other goals. Focusing on the Supreme Court, these scholars argue that institutional characteristics of the Court render other goals irrelevant (Epstein & Knight, 1998, pp. 36–49; Segal & Spaeth, 2002, pp. 92–96). One key attribute is the Court's ability to select the cases it will hear, so that it typically hears "difficult" cases in which decisions on both sides can readily be justified in legal terms.[6]

This rationale, though quite reasonable as far as it goes, is not entirely satisfying. Most important, the scholars who offer it consider only a limited range of goals that might compete with good legal policy, almost exclusively career considerations. They point out that career goals are irrelevant to at least the great majority of Supreme Court justices in the current era, since other positions are seldom attractive enough to entice justices away from the Court. But they do not consider other quite plausible goals, including those relating to life at work (such as the quality of the working environment) and to the justices' standing with colleagues and people outside the Court.

Even if all potentially competing goals could be dismissed as irrelevant, it would be useful to determine what basic motives of judges are satisfied through efforts to make good legal policy. Because other goals cannot easily be dismissed, that inquiry is even more important.

Judicial interest in good legal policy can be given firmer theoretical roots by subsuming it within general inventories of motivation. Of the various inventories that psychologists have offered (e.g., Beck, 2000, ch. 12; Fiske, 2003; Reeve, 2005, ch. 5), David Winter's (2002, 2003a) typology is especially relevant because it was developed to analyze political leaders.[7] In Winter's conception, leaders act on their needs for achievement, power, and affiliation. The power motive encompasses prestige, and it may be appropriate to treat the need for prestige as a separate category.

Judges' interest in making good legal policy might be fueled by each of these needs. To take an obvious example, the need for achievement could motivate efforts to advance what a judge sees as good public policy. Similarly, judges may gain prestige within the legal community by fostering the perception that they are devoted to accurate interpretation of the law. In combination, the needs that Winter posits provide a potentially strong motivational basis for the pursuit of legal and policy goals.

This does not mean that it is appropriate to rule out all other goals. The motives that support the goal of achieving good legal policy support other goals as well. For instance, the need for affiliation could motivate judges to take positions that are popular with salient audiences rather than positions they hold themselves. Further, because of Winter's purposes, his typology does not directly encompass basic needs such as economic security, needs that could shape the choices of public officials such as judges.

Another issue in the linkage between goals and motives relates to cognition as well. Pursuit of goals may operate with varying degrees of conscious thought, and psychologists have emphasized the role of nonconscious motives in shaping behavior (Bargh et al., 2001; Gollwitzer & Bargh, 2005; Moors & De Houwer, 2006). Almost surely, the motivations that underlie judicial decision making operate more consciously than those of people in most other situations. But even among political elites, motives that shape behavior are not always conscious (Winter, 2003b, p. 121).

One implication is that the goals that judges consciously try to advance and those they actually pursue through their choices may differ considerably. Some judges proclaim that they seek only to make good law, even though their patterns of votes and opinions indicate that their policy preferences have a powerful impact on their behavior. Such judges are not necessarily dissembling, because policy considerations may operate at an unconscious level. And in all likelihood, judges are often unaware of their own efforts to win favor from salient audiences through their decisions. For some analytic purposes, it is unnecessary to identify the degree of consciousness in judges' pursuit of their goals. But nonconscious motives should be taken into account in efforts to understand the purposive element in judicial behavior.

The Energizing Dimension

I have suggested that a full understanding of judicial behavior requires that the energizing dimension of motivation be considered alongside the directional dimension. If the assumption that judges always devote the maximum effort to advancing their goals is flawed, that inaccuracy has implications for judicial decision making.

The two dimensions of motivation are interrelated. If judges devoted all their time and energy to decision making, they still could not give every case the scrutiny needed to ensure that their choices were the best means to advance their goals (see D. Simon, 1998, pp. 82–83). But if judges devote some time and energy to other pursuits, the gap between the ideal and actual levels of scrutiny is wider.

One way that judges might deal with this gap is to rely on the efforts of others. In particular, they can defer to colleagues and delegate to law clerks and staff attorneys. The costs to their goals of yielding some control over their choices can be minimized if they rely on people whose judgment they trust. Thus policy-oriented judges may consult like-minded colleagues, and they may choose clerks who seem to mirror their own views (Ward & Weiden, 2006, pp. 99–107).

Judges may also rely on heuristics in making choices. One example concerns the selection of cases to hear in courts that have discretionary jurisdiction. Some of these courts, such as the California and U.S. Supreme Courts, face thousands of petitions for hearings each year. It is likely that members of these courts (and the law clerks who assist them in screening petitions) base their choices of cases to hear on a limited number of case characteristics. Indeed, that was the conclusion of one study based on interviews with Supreme Court justices and law clerks (Perry, 1991, ch. 5).

The same is true of decisions on the merits. Whatever they seek to accomplish with their decisions, judges must simplify the process by which they reach those decisions. For example, some scholars have posited that ·Supreme Court justices choose their positions in cases with the goal of avoiding congressional overrides of their decisions through new statutes (e.g., Eskridge, 1991; Bergara, Richman, & Spiller, 2003). The models that scholars have used to test this hypothesis incorporate complicated calculations by the justices about the ideological placement of potential decisions and of subsets of Congress (Segal, 1997; Bergara, Richman, & Spiller, 2003; Sala & Spriggs, 2004). But even these models leave aside relevant considerations such as the positions and activities of interest groups. If some justices do try to avoid overrides, undoubtedly they make their task less time-consuming by identifying a few variables that seem especially helpful in predicting congressional action and ignoring others. This example underlines the need to take into account both unavoidable and voluntary limits on judges' efforts to achieve their goals.

Variation by Judge and Situation

Despite the assumption of homogeneity that pervades most scholarship on judicial behavior, there is abundant evidence of differences in that behavior across judges and situations. Motivation is one important source of differences. In motivational terms, judges could be expected to differ in multiple ways.

First, judges may have different motivational profiles. Winter's empirical research, based on analysis of leaders' verbal outputs, has found considerable variation within groups such as U.S. presidents in the relative importance of the motives he describes (e.g., Winter, 2002). Barber (1965) found wide differences among legislators. It seems highly unlikely that judges are uniquely homogeneous in their mixes of motives. Indeed, two studies offer strong evidence of interpersonal differences in motivation among trial judges (Caldeira, 1977; Sarat, 1977), and Aliotta's (1988) application of Winter's scheme to Supreme Court justices produced evidence of variation in the justices' mixes of motivations.

Second, the same motives may translate into different goals for different judges. Supreme Court justices could seek prestige by taking policy positions that accord with the values of groups outside the Court that share those positions. Alternatively, they could demonstrate their skills in the legal craft and thus appeal to people in the legal community who appreciate those skills.

A third way in which judges differ is in the energizing dimension of motivation. There is considerable evidence of variation in the effort that public officials give to their work in bodies such as Congress (R. Hall, 1996) and state legislatures (Barber, 1965). Similar variation certainly exists in the judiciary. The anecdotal evidence that some judges make a limited commitment to their jobs sits alongside evidence that other judges work very hard to get their work done.

It is difficult to distinguish empirically among these three types of differences. That difficulty is illustrated by comparison of two Supreme Court justices. William O. Douglas and William Brennan were both strongly committed to liberal positions on civil liberties issues, and they voted together in a high proportion of decisions. But they were quite different in the extent of their efforts to win majorities on the Court. Douglas generally found it satisfying to take his own positions, regardless of the collective outcome in the Court (J. Simon, 1980). Exaggerating for effect, a colleague reported that "Bill Douglas is positively embarrassed if anyone on the court agrees with him" (*Time Magazine*, 1975). In contrast, Brennan worked regularly (and, in general, effectively) to put together coalitions in support of his positions (Eisler, 1993; Clark, 1995).

What underlay the differences between the two justices? Perhaps Douglas and Brennan simply gained a sense of achievement in quite different ways. Alternatively, Brennan's interactions with his colleagues to win majorities may have reflected a strong interest in affiliation or power that Douglas lacked. For that matter, the differences between the two justices may have resulted from Douglas's relatively limited commitment to his work on the Court (B. Murphy, 2003).

The recruitment process for judges undoubtedly limits variation in their motivational profiles, because it narrows the range of people who are selected for judgeships. However, as the examples of Douglas and Brennan suggest, even judges who reach the same court may differ considerably. And differences among courts in recruitment, such as the contrast between appointment and election, can foster differences in the mix of judges' motivations.

Of course, judges differ on many dimensions, not just those that involve motivation.[8] But variation in motivation is especially relevant to research on judicial behavior, because that research emphasizes motivation so heavily. Models built on the assumption that all judges want the same things are highly questionable. Political scientists and legal scholars need to follow the lead of psychologists in confronting interpersonal variation.

Two characteristics of the situations in which judges make their choices have already been considered. Institutional differences among courts, such as those between trial and appellate courts, can create quite different contexts for judges' choices. And the salience of cases could have multiple effects, the most obvious of which is on the energizing dimension of motivation. We would expect judges to expend more effort on behalf of their goals when they care more about the outcome.

One situational characteristic that social psychologists have emphasized is accountability. Their research has established the impact on behavior of several forms and dimensions of accountability (Lerner & Tetlock, 1999). Differences among types of cases in judges' perceptions of accountability could affect the weight they give to different criteria for decisions (Bartels, 2006) and the effort they devote to decision making. Whether or not a court produces a signed opinion, for instance, might affect the care with which a case is decided. In this and other respects, salience and accountability might have reinforcing or conflicting effects.

Motivation and Cognition

In discussing issues that concern judges' motivations, I have touched on issues of cognition as well. Those issues are unavoidable—or, at least, they *should* be unavoidable. Indeed, as a corrective to the implicitly motivation-centered perspective that dominates the study of judging, it makes sense to follow the common practice in psychology of putting motivation within a cognitive framework.

Of the frameworks and theories that psychologists have developed for the study of cognition, the concept of motivated reasoning has the most obvious relevance to judicial behavior as conceived by most legal scholars and political scientists. The accuracy and directional goals that Kunda (1990) and others (e.g., Baumeister & Newman, 1994; Lodge & Taber, 2000; see Hsee, 1996) describe map well onto legal and policy goals.

Braman (2004) has analyzed judicial decision making in terms of motivated reasoning. She demonstrates the insights that can be gained from this framework while noting some problems in its application to judicial decision making (see also Braman & Nelson, 2007). The concept of motivated reasoning provides a way to understand how judges' policy preferences could influence their choices in a less than fully conscious way. It also high-lights variation among cases in the balance between legal and policy con-siderations: the more that the law supports one side in a case, the more difficult it is for judges to reason their way to decisions that favor the other side.

Referring to motivated reasoning, Segal and Spaeth (2002, p. 433) argue that the legal ambiguity present in all Supreme Court cases frees the justices to pursue good policy without regard to the legal merits of cases. As Braman has shown, this argument can be contested. In any event, appellate courts that lack discretionary jurisdiction hear a mix of cases that vary in how "easy" they are to decide on a legal basis. The motivated reasoning framework seems well suited to an understanding of variation in the processes by which judges reach decisions in those courts.

Thus, the motivated reasoning framework addresses one important issue in decision making. Ideally, a cognitive framework would take into account each set of issues that I have considered: the motivational bases for goals, the two dimensions of motivation, and motivational variation across individuals and situations. One good candidate is the heuristic-systematic model of information processing that Shelly Chaiken and her collaborators have developed (Chaiken, Liberman, & Eagly, 1989; Chaiken, Giner-Sorolla, & Chen, 1996; Chen & Chaiken, 1999). The heuristic-systematic model is one of several dual-process theories of judgment (Chaiken & Trope, 1999). In such theories, individuals are "motivated tacticians" who select different cognitive strategies under different circumstances (Operario & Fiske, 1999, p. 67). In the heuristic-systematic model, as is typical of psychological models of cognition, the dependent variables are attitudes and beliefs rather than authoritative decisions. Even more than the distinction between ordinary people and political elites, this attribute calls for caution in applying the model to judicial behavior. Yet the basic insights of the model are clearly relevant to an understanding of judges' choices.

In the heuristic-systematic model, heuristic information processing is "relatively effortless . . . characterized by the application of simple decision rules," while the systematic mode is "more effortful and analytic" (Chaiken, Giner-Sorolla, & Chen, 1996, p. 553). The model incorporates three goals for individuals who make choices. As in the motivated reasoning framework, one goal is accuracy. The others are defense motivation, "an orientation toward reinforcing important self-related beliefs," and impression motivation, "an orientation toward holding and expressing beliefs dictated by the current interpersonal situation" (Chaiken, Giner-Sorolla, & Chen, 1996, p. 554).

Both the second and third motivations are intriguing. Defense motivation can be understood as a basis for acting on one's policy preferences, but for students of judicial behavior it is an unconventional formulation of the linkage between preferences and choice. However, this formulation offers a useful way of thinking about the weight of policy considerations in judicial decision making. For judges to depart from their preferred positions might detract from their sense of themselves. From this perspective, the popularity of concurring and dissenting opinions in the current era is understandable. There may be high personal costs to signing on to an opinion that does not reflect a judge's personal beliefs, and judges may gain considerable satisfaction from taking a position that perfectly reflects those beliefs. This satisfaction helps in understanding Justice Antonin Scalia's (1994, p. 42) lyrical description of writing an opinion "to express precisely" his own position as "an unparalleled pleasure."

Among the dominant models of judicial behavior, only strategic models incorporate the impression management motivation, and they do so only in a limited way. Strategic judges seek to affect the impressions of other people only for instrumental reasons—to win support for their positions from colleagues, to avoid negative reactions to their court's decisions from other policy makers and the public, to win reelection or reappointment so they can continue to make legal policy. Yet judges are not social isolates, so their interest in impression management cannot be instrumental alone. Inevitably, they also seek the regard of other people for its own sake. Thus self-presentation is at least as important to judges as it is to "ordinary" people (Goffman, 1959; Schlenker & Pontari, 2000). And judges are especially well situated to present themselves to relevant audiences.[9]

Impression motivation can help to explain the goals posited by the standard models of judicial behavior, in that judges' interest in the approval of salient audiences might reinforce their interest in good law or good policy. But social motives can lead people to make choices that diverge from both their conceptions of accuracy and their own directional preferences.[10] For this reason, separating impression motivation from other goals expands inquiry into the motives that drive judicial behavior.

In combination, defense motivation and impression motivation call attention to the role of individual and social identities in judging. Judges act in part to produce desired self-concepts and favorable images of themselves among audiences that are important to them. It is doubtful that judges' choices can be fully understood in terms of identity. But that concept provides a useful counterpoint to the usual ways of conceptualizing judicial behavior, which leave the human element out of judicial choice.

As a dual-process theory, the heuristic-systematic model takes the energizing dimension of motivation into account. Under the "sufficiency principle" (Chaiken, Giner-Sorolla, & Chen, 1996, p. 554), whether people engage in heuristic or systematic processing depends on what level of effort is sufficient to serve their needs. But very busy public officials must define sufficiency in relation to the time and effort that are available for decision making. One result is that judges sometimes engage in heuristic reasoning even though they would prefer the level of confidence in their choices that systematic reasoning would provide.

Undoubtedly, the dichotomy between two modes of reasoning oversimplifies variation in the effort that judges give to their decisions. Yet it is interesting that courts sometimes divide cases into two categories. Many intermediate courts explicitly differentiate between two classes of cases. A central staff of law clerks selects what appear to be easy cases, in the sense that one side clearly is right under the law, and makes tentative decisions in those cases before forwarding them to panels of judges who typically accept the staff recommendation (Chapper & Hanson, 1990, pp. 15–22; Symposium, 2002). In the U.S. and California Supreme Courts, court personnel assign petitions for hearings to two categories, and petitions in the two categories receive quite different levels of scrutiny from the justices (Caldeira & Wright, 1990; California Supreme Court, n.d.).[11]

In those examples, judges give more attention to classes of cases that they care more about, and the discussion of salience suggested the same result. But the impact of salience might be mediated by another factor. In decisions on the merits, as suggested by Lawrence Wrightsman's essay in this book, judges may engage in less systematic evaluation of cases that they can readily locate in ideological space, because ideology serves as the critical heuristic. In other words, issues that have clear ideological referents for judges tend to be easier than those that lack those referents (see Pollock, Lilie, & Vittes, 1993, p. 30).[12] On average, such "ideological" cases are probably more salient to judges than other cases.

The distinction between two modes of reasoning is one way that the heuristic-systematic model incorporates variation in motivation. As suggested earlier, the care with which judicial decisions are made can vary among judges as well as cases. Similarly, the absolute and relative importance of the three motives in the heuristic-systematic model surely differs among individuals and across situations.

Implications for Issues in Judicial Behavior

Most students of judicial behavior agree on some basic assumptions about the bases for judges' choices, but within the framework of those assumptions they disagree strongly about certain issues. I have discussed specific ways in which elements of psychological theory implicate both the disagreements and the broader agreement. In this section I pull together those discussions and take a broader look at the implications of psychological theory.

The Primacy of Legal Policy

The most widely shared assumption is that judges as decision makers act primarily or entirely on the goal of making good legal policy. That assumption is nearly universal in the study of the Supreme Court. The dominant models of judicial behavior incorporate that assumption but provide only limited justification for it. Can a justification be developed in psychological terms?

The dominant models do not connect the posited goals of judges to their basic motivations, to show the reasons that judges might be drawn to make good law or good policy as they define it. This limitation is relatively easy to overcome, and some scholars—primarily among those who work outside those models—have suggested a means to do so. In their account, judges act on an intrinsic motivation, the satisfaction they gain from efforts to make good law or good policy (Landes & Posner, 1975, p. 887; Posner, 1995, pp. 131, 133; Higgins & Rubin, 1980, p. 130; Klein, 2002, pp. 11–12; Cross, 2003, pp. 1473–1476). This account seems quite reasonable in light of the strength of lawyers' socialization in the task of making good law and the strength of the policy preferences that are held by most politically active people (including judges).

It also seems likely that this intrinsic motivation is reinforced by an extrinsic motivation: judges gain popularity and respect from people who are important to them by pursuing good law or good policy (see Baum, 2006). Other judges and lawyers respond positively to judges who demonstrate skill in the interpretation of the law and adherence to the task of interpreting the law faithfully. Salient audiences that range from political groups to circles of personal friends react to the content of judicial decisions as public policy. Like the satisfaction gained from pursuing good legal policy, this extrinsic motivation fits into Winter's typology of needs and the typology of motivations in the heuristic-systematic model.

Taking the motivational bases for legal and policy goals into account can help in understanding how those goals play out in practice. For example, the ideological dimensions that exist in judicial votes might be explained in part by judges' ideological self-identifications and the importance to them of audiences whose members define good policy on an ideological basis. Judges whose positions are more difficult to classify ideologically may stand at a moderate position on the ideological scale, but they may also identify themselves in less ideological terms.

A second motivational limitation of the dominant models is more difficult to overcome. It is far from obvious that judges devote themselves to good legal policy to the exclusion or near-exclusion of other goals. For one thing, judges' audiences may influence them to adopt positions that differ from both their reading of the law and their policy preferences. The effect of concerns about reelection on death penalty decisions in state supreme courts is an especially clear example of that phenomenon (M. Hall, 1992, 1995). Judges' interest in the regard of other people can shape their choices in more subtle ways as well.

Psychological theories of motivation treat effort as a dimension separate from the content of individual motives, but leisure can be considered a goal as well. As I have noted, the implicit assumption that judges devote the maximum possible effort to achieving good legal policy is highly questionable. This reality moves judges toward heuristic rather than systematic processing of relevant information. The result is to increase the distance between the actions that would advance a judge's interest in good law or good policy most effectively and the actions that the judge actually takes. Further, judges may take other actions that enhance their leisure at the expense of their interest in legal policy. One example is the large decline since the mid-1980s in the number of cases that the Supreme Court accepts for decisions on the merits (O'Brien, 2005).

Most courts have considerably less control over their workloads than the Supreme Court, and the inherent limits on the use of systematic processing impinge heavily on judges in these courts. In some courts, the press of cases is so great that simply disposing of them becomes a major concern—sometimes the central concern. Put differently, judges' most immediate goal may be to reach *any* conclusion rather than a specific conclusion (Kruglanski & Webster, 1996; Dhami, 2003). In intermediate appellate courts at least some judges appear to move consciously between systematic and heuristic processing modes, giving careful attention to law and policy in a minority of cases and more limited scrutiny to cases that they characterize as easy (Wold, 1978; Linder, 1985, pp. 498–499).

Thus the widely shared assumption that judges act only on the goal of achieving good legal policy applies to some courts and cases better than others. In no context does it fully fit the reality of judicial behavior, but in some—decisions on the merits in the Supreme Court, for instance—the fit may be good enough to make the assumption acceptable. In any context, however, scholars need to take into account the motivational bases for judges' interest in the content of legal policy. By doing so, they can better identify the ways that this interest affects judges' choices and the conditions that affect the linkage between the two.

Law Versus Policy

Among the scholars who think that judges devote themselves to making good legal policy, one continuing matter of disagreement is whether judges define that goal solely in terms of policy or whether good law is also important to them. Students of judicial behavior who espouse policy-only models treat their position as more realistic than its alternative. As noted earlier, this judgment is empirically based for the most part. In part, however, it is based on an unspoken assumption that judges have stronger motivations to pursue good policy.

The validity of scholars' conclusions from the empirical evidence can be contested (Baum, 1997, ch. 3), but the assumption about judges' motivations is my concern here. There is no inherent reason that judges should elevate policy over law. They can get satisfaction from advancing what they see as desirable public policy, but they can also do so by interpreting the law effectively. Similarly, they may be rewarded by their audiences in concrete or symbolic ways by taking either path.[13] In the terminology of the motivated reasoning framework, directional goals do not necessarily take primacy over accuracy goals.

Situational variation may be more important than any general rule. If the relative weights of accuracy and directional goals depend on the ease of identifying the more accurate result, then the extent of legal ambiguity in cases is a critical variable. Because the average degree of ambiguity is greater in cases before the Supreme Court than in those decided by the federal courts of appeals, directional goals can be expected to have greater impact in the Supreme Court. The salience of cases to judges affects the level of effort they give to decision making and perhaps the mix of considerations that shape their choices.

Variation among individual judges is less obvious but quite likely. Even if judges have the same motivational profiles, they may pursue their needs in different ways. Some judges might seek to gain prestige within the legal profession by developing a reputation for faithful and effective interpretation of the law. Others might pursue prestige within groups of people who share certain policy preferences by taking positions that accord with the prevailing views in those groups. Similarly, judges could gain a sense of personal achievement through either route. There is good reason to be wary of some judges' claims that they are more faithful to the law than their colleagues, but this does not mean that all judges balance law and policy in the same way.

Strategy

The growing popularity of strategic models of judicial behavior reflects a widespread belief that policy-minded judges *must* be strategic. If a judge has a policy position, why would the judge not do everything possible to bring public policy closer to that position? But from a motivational perspective, the reality is more complicated in several respects.

First, strategic judges gain nothing concrete for themselves by moving public policy closer to their positions. Thus they differ from people in many other situations, such as economic actors. Judges can gain a less concrete benefit from strategic action, the satisfaction of making a difference. But they might also get satisfaction simply by taking positions that fully accord with their conceptions of good policy. Indeed, judges would seem likely to satisfy their defense motivation more effectively by acting sincerely rather than strategically. To depart from the positions they favor for strategic reasons, when the ultimate outcome is uncertain, may be unsettling. Further, judges who are concerned with the impressions they make on relevant audiences may find it easier to make favorable impressions by casting votes and writing opinions that those audiences favor than by taking strategic positions that require justification. For judges, like legislators (Denzau, Riker, & Shepsle, 1985; Wilkerson, 1990), concern with the opinions of their audiences may work against strategic behavior.

Strategic behavior can provide symbolic benefits to judges through the satisfaction gained by influencing legal policy. But there is a complication here as well: even the optimal strategies are likely to have limited impact, thereby reducing these symbolic benefits. In general, neither judicial colleagues nor people outside the court are easy to move. One result is that strategic judges may suffer more defeats than victories. There is only so much that a liberal justice on a conservative Supreme Court can do to win liberal majorities. Judges can console themselves with the hope that short-term defeats ultimately will be reversed, but the tendency to discount the future reduces the value of this consolation (Loewenstein & Elster, 1992). Given this reality, a judge in an unfavorable situation may prefer not to play a game in which defeats are so common (Tushnet, 1992, pp. 2109–2110).

In contrast, if a judge's goal is simply to take the position that best reflects the judge's preferences, success is far easier to achieve. For such judges, as suggested earlier, being on the losing side does not detract from a sense of accomplishment and may actually enhance it. As a result, the nonstrategic judge is likely to get more reinforcement than does the strategic judge (see Shah & Kruglanski, 2000, pp. 118–123).

Further, optimal strategies are difficult to achieve. Psychologists and behavioral economists have amply demonstrated that even people with strong incentives to adopt optimal strategies make major, systematic errors (Barberis & Thaler, 2003). A strategic judge faces some relatively easy tasks, such as calculating what kinds of compromises will be necessary to win a colleague's support for an opinion. But other tasks are considerably more difficult. One example, discussed earlier, is determining whether a prospective decision would be overridden by Congress. Another is estimating the long-term effects of espousing doctrinal positions that command only minority support in a current case.

The most obvious implication of this difficulty is cognitive: strategic judges frequently will make mistakes. But the difficulty of achieving good strategy affects judges' motivations as well. Sincere behavior may be attractive on other grounds, and it has the additional advantage that it is less effortful. The uncertainties and frustrations of strategic behavior further reduce its attractiveness.

Undoubtedly, some judges are more willing than others to deal with the disadvantages of strategic behavior. Judges who have a strong need for power may gain considerable satisfaction from a perception that they are influencing collective outcomes in their own court and the broader course of public policy. But even those judges may be selective in their efforts at strategy, concentrating on strategies that are easiest to accomplish and that produce results most quickly. This is one reason that strategy aimed at shaping collective decisions within courts seems far more common than other forms of judicial strategy.[14] And judges who are willing to face more difficult strategic tasks can be expected to adopt heuristics as a means to limit the effort they put into strategic choices.

Conclusion

As the discussion of strategy illustrates, psychological theory provides new perspectives on judges' motivations and thus informs thinking and research on issues of motivation. This chapter's survey of relevant theory has been quite incomplete, but it should make clear the benefits of considering judicial motivation in psychological terms. By analyzing judges' motives more broadly and more deeply, scholars can gain a richer sense of the bases for judicial choice.

Two themes derived from psychological theory are especially important. The first is the limits that exist on the efforts of decision makers to pursue the goals that students of judicial behavior have posited. By choice and necessity, judges stop short of the comprehensive analysis that is implicitly assumed by the dominant models of judicial behavior. That reality provides a possible basis for some widely held conceptions of judicial behavior, such as the importance of ideological dimensions in judges' choices. It questions other conceptions, such as some elaborate formulations of judges' strategic calculations. Closer examination of the effects of limited efforts in decision making can provide insights on the processes of judicial choice.

The second theme is variation among cases and judges. Some scholars have recognized that judges may decide different kinds of cases on different bases, but this insight should be incorporated more directly into models of judicial behavior. Differences among judges in motivational profiles and in the links between their motives and choices have generally been left aside altogether. Taking into account differences among individuals and among situations will complicate the analysis of judicial behavior, but doing so will also lead to better conceptions of that behavior.

Notes

I appreciate the comments and suggestions by Kathleen McGraw and Tom Nelson.

1. Research in psychology concentrates on ordinary people who are engaged in ordinary behavior, and the insights of that research do not always apply well to judges and judicial decision making. Scholarship on political psychology gives primary attention to the mass public rather than government decision makers, and the portion of this scholarship that deals with government decision makers is concerned primarily with officials in the executive branch and with foreign policy decisions (see Sears, Huddy, & Jevis, 2003).
2. The discussion that follows draws from ideas in Baum (2006, ch. 1).
3. This does not mean that there is always a single correct decision in a case, because judges legitimately might adopt different rules of legal interpretation or apply them differently.
4. As noted earlier, studies of state judges who lack life tenure are an exception (Langer, 2002), though even for those judges continued tenure is typically treated as a means to the end of making legal policy. Students of Congress tend to give re-election greater weight as an end in itself (Fenno, 1973; Mayhew, 1974).
5. The use of psychological theory in research on judicial behavior is discussed in Baum (1997, pp. 135–141). In the decade since that time, psychologists, legal scholars, and political scientists have made additional use of theories in psychology to understand judicial behavior (e.g., [To distinguish from J.F. Simon, 1980) D. Simon, 1998; Gruenfeld & Preston, 2000; Guthrie, Rachlinski, &

Wistrich, 2001). Wrightsman (1999, 2006) has surveyed issues in Supreme Court decision making from a psychological perspective, identifying a variety of ways that psychological theory can inform our understanding of judicial behavior. During the same period, however, economic theory has been given considerably more use within law and political science.

6. These institutional characteristics are shared to varying degrees by other appellate courts. Because of that variation, some scholars have offered cautions about applying the dominant models to appellate courts other than the Supreme Court. This is especially true of state supreme courts, whose members depend on voters or the other branches of government to maintain their positions in the great majority of states (see Langer, 2002).

7. Another typology, developed specifically for analysis of politicians, is Payne and Woshinsky's (1972) categorization of motives for participation in politics. Caldeira (1977) and Sarat (1977) each used this typology in studies of trial judges, identifying their dominant motives and relating those motives to elements of the judges' behavior.

8. On variation in cognition, specifically cognitive complexity, see Tetlock, Bernzweig, & Gallant (1985) and Gruenfeld (1995).

9. I have developed this argument in Baum (2006). Concern with reputation as a judicial motive is also discussed in Miceli and Cosgel (1994) and Schauer (2000).

10. Judges' directional goals in the motivated reasoning framework could result from a variety of considerations. But the ways that Kunda and others describe directional goals relate most clearly to policy preferences as their source.

11. Trial judges who must impose criminal sentences or reach final resolutions of civil cases typically give much less attention to cases in which the two parties have agreed on a proposed resolution than they do to cases in which no such proposal exists. This dichotomy is understandable, perhaps inevitable, but it is also consequential.

12. In turn, this aspect of judges' perceptions of cases—like others—might be subject to framing effects (see Nelson, Oxley, & Clawson, 1997). Lawyers routinely engage in efforts to frame cases in ways that they perceive as favorable to their positions, but we know relatively little about the efficacy of those efforts.

13. Indeed, to the extent that judges' personal and social identities are based on a conception of judging as adherence to proper interpretation of the law, they may have powerful reasons to emphasize legal considerations in their decision making. To borrow terminology from Simonson and Staw (1992, p. 421), legal audiences may create perceptions of accountability for process as distinct from accountability for outcomes.

14. Another reason is that efforts to achieve consensus on appellate courts are regarded as desirable because they contribute to clarity and coherence in the law. Even judges whose only goal is to make good law as they see it would engage in those efforts (Kornhauser & Sager, 1993).

2

Multiple Constraint Satisfaction in Judging

Jennifer K. Robbennolt, Robert J. MacCoun,
and John M. Darley

> Under our law judges do in fact have considerable discretion in
> certain of their decisions: making findings of fact, interpreting
> language in the Constitution, statutes, and regulations; determining
> whether officials or the executive branch have abused their dis-
> cretion; and, fashioning remedies for violations of the law, including
> fairly sweeping powers to grant injunctive relief. The larger reality,
> however, is that judges exercise their powers subject to very signifi-
> cant constraints.
>
> Hon. Alex Kozinski, U.S. Court of Appeals for the Ninth Circuit

Judges make decisions for a living, and their decisions are unusually consequential, with direct effects on immediate cases, and a ripple of less direct effects
on future cases. Trial court judges must variously act as finders of fact in bench
trials, jury trial supervisors, and overall case managers. Appellate court judges
may, for example, make decisions about the merits of particular cases, determine whether to join an opinion and whether to write separately (see e.g., Taha,
2004), or participate in decisions about whether to grant cert or en banc review
(George, 1999). Chief judges face an additional set of administrative responsibilities, such as managing the docket and the budget, assigning opinion writing,
coordinating visiting judges and judges on senior status, hiring and firing staff,
and handling issues related to building maintenance and equipment (George &
Yoon, 2007). The Chief Justice of the U.S. Supreme Court has additional
responsibilities, such as appointing judges to the committees of the judicial
conference (Chutkow, 2007). Judges may even need to decide when it is the best
time to retire (see e.g., George & Yoon, 2007).

Each of the varied decisions that judges are called on to make inevitably evokes a range of possible goals. Different models of judicial decision making tend to highlight particular goals. For example, traditional legal theory posits that in making decisions judges strive to reach the correct legal decision as dictated by precedent. There are various legal realist and critical realist alternatives to this baseline account; of particular relevance here are the attitudinal, strategic, and managerial models. The *attitudinal model* focuses on the ways in which judges make decisions that further their preferred policy objectives (Segal & Spaeth, 1993, 2002). *Strategic models* incorporate consideration of the ways in which judges seek to effectuate their goals in the long term (Epstein & Knight, 1998; Maltzman, Spriggs, & Wahlbeck, 2000). The *managerial model* emphasizes the increasing caseload pressures that judges at all levels face (Resnik, 1982). Thus, as they make decisions, judges must balance their desire to reach the "right" legal result, their preferences for particular outcomes, their need to manage their workload, and many other objectives.

To view these models as competitive accounts—one more valid than the others—is probably misguided. We argue that each model accurately captures some of what every judge does some of the time, and that no single model is likely to describe any judge all of the time. A sophisticated understanding of judicial decision making should explicitly incorporate the notion that judges simultaneously attempt to further numerous, disparate, and often conflicting, objectives. In this chapter we attempt a preliminary account of a more psychologically plausible account of judicial cognition and motivation.

Goals in Judicial Decision Making

Traditional legal theory posits that judges ought to attempt to reach a correct legal decision through the proper application of legal rules and precedent (see review in Cross, 1997). As judge Harry Edwards (1985) argues, "it is the law—and not the personal politics of individual judges—that controls judicial decision-making." Consistent with this approach, there is evidence that the law does influence judicial decision making (see, e.g., Klein, 2002; Richards & Kritzer, 2002). However, substantial evidence demonstrates a range of additional objectives—beyond a correct legal holding—that judges seek to accomplish. For example, the attitudinal model of judicial decision making holds that judges make decisions that will maximize their policy preferences, voting in ways that are consistent with their political ideology (see Segal & Spaeth, 1993, 2002; see also George, 1998).

An influential approach to the attitudinal model of judging appears in the methodologically ambitious work of Andrew Martin, Kevin Quinn, and their colleagues (see, e.g., Martin & Quinn, 2002), who argue that Supreme Court votes across 47 consecutive terms are well represented by a single ideological dimension, and that at any given time, a justice can be located at a position—

an ideal point—on that dimension.[1] This model, or any attitudinal model that accounts for a good deal of the variance in judicial decisions, if correct, would not necessarily invalidate our constraint satisfaction account, but it would render our goal management principles superfluous, at least for justices of the Supreme Court. However, based on methodological considerations, we think it is plausible that the Quinn-Martin analysis could overlook other meaningful dimensions in justices' votes.[2]

We hope future research will attempt to cross-validate the Martin and Quinn analysis. For example, their unidimensional ideological scores could be validated against content analyses of how justices and decisions have been characterized in op-ed essays in U.S. newspapers,[3] and against ideal-point congressional data—for example, data on which representatives endorsed or opposed which justices. Without further validation, it is unclear whether Martin and Quinn are accurately characterizing the dimensional structure of the attitudes of Supreme Court justices. Still, we recognize that a unidimensional model might be a reasonable (and usefully simple) first approximation.

Related models have incorporated elements of strategic behavior in judicial decision making (Epstein & Knight, 1998; Maltzman, Spriggs, & Wahlbeck, 2000). These strategic models propose that judges do not simply vote in ways that are plainly consistent with their attitudes, but make decisions that take into account the ways that the predicted actions of other players (such as their colleagues or Congress) influence the feasibility of attaining their desired ends. Thus, judges may agree to decisions that do not completely effect their policy preferences to avoid results that depart even further from their preferences or may draft opinions in ways that do not perfectly represent their preferences in the instant case, but that will garner the necessary votes. Such models have primarily examined judges' use of strategy in effectuating their ideological goals, but strategic behavior could be employed in the service of other judicial objectives as well (Baum, 2006).

In contrast to an account of judicial decision making based on ideology, an account of judges as case managers highlights the effects of caseload pressures on judicial decision making (see Resnik, 1982). Managerial judges are thought to be concerned with saving time, reducing delays, and improving efficiency.[4] Thus, in this view, a primary goal for judges is to move the docket. For trial court judges, this goal may manifest itself in a desire to settle cases (Resnik, 2002), more judicial involvement at earlier stages of the case (Galanter, 2004), and decreased opinion writing (Taha, 2004). But a need to move the docket may be experienced at all levels of the judiciary. For example, judges may choose to dispose of cases on procedural grounds to limit the need to decide cases on the merits or to avoid the need to decide cases in areas where they have less expertise (see Macey, 1994; Resnik, 2002, describing "the profoundly challenging problems of rendering judgment"). Judges as case managers may strive to limit their workloads, minimize the amount of time they spend on aspects of their job they find less interesting in favor of decision tasks (or cases) they prefer, or attempt to achieve control (or a sense of control) over the nature and pace of their work.

One side effect of a focus on efficiency, coupled with the ability that courts now have to collect more data on court operations, is increasing opportunity for judges to attend to their "statistics"—for example, the number of cases they terminate, the number of motions they have ruled on, or the number of days they have spent in trial (Resnik, 1982; see also Darley, 2001). Thus, judges may have goals that relate to improving their performance on these types of measures.

Intertwined with the goals that are most central to legal, attitudinal, strategic, and managerial models of judicial decision making, judges may also be influenced by a range of additional objectives. For example, judges may seek to make decisions that will not be overturned by a higher court or on en banc review; they may seek to maximize their opportunities to exercise discretion; they may seek to cultivate their reputation with their peers or another constituency (e.g., the bar, academics, Congress, the press, particular interest groups, or the public), aspiring to be respected, influential, and frequently cited; they may seek to be reelected, to be promoted to a higher court, or to move to another position beyond the court; they may seek to build collegial relationships with their colleagues on the bench; they may seek to make decisions that are consistent with their self-identity; and they may seek to achieve a measure of consistency with their own past decisions (see generally Baum, 1997, 2006; Cohen, 1991; Posner, 1993; Wrightsman, 2006). While many of these disparate goals may be entertained consciously, others may be adopted or pursued without conscious awareness (see, e.g., Bargh & Chartrand, 1999; Shah, 2005; see also Guthrie, Rachlinski, & Wistrich, 2007). Furthermore, variations in the decision context—for example, whether and how the judge will be accountable for the decision—can serve to make particular goals temporarily operable or salient (see, e.g., Lerner & Tetlock, 1999).

While judges as a group may share this range of objectives to one degree or another, judges sitting on different courts or across jurisdictions face different sets of tasks and demands. Similarly, different decision tasks may evoke different judicial goals. For example, trial and appellate court judges are called on to make different kinds of decisions and face differing constraints on their decision making. U.S. Supreme Court justices enjoy a greater degree of control over their agenda and more discretion than do judges on other courts and may seek to effect a somewhat different set of objectives. For trial court judges, ruling on a pretrial motion may be subject to different constraints than reaching a verdict in a bench trial. Judges who sit in jurisdictions in which judges are elected may face different pressures than do judges who are appointed. This divergence in decision tasks and in the range of demands faced by judges sitting on different types of courts or across jurisdictions may lead to different (though overlapping) sets of salient goals.

Trial Court Judges

Trial court judges wear many different hats, variously serving as finders of fact, trial supervisors, and overall case managers. These judges decide some cases on the merits, but they also manage the trial process—ruling on objections and motions and instructing juries about the law. Trial court judges may hold Daubert hearings to determine the admissibility of scientific evidence, make determinations about the appropriate amount of bail, and conduct posttrial assessments of damage awards. In addition, trial court judges now spend much of their time managing the pretrial and case settlement processes as well as overseeing the implementation of remedies posttrial (Resnik, 1982).

As fact-finders, judges may struggle to simultaneously accomplish myriad goals—making accurate factual determinations and reaching a verdict consistent with the evidence (see Pennington & Hastie, 1993); accomplishing optimal deterrence (see Becker, 1969; Cooter & Ulen, 2007); awarding appropriate compensation (Darley & Pittman, 2003;); accomplishing some measure of distributive justice (see Deutsch, 1975); punishing when appropriate and to the extent that is fitting (see Darley et al., 2000); using the appropriate rules to guide decision making (see Robbennolt, Darley, & MacCoun, 2003); or expressing their values (see e.g., Sunstein, 1996; Robbennolt, Darley, & MacCoun, 2003). Indeed, as with jurors, judges have been shown to have difficulties with some of the decisions required by legal and economic models of decision making. Specifically, judges have been shown to have trouble ignoring inadmissible evidence (see e.g., Landsman & Rakos, 1994; Wistrich et al., 2005) and evaluating scientific, expert, or statistical evidence (Gatowski et al., 2001; Kovera & McAuliff, 2000; Redding & Repucci, 1999; Wells, 1992). In addition, judges have been found to be susceptible to a variety of cognitive heuristics such as anchoring, framing, hindsight bias, the representativeness heuristic, and the egocentric bias (Guthrie et al., 2001; Rachlinski et al., 2006).

Trial court judges, however, spend much of their time engaged in tasks other than presiding over trials. Indeed, judges are presiding over fewer and fewer trials (Galanter, 2004). In their role as case managers, trial court judges have different tasks and goals than they do in their role as fact-finders—they must negotiate with parties pretrial to settle cases, plan litigation, and manage discovery, and supervise the implementation of remedies posttrial (Resnik, 1982). In addition, trial court judges may be called on to manage complex class-action or multidistrict litigation (see, e.g., Galanter, 2004; Walker & Manahan, 2007).

As noted above, these case management responsibilities give rise to incentives to get cases resolved and off the docket. Judges may even utilize the symbolism of procedural justice to get cases settled. MacCoun (2005) relates an anecdote in which a judge conducted a settlement conference in which the attorneys negotiated a settlement in the clients' absence. When the plaintiff's attorney complained that his client might not accept the settlement without getting "her day in court," the judge put on his robe, called her into an empty courtroom, and sat her on the witness chair. After she told her story, she assented to the settlement.

These case management pressures provide an additional set of goals with which trial court judges, in particular, must contend.

Appellate Judges

Appellate judges face an overlapping, but somewhat different set of decision tasks than do trial court judges. Rather than acting as fact-finders, appellate court judges are primarily engaged in the business of judicial review. Accordingly, they face decisions—such as whether to grant cert to hear a case or whether to grant en banc review—that trial court judges do not. Similarly, appellate court judges must make decisions about whether to ask questions at oral argument and what the nature of those questions will be. Appellate court judges engage in more opinion writing and, in addition to determining how they will vote in a particular case, must decide whether to join a particular opinion, to write separately, or to author a dissenting opinion. Appellate judges at different levels may face differently structured decision tasks. For example, justices of the Supreme Court exercise more control over their agenda than do intermediate appellate judges.

Elected Judges

Judges who face reelection or some form of retention election face additional pressures attendant to such elections. There is evidence that judicial decision making is influenced by such political concerns. For example, there is evidence that in years in which they are up for reelection, judges are more likely to sentence criminal defendants to death (see Brace & Hall, 1997; Brooks & Raphael, 2003; see generally Bright & Keenan, 1995) or to sentence more harshly in general (Huber & Gordon, 2004). Other hot button issues such as tort reform also play a role in the politics of judicial elections and have the potential to influence judicial decision making (see generally Champagne, 2005; Ware, 1999).

Judges as Goal Managers

It is clear that judicial decision making implicates a wide variety of objectives. Judges may be required to balance, for example, a desire to follow precedent against preferred policy preferences, or to balance the effort needed to act strategically against a desire to limit workload, among other goal conflicts. Moreover, in attempting to balance these varied goals, judges have at their disposal a range of decision-making options, or choices about how to proceed (see, e.g., Molot, 1998, discussing the "wide array of tactics available" to judges as they attempt to manage their dockets). Models of decision making that portray judges as pursuing single objectives and that do not account for these intricacies are likely to miss important facets of the process. We therefore propose a model, the parallel constraint satisfaction model, that is explicitly designed to incorporate multiple objectives.

In an attempt to encourage the development of models of legal decision making that capture these types of complexities, we have argued that "legal decision making might profitably be conceived of as a process of parallel constraint satisfaction that can be represented using connectionist models" (Robbennolt, Darley, & MacCoun, 2003; also see Simon, 2004). Connectionist models endeavor to provide a framework for thinking about and modeling decision-making tasks that require the integration of a range of disparate, and potentially inconsistent, information and objectives (see Read & Miller, 1998; Read et al., 1997). Accordingly, such models are well suited to modeling decision-making by judges who must balance numerous, potentially inconsistent, goals.

Constraint satisfaction networks are made up of a set of nodes or elements connected by links in a neural-like network. Each element comprises a concept, item of evidence, legal proposition, or goal, and the links or connections between elements vary in strength and valence (indicating the degree of coherence or incoherence between elements) (Read et al., 1997). The links that connect the elements represent the constraints faced by decision makers—elements that are consistent, or mutually compatible, are said to be coherent and are connected with positively valenced links, while elements that are negatively related or that inhibit each other are said to be incoherent and are negatively linked (Read et al., 1997; Thagard, 2000). Such models are sophisticated enough to take account of differential initial priorities among goals—this would be done by initially linking favored goals to elements set to higher levels of activation and less favored goals to elements with lower levels of activation (see Thagard, 2000).

Under this framework, decisions are made by finding the action that best balances the constraints among the decision elements (Read & Marcus-Newhall, 1993; Thagard, 2000). In a parallel constraint satisfaction model, this balance is struck through a process of iterative updating of the model:

> In a parallel constraint satisfaction connectionist model, each element is assigned an equal initial activation value (e.g., .01). The central aspect of the model is that the activation level of each element in the model is then updated simultaneously based on four factors: (1) the number of other elements connected to it; (2) the level of activation of those elements; (3) the strength of the links to these other elements; and (4) the valence of those links. This updating process is iterated with activation of elements spreading through the network based on the configuration of links between the elements until the activation of each element stabilizes. Once the network settles, each element is accepted or rejected based on its final degree of activation (Robbennolt, Darley, & MacCoun, 2003, pp. 1149–1150).

Thus, a constraint satisfaction model is a mechanism for simultaneously accounting for all of the relevant constraints on the decision, including both consciously articulated and more intuitive objectives. Such models provide a useful framework for considering judicial decision making and are broad enough to encompass the range of decisions that judges have to make, including decisions in the role of fact-finder, legal decisions at trial or on appeal, strategic decisions, and administrative decisions.

For example, parallel constraint satisfaction models have been used to model trial level decision making (see, e.g., Byrne, 1995; Holyoak & Simon, 1999; Simon, 1998; Simon & Holyoak, 2002 Simon et al., 2004; Thagard, 1989). Indeed, it has been argued that "[p]rocesses of maximizing explanatory coherence are particularly well-suited for accounting for ... decision making where the task is to evaluate the coherence of accounts presented by the prosecution and the defense" (Thagard & Kunda, 1998, p. 13). In particular, fact-finders must engage in parallel constraint satisfaction as they attempt to integrate and account for the array of evidence presented at trial in an attempt to achieve explanatory coherence.[5] That is, fact-finders attempt to come to an understanding of the facts "that fits with the available information [i.e., trial evidence] better than alternative interpretations" (Thagard, 2000, p. 16). Moreover, "the best interpretation is one that provides the most coherent account of what we want to understand, considering both pieces of information that fit with each other and pieces of information that do not fit with each other" (Thagard, 2000, p. 16).

Importantly for our purposes here, parallel constraint satisfaction models can also be used to model the ways in which judges and other legal decision makers make decisions to maximize satisfaction of their varying goals, that is, to achieve what is referred to as deliberative coherence. In a model of deliberative coherence, decision makers faced with multiple, potentially inconsistent goals, seek a course of action that accomplishes the greatest coherence among competing goals. The competing goals and the potential avenues open to the decision maker are linked together in ways that signify the degree to which they are compatible or incompatible (Thagard & Millgram, 1995). Decision making, then, is:

> inference to the best plan. When people make decisions, they do not simply choose an action to perform, but rather adopt complex plans on the basis of a holistic assessment of various competing actions and goals. Choosing a plan is in part a matter of evaluating goals as well as actions. Choice is made by arriving at a plan or plans that involve actions and goals that are coherent with other actions and goals to which one is committed. (Thagard & Millgram, 1995, p. 440)

In essence, parallel constraint satisfaction models provide a way to account for the complex interplay among actions and goals. Specifically, we (Robbennolt, Darley, & MacCoun, 2003) have proposed a set of "goal management principles" that can describe the interrelations among the disparate goals and actions pursued by legal decision makers:

- *Principle of equifinality:* some goals may be alternately satisfied through any one of a number of actions (see Kruglanski et al., 2002; Anderson & MacCoun, 1999);
- *Principle of best fit:* a particular action may better fulfill some goals than others;
- *Principle of multifinality:* a particular action may sometimes accomplish multiple goals simultaneously (see Kruglanski et al., 2002);
- *Principle of goal incompatibility:* some goals will inevitably conflict and, thus, be difficult or impossible to satisfy concurrently.

Connectionist models of parallel constraint satisfaction accommodate these principles in various ways:

a goal might be connected by positive links to more than one action (*equifinality*) and each possible action may be connected by positive links to more than one goal (*multifinality*). At the same time, the links between a goal and several different actions may have different weights (*best fit*) and some of the links between two goals or two actions may be negatively valenced (*incompatibility*). The connectionist network updates activation of the elements (goals and actions) in parallel until the network stabilizes. In this case, the final activation of the elements represents the decision maker's chosen set of selected actions or goal valuations. (Robbennolt, Darley, & MacCoun, 2003, pp. 1154–1155)

Thus, examining deliberative coherence through parallel constraint satisfaction provides a way to formally model how decision makers such as judges "mediate among the influence of multiple, salient, and often conflicting goals and do so in a way that results in reasonable behavior that is sensitive both to the desires of the individual and the opportunities and constraints of the environment" (Read et al., 1997, p. 47).[6] Judges may, for example, be able to reach a particular desired outcome through two different analytic approaches (*equifinality*), but one approach may be contrary to precedent (*incompatibility*). A trial court judge may have at her disposal a number of case management approaches (*equifinality*): one may be the most effective at speeding the docket (*best fit*) but at the expense of party satisfaction (*incompatibility*), while another approach may simultaneously move the docket and achieve a good substantive result (*multifinality*). An appellate judge may weigh a desire to write a detailed dissenting opinion against strategic objectives or against an overwhelming workload (*incompatibility*).

Consider the following extended example as one illustration of how parallel constraint satisfaction can be used to model the complexity of judicial decision making.[7] Imagine a judge who is considering a motion to suppress key evidence in a criminal trial that raises a somewhat novel, but not unprecedented issue related to the exclusionary rule. The judge is faced with the related tasks of determining the content of her ruling and deciding whether to rule from the bench or to issue a written ruling. The judge, having reviewed the evidence, is aware of its strong probative value and (again, having seen the evidence) is of the opinion that the defendant quite likely committed the crime with which he is charged and ought to be punished accordingly. Given the nature of the other evidence in the case, the judge understands that it is unlikely that the prosecution will be able to proceed without the evidence. The judge is also aware of the public sentiment surrounding the case and predicts a strong negative public reaction if the case were to be dismissed. At the same time, the judge is strongly committed to the principles underlying the exclusionary rule and believes, as an empirical matter, that following the rule and excluding evidence in appropriate cases has had and continues to have positive effects on police procedure. The judge is strongly committed to following legal precedent. The relevant legal precedent in the judge's jurisdiction clearly requires that she find the evidence inadmissible. On the other hand, the prosecutor is urging her to follow an exception that another jurisdiction has recently carved out that would support the admission of the evidence. While the judge believes that following the approach suggested by this exception is analytically stronger than the approach currently followed in her jurisdiction and may apply to the facts of this case, she does not think that such an approach will be accepted in her jurisdiction and predicts that any ruling admitting the evidence stands a relatively high chance of being overturned on appeal. The judge enjoys writing opinions and would welcome the challenge of crafting an elegant analysis of an important legal issue; she views the appellate court as a more attractive audience for these scholarly efforts than she does the general public. She feels some need to explain her reasoning (particularly to the appellate court if she admits the evidence and to the public if she chooses not to admit it). However, as a busy trial judge, she does not have the luxury of spending a week or a month crafting a nuanced scholarly exposition of the issue.

Figure 2.1 diagrams these goals and constraints in a connectionist parallel constraint satisfaction network. Solid lines represent compatible links; dashed lines represent incompatible relationships. In the model, ruling the evidence inadmissible would be consistent with the judge's understanding of the relevant precedent and with the general purposes of the exclusionary rule, would minimize the chance of a reversal, and would move the docket (as the charges would most likely be dropped). Conversely, such a ruling would be inconsistent with the judge's own best legal analysis, would be inconsistent with the judge's view of just deserts by resulting in the release of a probably guilty defendant, and would inflame public sentiment. While ruling the evidence admissible would be consistent with the judge's notions of analytical rigor, would allow the prosecution of the defendant, and would comport with public sentiment and, therefore, build public confidence in the judicial

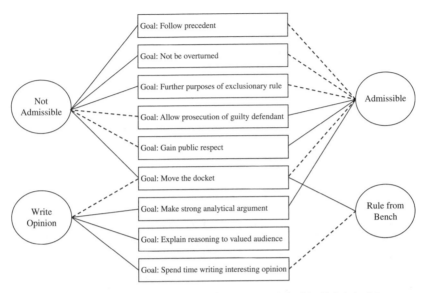

Figure 2.1 Parallel constraint satisfaction model of judicial decision.

system, the judge believes that it is contrary to the relevant precedent, opening the judge up to the possibility of reversal, and would be inconsistent with the aims of the exclusionary rule. Drafting an opinion on the ruling would further the judge's goals in being analytically rigorous and in spending time engaged in the intellectual enterprise of thorough legal analysis, and might catch the attention of the judge's judicial colleagues. However, the judge is simultaneously aware of the ever-present pressure to move the docket and spending time drafting such an opinion will not further this goal.

The judge's decisions, then, involve the elaborate interplay of these myriad goals, and subjectively, such decisions can feel rather mysterious.[8] One struggles and struggles with a decision, and then all of a sudden an internal threshold is crossed and the judgment is made. Though much of the deliberation is in the form of conscious internal dialogue, the cognitive process by which the various constraints are reconciled is largely unconscious, because serial consciousness cannot represent the kind of parallel processing required to reconcile all the conflicting positive and negative activations among elements. We experience the struggle, then we feel something settle, and we then begin a secondary process of trying to rationalize in words what we have decided.

Considering judges as decision makers who must reconcile numerous objectives in carrying out a variety of different decision tasks provides an avenue toward a more nuanced view of the cognitive complexity of judicial decision making and may lead to increasingly sophisticated hypotheses about judicial behavior. Identifying the distinctive constraints faced by judges with regard to particular decision tasks and settings can give rise to testable predictions involving those constraints. For example, concern about being overturned will be salient in some contexts and for some decisions, but not others, and differences in the constraints faced may lead to predictable differences in decision making across such contexts (e.g., differences in the citation of precedent or in the scope of the decision). Alternately, one might predict that alternate goals will have more influence on decision making when legal precedent is unclear (i.e., less constraining). Or consideration of workload constraints might lead one to predict more intuitive processing by judges facing greater workload pressures and more deliberation by those who are relatively unconstrained by such pressures (see Guthrie, Rachlinski, & Wistrich, 2007a). By guiding the generation of such predictions, conceiving of judges as decision makers who attempt to simultaneously satisfy myriad goals by engaging in a process of parallel constraint satisfaction offers a model for incorporating the range of considerations that influence judicial decision making and for understanding the interplay among them.

Notes

The authors would like to thank Matt Taksin for his helpful research assistance and Margareth Etienne and Kevin Quinn for their helpful comments on parts of this chapter.

1. The notion of ideal points has its origins in so-called *spatial models* of voting in the political science literature on legislatures (see Downs, 1957; Enelow & Hinch, 1990; McCarty, Poole, & Rosenthal, 2006).
2. Martin and Quinn (2002) attempt to identify the dimensionality of Supreme Court votes (to affirm or reverse) using a database of 3,450 cases from the 29 justices sitting on the Court during the 1953 through 1999 terms. They develop an innovative Bayesian Monte Carlo algorithm to infer ideal points for each justice. The details of the algorithm and its derivation are beyond the scope of this chapter, but our concern is less with the method than with the available data. In psychometric practice, the usual rule of thumb for fitting a latent dimensional model is that one needs a minimum of 5 to 10 respondents per measured item. The Martin-Quinn analysis reverses this inequality; with between 41 (in 2003) and 108 (in 1972) decisions per term and only nine seated Justices per term, there are far more items (41 to 108) than respondents (9 for any given item).

    It is difficult to correctly characterize an underlying multidimensional structure when the data are sparse (Fabrigar et al., 1999). For example, IQ tests are carefully and painstakingly constructed from a very large set of items selected to be homogeneous ("high g loading"), with thousands of respondents. Even so, with factor rotation algorithms, or with a confirmatory factor analysis using structural equation models, one can usually fit a multidimensional model to these seemingly unidimensional datasets, and many psychologists believe there are sound theoretical reasons to do so (see e.g., Cattell, 1963; Sternberg, 1999).

3. A new effort seems to proceed in the reverse direction, using Martin-Quinn scores to validate the ideologies of media outlets (see Ho & Quinn, 2007).
4. This concern is not unique to judges; citizens also seem to expect the courts to trade off efficiency and procedural thoroughness. MacCoun and Tyler (1988) found that citizens strongly preferred juries to judges (and 12-person unanimous juries to smaller or nonunanimous juries) for homicide cases, but preferred bench trials or small, majority-rule juries for shoplifting cases.
5. This view is consistent with the *story model* of juror cognition, in which jurors choose a verdict by constructing a "story" consistent with the trial evidence and matching that story to the available verdict choices (see Pennington & Hastie, 1986, 1988, 1992, 1993).
6. We have focused here on the decisions of individual judges. However, parallel constraint satisfaction network models can also be used to model the decisions made by groups, such as panels of judges. See, for example, Thagard, 2000 (describing a model of consensus decision making).
7. For other examples of constraint satisfaction models, see Byrne (1995); Thagard and Millgram, (1995).
8. For the sake of simplicity, we have focused on the links between goals and actions, and have not depicted relationships between and among goals. However, a full implementation of the model would include links showing the ways in which goals facilitate or compete with one another. For example, achieving the goal of following precedent facilitates achieving the goal of not being overturned; a link between these two goals would represent such a facilitative relationship. These extra links would help illustrate why a simple linear regression or cognitive averaging model is unlikely to accurately represent the relative impact of each goal.

3

Top-Down and Bottom-Up Models of Judicial Reasoning

Brandon L. Bartels

As is apparent from the other readings in this volume, the punchline of 50 years of behavioral research on Supreme Court decision making is that policy (or ideological) preferences[1] have a major, if not dominant, impact on justices' choices (Segal & Spaeth, 2002). Moreover, most perspectives assume that policy preferences—as well as other ingredients of decision making—exhibit generally uniform effects across all situations in which justices make decisions and between justices as well. While research focusing on the potent impact of policy preferences has increased our knowledge of judicial decision making, the work brings up nearly as many questions as it does answers. In other words, there is still a great deal we do not know about how judges make decisions.

In this essay, I offer a perspective on how social psychological insights on the cognitive processes of judgment can help enrich our understanding of judicial decision making. By highlighting a cognitive perspective of judicial reasoning, studies can move beyond "black box" models of decision making that ignore the crucial cognitive processes mediating the relationship between the judgmental considerations and the choices judges ultimately make. Such a focus can fill in the gaps regarding what we do not know about judicial decision making, namely, *when* ideology and legal considerations will exhibit greater or lesser effects on judges' choices. After reviewing some theories on cognitive processes of judgment and decision making, I posit a theoretical framework of judging focusing on top-down versus bottom-up reasoning processes. In providing one possible explanation for judges' reasoning processes, the theory suggests hypotheses specifying the conditions under which law and ideology will exhibit greater or lesser impacts on judges' choices. The theoretical perspective—and this essay in general—is primarily aimed toward explaining decision making by justices on the U.S. Supreme Court. However, the ideas have implications for judges at other levels of the judiciary.

Cognitive Processes of Decision Making

Motivational and Behavioral Heterogeneity

As Lawrence Baum's essay in this volume (ch. 1) highlights, political scientists of various theoretical persuasions have posited theoretical frameworks specifying justices as motivated primarily by policy goals, that is, as "single-minded seekers of legal policy" (George & Epstein, 1992). Yet it is possible that under certain conditions justices may be motivated by policy goals, under other conditions they may be motivated by legal goals, and under a third set of conditions they may be motivated concurrently by both goals—a desire to make both "good law and good policy" (Baum, 1997; Hausegger & Baum, 1999). A focus on judgmental reasoning processes makes one think more intently about what might be called "motivational heterogeneity," or the idea that under certain conditions justices might be motivated by something other than policy, or ideological, goals (Baum, 1994, 1997, 2006). Attitudinal and strategic perspectives of Supreme Court decision making have neglected such nuanced, multiple-goal frameworks and the broader notion of motivational heterogeneity. But it seems reasonable to think that context, case type, issue area, or other factors may determine which goals are operative in a given case for a given justice.

Social cognition theorists place an explicit focus on motivational heterogeneity (e.g., Fazio, 1986, 1990; Petty & Cacioppo, 1986; Fazio & Towles-Schwen, 1999; Kunda, 1990; Fiske & Taylor, 1991). Many social cognition theorists are first interested in what types of motivations may be at play. Then, one's motivation determines the nature of the cognitive process that produces a decision or judgment. In short, if we want more nuanced and realistic explanations of justices' behavior, we should think more broadly about justices' goal structures, and the conditions under which certain goals might become operative.

Behavioral heterogeneity is linked to motivational heterogeneity in that the types of motivations that are operative determine the nature of one's cognitive processes that will dictate the decision process, which in turn establishes the extent to which particular considerations will influence decisions. In the judicial context, Pritchett (1969, p. 42) alludes to a need to confront this particular type of heterogeneity, arguing that "[a]ny accurate analysis of judicial behavior must have as a major purpose a full clarification of the unique limiting conditions under which judicial policy making proceeds."

In the following section, I demonstrate how insights from theories of social cognition can illuminate the study of Supreme Court decision making. In particular, these theories are capable of explicating a more nuanced portrait of decision making addressing the following issues: (1) the multiple motivations that might be at play in the judicial context; (2) thinking about the relationship between policy preferences and behavior as a process of judgment as opposed to a stimulus-response relationship with an unexplained "black box"; and (3) specifying the conditions under which policy preferences or legal considerations influence behavior with greater or lesser force.

Top-Down and Bottom-Up Models of Reasoning and Judgment

Here, I describe and discuss two models of reasoning and judgment—*top-down* and *bottom-up* processes—that are prominent in various social cognition perspectives (Chaiken, 1980; Fazio & Towles-Schwen, 1999; Fiske & Taylor, 1991; Petty & Cacioppo, 1986). These models lay the theoretical foundation for my application of social cognition to the judicial domain. For both processes, I assume that reasoning is systematic as opposed to heuristic (Chaiken, 1980; Petty & Cacioppo, 1986). Systematic processing occurs when individuals engage in active and effortful processing of relevant stimuli and information in a decision context. On the other hand, heuristic processing is low-effort, passive processing, where individuals may skim over important stimuli and information and rely on more peripheral decision cues. In the context of judging, it is reasonable to assume that judges engage in systematic processing of the facts, briefs, oral arguments, and so forth, when making decisions (though see Guthrie et al., 2001, 2002). While both top-down and bottom-up processes involve systematic processing, the key difference between the two models relates to the extent to which ideological predispositions will bias the entire reasoning process. The two processes can be treated as a continuum of biased processing, where top-down processing represents the most biased reasoning process, and bottom-up processing represents the most unbiased process.[2]

In a top-down reasoning process, the generic predispositions, perceptions, or theories people bring to a judgment context dictate how they process the new information in front of them. Top-down processing is biased processing, and can be thought of as deductive—it is theory driven. In other words, the theories and predispositions people bring to a judgment context produce a biasing influence on how they process the relevant facts and information. These predispositions, then, dominate the final judgment by providing a lens through which the facts and evidence are evaluated and assessed. I use the term "theory" to mean a set of beliefs, based on a directional predisposition, that becomes an individual's "story of how the world works or ought to work." It is separate from the facts and evidence at hand. An example of top-down, or theory-driven, processing involves a police investigation of a murder case. The police may develop a theory early on about who the murderer is, based on their prior knowledge about the particular type of murder. For instance, if a child is killed inside the home, parents are typically suspects. The police may develop a theory about how and why the parents killed their child. In a top-down reasoning process, this theory would dominate the investigation process, leading to a biased search for the truth. The police will zone in on the parents, give less weight to alternative evidence suggesting a different suspect, and exclude other suspects. They view all evidence through the lens of the parent-centered theory they develop.

In contrast to top-down processing, bottom-up processing involves objective scrutiny of the information, facts, or evidence at hand. It involves objectively assessing the relevant information and making a judgment based solely on the facts, as opposed to predispositional biases. Bottom-up processing is usually referred to as inductive—it is "data driven." The theories or predispositions people bring to the judgment context do not dominate the decision process. Returning to the police investigation example, police would engage in bottom-up reasoning if they are able suppress the biasing influence of a particular theory that may develop during a murder investigation. They engage in an objective search for the truth, considering all the relevant facts and evidence.

Fazio's MODE model (1990; Fazio & Towles-Schwen, 1999), which explains the processes by which and extent to which attitudes guide behavior, sheds further light on top-down versus bottom-up processing. MODE stands for *M*otivation and *O*pportunity as *DE*terminants, and these determinants regulate whether people will enter into one of two attitude-behavior processes: a deliberative process or a spontaneous process. The deliberative process is a data-driven, bottom-up process, in which an individual closely and systematically scrutinizes information, or the "data," that is, the "the attributes of the behavioral alternative" (Fazio & Towles-Schwen, 1999, p. 99; see also Ajzen & Fishbein, 1980). Thus, it is an objective form of processing, where attitudes may play a role in guiding behavior, but their influence is diminished in the presence of the other attribute-based considerations.

A spontaneous attitude-behavior process is a top-down, theory-driven process, where an automatically activated attitude is triggered, which then biases how the individual processes the data and the attributes of the alternatives. In short, the attitude triggered by the immediate appraisal of the decision context biases how one processes and perceives subsequent information in an automatic, unconscious fashion. This strong attitude functions like a theory, discussed above. The stronger the attitude, the more likely that attitude will dominate the decision process at the expense of objectively assessing the facts and evidence at hand.

Importantly, a mixed, controlled process may also occur whereby people can "overcome the potential biasing influences of even a relatively accessible attitude when they [are] properly motivated"; they can objectively process the attributes of the alternatives "instead of readily accepting the interpretation implied by their attitudes" (Fazio & Towles-Schwen, 1999, p. 102). Petty and

Wegener's (1993; see also Wegener & Petty, 1995) "flexible correction model" is akin to this mixed model. Upon entering a judgment context, an attitude may be automatically activated, but "the activation of knowledge regarding the normative requirements induces an individual to define the event as one in which he or she needs to control and monitor impulsive behavior carefully" (Fazio & Towles-Schwen, 1999, p. 103). This controlled process means that people will recognize their biases and, if motivated, will correct for those biases, inducing one to engage in more data-driven processing, which will "attenuate the impact of the automatically activated attitude" (Fazio & Towles-Schwen, 1999, p. 103).

Conditions Under Which People Engage in Top-Down or Bottom-Up Reasoning

Social cognition theorists have specified the conditions under which we might expect people to engage in top-down or bottom-up processing, and the issue of "motivational heterogeneity" is directly implicated. That is, the motivations, or goals, of the actor determine which type of processing the decision maker will engage in. First, when a *fear of invalidity* motivation is operative, people will tend to process information more objectively, in a bottom-up fashion, and rely less on their predispositions (Fazio & Towles-Schwen, 1999; Fiske & Taylor, 1991). Related to this motivation, when people feel *accountable* for their decisions, they are more likely to be objective, bottom-up processors (Lerner & Tetlock, 1999; Fiske & Taylor, 1991). The possibility of having to justify one's decision to another person or group leads to more careful scrutinizing of the attributes and information specific to the context, and less of a reliance on the potentially biasing predisposition one brings to the case.

The motivated reasoning perspective also highlights conditions under which people will engage in different reasoning processes. As Kunda (1990, p. 480) states, "People rely on cognitive processes and representations to arrive at their desired conclusions, but motivation plays a role in determining which of these will be used on a given occasion." Motivation is defined as "any wish, desire, or preference that concerns the outcome of a given reasoning task" (Kunda, 1990, p. 480). The motivations one possesses entering the decision context bias the reasoning process toward achieving the end state specified in that motivation. Kunda discusses two motivations in particular: *accuracy* and *directional* goals. The core theoretical contention is that "goals affect reasoning by influencing the choice of beliefs and strategies applied to a given problem" (Kunda, 1990, p. 481). Braman and Nelson (2007) use the motivated reasoning framework to explain when biases will occur in legal decision making.

A motivation to be accurate leads to a reasoning process akin to a bottom-up, data-driven process. Accuracy goals "lead to an elimination or reduction of cognitive biases" (Kunda, 1990, p. 481); they reduce top-down, biased processing and induce objective, data-driven processing. Accountability, self-presentation considerations, and fear of invalidity induce accuracy goals, which then lead to more careful, objective processing of the information, evidence, and data. Directional goals lead people to "construct a justification of their desired conclusion that would persuade a dispassionate observer.... In other words, they maintain an illusion of objectivity" (Kunda, 1990, pp. 482–483). Unlike a bottom-up reasoning process, directional goals bias memory search and belief formation processes. One important constraint on the biasing role of directional goals is the presence of strong arguments. In the persuasion context, bottom-up processing involves yielding to strong and influential arguments, even if they promote a counterattitudinal position (Petty & Cacioppo, 1986; Kunda, 1990).

According to the MODE model, motivation and opportunity determine the type of attitude-behavior process one enters into. Fazio and Towles-Schwen (1999) specifically discuss fear of invalidity as an important motivation that induces a deliberative, bottom-up attitude-behavior process. Opportunity relates to the availability of time and resources. The more time and resources one has, the more likely one will engage in a deliberative process. The key variable that moderates the attitude-behavior relationship is attitude accessibility, which is the strength of the association in memory between an attitude object and its summary evaluation (Fazio et al., 1982; Fazio & Willams, 1986). Accessibility ranges from nonattitudes, where there is absolutely no association between an object and a summary evaluation, to complete accessibility, where attitudes are automatically activated when one encounters the object. According to Fazio, attitudes will guide behavior to the extent that they are accessible in memory.

Schuette and Fazio (1995) report compelling experimental findings that make several connections to the judicial context. Their findings support a mixed, controlled process (see also Petty & Wegener, 1993; Wegener & Petty, 1995). They manipulate attitude accessibility and motivation (i.e., fear of invalidity) and examine how each factor influences how subjects assess the quality of a death penalty study. As expected, the low motivation (i.e., no fear of invalidity), high accessibility subjects were more likely to assess the studies in accord with their attitudes, evidence of attitudinally biased, top-down processing. Increases in accessibility enhanced this biasing effect. However, increasing fear of invalidity reduced this biasing effect, inducing more bottom-up reasoning, even for those with highly accessible attitudes. Importantly, the findings suggest that individuals are capable of controlling the potentially biasing role of attitudes and predispositions when they are properly motivated.

Processes of Supreme Court Decision Making

Adopting insights from the work discussed above, I posit a cognitive model of judging specifying the reasoning processes—top-down and bottom-up processes—by which Supreme Court justices make decisions. The model posits conditions under which justices will engage in either type of process.

It also produces empirical implications suggesting when policy preferences and legal considerations will have greater or lesser impacts on justices' choices.

Attitudes, Policy Preferences, and Ideological Values

Before launching into the theoretical framework, I discuss a conceptual issue regarding the concepts *attitudes, policy preferences, values,* and *predispositions.* Thus far, I have used these terms somewhat interchangeably, which follows the tradition in judicial behavior scholarship (e.g., Segal & Cover, 1989; Gibson, 1991; Segal & Spaeth, 2002). In general, all relate to a justice's ideological predispositions toward legal policy issues, and I will treat them—particularly attitudes and policy preferences—as synonymous. Many scholars tend to use these terms without providing explicit definitions. Referring to Eagly and Chaiken's (1993) definition of an "attitude," I will define justices' policy preferences/attitudes as evaluative tendencies—in terms of favoring or disfavoring— toward legal policy. Note that the attitude object is legal policy. Using Fazio's (1995) definition, we could refer to justices' policy preferences/attitudes as associations in memory between legal policy and evaluative orientations.

Judicial scholars tend to think of justices' policy preferences as global as opposed to issue-specific. That is, policy preferences are thought of as more global views toward broad legal policy areas, like civil liberties and economics (e.g., Segal & Spaeth, 2002; Segal & Cover, 1989). In this sense, ideological values may come closer to how scholars conceive of policy preferences both conceptually and operationally (see Segal & Cover, 1989). Values can be thought of as attitudes toward "relatively abstract goals" (Eagly & Chaiken, 1993, p. 270). The difference between attitudes and values, then, is in the specificity of the object toward which the evaluation is directed. Justices' global policy preferences resemble abstract formulations regarding their ideological tendencies toward broader issue areas, like civil liberties. Those with more liberal values on the civil liberties issue area favor the protection of individual liberties and rights, while conservatives favor the government's capacity to impose certain restrictions on those rights. For this essay, I will not distinguish between "values" and "attitudes" in terms of the attitude object's degree of specificity. Following in the tradition of judicial behavior scholarship (e.g., Segal & Spaeth, 2002), I will refer to policy preferences in more global terms—as an ideological orientation toward a broad legal policy area.

Top-Down and Bottom-Up Processes of Judicial Decision Making

The top-down and bottom-up reasoning processes I have discussed above distinguish between *theory* and *data* in a judgment process. The "theory" a justice brings to a decision setting can be thought of as a set of beliefs on a given legal issue, rooted in one's general ideological predispositions. These predispositions, or policy preferences, have the potential to bias the reasoning process. The "data" in a decision setting are the facts of the case, past precedent(s) and legal doctrine, the arguments in the briefs, oral arguments, and other legal considerations.

The top-down model is a theory-driven reasoning process whereby the policy predispositions a justice brings to a decision context determine how the justice will both process the information at hand and make the judgment. In this process, predispositions, in the form of policy preferences, dictate how the data will be processed. For a top-down processor, one's predisposition provide a lens through which one views the data, therefore biasing the reasoning process. Instead of letting the data guide the decision-maker, the decision-maker finds the data that best supports his or her desired conclusion (á la Segal & Spaeth, 2002). Akin to the MODE model's spontaneous attitude-behavior process, ideological predispositions condition the entire reasoning process by determining how one appraises the cases, how one processes relevant information, and ultimately, how one makes a decision.

The bottom-up model is a data-driven reasoning process whereby the evidence, information, facts, and legal considerations objectively guide the decision maker. Bottom-up processing is objective, unbiased processing of the information and facts, untainted by the ideological predispositions one may possess about the attributes in the decision context. Accuracy, fear of invalidity, and accountability motivations drive one to engage in bottom-up reasoning, to let the data determine how the decision is made, as opposed to finding the evidence that best supports an ideological predisposition. Therefore, given sufficient motivation, the impact of even a relatively accessible attitude will be attenuated throughout the reasoning process, with the justice instead focused on the facts and legal considerations.

Before moving on, a few caveats are in order. First, legal scholars and political scientists recognize that facts, legal rules, and precedent are never completely self-evident. The discovery of these factors can often involve subjective choices based on differences of interpretation. Braman and Nelson (2007), for example, report how the ascertainment of case similarity—choosing which precedent most closely resembles the current case—in legal reasoning can be biased by policy preferences. Thus, rarely would we ever witness a judge engaging in pure bottom-up reasoning. This leads directly to the second caveat. I do not mean to depict judicial reasoning processes as either strictly top-down or strictly bottom-up. Instead, I view these two processes as endpoints of a reasoning continuum, with various hybrid processes falling in between. Social cognition perspectives, and my own perspective, tend to focus on factors that serve to reduce the amount of top-down processing or increase the amount of bottom-up processing. These perspectives recognize that under certain conditions, bias may not be completely eliminated, but instead reduced, with one's predispositions *and* the data guiding the decision process. I recognize this nuance and do not necessarily examine the conditions under which the effects of policy preferences in the decision making process are completely eliminated, which would suggest a purely bottom-up process, or are completely determinant, which would suggest a purely top-down process.

Thus, while a pure bottom-up process would suggest that facts and legal doctrine are essentially self-evident, recall that it represents an endpoint on a continuum. Processes that move away from that endpoint can more realistically capture the subjectivity of interpretation that is inherent in legal reasoning. It is helpful, however, to depict and describe the full range of variation in order to proffer a comprehensive explanation of judicial reasoning.

Sequence of Justices' Decision Processes

To understand justices' reasoning processes, it is instructive to describe first the sequence of processes justices go through when they are confronted with a case. The sequence, depicted in Figure 3.1, begins at the merits stage. Upon

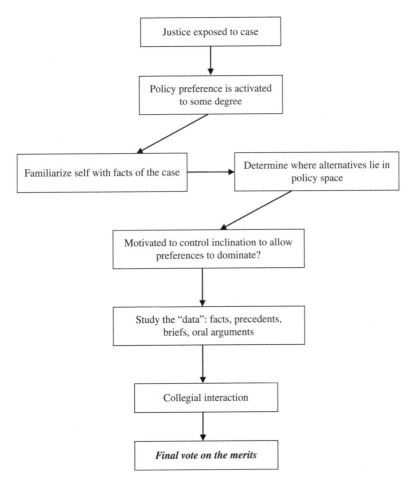

Figure 3.1 Sequence of justices' processes of judgment.

exposure to a case, a justice's policy preference is activated to a certain extent. What I refer to as degree of "activation" is akin to Fazio's conception of attitude accessibility. I do not necessarily assume that a justice's policy preference is automatically activated upon confronting a case. In a death penalty case, for instance, we might assume that a justice's policy preferences toward this issue are highly accessible, and therefore, automatically activated. However, in a case that involves a new, emerging issue area on which the Court has not frequently decided, we might expect less accessible policy preferences. For these latter cases, a policy preference is not strongly activated because the justice has not had much experience with the issue. Since judges are legal experts, though, and have seen a wide variety of cases, they can probably access a policy preference on just about every case that comes before them But this does not mean that the degree of preference activation is uniform across all cases.

After the policy preference is activated to a certain degree, a justice becomes familiar with the facts of the case. This contributes to the determination of where the alternatives (i.e., potential outcomes) lie in an ideological issue space. Note that this stage is at the heart of the attitudinal model (Segal & Spaeth, 1993, p. 65), which states that justices "decide disputes in light of the facts of the case vis-á-vis [their] ideological attitudes and values." Modern conceptions of the attitudinal model are akin to a proximity spatial model, where a justice possesses an ideal point in an issue space, determines where the two alternatives are in the issue space, and votes for the alternative closest to his or her ideal point. My perspective thus far subscribes to the process by which justices come to realize the location of their policy preference relative to the alternatives; they attain this information by consuming the case facts, relevant precedents, and the arguments made by the parties.

In a cognitive account, the next stage in justices' decision processes is crucial. What justices do at this stage depends on the extent to which they are motivated to control an inclination to allow their personal policy preferences to dominate and bias the remainder of their decision processes. This stage may occur either consciously or unconsciously.[3] Fear of invalidity, accountability, or accuracy goals help motivate justices to control these predispositional biases, whatever their strength. Note the similarities to the mixed, controlled processes discussed earlier (Petty & Wegener, 1993; Schuette & Fazio, 1995; Wegener & Petty, 1995). This is both an original and controversial way of thinking about motivations in the judicial context. To clarify, when I talk about motivations, I am referring to the goals that push a justice to reason in one way or another. Recall that typical treatments of Supreme Court decision making have posited a one-goal framework assuming at the outset that justices are "single-minded seekers of legal policy." Adopting Baum's (1994, 1997, 2006) multiple goals framework, a cognitive approach can more easily incorporate the idea of motivational heterogeneity. The motivation a justice possesses under a particular condition will determine the relative impact of predispositional biases versus "data." In Supreme Court decision making, this has implications for explaining the relative impact of policy preferences versus legal considerations.

Following this stage, justices must go through the legal reasoning process: study the facts, read the parties' briefs and amicus curiae briefs, examine past precedents and legal doctrines, and engage in oral arguments. During this "data processing" stage the justices sort through the information and attributes associated with the case. The degree to which a justice is motivated to control predispositional biases will determine how the justice processes the data. It is at this stage that theory and data collide—a justice begins reasoning either in a more top-down, theory-driven process or a bottom-up, data-driven process. In a top-down process, a justice assesses the data through the biasing lens of his or her policy preferences. In a bottom-up process, a justice suppresses this bias and assesses the data through a more objective lens. In a hybrid process, a justice processes information via a mixed process—a weighted combination of top-down versus bottom-up processing, where the weights are determined by the operative motivation(s).[4]

Ideal Types of Justices' Decision Processes

To summarize, I posit that there are two key stages in the sequence of a justice's decision process where there is variation crucial to explaining the relative influence of policy preferences and legal considerations on justices' decisions. First, upon exposure to a particular case, a preference will be activated to a certain degree, such that less than complete preference accessibility will set the stage for a process where the biasing impact of policy preferences in the decision process will be attenuated and the impact of objective considerations will be elevated. At the second stage in the process, a justice's motivation to control bias is central. As this motivation increases, bottom-up processing is more likely to occur, and the impact of policy preferences in the decision process will be attenuated. Below, I construct ideal types of justices' decision processes based on combinations of these two key factors. These ideal types provide predictions about the type of reasoning process under various conditions, and predictions about the effects of policy preferences and legal considerations.

The four ideal types summarized in Table 3.1 consist of all combinations of whether or not a justice's preference accessibility is high or low and whether or not a justice is motivated to control an inclination to act solely on the basis of policy preferences. As ideal types, these four models focus on high and low values of both accessibility and motivation to control bias in order to explore the full theoretical spectrum of processes of behavior. I begin by discussing the two most extreme ideal types. The first ideal type encompasses a situation where a justice's policy preference is highly accessible, and moreover, the justice is not motivated to control bias—perhaps the justice does not feel accountable to another entity, possesses no fear of invalidity, and is driven primarily by ideological goals. This motivational type produces a

Table 3.1 Ideal Types of Justices' Decision Processes

| | | | Predictions | |
| | | | --- | --- |
Preference Accessibility	Motivation to Control Predispositional Biases?	Type of Process	Preference-Behavior Relationship	Impact of Legal Considerations
High	No	Top-Down	Intensified	Minimal
Low	Yes	Bottom-Up	Significantly Attenuated	Significantly Large
High	Yes	Mixed, Controlled	Attenuated	Moderate
Low	No	Mixed	Attenuated	Moderate

strongly top-down reasoning process. It is akin to Fazio's spontaneous atti-tude-behavior process, where an attitude is highly accessible and hence dominates the information processing stage and serves as the predominant influence on reasoning and choice. This top-down ideal type of justices' judgment processes can be considered a cognitive analogue to the contem-porary attitudinal model, where a justice possesses fixed preferences over policy issues and is uninhibited by legal, political, and normative constraints, leaving unbridled discretion to decide cases in an ideological fashion. The predictions that flow from this ideal type, then, are: *(1)* the preference-behavior relationship will be very potent, and *(2)* the impact of legal con-siderations will be minimal.

The second ideal type produces a polar opposite reasoning process from the first type. In this situation, a justice's policy preference is not highly accessible. Low accessibility means that a justice's preference will not dom-inate the decision process to the extent that it will in the spontaneous process. Moreover, the justice is motivated to control an inclination to act in a biased fashion. The situation in front of the justice induces a fear of invalidity, accountability, or accuracy motivation, whereby the justice suppresses pre-dispositional biases and instead, processes the attributes of the case, legal doctrine, and other relevant information in an objective manner. This process strongly resembles a bottom-up reasoning process. The following predictions emerge from this ideal type: *(1)* the preference-behavior relationship will be significantly attenuated, and *(2)* the impact of legal considerations will be significantly large.

The next two ideal types represent reasoning processes somewhere in between top-down and bottom-up processes. First is a situation where a justice's policy preference is highly accessible upon exposure to a case. Thus, the justice's reasoning process is capable of being biased and dominated by the justice's policy preference. However, the justice simultaneously pos-sesses a motivation to control such bias. As mentioned above, the decision context could induce a fear of invalidity, accountability, or accuracy motivation that competes with a justice's highly accessible policy preference. This motivation causes a justice to suppress the inclination to engage in a pure top-down process, and instead to focus on the legal considerations and the particular attributes of the case in an optimally objective manner. This mixed, or controlled, process falls somewhere in between a top-down and bottom-up reasoning process since it is possible for a top-down process to take over, but a motivation to suppress this top-down inclination also exists, which increases the prospects for bottom-up type behavior. In the psychological literature, this process resembles both a controlled, mixed attitude-behavior process (Fazio & Towles-Schwen, 1999) and a flexible correction model (Petty & Wegener, 1993; Wegener & Petty, 1995). Recall that in both models, an individual recognizes his or her bias, is motivated to control that bias, and implements a mechanism that corrects for the bias. From this mixed, controlled process of a justice's reasoning process, a prediction emerges that the relationship between policy preferences and behavior will be attenuated. Also, the impact of legal considerations of various objective criteria will be accentuated.

The final ideal type is the case where a justice's policy preference is not highly accessible, but he or she also possesses no motivation to control the inclination for biased reasoning. This combination is probably the least likely to occur in reality, given the odd combination of low accessibility and a high likelihood for biased processing. Nevertheless, it is a mixed reasoning process since the justice's policy preference is something less than completely accessible, which suggests that a pure top-down reasoning process will not take hold. Thus, the justice is likely to focus more on the attributes of the case, including the legal aspects, in the absence of a strong policy predisposition. However, the justice is also not motivated to control an inclination to behave in a top-down manner, even though the capacity to do so is suppressed due to the low accessibility of preferences. Thus, the low accessibility pushes the justice to be more bottom-up, but the lack of a motivation to control bias pushes the justice to reason via a top-down process. The predictions flowing from this ideal type are similar to the previously discussed type: the preference-behavior relationship will be attenuated, and the impact of legal considerations will be elevated.

Conclusion

In this essay, I have presented a broad cognitive perspective of judging. In this section, I touch on some more tangible issues and obstacles, particularly with respect to testing some of the empirical implications of the model. First, what factors are associated with preference accessibility and motivation to control predispositional biases? In other words, what situations or conditions would induce the accessibility of policy preferences and what situations would induce accountability, fear of invalidity, or accuracy goals? In other work (Bartels, 2005, 2006), I suggest that certain case-level, situational factors are capable of shaping the degree of preference accessibility (or preference strength) and accountability. In particular, I posit that increases in issue salience and issue familiarity and decreases in case complexity activate strong policy preferences among the justices, leading to the possibility of more top-down processing and a stronger preference-behavior relationship. Pertaining to accountability, I posit that the interest group environment, participation by the solicitor general, and whether the case involves a statutory or constitutional question will trigger varying levels of accountability. Higher levels of accountability among the justices lead to a greater possibility of bottom-up processing and a weaker preference-behavior relationship. Another factor associated with preference accessibility relates to so-called "freshmen effects" (e.g., Hagle, 1993). Do new justices have less accessible preferences than veteran justices? Another factor associated with accountability includes the ideological configuration of Congress and the president (Bartels, 2006), which would relate to debates about whether and how the separation-of-powers structure constrains the justices (Epstein & Knight, 1998; Segal, 1997; Segal & Spaeth, 2002; Bergara et al., 2003).

The second empirically oriented issue pertains to the issue of observational, or behavioral, equivalence. In particular, one might find support for the empirical implications of a cognitive perspective of judging, but one could argue that these empirical implications are also consistent with implications emerging from a rational choice, attitudinal, or some type of legal perspective. If observational equivalence is an issue, as it almost certainly would be in this context, empirical evidence in favor of the cognitive model's empirical implications would not necessarily indicate support for the cognitive model itself—that is, the processes underlying the model—because this evidence might also support, for example, a rational choice approach. Since the predictions would not be unique to the cognitive model, it would be necessary to test empirically the processes underlying the cognitive model via experimental methods.

This last point transitions to the third and final empirical issue I discuss—how to test the cognitive processes of judging. If legal researchers had their way, we would recruit judges as experimental subjects, design an experiment that manipulates some factors (e.g., preference accessibility and motivation to control bias), randomly assign the judges to experimental conditions, and test for causal processes underlying judging. Guthrie et al.'s (2001, 2002, 2007a) innovative experiments on judges provide a valuable template for conducting such work. My theoretical framework requires an experimental approach that would allow researchers to "get inside the heads" of judges to explain how they reason about cases. Recruiting currently serving judges as experimental subjects for this type of study might be improbable, given judges' sensitivity to rendering judgments on hypothetical cases. This presents an obstacle for testing the cognitive processes of judging, but the obstacles are not insurmountable, as Guthrie et al show. Moreover, Braman and Nelson (2007) used law students as experimental subjects to explore biases in legal reasoning. To test a theoretical framework like the one I have proposed, one possibility is to recruit retired judges as experimental subjects and perform a survey experiment.[5] Retired judges may be more likely to respond to such a survey experiment with considerable candor, given they no longer have an active stake in the judiciary. Obviously, the pool of retired Supreme Court justices is extremely limited, but recruiting retired U.S. Courts of Appeals or District Court judges is a possibility.

In conclusion, the cognitive perspective presented in this essay has the potential for providing a more realistic, nuanced explanation of judging. By focusing on the cognitive processes inside the judicial mind, the cognitive approach has the ability to improve on existing models of judicial decision making that treat judicial reasoning processes as a black box. While I have aimed the essay toward justices of the U.S. Supreme Court, the theoretical framework I have presented has implications for judging at other levels in the judicial hierarchy.

Notes

I am grateful to Lawrence Baum, Eileen Braman, David Klein, and Howard Lavine for extremely helpful feedback and suggestions on this essay.

1. I use the terms "policy preferences," "ideology," and "attitudes toward legal policy" interchangeably.
2. Posner (1992) has distinguished between top-down and bottom-up legal reasoning processes. While there are some general similarities between his approach and mine (e.g., emphasis on "theory-driven" reasoning), some key differences exist. Namely, his conceptual framework is not psychologically oriented. My focus is on the extent to which, and conditions under which, ideological predispositions bias legal reasoning processes.
3. The issue of whether this is a conscious or unconscious process would require a more in-depth discussion, which is beyond this essay's central scope of inquiry. What is most important in this discussion is whether and to what degree justices are motivated to control their biases. It is quite conceivable that such a process could be either conscious or unconscious, a question I leave for future research.
4. I exclude from this discussion any collegial interaction that occurs in the opinion drafting stage (e.g., Maltzman, Spriggs, & Wahlbeck, 2000). Incorporating small-group dynamics (see Martinek's essay in this volume) would offer a compelling addition to the framework I have laid out.
5. I thank Pete Rowland for suggesting this idea in a conversation.

4

Persuasion in the Decision Making of U.S. Supreme Court Justices

Lawrence S. Wrightsman

The purpose of this paper is to provide some thoughts about the role of persuasion in judicial decision making. Herein, persuasion is treated broadly as the process of influence, which covers not only overt attempts at influence (by the media, by the advocates, and by other judges) but also the judges' responses to attempts at influence. Emphasis is on the question: What influences how a judge forms an initial opinion about a case? The coverage and examples refer to the United States Supreme Court, but the ideas are applicable to other appellate panels and in some respects to trial judges.

Basic Assumptions

This paper assumes that justices are more susceptible to persuasion depending on the nature of the case; some cases deal with matters to which the justices have given much prior thought. Certain cases may reflect issues on which they have developed strong views long in their past. Research on persuasion certainly indicates that the nature of the material affects the willingness to be responsive to an attempt to persuade. But individual differences may exist in justices' readiness to be persuaded on all issues; some may possess personality characteristics that inhibit change. Thus, this paper reflects two assumptions:

1. Persuasion operates differently depending on the type of case.
2. Persuasion operates differently depending on the particular justice.

The body of the paper elaborates on these assumptions and presents some data and examples to evaluate the paper's claims.

Testing the First Assumption: Ideological Versus Nonideological Cases

Cases that are granted certiorari by the Supreme Court can be classified in many different ways: by their topic, by whether they reflect ordinary litigation or political litigation (Baum, 2007), by the presence or absence of the government as a party, by whether they come from the liberal 9th Circuit Court or the conservative 4th and 5th Circuits, and so on. This paper hypothesizes that persuasion, and thus the decision-making process, operates differently in ideological cases than in nonideological cases. By "ideological cases," I mean cases whose content is related to an attitude or value held by a justice. Hot-button issues lead to ideological cases. In general, agreement exists on just where positions on salient ideological issues can be placed along a liberal-versus-conservative political dimension. For example, "in criminal cases, liberals are relatively sympathetic toward criminal defendants and their procedural rights, while conservatives give more emphasis to the effectiveness of the criminal justice system in fighting crime" (Baum, 1990, Table 1–3, p. 13). This paper employs Lawrence Baum's distinctions between liberal and conservative positions on judicial issues as a convenient summary.

Nonideological cases are those in which the central issues do not tap into deeply felt values of the justices. In the studies to be described subsequently I asked two raters to independently classify cases as nonideological if their content did not deal with the various topics that distinguished between liberals and conservatives, using Baum's detailed distinctions. Thus, non-ideological cases are less easily classified by content, but disputes between two states, patent disputes, and conflicts between two businesses usually are nonideological cases. The case of *Wachovia Bank v. Schmidt* (2006) dealt with the question of whether a bank with many branches was a "person" in every state where it had a branch or only in its headquarters state. The case was decided unanimously and did not seem to provoke any ideological biases. Another nonideological example is the case of *Kansas v. Colorado*, to which the Supreme Court granted cert in 2001. The Arkansas River begins in the Rockies, flows across Kansas, part of Oklahoma, and across Arkansas before emptying into the Mississippi. A dispute between Colorado and Kansas over diversion of river water had seemingly been settled by the passage of the Arkansas River Compact by Congress in 1949. But for a number of years Kansas had complained that Colorado had violated the compact. After the Court had so ruled in 1995, it remanded the case to a Special Master. But Kansas claimed that Colorado continued to violate the rules. In 2001 the Court again sided with Kansas, including a judgment that Colorado should pay interest on the damages accrued. While the question of an interpretation of the Eleventh Amendment was part of the issue at hand, the Supreme Court ruled unanimously in favor of Kansas in 2001, and the basis appears to be simply what the law says. Thus the case appears to be free of ideological triggers.

How does persuasion operate differently in ideological cases than in nonideological cases? First, it is proposed that justices are aware of ideological cases earlier than they are about nonideological cases. Well before their conference to decide which cases to grant cert, even well before a petition is submitted, the typical ideological case has generated publicity. A state passes a law that critically restricts abortions, a university's admissions program to increase diversity is challenged in a lower court, the Bush administration places prisoners of war at Guantanamo Bay and denies them rights to a trial— such decisions draw attention from the media, and the justices read the newspapers and watch television news as many members of the citizenry do. In contrast, for many nonideological cases, the first awareness may come when the justice reads the recommendations from a law clerk who has processed the case as part of the cert pool.

Second, at the point of granting cert, justices know more about the issues in ideological cases than nonideological ones. Issues of search and seizure, for example, are frequently before the Court; in the October 2003 Term the Court dealt with ten cases involving claims of a violation of Fourth Amendment rights. More often, nonideological cases deal with a relatively obscure federal law, so that during the process leading up to the decision to grant cert, most justices have to do more review. For example, a case during the October 2003 Term (*BedRoc Limited v. United States*) dealt with the terminology in the Pittman Underground Water Act of 1919, a legislative decision probably not on the forefront of each justice's awareness prior to preparing for the cert conference.

Justices' Values and Ideological Cases

But the most important difference is what makes the case ideological— whether its issues generate a value-based predisposition. Many years ago psychologist Fred Kerlinger (1967) proposed that in conceptualizing attitudes and values, it was useful not to think of each as a bipolar continuum, but rather to focus on what he called "criterial referents." Certain objects, topics, or issues may serve as anchors, or criterial referents, which define one's values. For each justice, different issues may serve as criterial referents; for some, abortion; for some, the death penalty; and for some, racial or gender dis- crimination. These serve as triggers to at least a preliminary leaning in one direction. Sometimes it is more than a leaning; it is an irrevocable response. For example, toward the end of Justice Harry Blackmun's service on the

Court, his position on any case coming before the Court that dealt with the death penalty was clear. In 1994, his dissent in *Callins v. Collins* states:

> From this day forward, I no longer shall tinker with the machinery of death. . . . It is virtually self evident to me now that no combination of procedural rules or substantive regulations can ever save the death penalty from its inherent constitutional deficiencies. . . . The problem is that the inevitability of factual, legal, and moral error gives us a system that we know must wrongly kill some defendants, a system that fails to deliver the fair. . . and reliable sentences of death required by the Constitution. (p. 1145)

More recently, Justice Antonin Scalia has made it clear that on certain matters before the Court, he had made his mind up before the process of considering the issues had been completed. On one occasion—the issue was the constitutionality of the words "under God" included in the Pledge of Allegiance—he recused himself because of public statements he had made.

But in another notable case, that of *Hamdan v. Rumsfeld*, he did not. This case required the Court to decide whether an enemy combatant who was detained at Guantanamo Bay was protected by the articles of the 1949 Geneva Conventions as a prisoner of war. In a speech a few weeks before this case's oral arguments, Scalia ridiculed the suggestion that detainees captured "on the battlefield" should receive a trial in civil courts; that proposition, he said, was a "crazy idea." He interrupted a subsequent question by claiming: "If he was captured by my army on a battlefield, that is where he belongs. I have a son on that battlefield and they were shooting at my son. And I am not about to give this man who was captured in a war a full jury trial. I mean it's crazy" (Isikoff, 2006, p. 6).

Justice Scalia's comments drew strong criticism and calls for recusal from several sources (Isikoff, 2006). But Justice Scalia was not deterred; he participated actively at the oral arguments and voted in the case. In fairness to Justice Scalia, he is certainly not the only justice and this was not the only case in which a justice's eventual vote was fixed in concrete before the oral arguments; the matter came to light because of his provocative style and willingness to express his opinion in public. For him, if not every justice, this was an ideological case, and his actions support the argument that in such cases, opinions are formed early and not susceptible to persuasion. Thus, even though the focus of this paper is on persuasion, it questions how much opportunity exists to persuade justices on certain cases; their minds may be made up very quickly.

Ideological Cases and Automatic Responses

Thus, for some justices on some cases, it is proposed that their reaction is emotional and their response is instantaneous. (For a sharp contrast in very well formed values between two justices, read Justice Scalia's opinion for the Court and Justice Brennan's dissent in the case of *Michael H. v. Gerald*

D., 1989.) Social psychologists have concluded that the evaluations of stimuli—events, persons, issues—are often automatic; that is, they are so primed by the stimulus that they are given without further processing (Bargh & Ferguson, 2000; Duckworth, Bargh, Garcia, & Chaiken, 2002). There is even some evidence that we may have two systems

> for evaluating various aspects of the social world; one that operates in an automatic manner and the other that operates in a systematic and controlled manner.... In fact, studies conducted from the perspective of social neuroscience indicate that these differences exist. Certain parts of the brain, especially the amygdala, may be involved in automatic evaluative reactions, simple good-bad judgments that occur in a rapid and nonconscious manner. In contrast, portions of the prefrontal cortex (especially the medial prefrontal cortex and ventrolateral prefrontal cortex) may play a key role in more controlled executive reactions—the kinds about which we think carefully and consciously. (Baron, Byrne, & Branscomb, 2006, p. 54)

Are some values so entrenched and so relevant to case decisions that they produce automatic reactions that do not receive review? If Justice Scalia (rather than the ubiquitous freshman psychology student) were a respondent in the kind of experiment used by psychologists to demonstrate automatic responses, how would he respond if "abortion" were flashed on the screen? We cannot say, but the emphasis on automaticity of responses is provocative.

Attitudinal and Legal Models of Judicial Decision Making

The distinction between ideological and nonideological cases may help to understand the long-standing conflict between two models of judicial decision making. Both the legal model and the attitudinal model have been extensively considered and debated in the political-science literature. (Other chapters in this book describe shifts in the attitudinal model toward a more strategic orientation.) Indirect support for the attitudinal model has also been demonstrated in several extensive analyses of the voting records of federal district court and circuit court judges; for example, Rowland and Carp (1996) showed how district judges appointed by Republican presidents decided cases on civil liberties and civil rights, for example, in a different direction from similar cases decided by judges appointed by Democrats. More recently, Sunstein, Schkade, Ellman, and Sawicki (2006) presented data on how the composition of judges on federal circuit-court panels (specifically the political party of the president who appointed them) affected their votes on what we would call ideological issues.

Each of these models (especially the attitudinal model) has its adherents (see, for example, Segal & Spaeth, 1993, 2002), but the possibility that each may apply in certain types of cases is less often emphasized. Another possibility is that in a particular case, the attitudinal model may describe the reaction of some justices, while others may struggle to maintain a basis in the legal model.

The wealth of empirical data used by adherents of the attitudinal model (consistency in votes, correlation of votes of individual justices with their ideological pronouncements in speeches, books, or articles) to support their claim may apply in ideological cases, but in those cases where no personal values are salient, the justices are more likely to examine the statutes, the precedents, and, if applicable, the Constitution in a dispassionate manner. (See, for example, the recent article by Lindquist and Klein, 2006, that revives support for the role played by legal reasoning in Supreme Court decisions.)

Predictions

In summary, it is proposed that, compared to their response to nonideological cases, individual justices in ideological cases are less responsive to the persuasion expressed in merit briefs and oral arguments. Specifically, it is hypothesized that they:

1. Form initial opinions more quickly.
2. Are less likely to change their opinions.
3. Have formed opinions by the time of oral arguments, so that their questioning reflects their already-formed opinions.
4. Are less responsive to outside influences.
5. Are more predictable with regard to their final votes.

Furthermore, this paper suggests that the degree to which a case is ideological can be reflected in several qualities of the dispensation of the case. Specifically, in ideological cases, compared to nonideological cases:

1. The final vote will less often be a unanimous vote, because the current composition of the Court is divided ideologically.
2. It will take longer for the Court to announce the decision in the case, because the minority will more likely write dissents and the opinion of the Court will go through more drafts.

As part of an ongoing project (see Wrightsman, 2008), data have been collected from several recent terms of the Supreme Court that sometimes directly and sometimes indirectly respond to these hypotheses.

For four recent terms each case has been classified as ideological, borderline, or nonideological. The following variables have been determined:

1. In the oral arguments, the length of time (measured in words) that the petitioner spoke and the respondent spoke before they were interrupted by a justice.
2. The number of questions asked each advocate by the justices during the oral arguments.

3. Whether or not a representative of the Office of the Solicitor General participated in the oral arguments, and if so, on which side.
4. The length of time (measured in days) from the oral argument to the announcement of the decision.
5. The announced vote.
6. For the October 2002 Term, the predicted votes and case outcomes as determined by the Supreme Court Forecasting Project at the School of Law at Washington University in St. Louis. (Although this project calculated statistical predictions of the outcomes in some cases in the next term, the October 2003 Term, the data analysis was discontinued in the middle of this second term.)

Empirical Tests of the Predictions

Data from the Supreme Court website were used to test the above predictions. For example, it was hypothesized that in ideological cases, justices form opinions quickly, they are less likely to change their opinions, and their questioning during oral arguments reflects their already-formed opinions. How can these hypotheses be tested empirically?

Over the last three years, two findings have been published that have concluded that during oral arguments, justices as a group ask more questions to the advocates representing the eventual losing side than they do to the advocates whose side eventually wins. The first was a study done by Sarah Shullman (2004), who observed ten oral arguments during the October 2002 Term. She reported, "All nine justices seemed to ask fewer questions of the party in whose favor they would ultimately decide" (2004, p. 278). But there are numerous methodological problems in her study. With only one observer, there is no test of inter-rater reliability. The task of doing these ratings on the spur of the moment seems very challenging; a typical 30-minute presentation by one side generates anywhere from 30 to 100 questions/comments by the justices. And when my students and I set forth to replicate and extend her findings, we found it is not easy to say just what is a question. Justices interrupt each other, their questions are sometimes answered before they are finished, there are numerous brief comments ("Okay." "I see." "Right.") which may or may not be counted as questions. But despite these, Shullman's study drew attention. Tony Mauro devoted an article in the *American Lawyer* to it, and it certainly provoked me to determine if the effect was genuine and widespread.

Just about the same time as the publication of Shullman's article, John Roberts (before he was named Chief Justice) addressed the Supreme Court Historical Society at its annual meeting. Although most of his talk dealt with the reemergence of a Supreme Court bar, he did report on an analysis he had conducted. He took the first and last cases in each of the two-week argument sessions for the October 1980 Term and for the October 2003 Term, and determined, for each case, the number of questions directed at the petitioner and the number directed at the respondent. Then he examined which side won. He reported: "In the 28 cases I looked at, 14 from the 1980 Term and 14 from 2003, the most-questions-asked 'rule' predicted the winner—or, more accurately, the loser—in 24 of those 28 cases, an 86 percent prediction rate" (2005, p. 75). Then he drily added, "The secret to successful advocacy is simply to get the Court to ask your opponent more questions" (2005, p. 75). Like Shullman, Roberts did not define what a "question" was, and neither study distinguished between ideological and nonideological cases. But the methodology seemed to provide an entry into determining if any difference related to persuadability existed. Does the more-questions-to-the loser rule hold when all cases in a term are examined? Does it hold more strongly for ideological cases?

Testing the Accuracy of the "More Questions to the Loser" Rule

In our research (Wrightsman, 2008), we quantified "questions" by referring to the transcript of the case and counting any comment or question by a justice, even if it was interrupted or fragmentary. The virtue of this operational definition is that it provides reliability. We investigated other ways of counting questions, such as combining interrupted statements or questions; such procedures lacked reliability; it is not as easy to say what is and what is not one "question" as one might think. The analysis my students and I did revealed the following: For the October 2001 Term, the eventual losing side was asked more questions in 29 of 41 ideological cases, or 70.7%; this success rate contrasts strongly with those in the borderline ideological cases—6 of 14, or 42.8%—and the nonideological cases—8 of 16, or 50%. For the October 2002 Term, the same differences were observed; the eventual losing side was asked more questions in 21 of the 33 ideological cases, or 63.6%; in 9 of 16 borderline ideological cases, or 56.2%, and in only 11 of 23 nonideological cases, or 47.8% (Overall, in each of these terms, while the eventual loser did get more questions, the percentage of outcomes predicted accurately, 60% in each term, was much lower than what was found in the previous studies.)

For the October 2005 Term, the results were consistent with the October 2001 and 2002 terms, although the differences between types of cases were smaller. More questions were asked of the losing side in 28 of 43 ideological cases (65.1%), in 9 of 14 borderline ideological cases (64.3%), and 9 of 15 nonideological cases (60%). Overall, the rate was 46 out of 72 cases, or 64%.

Thus, the rule does seem to have some validity, although not as great a predictability as the early studies promised. The fact that it holds more strongly in ideological cases (albeit the differences are not huge) indicates that to some extent, the nature of the case has led to an earlier formation of opinions by justices.

Agreement with the Office of the Solicitor General

Another measure that supports the distinction between ideological and non-ideological cases is the degree to which the eventual decision was consistent with the position advocated by the Office of the Solicitor General. As has been well documented (Baum, 1997; McGuire, 1996), the side supported by the solicitor general, as advocate or amicus curiae, more often wins. In those terms studied in this project, this was true: in the October 2002 Term, the solicitor general's side won in 43 of 61 cases, or 65%, and in the October 2005 Term, 38 of 56 cases, or 68%. But in each of these terms, in ideological cases the solicitor general's side won less often than it did overall—only 60.7% in 2002 and 61% in 2005. In the October 2001 Term, the Court's decision was consistent with the solicitor general's position in a whopping 89% of the ideological cases and 93% of the nonideological cases. Again, the differences are small, and subject to several interpretations, but one possible interpretation is that in ideological cases the justices are less susceptible to persuasion from the Office of the Solicitor General, despite the high regard with which these attorneys are held, because their minds have been made up.

It was also predicted that differences in the dispensation of cases would be based on the degree to which their content was ideological. Two measures were employed to test these predictions: percentage of cases in which the final decision was unanimous, and length of time to reach a decision.

Do Ideological Cases More Often Lead to Nonunanimous Decisions by the Court?

During the October 2001 Term, of 72 decisions, only 26, or 36%, were unanimous. As predicted, unanimous decisions were reached less often in ideological cases (32.5%) than in nonideological cases (43.7%). Borderline-ideological cases produced just about the same level of unanimity (33.3%) as ideological cases.

While the overall degree of unanimity increased slightly in the October 2002 Term, the pattern was consistent with the earlier term. Only 12 of 33 ideological cases resulted in unanimous decisions (36.4%), compared to 7 of 16 borderline-ideological cases (43.7%), and 13 of 23 nonideological cases (56.5%). Overall, 32 of 72 decisions, or 44.4%, were unanimous. For the October 2005 Term, the effect of the type of case is quite similar: unanimity in 20 of 43 ideological cases (45.6%), in 8 of 14 borderline-ideological cases (57.1%), and 10 of 15 nonideological cases, or 66.7%). Overall, in 2005–2006, 38 of 72 decisions were unanimous, or 52.8%. (The latter term, Chief Justice Roberts' first, led to a higher rate of unanimous decisions than in any recent term, perhaps reflecting his aspirations for greater consensus in decisions.)

How Long Does the Court Take to Reach a Decision?

It was also predicted that the justices would take longer to announce decisions in ideological cases. Decision latency was measured by the number of days between the oral argument and the announcement of the decision. For the October 2002 Term, the average latency for ideological cases was 81 days, for borderline ideological 75 days, and for nonideological 67 days. For the October 2005 Term, these average latencies were 84, 78, and 66 days. In both terms, ideological cases took longer to reach final resolution. But in the October 2001 Term, the justices took less time to decide ideological cases—82 days versus 92 days for nonideological cases.

Reanalyzing Data from the Supreme Court Forecasting Project

Finally, with regard to predictions generated from the initial hypothesis that persuasion operates differently based on the nature of the case, a further analysis was done of some data generated by researchers at the School of Law at Washington University in St. Louis (Ruger, Kim, Martin, & Quinn, 2004). The Supreme Court Forecasting Project has been an exceedingly useful vehicle for anyone interested in Supreme Court decision making. For all cases in the October 2002 Term, the staff developed a prediction of votes and decisions based on a statistical formula that employed only six generally straightforward variables. These were the following:

1. The circuit court of origin.
2. The issue area of the case (using the 15 topic areas developed by Harold J. Spaeth in his U.S. Supreme Court Judicial Database).
3. The type of petitioner (e.g., the federal government, an employer, a defendant, etc.)
4. The type of respondent.
5. The ideological direction (liberal or conservative) of the ruling by the lower court.
6. Whether the petitioner argued that the law or practice was unconstitutional (Ruger et al., 2004, p. 1163).

This information was fed into classification trees and generated predictions for the votes of each justice and hence the outcome of the case. The classification trees differed from justice to justice; a variable that was prominent in the decision tree of one justice might be "relatively unimportant or altogether absent in another" (Ruger et al., 2004, p. 1165). But also, the decision trees of the different justices are not independent of one another; for example, a branch point in Justice Thomas's decision tree is based on Justice Scalia's anticipated vote (Ruger et al., 2004, Figure 9, p. 1198).

The staff also identified a pool of 83 experts, 71 law professors, and 12 appellate attorneys (including 38 former Supreme Court law clerks), and, for each case, asked as many as three who had specialized knowledge in the type of case to predict the votes and outcome. Experts were asked to predict the outcomes of cases within only their areas of expertise. Like the predictions from the statistical formula, all predictions by the experts were made prior to oral arguments. Experts were provided a copy of the lower court opinion and citations to the parties' Supreme Court briefs, but they were free to consider any sources of information they considered relevant.

Overall, the statistical model correctly predicted 75% of the decisions in the October 2002 Term, while the experts, as a group, were correct only 59.1% of the time (Ruger et al., 2004, Table 1, p. 1171). It was hypothesized that decisions in the ideological cases would be more predictable than those in the nonideological cases, and so a further analysis was done of data that were available on the project's website (www.wusct.wustl.edu). Considering the statistical model first, it was found that it was correct in 26 of 33 ideological cases or 78.8%, correct in 11 of 15 borderline-ideological cases, or 73.3%, and correct in 16 of 23 nonideological cases, or 69.6%. Thus the predicted difference was obtained. For the experts, in ideological cases, 53 of 88 were correct or 60.2%, while 18 of 35 were correct in borderline-ideological cases, or 51.4%, and 32 of 55 were correct in nonideological cases, or 58.2%. For the experts, the differences are not linear, as they are with the statistical model, and the experts did not do appreciably better in the ideological cases than in the nonideological ones.

Interim Summary

In summary, persuasion does appear to operate somewhat differently based on whether the case is an ideological one or not. Data from several terms indicate that:

1. In ideological cases, the final vote less often is unanimous.
2. In ideological cases, the time it takes to reach a decision is longer, at least in the majority of terms.
3. In oral arguments in ideological cases, justices direct more questions to the advocate or advocates who represent what later becomes the losing side, implying that to some extent justices have already formed an opinion in ideological cases before the oral argument.
4. In ideological cases, the decision of the Court is less often consistent with the position of the Office of the Solicitor General, again reflecting the power of the justices' own ideologies in deciding such cases.

Most of the empirical tests of the hypothesis produce small differences, although the pattern is strongly in the expected direction. The smallness of the differences is perhaps not surprising, given the rather broad means of distinguishing between ideological and nonideological cases. For example, abortion cases were classified as ideological; in actuality, the topic of abortion triggers an instantaneous, value-drive reaction in some justices more than it does in others. More work is needed in specifying the interaction between type of case and the individual justice.

To conclude that justices react in different ways to ideological and non-ideological cases may, to many readers, seem to be less than a surprising conclusion. But this variable may be useful in helping us understand the role of persuasion in judicial decision making. A next step is to examine the content (rather than the frequency) of justices' questions during oral arguments, to determine if evaluative comments are made more often in ideological cases. In an analysis of 24 oral arguments during the October 2004 Term, Jacqueline Austin and I recorded 109 instances of a justice's question or comment that was unsympathetic to the advocate's position. In 87 of the 109, the justice later voted against that side. Do these reflect values that play a role in ideological cases?

Testing the Second Assumption

The second assumption offered at the beginning of this paper proposed that persuasion operates differently depending on the particular justice. Here an individual-differences approach may be fruitful. What makes certain justices more persuasive and what make certain justices more resistant to persuasion?

Justices Who Were Effective Persuaders

If we consider justices over the last 50 years, certain ones stand out for their ability to persuade their colleagues. Earl Warren is recognized for taking a conflict-riddled Court that was divided on *Brown v. Board of Education* and persuading its holdouts so that the Court was able to announce a unanimous decision on May 17, 1954. Chief Justice Warren was not a legal scholar, but the other justices were influenced by his charisma and his political skills. During that period, and even after Warren had left the bench, William Brennan was very influential, even bringing conservatives to his side in some cases, because of his genuine interest in people and his willingness and ability to craft majority opinions that reflected the wishes of justices who did not completely agree with everything that Brennan would have wished to achieve. Consideration of the Court during those years leads to a conclusion that sheer brilliance is not, in and of itself, enough to make justices effective in their attempts to persuade their colleagues (Rosen, 2007). Felix Frankfurter came to the Court with everything going for him: a professorship in constitutional law at Harvard Law School, a number of articles and books on the Supreme Court, and a network of friends and former students in high places in the government. Yet Frankfurter's attempts to ingratiate and manipulate other justices were largely unsuccessful, and, in fact, some justices (Douglas and Black and even, eventually, Whittaker) came to ignore and even ridicule his efforts to persuade.

Justices as Recipients of Persuasion

Judges, as recipients of persuasion, can be studied through several approaches. For example, an appellate court is like any other small problem-solving group in that pressures toward uniformity exist and that some group participants succumb to them. Solomon Asch (1955, 1956), a social psychologist, demonstrated in what has become a classic study, that it is very hard for a sole participant in a group project to maintain his or her response when all the other participants differ in response, *even if he or she is the only participant who is correct*. That such pressures to conformity often cause the outlier to succumb has been demonstrated in everything from jury deliberations to decisions by the advisers to the United States president. Justice O'Connor is quoted in a recent book as saying that justices would never change their vote simply to be a part of the majority (Greenburg, 2007) but it does happen. Certainly on occasion justices join the majority opinion even when they have reservations. A memo from Chief Justice Burger to Justice Black in a 1971 case said: "I do not really agree but the case is narrow and unimportant except to one man. . . . I will join you in spite of my reservations" (Maltzman, Spriggs, & Wahlbeck, 2000, p. 22). The justices even have a name for this reaction, as illustrated in a communication from Justice White to Justice Marshall: "I was the other way, but I acquiesce, i.e., a graveyard dissent" (Maltzman et al., 2000, p. 7).

Responses to Pressures Toward Uniformity

The claim that even justices frequently respond to pressures to uniformity is illustrated in an analysis of the data generated by the Supreme Court Forecasting Project (Wrightsman, 2006, Chapter 10). Recall that this project generated predictions of each justice's vote in each case for the October 2002 Term. The project then took these anticipated votes to make predictions of the outcomes. But the procedure did not have any means to add in what might be called a "conformity correction." Thus the statistical model predicted that in this term there would be only 7 unanimous decisions out of 72 cases. In actuality there were 31. The model predicted there would be 20 8-to-1 decisions, but in actuality there were only 4 (Wrightsman, 2006). Clearly, when most justices vote one way, pressures exist on the holdout justice to go along, and often they do. An analysis by Granberg and Bartels (2005) of voting patterns in the Court extending back to the 1950s found that 8-to-1 votes were the least frequent type, accounting for only 10% of the decisions. In contrast, over this period of 48 terms, unanimous votes occurred in 35% of the cases and 5-to-4 votes in 21%. William O. Douglas, who served on the Court for 36 years, the longest of any justice, also has the record for the most sole dissents, 106, or about 3 a year. But William Brennan, on the Court for almost as long as Justice Douglas, had only 11 in 34 years, reflecting his desire to be conciliatory. And Chief Justice Burger, who did not like other justices to write dissents, or even concurrences, was a sole dissenter only 4 times in his 17 years on the Court.

Such individual differences are also apparent among current justices; in the last five terms, Justice Stevens has been a sole dissenter 10 times, Justice Thomas 6 times, and Justice Scalia 4 times. In contrast, Justice Ginsburg never was a sole dissenter in that time period, and neither Chief Justice Roberts nor Justice Alito have been sole dissenters in their briefer times on the Court. (As noted, Chief Justice Roberts, during this term, has been advocating for more narrow, unanimous decisions.)

What contributes to a justice's being a sole dissenter? Strongly held opinions and a relative lack of concern about the opinions of others would seem to be determinants. In his 30 years on the Court, Justice Stevens has always gone his own way. Kenneth Starr has written that "he has taken on the role of a naysayer" (2002, p. 43). Jan Crawford Greenburg's recent book calls him "an iconoclast" and has this description of him:

> Stevens was a maverick who didn't ascribe to a particular theory. He was fiercely independent in his writings and actions. When the justices donned their robes before taking the bench, Stevens was the only one who refused assistance from the aides in the robing room. He always insisted on putting on his own robe. He took his own path in his opinions, too. (2007, p. 180)

Justice Thomas has, of course, been subjected to intense scrutiny from the time of his nomination to the Court; within the last year two books have been published that direct attention to his style of decision making. *Supreme Discomfort* (2007) by Kevin Merida and Michael Fletcher provides an insight into Justice Thomas's background and possible reasons for his adamant position on ideological issues. Jan Crawford Greenburg's (2007) book illustrates that even from his first months on the Court, Justice Thomas had an independent streak. At his very first conference after the oral arguments (*Foucha v. Louisiana*, 1992) he chose to dissent from the majority, and it initially appeared that he would be the sole dissenter. (Several months later, after he had circulated his written dissent—which was sharply critical of the majority opinion by Justice White—three other justices shifted from the majority to his minority side.) In his second week of oral arguments, he again chose to be a sole dissenter, in the Eighth Amendment case *Hudson v. McMillian* (2002). His dissent drew wide condemnation in the media (the *New York Times* editorialized that he was "the youngest cruelest justice") but again it drew the support of one other justice (Scalia).

Greenburg's view is the following:

> Though quiet on the bench during public sessions, Thomas wasted no time sharing his views in conference. Pundits and analysts would disparage Thomas as Scalia's intellectual understudy, but from the beginning that portrayal was grossly inaccurate.... Thomas made clear that he was willing to be the solo dissenter, sending other justices the strong signal that he would not moderate his opinions for the sake of comity. (Greenburg, 2007, p. 115)

According to Mark Tushnet, Justice Thomas's strong will and uncompromising positions created problems when he was assigned majority opinions by Chief Justice Rehnquist. Tushnet writes:

> Thomas was rarely unsure about the positions he took, so strategy never counseled in favor of giving him an important opinion. Indeed, his very certainty sometimes recommended against doing so. Thomas tended to write strong opinions, drawing sharp lines and rarely acknowledging that different circumstances might produce different outcomes. O'Connor and Kennedy sometimes preferred a more nuanced doctrine than Thomas's opinions articulated. Also, Thomas was more reluctant that other justices to accommodate such concerns. As a result, Thomas "lost a Court" more often than other justices given opinion assignments. That is, instead of gaining the five votes that seemed to be available when the opinions were assigned, his opinions might get only four votes. (Tushnet, 2005, p. 86)

Tushnet makes an interesting observation. It seems to predict that, at least when Chief Justice Rehnquist was assigning opinions, Justice Thomas was more likely to be assigned "safe" ones. An examination of the opinion assignments for the last two terms when Rehnquist was Chief Justice (October 2003 and October 2004 terms) finds that Justice Thomas wrote 16 opinions for the Court, and 9 of the 16, or 56%, were unanimous. Of the remaining 7, 3 were 7-to-2 or 6-to-2, 2 were 6-to-3, and 2 were 5-to-4. The percentage of 9-to-0 decisions in cases in which Justice Thomas authored the Court's opinion was much higher than the 35% to 40% unanimity in those terms.

Justice Thomas's response to his critics is to say, "I don't care what they think. I am free to live up to my oath" (Greenburg, 2007, p. 121). And it is certainly true that his independence is manifested in a number of ways, some related to his work on the Court and some not. His failure to participate in oral arguments has been noted here and elsewhere. During a visit to the University of Kansas Law School, he was interviewed by the local newspaper; when asked about oral arguments, he told the reporter, "I don't see the need for all those questions. I think justices, 99 percent of the time, have their minds made up when they go to the bench" (Rombeck, 2002, p. 5B). Justice Thomas also demonstrates his nonconformity in his off-the-Court preferences, including—in what seems to be a deliberate act of perversity in Washington, D.C., where everyone lives and dies with the results of the Redskins' football fortunes—his identification as a Dallas Cowboys fan.

Individual Differences Variables and Personality Variables

Psychologists interested in personality and individual differences have generated concepts applicable to resistance to persuasion, going all the way back to work on dogmatism in the 1950s. Tetlock's (1983a; Tetlock, Bernzweig, & Gallant, 1985; Gruenfeld, 1995) work on integrative complexity or cognitive complexity led him to analyze majority and dissenting opinions by the Supreme Court, and such concepts could be applied to resistance to persuasion. As discussed in the Mitchell and Tetlock chapter in this book, Isaiah Berlin's prototypes of the hedgehog and the fox can be used to identify formulaic approaches to decision making, including that by judges and justices. These and other related traits, such as need for cognition, dogmatism, and the need for cognitive closure are worthy of the attention of scholars studying persuasion in judging.

Conclusion

In the preface to *The Puzzle of Judicial Behavior,* Lawrence Baum expresses his belief "that we are a long way from achieving explanations of judicial behavior that are fully satisfactory" (1997, p. xi). That was more than 10 years ago; this chapter has presented a modest effort toward an explanation, by identifying ways that persuasion operates differently on judges as they form their opinions, depending on their biases and the nature of the case. Beyond this, scholars are beginning the hard work of examining the files of several recent justices, especially the detailed records of Justice Blackmun, to illustrate the role of persuasion during the process of moving from the initial decision draft to the final opinion of the Court. The recent article by Johnson, Spriggs, and Wahlbeck (2007) is an excellent example. We can look forward to a greater understanding of the role of persuasion at all stages of judicial decision making.

5

Judges as Members of Small Groups

Wendy L. Martinek

Though most judges are trial court judges, and most judicial decisions are made by trial court judges, appellate courts and the judges who populate them have attracted a considerable (disproportionate?) share of scholarly attention. This focus is perhaps lamentable but understandable given that judicial policymaking falls more centrally in the province of appellate courts rather than trial courts.[1] In fact, some legal scholars have gone so far as to suggest that policymaking is the primary function of appellate courts (Landes & Posner, 1979).[2] The importance of the decisions appellate courts make is reflected in the fact that virtually all appellate courts use groups of judges to render decisions. Sometimes this includes the full complement of judges on a court (e.g., the U.S. Supreme Court) and sometimes merely a subset of those judges (e.g., the South African Appellate Division) but, with exceedingly rare exceptions, appellate court decisions are group decisions. The logic underlying the use of groups of judges at the appellate stage is straightforward: deliberation among a set of judges is intended to enhance the likelihood of arriving at the correct decision; that is, reduce the likelihood of erroneously reversing a correct lower court decision or erroneously affirming an incorrect lower court decision (Drahozal, 1998).

The fact that appellate courts are collegial (that is, multimember) courts has not been lost on students of judicial behavior. In particular, those scholars who approach judicial choice through the lens of strategic behavior explicitly recognize that, to achieve their most preferred policy outcome, judges on collegial courts must consider the likely actions of their colleagues on the bench to determine their best course of action:

> [J]ustices may be primarily seekers of legal policy, but they are not unconstrained actors who make decisions based only on their own ideological attitudes. Rather, justices are strategic actors who realize their ability to achieve their goals depends on a consideration of the preferences of other actors, the choices they expect others to make, and the institutional context in which they act. (Epstein & Knight, 1998, p. 10)

Though Epstein and Knight were writing about members of the U.S. Supreme Court bench, their description of strategic behavior by members of that court is equally applicable to judges on other appellate courts, both domestic (e.g., Hettinger, Lindquist, & Martinek, 2006; Langer, 2002) and foreign (Helmke, 2005; Vanberg, 2005).

Such scholarship takes seriously the fact that judicial decisions on collegial courts are the product of group choices and, in that regard, takes into account the small group environment of collegial court decision making. The focus of the majority of this scholarship is unduly narrow, however, in that it almost always presumes a single goal (policy) and neglects to consider nonstrategic aspects of appellate court decision making (see Baum, 2006, pp. 6–8). But the small group context of appellate court decision making has meaningful consequences beyond serving as a venue for strategic calculations. This is where psychology, especially the insights of social and organizational psychology scholarship, focused on the behavior of small groups, can be profitably deployed to further our understanding of how judges on collegial courts behave. This is by no means the first time such an approach has been suggested. Schubert (1964), Murphy (1966), and Ulmer (1971), among others,[3] made this same argument quite some time ago. But since then, researchers approaching collegial court decision making as a type of small group behavior have been few and far between.[4] This is an unfortunate state of affairs.

Taking a small group approach to the study of judicial decision making is very much an interdisciplinary activity. Sociologists, organizational behavior researchers, social psychologists, and anthropologists have all applied small group theory to their work.[5] Regardless of the disciplinary context, however, a key preliminary issue is determining what constitutes a small group. Levine and Moreland offer a useful definition of a small group: a group of individuals who "interact on a regular basis, have affective ties with one another, share a common frame of reference, and are behaviorally interdependent" (1994, p. 306). Notwithstanding their enormous institutional variation, this definition certainly fits the situation of virtually all appellate courts.[6]

First, judges serving on appellate courts must interact on a regular basis to dispose of their caseloads. For example, many appellate court judges, such as the justices of the U.S. Supreme Court and some members of state courts of last resort, come together in conference to make decisions about which cases to accept for review (Langer, 2002; Perry, 1991). And all members of an appellate court or appellate court panel must come together for oral arguments (Cohen, 2002, pp. 133–136; Johnson, 2004) when they are held.[7] Further, a written opinion that formally disposes of a case may be the product of an intensive and iterative process among the judges (Maltzman, Spriggs, & Wahlbeck, 2000) or a less interactive process but, nevertheless, does entail at least some level of interaction if for no other reason than a majority of the judges on an appellate panel must sign off on an opinion to make it a majority opinion.

Second, judges serving on appellate courts may squabble like children, bond like family, or behave toward one another in a more detached, professional manner, but both anecdotal (Cooper, 1995; Hirsch, 1981; Schick, 1970) and systematic (Cohen, 2002; Howard, 1981) evidence make clear that there is an affective component to the interactions between and among judges serving on appellate courts. The personal closeness between Chief Justice Warren Burger and Justice Harry Blackmun, which devolved into a relationship that could be called strained, at best, is one well-known example. Further, Justices Brennan and Marshall were considered close colleagues, both on and off the bench, while Justices Ginsburg and Scalia, though ideologically dissimilar, are known to be personally quite friendly. Even in the absence of personal affect—either positive or negative—for one another judges on appellate courts share affective ties to the institutions on which they serve.

Third, colleagues on a given appellate bench possess a common frame of reference provided by the institutional environment within which they operate. That institutional environment includes rules regarding case selection, oral argument, opinion assignment, and the like. It also includes a common body of law, which they are charged with interpreting and applying. While nonjudges may recognize and acknowledge this common frame of reference, they are viewing it as outsiders rather than partaking of it as judges themselves do. In other words, colleagues on the bench "function as a true peer group, people who share the same position and work in the same situation" (Baum, 2006, p. 54).

And, fourth, appellate court judges are behaviorally interdependent by definition. No single judge on an appellate court, not even the majority opinion author, can individually determine the winner and loser in a given case or dictate the content of the legal rule embedded in a particular written opinion. Those are functions of the collective choices of the judges on that appellate court. While it is true that some judges may be more influential than others both as to the winners and losers in a case and as to the reasoning subscribed to by an appellate court in determining those winners and losers, no single judge can be determinative in the disposition of an appellate court decision. In short, "[a]ppellate court decisions are inherently collective products. The outcome for the litigants and the legal doctrine that a court promulgates are determined by where a majority of judges stand" (Baum, 2006, p. 51).

Though individual collegial courts may differ in their proximity to the archetype of a small group as defined by social psychologists and organizational behavioral specialists, as a class they fall quite comfortably under the rubric of small groups. This makes small group theory very inviting as a tool for the investigation of a plethora of appellate court decision-making processes. Two aspects of appellate court decision-making are particularly ripe for the application of theories emerging from small group research. First, scholarship devoted to group cognition can aid students of judicial decision making in their quest to understand when and how legal versus nonlegal factors influence judicial choices. Second, the small group literature can shed valuable light on how group roles—both formally and informally defined— occupied by members of collegial courts matter for the decision making of both those who occupy a given role and those with whom such individuals make decisions.

Legal Versus Nonlegal Factors and Collegial Court Decision Making

A persistent debate in the law and courts community is over the relative influence of legal and nonlegal factors in the decision calculi of judges. The view of judging as a mechanistic legal process in which judges simply match cases with the relevant legal factors (e.g., the language of the relevant statute, the principle of law articulated in the pertinent precedent) was unsatisfying to the group of judges and legal scholars who were the progenitors of what became known as legal realism (Duxbury, 1995, ch. 1). Though hardly all of like mind in terms of the proximate cause of judicial decisions,[8] the legal realists did all agree that a focus on the "law on the books" was uninformative—and, in fact, misleading—when compared to a focus on "law in action" (Duxbury, 1995, pp. 67–68). The legal realists ultimately inspired the attitudinal model of judicial decision making (Pritchett, 1948; Schubert, 1965), which "holds that the Supreme Court decides disputes in light of the facts of the case vis-à-vis the ideological attitudes and values of the justices" (Segal & Spaeth, 2002, p. 86).

Notwithstanding the fact that it has proven to be useful for understanding judicial decision making in a variety of courts, the attitudinal model has not been without its critics.[9] Some of the sharpest criticisms of the attitudinal model have focused on its perceived failure to fairly evaluate the evidence with regard to the influence of factors other than the attitudes of judges; in particular, the influence of the law. Segal and Spaeth (1996; Spaeth & Segal, 1999), the standard bearers of the contemporary attitudinal model, offered an empirical test of one aspect of the traditional legal model: the role of precedent as a determinative influence on judicial vote choice. They found little evidence that precedent was a meaningful constraint on judicial choice but were taken to task by a range of scholars for defining the influence of law in narrow, mechanistic terms.[10] Some of these critics have argued that the influence of precedent, and of law more broadly defined, should be seen in a nuanced fashion as drawing the attention of judges to particular aspects of subsequent cases that merit special attention in the decision process (Richards & Kritzer, 2002; see, also, Kritzer & Richards, 2003, 2005) rather than mandating particular outcomes.

Though numerous scholars have extended our collective knowledge about the role of law in judicial choice, virtually none have paid attention to how the small group context of collegial court decision making might matter for understanding the influence of legal factors in appellate adjudication. The fact that appellate court judges are rendering decisions collectively, however, means that those charged with crafting the written opinion of the court must convince their colleagues (or, at least, a majority of their colleagues) as to the "correctness" of the opinion they have crafted. The work of social psychologists that considers the effect of group membership on attitudes and behavior is particularly promising in terms of understanding how opinion authors might go about doing this. Though membership in a group as denoted by a set of objective criteria is neither necessary nor sufficient to give rise to an internalized sense of group membership (Abrams et al., 1990), the fact that appellate court judges are readily recognized by themselves and others as belonging to an unambiguously defined group (a court) may enhance the likelihood that they will incorporate their group membership into their concept of themselves. In other words, the fact that judges see themselves as members of a distinctive institution (a court) and that others (e.g., litigants, attorneys, other judges) see them that way, too, suggests that judges might be especially attentive to the norms and expectations that attach to the members of their small group.

In this regard, there is perhaps no other norm that has a stronger prima facie claim on judges than the norm that the decision making of judges should be governed by a consideration of the relevant legal factors. This norm is woven tightly into the fabric of legal education and the legal profession. Judges, then, come to the bench already well inculcated with this norm. A judge's self-identification as a member of a court may lead to an enhanced reliance on conventional legal factors in arriving at a case disposition; not because she sees it as an instrumental way to marshal the support of her colleagues, as the strategic theorist might have it (Epstein & Knight, 1998; Maltzman, Spriggs, & Wahlbeck, 2000), or as a cloak to mask the brazen influence of personal ideology, as the attitudinalists might have it (Segal & Spaeth, 1993, 2002), but because she views legal factors as those most relevant for her decision making precisely because of her membership in the small group constituted by her court.

Theorizing about if and how the law matters in the decision making of appellate court judges would substantially benefit from an even more direct consideration of how the members of the small group constituted by a court affect one another when it comes to reasoning to resolve a case. In particular, a natural question is whether a judge's reliance on legal factors is conditioned by the extent to which his colleagues on the bench rely on such factors. Small group researchers have argued that the social exchanges among group members "produce shared cognitive products, including memories, norms, scripts, schemas, and interpretations of shared events and activities" (Gruenfeld & Hollingshead, 1993, p. 384). This suggests the possibility of an iteratively reinforcing process in which reliance on legal factors becomes even more ingrained as the "correct" approach to the disposition of cases as appellate court judges continue to decide cases together.

This conjecture gives rise to two questions for which research on small groups and small group decision processes can provide important insights. First, what initial conditions are necessary for legal (as opposed to nonlegal) factors to dominate the group decision-making process? Is it sufficient for one judge to be self-conscious about locating persuasive legal arguments to guide the resolution of a case to prompt all judges on the court to do so or is there a necessary critical mass of such judges on a given court? Second, does the stability of the membership of the appellate court matter for the extent to which any single judge or group of judges can influence colleagues to pay special attention to legal factors in arriving at a case outcome? This question takes on special importance for courts with frequent membership changes and those in which decision making is done via panels of judges rather than en banc; for example, the U.S. Court of Appeals (Howard, 1981) and the Supreme Court of Canada (Hausegger & Haynie, 2003).

Group Roles and Collegial Court Decision Making

Another means by which a small group perspective may inform the work of students of judicial behavior is the attention it directs to the roles members of small groups occupy. Though any given judge may be formally fungible with his colleagues on a particular court, in reality there are often tangible differences among judges operating on a court, differences of which the judges are themselves aware and that are rife with potential behavioral consequences. Some of these differences come in terms of a formally defined role, such as the Chief Justice of the United States, the Chief Judge of the Appellate Division of the Supreme Court of South Africa, or the chief judge of the U.S. Court of Appeals for the Ninth Circuit. Other differences arise from roles that judges occupy on a temporary basis. For example, there is considerable evidence that judges new to the bench experience acclimation effects (e.g., Hurwitz & Stefko, 2004; Hettinger, Lindquist, & Martinek, 2006). But, assuming a long enough tenure, every freshman judge will eventually lose his newcomer status. Moreover, some judges are not regular members of an appellate court but participate on a temporary basis, such as certificated judges in the New York judicial system[11] and district court judges serving by designation on the U.S. Courts of Appeals.[12] All of these differences—whether informal or formal, subjective or objective—have potential import both for the behavior of individual judges possessing a given characteristic as well as the behavior of those with whom that individual is making decisions.

Perhaps the quintessential group role is that of group leader. Leadership is a staple topic in the study of judicial behavior (e.g., Atkins & Zavoina, 1974; Haynie, 1992), and there is a voluminous set of organizational psychology research devoted to leadership in small groups that can be usefully brought to bear in theorizing about leadership on appellate courts. The concept of leadership has been profitably parsed into task and social leadership (Bales, 1950): "The former seeks to complete the present task in the most effective and efficient manner; the latter seeks to provide the friendly atmosphere that eases cooperation" (Murphy, 1966, p. 1567). A single individual—such as the Chief Justice—may or may not exercise both types of leadership. Danelski found, for example, that Chief Justice William H. Taft provided social leadership while his colleague and friend, Associate Justice Willis Van Devanter, provided task leadership (1960, pp. 490–491), and that Chief Justice Charles E. Hughes exercised both (1960, p. 491).

Thinking about leadership on a court from the perspective of organizational behavior, one question is whether the formal role of chief justice or chief judge is sufficient for the individual occupying that role to exercise leadership of either variety. Some of the existing judicial behavior literature suggests that formally occupying such a role can have some effect on group deliberations. For example, Hettinger and her colleagues (2006, ch. 5) found that the presence of a chief judge of a U.S. Court of Appeals on a decision-making panel made the reversal of a lower court decision more likely. They speculated that this was a function of a chief judge's being more attentive to the need to reverse errant lower courts due to their institutional responsibilities as the head of their respective circuits. They also found that chief judges were less likely to express disagreement by filing separate opinions (2006, ch. 4), which was attributed to a desire to maintain collegiality among the judges on the circuit. Other literature, however, suggests that the magnitude of the effect of possessing a formal leadership role on a court pales in comparison to the influence attributable to characteristics such as collegiality, intellect, and administrative competence (Wrightsman, 1999, pp. 83–103). This is exactly where the psychology of small groups has the potential to help students of judicial behavior determine how and under what conditions those occupying formal leadership positions on a court can wield influence on that court.

Particularly promising in this regard is work by Ridgeway and her colleagues (Ridgeway & Berger, 1986; Ridgeway, Johnson, & Diekema, 1994) devoted to understanding how the external status of group members affects their perceived legitimacy and, hence, the propensity of colleagues to comply with the authority of formal leaders. Those who occupy formal leadership positions on an appellate court typically have few coercive mechanisms at their disposal for inducing compliance with (or deference to) their wishes. Neither the Chief Justice of the United States nor the chief judges of the U.S. Courts of Appeals, for example, play a role in the selection or removal of their colleagues.[13] Nor do such formal leaders possess the ability to "dock the pay" of those colleagues they see as recalcitrant. This is not to say that formal leaders such as chief justices have no punitive measures they can impose. The opinion assignment authority of the Chief Justice of the United States is an example of a power that could be used punitively through the withholding of desirable opinion assignments, though the discretion to use opinion assignment in this fashion is not infinitely elastic given efficiency concerns (Maltzman & Wahlbeck, 1996). Compliance with or deference to the wishes of an appellate court leader is secured in large part voluntarily or not at all. The question remains, however: when can a person occupying a formally defined leadership position on an appellate court effectively influence his colleagues? Small group theory can provide useful guidance in answering this question.

Likewise, small group theory can profitably inform our work regarding the behavioral effects of other types of roles. For example, the evidence to date suggests that judges who are new to their positions are likely to face an acclimation or socialization process (Alpert, Atkins, & Ziller, 1979; Hurwitz & Stefko, 2004; Wood et al., 1998). Louis defines organizational socialization as "the process by which an individual comes to appreciate the values, abilities, expected behaviors, and social knowledge essential for assuming an organizational role" (1980, p. 229). In other words, organizational newcomers must gather a great deal of information about an institution before they can become fully fledged members of that organization. A natural source for that information is the other members of the organization. Freshman judges, in effect, may cue off the behavior of their more senior colleagues. Small group theory can guide our thinking about how freshman judges determine which colleagues to rely on as cues for their own behaviors. Is ideological proximity key or is it, perhaps, respect that comes from demonstrated expertise? Alternatively, selecting a cue giver may be a function of demographic and experiential similarities or the recognition of the status accorded to a particular member of a court by other members of that court.

Research devoted to understanding conformity and status attainment in small groups holds promise vis-à-vis its utility for understanding when and how new members of collegial courts select cue givers from among their colleagues, as well as how more senior group members behave toward new colleagues. Specifically, expectation states theory suggests that group members have expectations for themselves and for other members of the group regarding their ability to contribute toward the completion of the group's tasks (Berger et al., 1977; Berger, Wagner, & Zelditch, 1985). These expectations are based on both external status characteristics and specific information regarding task competency. External status characteristics include gender and race, demographic characteristics that shape beliefs about task competence. For example, women are generally disadvantaged compared to men in terms of their perceived competence in economics and foreign affairs but advantaged when it comes to their perceived competence in social welfare issues (Sapiro, 1983). Further, African Americans are seen as less able to engage in abstract thinking compared to whites (Plous & Williams, 1995).

Specific information regarding task competency may come from the personal observation of group members but may also be a product of reputational factors.[14] Newcomers to an appellate court generally have had no prior means for acquiring information about the competence of their peers through direct observation. They can, however, readily observe demographic characteristics and are likely to know something about the reputations of their new colleagues. Small group research can help us understand the relative contributions of these two types of information to the expectations judges new to a court have about their colleagues' skills and abilities, and in the process, can help us understand which of those colleagues are likely to be influential on newcomer judges because of their status as cue givers.

Expectation states theory can also shed light on how senior members of a collegial court interact with newly appointed members. Not all freshman judges are created equal. Some judges new to an appellate court come with a wealth of prior experience on another appellate court. Others come with little to no experience as a judge—appellate or otherwise—but have other experience as prosecutors, public defenders, legislators, or other elected officials. These experiences have the potential to shape how newcomers are received by their senior colleagues because they contribute to the expectations those senior colleagues have about the competence of their newly arrived brethren. Ignoring these differences in past experience and the expectations they generate about how the competence of new members of a collegial court are perceived by senior colleagues on the bench is risky. For example, one strand of the literature devoted to the study of freshman effects considers whether chief justices and/or senior associate justices on the U.S. Supreme Court treat newly appointed members of the Court differently when it comes to opinion assignment (e.g., Slotnick, 1979; Bowen & Scheb, 1993; Brenner & Hagle, 1996). The inconsistencies in the empirical findings to date may, in fact, be due to ignoring a consideration of how preappointment experiences matter in terms of the reputations newcomers bring to the bench. A small group perspective, especially that embodied by expectation states theory, may help reconcile those findings as well as, more generally, refocus attention on how reputations of group members might matter for appellate court adjudication.

Appellate Courts as Small Groups and the Quality of Adjudication

The utility of approaching the study of appellate court decision making as a variety of small group decision making is not limited to understanding the role of legal factors in the judicial calculus or how the roles appellate court members occupy influence their behavior and the behavior of their colleagues. More generally, thinking about appellate court adjudication from this perspective can help students of the courts consider how the nature of the small group constituted by a collegial court might matter for the quality of adjudication. As noted at the beginning of this chapter, appellate courts consist of more than one member on the presumption that groups of judges will be less likely to err than single judges. In theory, each member of a collegial court will engage in a deliberative process with his colleagues in which the decision-making biases and other cognitive deficiencies of each judge will be compensated for by his fellow judges on the bench. The end result will be adjudication that, though a function of the decisions of individual judges on the bench, goes beyond the mere sum of those individual decisions. Work by Gruenfeld and Hollingshead suggests that a group cognition process such as this ideal conception of adjudication is possible: "[I]ndividuals in social interaction do more than trade individually produced cognitions. They also engage in active reconciliation and integration processes, leading to the emergence of unique, collectively produced conceptualizations—including ideas, representations, solutions, and arguments—that no individual had to begin with" (1993, p. 385). As a consequence, the quality of a group decision has the potential to exceed that of even the most skilled individual member of the group under ceteris paribus conditions. Ceteris paribus conditions, however, are rare rather than common.

There are a host of factors that can compromise the quality of adjudication, factors to which our attention is directed by the extant body of small group research. One of these factors is undue deference on the part of some members of a collegial court to other members. Such deference may result from a status differential between and among judges. For example, the nature of the judicial hierarchy implies that judges serving on appellate courts occupy more prestigious positions than those serving on trial courts. This, in turn, suggests that U.S. District Court judges serving temporarily by designation on the U.S. Courts of Appeals or with circuit court judges on three-judge district courts may defer to the circuit court judges with whom they serve (Brudney & Ditslear, 2001; Walker, 1973). And, as previously discussed, judges new to the appellate bench may similarly be deferential to their more senior colleagues (Hettinger, Lindquist, & Martinek, 2003). Certainly there are conditions under which such deference may be desirable, as when neophyte judges pay heed to senior colleagues with more expertise. Regardless, the roles group members occupy can result in less than the full-throated deliberations among equals that the ideal of appellate adjudication suggests.

Even assuming equal status among all members of an appellate court, there are reasons to be concerned about the quality of the adjudication process that derive from the fact that it is decision making by a small group. Specifically, individuals participating in group decision making processes are susceptible to conformity effects (Sunstein, 2003). Part of this may be attributable to the fact that members of a group care about the evaluations of their fellow group members and, all things being equal, prefer higher to lower status within the group. And at least some research on organizational behavior indicates that conformity initially contributes to the attainment of status within a group (e.g., Hollander, 1960; Warhman & Pugh, 1972; Ridgeway, 1978). In the specific context of collegial court decision making, the evidence is that appellate judges are profoundly affected by those with whom they render decisions (Sunstein, 2003, ch. 8; Sunstein et al., 2006). In particular, they are subject to conformity effects, another deviation from the ideal of appellate adjudication.

Whether the goal is to extend our understanding of the choices made by appellate court judges or to identify threats to the ideal appellate court decision process, small group theory offers rich possibilities. Appellate courts are small groups. Hence, what we know about small group dynamics from social psychology and organizational behavior can (and should) inform research on appellate court decision making. This is not an argument that small group theory entirely replace the attitudinal or strategic theories of judicial choice. The attitudes of at least some judges certainly matter at least some of the time; and at least some judges can and do engage in strategic calculations in at least some circumstances. The evidence is too overwhelming to assert the contrary without being, at best, naive or, at worst, disingenuous. But paying attention to the small group context within which appellate court adjudication takes place will enrich our understanding of judicial choice well beyond the confines of the attitudinal and strategic paradigms by offering a more realistic view of the psychology of judicial behavior.

Notes

Special thanks are due to Paul M. Collins Jr. and Raymond V. Carman Jr. for their thoughts about the utility of small group theories for understanding judicial behavior on collegial courts and Harold J. Spaeth for his insights on this and related projects.

1. There is also a very practical reason for the focus on appellate courts—and appellate courts of last resort, such as the United States Supreme Court, in particular—that has to do with the comparative ease of collecting the requisite data to answer questions about how and why judges make the decisions they make for appellate courts. The very fact that there are so many more trial courts makes it a daunting task to gather information on a representative set of courts, judges, and decisions sufficient for the purposes of inference.
2. Of course, trial court judges arguably make policy in the pattern of decisions they render (Rowland & Carp, 1996).
3. Other notable work drawing on the psychology of small groups includes work by Snyder (1958) and a series of articles by Walker (1973, 1974, 1976).
4. There is a similar dearth of recent political science scholarship that takes a small group approach outside the context of judicial behavior, despite Kirkpatrick's (1976) exhortation and some promising work from the late 1970s and early 1980s (e.g., Dorff & Steiner, 1981; Fiorina & Plott, 1978; Hinckley, 1979).

5. Hare, Borgatta, and Bales (1965) contains an excellent set of readings that nicely illustrates the interdisciplinary history of small group theory.
6. This is consistent with Murphy: "Collegial courts. . . use small groups in a face-to-face relationship that interact under an obligation to solve a specific problem or set of problems" (1966, p. 1565).
7. Of course, not all appellate court cases are disposed of with the aid of oral argument. On some appellate courts, in fact, a sizable proportion of the cases are disposed of without oral argument (Cohen, 2002, pp. 60–62).
8. One school of thought among the legal realists focused on the role of social forces, while the other focused on the characteristics of individual judges.
9. The symposium appearing in the Spring 1994 issue of *Law & Courts* and the symposium appearing in the Summer 2003 issue of that same newsletter offer a representative sampling of the criticisms of the attitudinal model.
10. Issue 3 of volume 40 of the *American Journal of Political Science* (1996) was specifically devoted to Segal and Spaeth's empirical test of the influence of precedent and critiques of that approach.
11. Certificated judges are retired judges who are certified to be both willing and able to serve on a New York State court.
12. Designated district court judges serve for temporary periods of time on the appeals court bench. Those coming from within the circuit are so designated at the discretion of the chief judge of the circuit. Those coming from outside the circuit are so designated only with the permission of the Chief Justice of the United States. Similarly, circuit judges from one circuit may serve temporarily in another circuit with the permission of the Chief Justice. Service by these judges "visiting" the appellate bench from outside the circuit or from the district court bench provides considerable service to the U.S. Courts of Appeals (Cohen, 2002, pp. 194–195).
13. There are notable exceptions, of course, such as the influence of Chief Justice Warren Burger in President Richard Nixon's selection of Burger's boyhood friend Harry Blackmun for a spot on the Supreme Court.
14. The empirical evidence suggests that judicial reputations do have tangible effects. For example, the reputations of United States Courts of Appeals judges make a difference in the extent to which individual judges are influential in the development of intra- and intercircuit law (Klein, 2002). Further, Caminker (1994) makes the case that judges care about their reputations for reasons of advancement.

6

The Supreme Court, Social Psychology, and Group Formation

Neal Devins and Will Federspiel

The justices of the Supreme Court function not only as individuals, but as members of groups. One group of which they are part is the Court itself, as discussed in Wendy Martinek's chapter in this volume (ch. 5). But they can also come together to form important subgroups. In this chapter, we examine a particular type of subgroup that we refer to as a majority coalition—a group of ideologically simpatico justices who are able to issue unambiguous, far-reaching decisions, as opposed to fact-specific decisions of limited consequence. We employ social psychology literature to better understand when the Court will and will not function as a cohesive coalition. In so doing, we also comment on the models political scientists use to describe Supreme Court decision making.

Our principal claim is intuitively obvious but in tension with much of the political science literature. Political science models of Supreme Court decision making typically focus on the legal and policy goals of individual justices—so that the key question concerns the legal policy preferences of the median justice and the ideological gap between the median justice and other members of the Court. We think the political science models focus too much on the individual and not enough on the group (including the reasons why individuals do or do not join groups). Specifically, when there is an ideologically simpatico majority coalition, intragroup dynamics play a prominent role in determining the reach of Supreme Court decisions. More to the point, the individual preferences of the median justice are less consequential on a cohesive Court—since the median justice will (up to a point) give in to intragroup pressures to uniformity. In contrast, the preferences of the median justice play a more prominent role on an ideologically diverse

Court. At the same time, these preferences may not mirror the policy views of the median justice. In refusing to join forces with an ideologically cohesive coalition, the median justice is likely to place a high value on personal power and reputation. In other words, median justices on ideologically diverse Courts have comparatively weaker legal policy preferences and are willing (up to a point) to sublimate those preferences in order to pursue other goals.

We begin with a brief tour of the chief political science models, highlighting the ways in which those models focus on individuated legal and policy preferences. We then turn to social psychology to examine both the importance of and obstacles to group formation. Finally, by comparing differences in decision-making styles of the (largely simpatico) New Deal Court and the (very diverse) Rehnquist Court, we illustrate how social psychology can contribute to an understanding of Supreme Court decision making.

The Political Science Models

The dominant political science models posit that Supreme Court justices are principally interested in pursuing favored policies. The attitudinal model assumes that judges vote "reflexively in each case; that is, they cast their votes based solely on their individual reactions to the facts and legal issues presented, rather than by considering, in addition, how judges or institutions are likely to react to the decision" (Merrill, 2003, p. 591; Segal & Spaeth, 2002). A second model, the strategic model, posits that judges take the reaction of others into account when advancing their policy preferences. A Supreme Court justice, for example, might calibrate a decision in order to secure the votes of other justices—so that the Court will embrace a decision that most closely matches the justice's preferred policy outcome (Epstein & Knight, 1998; Maltzman, Spriggs, & Wahlbeck, 2000). Alternatively, a justice might take implementation concerns into account and, with it, potential resistance from either elected officials (Epstein & Knight, 1998; Segal, 1997) or the American people (Mishler & Sheehan, 1996). In recent years, some political scientists have tweaked the attitudinal and strategic models. Institutionalists "shift their focus away from the long-standing question of how institutions are affected by the personal characteristics of judges and toward the question of how judges are affected by the institutional characteristics within which they are embedded" (Gillman, 1999, p. 66). In this way, judges act strategically to pursue both policy and legal goals (federalism, separation of powers, adherence to precedent). At the same time, institutionalists focus on an individual justice's pursuit of legal policy goals.

The "most influential models of judicial behavior share not only a basic assumption but also a limitation, the lack of a persuasive theory of judges' motivations" (Baum, 2006, p. 19; see also Baum in this volume, ch. 1). Notwithstanding their differences, the attitudinal, strategic, and institutional models all assume that justices are single-minded maximizers of legal and policy preferences. Differences between the models turn on whether justices act strategically and whether justices are pursuing legal or policy objectives. For this very reason, the median justice plays a central role in all three models. All models, for example, think that power resides at the median—so that the most powerful justice is "the Justice in the middle of a distribution of Justices, such that (in an ideological distribution, for example) half the Justices are to the right of (more 'conservative' than) the median and half are to the left of (more 'liberal' than) the median" (Martin et al., 2005, p. 1277). To pick a simple example, if the Court is split 5 to 4, the median justice would be the weakest member of the majority coalition. Under the attitudinal model, the median justice would only sign an opinion she agreed with and, as such, the majority might move closer to her position (so long as they too agreed with the final opinion) or, alternatively, the median Justice might write a consequential concurring opinion that would limit the reach of the majority or plurality opinion. The strategic and institutional models likewise see the median's view as controlling. Not only might the median write a consequential concurring opinion, but other justices in the majority—fearing possible defection—might move their opinion closer to the median's preferred legal or policy position.

The power of the median justice is variable, and that variability will call attention both to commonalities and differences between the political science models and a model that makes use of social psychology. For the political science models, medians are most powerful when there is substantial ideological distance between the median and other members of the Court—so that the median sits between one group of justices substantially to the right and another group of justices substantially to the left (Epstein & Jacobi, 2008). During the 2006 term, for example, Justice Anthony Kennedy was a "supermedian"; among other measures, he was a member of the winning coalition in each case decided by a 5-to-4 vote. In sharp contrast, medians are least powerful when their preferences overlap with the preferences of justices to their right or left. This convergence of preferences, moreover, makes it more likely that there will be an ideologically simpatico majority coalition of justices. When this happens, the Court is likely to issue consequential opinions, for a "majority coalition sharing great unity of mind has the ability to adopt whatever rule it would like" (Staudt et al., 2008, p. 369).

We agree with these conclusions but nevertheless feel that the political science models are incomplete because their policy-preference-driven focus is too narrow and ignores basic psychological concepts. As we discuss below, the power of the median is diminished on an ideologically simpatico Court because the median justice is a member of a majority coalition and pressures toward uniformity will diminish the preferences of any individual justice. Correspondingly, although median justices are more likely to assume power on an ideologically diverse Court, the unwillingness of a median justice to join one or another group is not simply a matter of ideological or jurisprudential divergence. Median justices do not join groups because they are less interested in the pursuit of some ideological or legal vision and more interested in competing values, most notably power and image.

We are not the first to observe that justices think about more than their legal and/or policy preferences. Lawrence Baum, both in his 2006 study *Judges and their Audiences* and in his chapter in this volume, criticizes the leading political science models for failing to take into account the desires of judges to win approval from audiences they care about. Noting that the "Spock-like judges of the dominant models have no interest in public approval as an end in itself," Baum argues that political scientists need to take into account the commonsense notion that judges, like other people, "care a great deal about what people think of them" (Baum, 2006, p. 22). We agree and will discuss how impression management figures into the willingness of a justice to be part of a coalition of justices. Unlike Baum, however, the approach taken in this chapter also applies social psychology to describe the interplay between the justices themselves.

Social Psychology and Coalition Formation on the Supreme Court

Before turning to what the psychological literature teaches us about group formation, let us begin by clarifying our central concept. By a coalition, we do not necessarily mean a set of justices who vote together all or nearly all the time. Instead, a coalition of justices is a set of justices who coalesce around an issue or a set of issues that are highly important or salient to the justices involved, and who vote and act together in the relevant issue space. This coalescing need not be a conscious decision made by the justices in the sense that they consciously choose to form a coalition on a particular issue, but is rather a recognition on the part of the justices involved of a shared set of goals or opinions that are salient for each individual justice. Unlike in the dominant political science models, coalitions of justices are not simply individuals who share a similar legal and/or policy preference. Instead, social psychology indicates that where a coalition forms, the very presence of such a subgroup will have profound effects both on the action of other coalition members and on the development of the opinions and reasoning of other coalition members (Stangor, 2004, p. 3; Cartwright & Zander, 1968, pp. 3–21). This, of course, is not to say that legal policy preferences are irrelevant to the formation of subgroups of justices. An individual's personal beliefs are key to coalition formation. At the same time, membership in a coalition transcends the individualized preferences of coalition members.

Importance of Group Formation

When a majority coalition forms, group dynamics play a crucial role in the Court's decision making. This is because when people align themselves as part of a group, powerful psychological pressures begin to bear on the members of the group. The most important of these pressures is the pressure to uniformity that occurs in groups. Pressures to uniformity in group decision making have long been recognized as a hallmark of group behavior and they present themselves in several contexts (Festinger et al., 1968). First, and most intuitively, membership in a group creates pressure to go along with the group in order to achieve the goals for which the group was formed initially. The more important a goal is, the more powerful this pressure is (Cartwright & Zander, 1968). The amount of pressure to conform to a group's decision also increases when the members are more dependent on one another in order to achieve their goals (Festinger, 1968).

There is also evidence that the opinions of group members become more influential for other group members. Some studies indicate that the opinions of group members actually converge once the group has made a decision. Even in situations where consensus among the group is not required, the opinions of group members are influential to other members as they form their opinions (Tinsdale et al., 2000, p. 10). Interestingly, group dynamics may actually push group members to take more extreme positions than they might otherwise be inclined to take (Stangor, 2004, pp. 202–203; Forsyth, 1999, p. 320). Experiments examining this phenomenon may have special relevance to the Court as they examined the decision making of people in a judicial setting. Mock jury experiments indicate that where a group is predisposed to a particular outcome, discussion of the issues presented to the group has a tendency to lead the group to adopt more extreme positions than the average group member held prior to discussing the issues (Stangor, 2003, pp. 202–203).

Social Judgment Theory posits that people generally are most persuaded by positions that are slightly different from the positions they already hold, but that they are not particularly persuaded by positions that are very different (Tindale et al., 2000, pp. 9–10; Kerr & Tindale, 2004, p. 635). Because members of a coalition on the Court will tend to hold similar, but not identical, views on a given issue, the opinions of the other members of the coalition will tend to be more influential to each other than any opinions of noncoalition members. In other words, when justices associate as a coalition, the median member of the Court (i.e., the most moderate member of the group) will be most susceptible to being pulled in a more liberal or conservative direction by the other members of the coalition instead of by noncoalition members.

Taken together, these psychological processes suggest that Court decision making may be substantially affected when the justices coalesce in a majority coalition. First, pressures to uniformity in the group indicate that members of a group are more willing to sublimate personal preferences, as long as the members remain committed to the core purposes of the group. Thus, where there is a majority coalition of justices, the members will be likely to join an opinion that may be more reflective of the coalition's preference, not necessarily the justice's individual preferences.

Further, where there is a majority coalition on the Court, the members should tend to show greater deference to the opinion writer. The members should also be more likely to go along with the coalition without issuing a consequential concurrence. This should be especially true when the issue at hand is particularly important or salient to the group's core beliefs. And, the opinions issued by a majority coalition of justices will not reflect the preferences of the median justice on the Court. Instead, it will be the product of the group dynamics of the majority and may be a more extreme position than some members of the group would have preferred on their own.

Finally, depending on the cohesiveness of the coalition, there may be a willingness among the members to vote together on other issues, provided the votes on those issues are not central and opposed to a justice's personal beliefs. The more group members see the group as "significant, important," the more likely it is that the group will "bond together and stick together" (Stangor, 2004, PIN/24). With respect to Supreme Court justices, norms of independence (which typically cut against the formation of a cohesive majority coalition) are likely to limit the willingness of group members to form a group that cuts across all issues. It is far more likely that the group will coalesce around a set of core issues and that the justices will act in a more disparate way on issues that are not central to the group's identity. For example, the New Deal Court—as we will soon discuss—was formed around the core issue of governmental power to regulate economic conditions. Civil rights and liberties issues were not core to the formation of this coalition and, not surprisingly, the majority coalition broke apart on civil liberties questions.

Indeed, the bitterness that subsets of New Deal justices expressed about each other in connection with civil rights and liberties issues backs up the central point of this chapter: Although justices can come together to act as a coalition on one set of core issues, at the same time, the social psychology barriers that stand in the way of group formation also make it likely that these justices will splinter on issues that are not central to the group's mission. We turn to a discussion of those barriers now.

Barriers to Forming a Majority Coalition

From a group dynamics perspective, "attraction to a group for a given individual will depend on his assessment of the desirable and undesirable consequences attendant upon membership in the group" (Cartwright, 1968, p. 95). For reasons we will now detail, social psychology identifies numerous roadblocks that stand in the way of a majority coalition forming on the Supreme Court. The most obvious roadblock (and the one hurdle that political scientists and social psychologist agree on) is ideological diversity among the justices. An individual will not act in ways that are inconsistent with matters central to their cognitive network. In particular, group membership is a basic part of individual self-conception; it is a key component of how we perceive our place in the world, throughout our lives (Forsyth, 1999, pp. 66–80). Because of the fundamental importance of group identification in our lives, individuals are only willing to associate themselves meaningfully with groups that are in sync with their core beliefs (Arrow et al., 2000, pp. 70–77; Stangor, 2004, p. 25).

A second potential barrier to group formation is tied to an individual justice's motivations, specifically, the need for power (Baum, ch. 1 in this volume). An individual's need to influence others and to control or shape the world around them, the need for power, is a basic psychological need; but it is valued differently by different individuals, and it manifests itself differently in different situations. In some settings, membership in a group may actually provide an outlet for people with high needs for power because groups present opportunities for leadership (Forsyth, 1999, p. 92). Also, an ideologically simpatico coalition may join together in order to decisively advance the individual preferences of coalition members. However, people with a high need for power may find it best to refrain from joining a group and instead play the role of power broker, or "decider," between rival factions. And, of course, for some people the need for power is simply not a sufficient enticement to join any group.

Consider, for example, the so-called swing justices who cast the deciding votes on controversial cases. "Swing" justices exercise power by writing consequential concurring opinions that limit the reach of the majority's ruling or by insisting that their legal policy preferences are reflected in the majority opinion. Like any justice, a "swing" justice will not cast votes at odds with core beliefs. But a "swing" justice might have comparatively weak legal policy preferences and a comparatively strong desire to exercise power. To exercise power meaningfully, however, the Court must be ideologically diverse (Epstein & Jacobi, 2008). An ideologically cohesive Court (with a majority coalition of 5 or more justices) will not need the "swing" justice's vote to advance their legal policy preferences. In this situation, the "swing" justice might seek to exercise power by joining that coalition in the hopes of playing a leadership role in that group (assuming that the coalition is acting in ways consistent with her core beliefs). Alternatively, the "swing" justice might not want to join that coalition—even if that will mean fewer opportunities to exercise power. For example, the "swing" justice (or, for that matter, any justice) might place a high value on external variables—most notably, how she is perceived by audiences that she cares about. These audiences might include journalists, law professors, lawyers' groups, other judges and justices, political parties, interest groups, and even the public (Baum, 2006).

In paying attention to "audiences," justices engage in impression management, that is, the "process of controlling how one is perceived by other people" (Leary, 1996, p. 2). Like group dynamics generally, impression management is a universal phenomenon. Everyone engages in some form of impression management every day. It is an "essential component of social interaction" (Leary, 1996, p. 3). Like an individual's desire to exercise power, the amount of impression management engaged in by individuals varies significantly with the situation and the individual. For Supreme Court justices, there are countless opportunities to take into account their standing with various audiences—oral argument, opinion writing, the giving of speeches and interviews, attending social gatherings, so on and so forth. In other words, judging on the Court is in many ways an exercise in self-presentation, and the behavior of the justices is shaped in important ways by the opinions of outside groups that the justices care about. More than that, the very process by which we select justices tends "to favor those with an especially strong interest in the esteem of other people" (Baum, 2006, p. 32). Accepting a judgeship entails accepting relatively significant constraints on personal activities and behaviors as well as a significant reduction in monetary compensation. The inducement for accepting these losses is an increase in prestige (and an increase in potential power). As a result, the types of people who end up with judicial positions tend to be those who care a great deal about the esteem of others.

Impression management figures prominently in the willingness of a Supreme Court justice to join forces with others and forge a majority coalition. To start, a justice will not join a coalition if that will harm her reputation among groups that are important to her. Just as a justice will not join a group that would require her to vote in ways not in sync with her personal beliefs, a justice will not hurt her standing with groups she cares about. And while some of these groups may have identifiable ideologies (Federalist Society, American Constitution Society), externally focused justices are well aware that the norm of judging in the United States is that the judge is a neutral, impartial arbiter of disputes. For some (but not all) justices, this norm tends to act as a disincentive to be part of a unified, ideologically identifiable subgroup of justices, because "people try to project images of themselves that are consistent with the norms in a particular social setting and with the roles they occupy" (Leary, 1996, p. 67). In this way, justices have incentives to act like an independent judge and not a member of an ideologically identifiable group. As such, an externally focused judge—especially as compared to public officials whose status is tied to political battles that play out in public view—has little reason to curry favor with one or another ideologically identifiable constituency. Justices with strong ideological precommitments, however, will place a higher value on winning the esteem of some ideologically identifiable group. For these justices, approval by such groups may matter more than engaging in self-presentation that is aimed at reinforcing the norm of neutral, impartial arbiter.

Consider again our so-called swing justice. If all she cared about was power, she would pay no mind to her reputation. Her decision to join one or another side of a dispute would simply be an exercise in power—her efforts to wield as much as influence as possible (either by filing a consequential concurring opinion or by joining one or the other side of a dispute). In particular, she would want to maintain her "swing" justice status—so that her vote would be critical to the resolution of any dispute. Along these lines, she would want to locate herself at the Court's median (and, to the extent possible, distance herself from justices to her immediate right and left) (Epstein & Jacobi, 2008, p. 74–81). An externally focused "swing" justice, instead, would focus on how others perceive her. Perhaps she would cultivate a reputation of neutrality; perhaps she would want to be known as the "critical vote"; perhaps she would want groups with disparate ideologies to view her vote as gettable. Whatever her methodology or motivation, the externally focused swing justice will place a high value on cultivating a positive image with groups that do not demand ideological conformity.

Indeed, the desire to appear independent may prompt some justices to engage in a type of behavior known as reactance. Reactance speaks to the desire of individuals to resist challenges to their autonomy (Brehm & Brehm, 1981). In particular, when people feel their independence is threatened, they will take steps to demonstrate that they are in control of their own behavior. For example, the Supreme Court's 1992 reaffirmation of abortion rights in *Planned Parenthood v Casey* may well be tied to the desires of Justices O'Connor, Kennedy, and Souter to demonstrate that they were not the political lackeys of the presidents (Reagan and Bush I) who appointed them to the Court. Proclaiming that the Court's legitimacy is tied to its ability to withstand political attacks, these justices made clear that they would not facilitate efforts by the Reagan and Bush administrations to push for the overruling of *Roe v. Wade*. Taken together, these psychological concepts illustrate some of the difficulties of forming a majority coalition on the Court. A justice, of course, will not choose to join a coalition if doing so means they have to cast a vote on a core issue that does not match her central beliefs. In addition to legal and/or policy preferences, the desire for power, impression management, and reactance may all contribute to a justice's refusal to join a coalition. In other words, even if a justice's legal policy preferences are largely in sync with an existing subgroup on the Court, a justice might not join it. Put another way: Without strong ideological pre-commitments to a particular group, Supreme Court justices are likely to value power and image in ways that make them resistant to forging a majority coalition.

On the other hand, justices with strong ideological precommitments may be especially likely to join coalitions. Members of ideologically simpatico coalitions will agree with each other on issues of high salience to coalition members; consequently, they will more likely seek to assume power by forcefully advancing a shared agenda. In other words, members of such a group have less interest in exercising individualized power by casting the decisive swing vote; for them, the pursuit of a shared agenda is the most important manifestation of power. Likewise, justices with strong ideological precommitments may be less interested in fostering the norm of an impartial, independent jurist. Rather, when it comes to impression management, the outside groups they care about are those who share their values and objectives. Compare, for example, Justices Anthony Kennedy and Clarence Thomas. Kennedy—consistent with "swing" justice behavior—places a high value on the opinions of the news media and other elites; Thomas identifies closely with ideologically conservative groups (Baum, 2006, pp. 132, 142–144). If there are 5 or more ideologically simpatico justices, a majority coalition may form. The key variable, as noted above, is whether these justices have sufficiently strong ideological precommitments to overcome the basic obstacles to group formation. For example, in determining whether a justice will join a group, it may require more than the justice agreeing with other members on the preferred outcome and legal reasoning in any given issue space. A justice not strongly precommitted to the group's agenda may place a higher value on the exercise of individual power or cultivating a reputation for judicial independence. Perhaps for this reason, Justice Anthony Kennedy broke ranks with the Rehnquist Court's "conservative bloc" by switching his initial conference votes in high visibility school prayer and abortion cases. (Greenburg, 2007, pp. 145–160).

The appointments-confirmation process also stands as a substantial obstacle to the formation of an ideologically simpatico majority coalition, especially with regard to controversial, highly salient issues. Because justices have life tenure, it is very unlikely that appointments to the Court will be clustered closely together. Such clustering of appointments facilitates group formation (Arrow et al., 2000, p. 69). In the case of the Court, this is both because people who join an existing organization tend to identify with others who join at the same time and because such clustering means that the same president and Senate will be making the appointments, increasing the likelihood of clustered appointees being relatively closely aligned ideologically. For example, as we will discuss near the end of this chapter, President Roosevelt's clustering of Supreme Court appointments from 1938 to 1943 figured prominently in the New Deal Court's dramatic expansion of government power over the economy. At the same time, this perfect storm of closely clustered appointments and other factors that would help overcome the barriers to group formation rarely occurs.

Applying the Psychological Perspective

Social psychology explains both the ramifications of group formation on the Supreme Court and the innumerable roadblocks that typically stand in the way of group formation. When there is no dominant majority coalition on the Court, social psychology suggests that concerns of power and image (including reactance) stand in the way of justices voting their true legal and/or policy preferences. And when there is an ideologically cohesive majority, social psychology suggests that intragroup dynamics will play an important role in defining the Court's decision as well as the willingness of justices to stick with the coalition on issues that are not core to the group's identity. This section will provide a preliminary test of the social psychology model. We will compare the willingness of the Rehnquist and New Deal

Courts both to overrule precedent and to issue consequential rule-like (as opposed to minimalist fact-specific) decisions. For both Courts, we will focus on two issue sets—congressional power and individual rights.

Before turning to our discussion of these two Courts, two clarifying comments: First, even though this paper highlights significant differences between the social psychology and dominant political science models, these models overlap in significant respects. Most important, just as political science models talk about the pursuit of legal policy preferences, social psychology likewise talks about the importance of personal beliefs to an individual's willingness to join a group. For this very reason, it is often the case that the social psychology model and the political science models will both point to personal beliefs as a principal motivation for a justice's decisions. More to the point, the social psychology and political science models both anticipate that the Court is more likely to generate consequential precedents when there is an ideologically simpatico coalition of five or more justices. Likewise, when there is no such coalition, each of these models recognizes that the median justices' views are often controlling. At the same time, social psychology provides a much more nuanced explanation for Supreme Court decision making. That explanation has strong empirical foundations and, as such, we think that political scientists must do more than demonstrate the predictive powers of their models. They must also explain why Supreme Court Justices do not function like other individuals who operate in a group dynamic. Second, in discussing the Rehnquist and New Deal Courts, our objective is quite limited. Specifically, we want to see if these two Courts superficially track the social psychology model discussed in the preceding section. A more detailed, empirical assessment still needs to be done—and we hope to do that in another paper. For reasons we will now discuss, Rehnquist and New Deal Court decision making seem to follow the social psychology model discussed in this chapter.

The New Deal Court

The New Deal Court (1937–1949) was, in critical respects, two Courts. On issues involving Congress's power to regulate the economy, an ideologically simpatico majority coalition operated as a cohesive group. Those issues were central to the group's identity. On individual rights issues, however, the Court was anything but coherent. These issues, while of great national significance, were not central to the group's identity.

To start, the New Deal Court was forged by President Franklin Delano Roosevelt. Roosevelt used his appointments power to nominate eight justices during a five-year period, 1938–1943. More than that, Roosevelt used his appointments power to celebrate the New Deal's embrace of big government, especially the power of government to regulate the economy. Roosevelt felt compelled to do so because the pre-1937 Supreme Court had taken the country back to its "horse and buggy" days by overturning several New

Deal initiatives; indeed, Roosevelt promised—when introducing his ill-fated Court-packing plan—to appoint justices who "will not undertake to override the judgment of Congress on legislative policy" (quoted in Devins & Fisher, 2004, p. 61).

Roosevelt did just that; his appointees were committed New Dealers who, from the moment they joined the Court, advanced an expansive view of the federal government's power to regulate the national economy. From 1937 to 1944, the New Deal Court had created a "new constitutional order," over-ruling thirty cases—"two thirds as many as had been overruled in the Court's previous history" (Leuchtenburg, 1995, pp. 208–215). Over the course of its twelve-year tenure (1937–1949), the Court "throroughly repudiated the entire doctrinal system of constitutional limitations of federal power over the national economy" (Ackerman, 1999, p. 47). It handed down 42 rulings that overturned at least 59 of its prior decisions. The majority of these decisions had broad support—only five were decided by a 5-to-4 vote (as compared to 10 unanimous overruling decisions).

Group dynamics, as well as the legal policy preferences of the justices, likely figured into New Deal Court decision making. As discussed earlier, justices who are part of an ideologically simpatico majority coalition seek power by voting with the coalition. Likewise, rather than cultivate an image of impartiality by refusing to join a coalition, justices who are part of a majority coalition pay attention to audiences that agree with the core agenda of that coalition. Perhaps most significant, justices on an ideologically simpatico majority do not necessarily vote their personal preferences—instead, they allow the group dynamic to shape their final vote.

Consider, for example, the New Deal Court's 1942 decision in *Wickard v. Filburn*. *Wickard* concerned the power of the secretary of agriculture, acting pursuant to the Agriculture Adjustment Act, to extend a quota on wheat production to a farmer who grew wheat for home consumption. In upholding the secretary's power, the Court issued a sweeping opinion—ruling that Congress may regulate economic conduct "trivial by itself" so long as the aggregation of similar activity by other actors affects interstate commerce (*Wickard v. Filburn*, 1942, pp. 127–128). For our purposes, *Wickard* is especially instructive because some justices on the Court put aside personal misgivings about the decision's reach in order to forge a pathbreaking ruling that reflected the core beliefs of the New Deal.

Before *Wickard*, the Court encouraged Congress to make findings that commerce indeed was affected. In this way, the justices placed the ball in Congress's court, for once Congress found facts, it would be very difficult for the Court to meaningfully check Congress. Nonetheless, in the years pre-ceding *Wickard*, Congress contributed to the Court's approval of New Deal initiatives through its "sustained and thoughtful" showing that there was, in fact, an integrated national economy (Frickey, 1996, pp. 711–712). When Congress enacted the Agriculture Adjustment Act, however, lawmakers made no factual findings. For this very reason, Justice Robert Jackson, who had been tasked to write the decision, initially drafted an opinion that would have remanded the case so that a trial court could make additional factual findings (Cushman, 2000, p. 1138). Jackson nevertheless backed away from his original opinion and wrote a decision that effectively granted Congress carte blanche power to regulate anything arguably economic. In private correspondence, Jackson signaled his discomfort with his handiwork. Recognizing that we no longer have "legal judgment upon economic effects which we can oppose to the policy judgment made by the Congress in legislation," Jackson observed: "I really know of no place ... where we can bound the doctrine" (quoted in Cushman, 2000, pp. 1143, 1145).

Wickard exemplifies what a coherent Court can do. Committed to a shared agenda, group members can work together to advance an expansive vision of the law. *Wickard* also stands in sharp contrast to New Deal Court decisions on individual rights. Unlike economic issues (which were core to the group's formation), civil and individual rights were irrelevant to the formation of the New Deal Court. Roosevelt wanted justices who would validate the regulatory state; he was not especially interested in constitutionalizing civil liberties and civil rights. At the time of Court-packing, the Court's docket had almost no cases implicating civil and individual rights. But with the Court's approval of sweeping legislative power over economic issues, the Court inevitably turned its attention to other matters. Reflecting both changing social conditions and their personal interest in asserting power, "judges created for themselves a new role in the political system, one that involved identifying those 'preferred freedoms' or 'suspect classifications' that might provide a basis for trumping the otherwise unrestrained power of the modern legislature" (Gillman, 1993, pp. 202–203). Here, the New Deal Justices divided—reflecting the fact that groups organize around clusters of core issues, that justices will not vote against their legal policy beliefs on issues of consequence, and that the norm of impartiality pushes justices away from groups that do not share their core beliefs. In other words, just as social psychology helps explain why the New Deal Court acted as a coherent group on economic questions, social psychology is also useful in understanding why the justices were unwilling to forge a majority coalition on issues involving civil and individual rights.

The Rehnquist Court

The Rehnquist Court (1986–2005) likewise exemplifies the forces that push against group formation on the Supreme Court. Throughout its history, the Rehnquist Court was fractured on issues involving civil and individual rights. But even its much ballyhooed efforts to reinvigorate federalism-based limits on congressional power proved to be a bust—principally because a majority coalition was never able to coalesce around these issues. The inability of the Rehnquist Court to fundamentally transform doctrine, as we will now explain, is to be expected. Without five justices strongly committed to the pursuit of some shared agenda, concerns of power, impression management, and reactivity stand in the way of group formation.

On civil and individual rights issues, the Rehnquist Court seemed destined to embrace Reagan's vision of judicial conservatism. When running for president in 1980 and 1984, Ronald Reagan both pledged to appoint judges "who share our commitment to judicial restraint" and reached out to social conservatives by condemning Supreme Court decisions on school prayer, busing, and especially abortion (Devins & Fisher, 2004, quoting Republican party platform). But two of Reagan's four nominees, Sandra Day O'Connor and Anthony Kennedy, refused to embrace the social conservative agenda—so much so that "Republican domination of the Court" did not result "in the overruling of a single revolutionary Warren [or Burger] Court decision" (Nagel, 2006).

On social issues, Justices Kennedy and O'Connor were anything but precommitted to the social conservative agenda. Reagan picked O'Connor to fulfill his pledge to nominate the first woman to the Supreme Court. Accounts of his decision to nominate her make clear that ideology was not central to Reagan's decision (Toobin, 2007, pp. 17–18). Kennedy's selection is even more telling. Reagan initially nominated Robert Bork for that seat—but civil rights and abortion rights groups strenuously objected to that nomination and the Senate rejected Bork. Reagan's second choice, Douglas Ginsburg, withdrew from consideration after newspapers revealed embarrassing personal details. Kennedy was selected to stave off further embarrassments; ideology entered the calculus but it was not figural in Kennedy's nomination (Greenburg, 2007, pp. 35–65).

Kennedy and O'Connor repudiated the social conservative agenda by, among other things, voting to reaffirm earlier rulings on school prayer and abortion rights. Reactance may well have been a contributing factor to these decisions. O'Connor and Kennedy also acted in ways that expanded their personal power and fostered their reputation for judicial independence. Kennedy, in particular, seemed concerned with his public persona. His decisions to reaffirm Court rulings on school prayer and abortion rights may not have reflected his true preferences—but, instead, his desire to exercise power in ways that would distance himself from the Reagan administration's social conservative agenda. According to one of his law clerks, Kennedy "would constantly refer to how it's going to be perceived, how the papers are going to do it, and how it's going to look" (Tushnet, 2005, p. 176, quoting an anonymous Kennedy clerk). On the very day that the Court reaffirmed Roe, Kennedy told a reporter, "[s]ometimes you don't know if you're Caesar about to cross the Rubicon or Captain Queeg cutting your own tow line." (quoted in Greenburg, 2007, p. 159). Kennedy, moreover, seemed determined to "occupy the pivot" on the Court. According to one account, Kennedy sought to maneuver himself to the center—and "even boasted of employing this strategy" (Lithwick, 2004, p. 25; Lazarus, 1998, p. 515). Kennedy's concerns for power are further revealed in a 2005 interview; he spoke about Supreme Court justices' "shap[ing] the destiny of the country," noting that "in any given year, we make more important decisions than the legislative branch does" (quoted in Rosen, 2007b, p. 17).

For her part, Justice O'Connor made extensive use of fact-specific concurring opinions to keep her options open in future cases and, more importantly, to tell litigants that "the outcome of a case goes through her"—so much so that litigants spoke about "writing for an audience of one" when crafting Supreme Court briefs (Brust, 2005, p. 37; Estrich & Sullivan, 1989, p. 119). "As Justice Sandra Day O'Connor votes, so goes the Court," wrote one commentator, and it is undeniable that O'Connor was aware of both the power she wielded and her legacy as the Court's first women justice (Lazarus, 2000). O'Connor's "flexible, context specific approach" was most pronounced in cases implicating civil and individual rights (Maveety, 1996, p. 31). In a prominent voting rights case, O'Connor filed a concurrence to a decision she authored (*Bush v. Vera*, 1996, pp. 990–995). When concurring to a decision rejecting a constitutional right to physician assisted suicide, O'Connor's reasoning fundamentally limited the majority opinion—so much so that Justice Stephen Breyer joined the concurrence "except insofar as it joins the majority"(*Washington v. Glucksberg*, 1997, p. 789). Whatever her motivations, O'Connor did not want to be pinned down. She wanted to make her mark through individuated fact-specific decisions of limited reach, decisions that would make her the focal point of subsequent cases.

Without a solid coalition of five ideologically simpatico justices, the Rehnquist Court's civil and individual rights legacy was inconsequential. The Court did not "make a single move that would radically change or unsettle existing constitutional doctrine" (Friedman, 2002, p. 146). The Rehnquist Court's federalism revival, for the most part, tells a similar story. Unlike civil and individual rights, the Rehnquist Court did pursue doctrinal innovations on federalism (Merrill, 2003, p. 584–86). More than that, commentators initially labeled a group consisting of Justices O'Connor, Kennedy, Scalia, Thomas, and Chief Justice Rehnquist as the "federalism five." But the federalism revival, ultimately, was more bust than boom; the Court overturned only one significant precedent and, ultimately, backed away from its campaign to limit congressional power under the Commerce Clause and section 5 of the Fourteenth Amendment. In cases decided in 2003, 2004, and 2005, four of the five so-called federalism five distinguished earlier Rehnquist Court rulings in order to back up congressional power. The only justice to consistently vote in favor of limits on Congress was Clarence Thomas.

The failure of the federalism revival is tied to the simple fact that federalism-qua-federalism was never a core issue to the so-called federalism five. Presidents Reagan and Bush never used federalism as a measuring stick when screening candidates; the Senate paid no mind to federalism during its confirmation hearings. The focus, instead, was on first-order policy issues—race, privacy, religion. Unlike the New Deal era (where Court limits on congressional power frustrated Roosevelt's pursuit of a fundamental restructuring of the regulatory state), elected officials neither pushed for nor resisted Rehnquist Court efforts to place some federalism-based limits on congressional power (Devins, 2004). Against this backdrop, it is not surprising that a core group could not form around this low salience issue and, in so doing, invalidate laws that they otherwise supported.

For our purposes, the Rehnquist Court highlights the various roadblocks that stand in the way of group formation on the Supreme Court. Groups form around core issues and, in part, that requires the appointment and confirmation of justices who are precommitted to the pursuit of some agenda. Otherwise, median or "swing" justices will resist banding together with other justices—for these "swing" justices are likely to place a high value on power and/or their image. Indeed, the Reagan administration's embrace of the social conservative agenda may well have boomeranged, in that, "swing" justices—consistent with reactance—felt that their independence was threatened by the administration's assault on the Court.

Conclusion

Social psychology provides important insights into group formation on the Supreme Court. In particular, unlike political science models, which emphasize the pursuit of legal and policy preferences, social psychology highlights the importance of group processes and how issues of power and reputation also contribute to group formation on the Supreme Court. In so doing, social psychology suggests that political scientists overemphasize the median justice benchmark. When a majority coalition forms, intragroup dynamics define the scope of the Court's ruling. Those dynamics reflect group preferences, not the preferences of the median justice. And when there is no majority coalition, the median justice may well be influenced by concerns of power and reputation—concerns that may lead the median justice to vote in ways that do not necessarily reflect her true legal policy preferences. Through limited case studies on the New Deal and Rehnquist Courts, there is reason to think that justices—like other humans—operate within the boundaries of group dynamics. That, of course, is not to denigrate the profoundly important role of legal policy preferences. Justices, according to the social psychology model, will never cast votes that do not jibe with their core beliefs. At the same time, the dominant political science models offer a too simplistic picture of Supreme Court decision making.

Note

Thanks to David Klein, Greg Mitchell, Lee Epstein, Larry Baum, and especially John Nezlek.

Part II

JUDGING AS SPECIALIZED ACTIVITY

7

Is There a Psychology of Judging?

Frederick Schauer

In the United States, as in most countries, judges share three prominent characteristics. First, and tautologically, they are judges. Second, and with the exception of the lay magistrates who hear small cases in many states, they are lawyers. And third, the opinions of some attorneys and litigants notwithstanding, they are human beings. My goal in this paper is to examine in a preliminary way the relative contributions of each of these three characteristics in explaining judicial cognition and judicial behavior.

The potential value of such an inquiry lies in its contrast with the (small) existing literature (e.g., Guthrie, Rachlinski, & Wistrich, 2001; Wistrich, Guthrie, & Rachlinski, 2005) on the psychology of judging.[1] That literature, with few exceptions, aligns itself with the conclusion that it is the third and not the first or second of the items on the above list—the judge as human being and not the judge as judge or the judge as lawyer—that has the greatest explanatory power in accounting for judicial behavior, and that holds out the greatest promise for setting a research agenda for law and psychology and for the psychology of judging (Spellman, 2007). More often implicitly than explicitly, the existing research tends to support the view that a judge's attributes as a human being reveal more about the psychology of judging than does anything a judge might have learned in law school, acquired in the practice of law, or internalized by virtue of serving in the judicial role.

The conclusion that judges share (some) important decision-making characteristics with their fellow human beings is occasionally supported by empirical findings (Guthrie, Rachlinski, & Wistrich, 2001; Wistrich, Guthrie, & Rachlinski, 2005). More often, however, this conclusion lurks in the background as an undocumented and unargued premise of the research on the psychological dimensions of judicial behavior. Researchers commonly assume that what is known about human decision making and cognition will apply to judges, and thus conclude that nonjudge experimental results can be applied to explain and predict judicial behavior. One survey of (nonjudicial and nonlegal) analogy research (Holyoak, 2005), for example, asserts that the legal system's use of precedent is but a formalized application of the nonlegal and nonjudicial human practice of analogizing, while another study (Simon, Krawczyk, & Holyoak, 2004) describes two of the authors' earlier study using undergraduate research subjects (Holyoak & Simon, 1999) as being about "legal decision making." And in the law review literature, it is routine to take the teachings of contemporary cognitive and social psychology as substantially applicable to the decisions of lawyers and judges (Arlen, 1998; Hanson & Yosifon, 2004; Schauer, 2006a, 2006b; Simon, 1998, 2002, 2004).

Although applying the research on lay decision makers to judges is thus relatively common, research on real judges has to date been quite limited.[2] And even when there has been serious research on the psychological dimensions of actual judicial decision making, it is of less pervasive value than it might be because the research has focused almost exclusively on the fact-finding[3] and verdict-rendering dimensions of the judicial role. Judges are indeed often required to determine simply what happened, and then, in place of a jury, are often in the position of delivering a final verdict. Thus, judges must frequently decide which of multiple opposing factual accounts is most likely true.[4] And in engaging in such tasks, judges perform functions similar to those performed by a jury.[5] So insofar as people tended to believe that judges would be superior to jurors as fact-finders or verdict-renderers, or to believe that judges would be largely immune from the cognitive biases of mere mortals, much of the current research on the psychology of judging has usefully cast doubt on the view that judges by virtue of their intelligence or legal training or judicial position could significantly outperform juries with respect to the same fact-focused inquiries.

By concentrating so dominantly on the fact-finding and verdict-rendering tasks that judges share with jurors, however, the existing research tends to slight those aspects of judging—most obviously selecting the relevant law, interpreting the law, and sometimes making law—that are more or less the exclusive province of the judge. Because judges thus appear to take on many tasks that jurors and everyday decision makers do not, and also because judges likely possess some characteristics that experimental subjects do not,[6] perhaps the conclusion (or the assumption) that judicial decision making is substantially similar to the decision making of those who are not judges is open to question. Just as it would be a mistake to conclude very much about the mathematical reasoning of the Harvard mathematics faculty from studies about how ordinary people make mathematical calculations at the supermarket or when balancing their checkbooks, so too might it be a mistake to draw conclusions about how judges reasons with rules and precedents and authorities from the way in which the man on the Clapham omnibus[7] deals with similar inputs into and constraints on his decision-making processes. And if it is a mistake to move too quickly from what we know about how lay people perform certain tasks to conclusions about how judges perform some of those same tasks, it certainly would be a mistake to draw conclusions about how judges perform a range of judge-specific tasks from what we have found about how lay people perform quite different tasks.

Thus, one question—a question and not a conclusion—is whether the experience of studying to be a lawyer and then of practicing law causes decision making in law, especially about legal (as opposed to factual) matters, to diverge in deep and cognitively substantial ways from the decision making of human beings who do not possess such training and experience.[8] And a further question is whether those who self-select to be judges, who are selected as judges, and who have the experience of serving as judges make decisions differently from nonjudge lawyers, thus causing further gaps between judicial decision making and the decision making even of similarly trained and experienced people holding different roles.[9] Consequently, there are hypotheses worthy of investigation about whether in law-focused decision making there are divides between lawyers and people in general, between judges and nonjudge lawyers, and consequently even larger divides between judges and people in general.

Indeed it is likely that multiple phenomena are at work. Self-selection into law, subsequent legal training, subsequent legal experience, self-selection into judging, and then finally serving in the judicial role may all interact with each other to produce considerable differences between how judges and lay people reason and decide. To the extent that this is so, the interaction among legal training, legal acculturation, legal experience, and the judicial role may even generate process- and not just content-based differences between the cognitive mechanisms of judges and those of nonjudge humanity. If so, there may be differences, at least with respect to some highly important judicial tasks, between *how* judges and lay people think and not merely differences in *what* they think about.

The battery of possibilities offered in the previous paragraphs is no more than an array of testable hypotheses. If even some of these hypotheses turn out to be true, however, then there actually may be a genuine psychology of judging. But if on the other hand these hypothesized differences between judges and lay people turn out not to exist, and if instead the assumptions and premises of judge as human being lying behind most of the existing research are sound, then research into the psychology of judging will be an interesting application of larger psychological issues, but will not in any fundamental way constitute a discrete area of inquiry. If the most important or only determinant of judicial decision-making characteristics is the fact that the judge is human, after all, then a psychology of judging will be little different from a psychology of dentistry or a psychology of plumbing. It would be interesting and possibly even important to know what psychology could teach us about how dentists and plumbers think, but the application of research findings about human beings generally to the human beings who fill these socially vital roles is a long way from saying that there is a psychology *of* dentistry or plumbing. Perhaps the psychological dimensions of judging are different from those of dentistry or plumbing, but we will not know that unless we depart from the assumption that what we know about people is necessarily applicable to judges. And because I suspect that there might be more to the psychology of judging than there is to the psychology of dentistry or plumbing,[10] and because I suspect as well that there are reasons to believe that legal and judicial attributes may cause judicial decision making to depart in relevant ways from the decision making of lay people, my aim in this paper is to examine in a preliminary and nonempirical way—hypothesis offering but not hypothesis testing—what a genuine psychology of judging might look like, and why, most of the existing literature on the psychology of judging notwithstanding, we ought to take this possibility seriously.[11]

The Promises and Premises of Legal Reasoning

Lord Coke wrote of the "artificial" reason of the law (Coke, 1628/1985; Fried, 1981) hundreds of years before even the advent of university-based formal training in law. Now that such training is ubiquitous, Lord Coke's premise is more important yet, because the view that there is a special reason of and for law has become the guiding principle for the vast numbers of American law schools and their equivalents[12] in other countries. These schools purport to teach their students the mysterious art of "legal reasoning," and they hold out the hope that at the end of law study a student will have learned how to "think like a lawyer" (Schauer, 2003, 2004a, 2009).

The belief that thinking like a lawyer is fundamentally different from simply thinking has declined a bit in the past several generations, but not much. Law schools these days pay more attention than previously to philosophy, literature, economics, and the empirical social sciences, among others, but they have scarcely abandoned their commitment to there being such a thing as legal reasoning, to legal reasoning being a somewhat autonomous skill, and to the responsibility of law schools to inculcate this skill in those who would be lawyers and judges. Moreover, law schools subscribe to the view that legal reasoning is not easily picked up on one's own, and that formal training and subsequent experience in thinking like a lawyer can and characteristically do produce a genuinely transformed method of thinking, reasoning, arguing, and decision making.

Although I will discuss presently my view of what legal reasoning just *is*, I want to be careful not to overstate the claim about the alleged distinctiveness of legal reasoning. Law schools and the legal culture do not typically maintain that legal reasoning is totally or even almost totally unconnected with ordinary reasoning,[13] in the way that Estonian is unconnected with English, for example, or that literary interpretation is unconnected with multivariate calculus. Nor could they. Rather, the most plausible version of the claim to distinctiveness in legal reasoning would be the comparative statistical claim that some of the methods of reasoning that are located outside of legal reasoning—arguments from precedent,[14] reasoning from rules, and reliance on authority, most prominently—are more highly concentrated in legal argument and decision making than in ordinary reasoning and decision making, the difference being sufficiently great as to support the conclusion that legal reasoning is, in the aggregate, substantially unlike the kind of reasoning that takes place in other decision making domains. So although lawyers and judges necessarily employ nonlegal forms of reasoning as they argue cases and make decisions, and although nonlawyers occasionally make use of the characteristic modalities of legal argument, the concentration of these modalities in legal argument is so great, the law schools' view of the world appears to maintain, as to justify the claim that something very different is going on when lawyers and judges tackle a problem or face a decision.

So what then *is* legal reasoning, or at least what is it alleged to be? What is it to think like a lawyer, as opposed to just thinking? These are neither easy nor uncontroversial questions, and so we find in the literature on legal reasoning and argument the claims that legal thinking is about the ability to seek and do justice in the individual case (Bartlett, 1990; Burton, 2005 Henderson, 1987; Minow & Spelman, 1990; Solum, 1988; Sunstein, 1996, 1999), or about the capacity for self-critically seeing and appreciating viewpoints opposed to one's own (Sherry, 2007), or about a tendency toward clarity and analytic precision (Sherry, 2007; Vandevelde, 1996), or about a talent for understanding and dealing with facts (Bandstra, 2005), or about a facility in argument and debate (Bandstra, 2005), or about the capability of engaging in analogical reasoning (Brewer, 1996; Levi, 1948; Weinreb, 2005).[15] Yet although there can be little doubt that all of these skills and many more are necessary for successful lawyering (and judging), and equally little doubt that good lawyers tend to have them in greater abundance than poor ones, these are not skills that seem especially of greater importance for lawyers than they are for police officers, physicians, social workers, politicians, and countless others. Most of these skills, even including the skill of analogical reasoning,[16] are domain-general reasoning abilities, and while lawyers may on average be better at some of them than other people, it is probable that any differential ability with respect to these and similar tasks is explained almost entirely by the fact that lawyers are on average somewhat better educated, smarter, and possibly even more motivated than the population at large.

But although many of the posited components of legal reasoning are neither unique to nor even much concentrated in lawyers and legal argument, there is one form of reasoning—or one cluster of associated forms of reasoning—that can plausibly be understood to set lawyers apart from others, and it is one that can be described as *second-order reasoning* (Raz,

1979; Schauer, 1991, 2004b; Sunstein & Ullman-Margalit, 1999). When engaged in ordinary (first-order) reasoning and decision making, people tend, not surprisingly, to try to make the best decision for the problem or task at hand. Their aim is typically to reach the right result for *this* case—the present case. That this is so for ordinary people, however, is not to say that it is so for lawyers and judges, for one of the things that law schools attempt to teach their students is precisely to *avoid* thinking that the right result for *this* present case is necessarily the right result all things considered. So consider, for example, the typical allegedly Socratic[17] dialogue that takes place between student and teacher in the first year of law school. After eventually being coaxed into reciting the facts of some reported case correctly and accurately, the student is then asked what the correct result should be for the present case, and she commonly responds by announcing what she believes to be the most fair or just outcome as between the opposing positions of the particular parties. At this point the student is asked to give the rule or principle that would support this outcome, and here the characteristic pattern of Socratic inquiry begins. By a series of patterned and well-planned hypotheticals, the professor challenges the student's initially proffered rule, with the aim of demonstrating that the rule that would generate a just or fair or efficient outcome in the present case would generate less just, less fair, or otherwise less satisfactory results in other cases. And in taking the student through this series of uncomfortable applications of the student's initially chosen rule, the professor attempts to get the students to understand that the best legal rule may be one which produces an unjust result in the present case, but which will produce better results in a larger number of cases, the result in the present case notwithstanding.

This form of Socratic inquiry is not restricted to the law school class-room, and it is noteworthy that it is the common form of judicial questioning in appellate argument.[18] Because appellate courts see themselves as setting forth rules that will control other and future factual situations and as writing opinions that will serve as precedent for future cases, appellate judges often focus as much on the effect of this ruling on future cases as on reaching the best result in the present case. As a consequence, appellate advocates often find themselves asked how the rule or result they are advocating will play out in various hypothetical cases. As in the law school classroom, these hypothetical situations are offered against the background of the view that the right result in the particular dispute before the court will only be the actual outcome if it can be justified in a way that will not produce the wrong outcomes in too many expected future cases (Golding, 1963; Greenawalt, 1978).[19]

In seeking to demonstrate to the hapless student or struggling advocate how the best legal outcome may be something other than the best outcome in the immediate case, the prototypical Socratic interrogation aligns itself with an even more important dimension of legal reasoning and argument, the way in which the backward-looking, constraining, and limiting dimensions of law (Levi, 1948; MacCormick, 2005; Raz, 1979; Wasserstrom, 1961, pp. 25–26)[20] often mandate a result other than the one that is optimally fair or maximally wise, all things considered, in the particular case—a result that "will sometimes be wrong" for the particular dispute (Sherwin, 1999). It may seem unfair on the balance of all reasons to deprive a person of property (*United States v. Locke*, 1985) or a place on a ballot (*Hunter v. Norman*, described in Schauer, 1988a) just because he has missed a statutory deadline for understandable, innocent, and ultimately inconsequential reasons, but the law characteristically even if not universally enforces the literal meaning of authoritative language even when such an action produces a bad outcome in the particular case (Manning, 2003; Schauer, 1992). And it may seem equally unfair to take the existence of clear precedent as commanding a suboptimal result, especially from the vantage point of a decision maker who thinks the precedent mistaken, but following even a precedent perceived to be erroneous is what, under the traditional understanding, the law expects its decision makers to do.[21]

The second-order reasoning I describe here is not about what *is*, but instead about what to *do*. The law must frequently engage in factual inquiry to determine who fired the gun, how much toxic waste was discharged into the river, whether someone was in possession of inside information when they purchased a quantity of securities, or whether the driver of some car had consumed alcohol prior to being involved in an accident. But in the law such factual determinations are typically precursors to a judgment about what the law requires to be *done* on the basis of these facts; and what the law requires to be done may be something other than that which a nonlegal decision maker would decide, all things considered, should be done. So although the legal system engages in factual inquiry, it is precisely in moving from factual inquiry to action-producing consequence that legal reasoning potentially differs in fundamental ways from the reasoning of other action-producing agents. These other agents, we typically think, are focused on producing the right decision for *this* decision making event, but if the characteristic decision-making modality of law is different from the decision-making modalities of other domains, than legal reasoning and decision making may be different as well. Legal reasoning, on this widespread account, is "artificial" not only because of the way in which it is deliberately *not* focused on reaching the best for just this case, but also because decisions having legal consequences differ for just this reason from the practical reasoning in which nonlawyers ordinarily engage.

The Realist Challenge

Although a widely believed traditional conception of legal reasoning is consistent with the foregoing account,[22] the descriptive accuracy of the traditional conception has hardly gone unchallenged. More particularly, an array of perspectives collected under the heading of Legal Realism[23] can be understood as presenting not only a challenge to the traditional conception of legal and judicial reasoning, but also, and more germane here, a challenge to the view that judicial reasoning is substantially different from the reasoning of ordinary people.[24] For the Realists, judges were less different from people in general, and from other public and private decision makers, than the traditional "artificial reason" view maintained. The Realists saw legal reason as human reason, and thus traditional claims for the distinctiveness of legal reasoning were to the Realists largely pretense. Because the Realists therefore implicitly (and sometimes explicitly) subscribed to the view that judges were best seen simply as human decision makers with few distinctive methods, most of the existing research on the psychology of judging can be understood as incorporating an unexpressed—and typically unresearched—Legal Realist outlook on what judges do and how they do it.

The connection between Legal Realism and the psychology of judging can be traced to the earliest days of Realism. In *Law and the Modern Mind* (Frank, 1930), Jerome Frank, then in the aftermath of his own recent psychoanalysis, claimed that it was impossible for judges to engage in the second-order decision making then and now associated with the traditional account of legal reasoning.[25] Frank argued that judges, like other human beings, invariably trained their attention on the facts and details of this particular case, and, moreover, unavoidably strove to make the best decision for this case and this dispute. Having done that, Frank insisted, the judges would then seek to find conventional legal materials—cases, statutes, regulations, constitutional provisions, maxims, canons, and so forth—that would provide ex post justifications or rationalizations for decisions that were causally uninfluenced by those materials. For Frank and others (Hutcheson, 1929; Radin, 1925), the key challenges to the traditional account lay first in the way in which they saw judges as focused on reaching the best result for the particular case, and, second, in the fact that the *law* was used by judges not to produce decisions, but instead to justify ex post decisions made on decidedly nonlegal grounds.[26]

Not all of what ordinarily rides under the banner of Legal Realism fits this mold. When Karl Llewellyn, for example, suggested that judges often made decisions based on rules that diverged from the rules that one would find in the law books (Llewellyn, 1930, 1960; Twining, 1973), he was denying neither the possibility nor even the desirability of rule-based second-order decision making. What he did deny, however, was the view that formal official written law provided the source for the actual rules that judges and other decision makers employed in making their decisions (Dagan, 2007). There *were* rules, Llewellyn agreed, but those rules came not from the law books or the decided cases, but instead from the judges' own policy views and from the social and professional culture within which the judge operated.

Even for Llewellyn at times, however, and for other Realists more pervasively, the challenge offered to the traditional model of legal reasoning was a challenge to the possibility that judges could avoid what they saw as the best result for the case at hand in the service of other and larger law-based, rule-based, precedent-based, or process-based goals. In this regard, therefore, the Realists saw judges first and foremost as human beings, and saw the (natural) human desire to reach the best outcome for *this* case as the primary determinant of judicial behavior and judicial decision making. What judges learned in law school or in practicing law might make some difference at the margins, and so too would what judges internalized in taking on the role and duties of a judge, but these minor differences, many Realists insisted, were overshadowed by the particularistic proclivities which judges shared with their fellow human beings. And it is precisely in this respect that most of the existing research on the psychology of judging, research that also sees the pervasively human characteristics of judges as the primary determinant of judicial behavior and judicial decision, is best understood as embodying a Realist outlook on adjudication in particular and law more generally.

The Issue Joined

The contrast between Realist and traditional views of legal reasoning—between Frank and Coke, if you will—is an important window through which to view questions about the psychology of judging. And although I have stressed the contrast between Realist and traditional views in terms of particularism and generality, and in the distinction between first-order and second-order reasoning, my larger point hinges on neither of these distinctions. Rather, the central claim is that the Realists, or at least many of them, were concerned with challenging the larger view that there is something distinctive about legal reasoning. The traditional view, captured well by Coke's appeal to artificiality, is that lawyers and judges are engaged in demonstrably different cognitive processes from other reasoners and decision makers. And the Realist view, exemplified by Frank, is that the alleged cognitive differences between judges (or lawyers) and the rest of humanity are exaggerated, with judges engaged in forms of cognition not appreciably different from those of the human species in general, a species of which judges are of course a part.

If the Realists were right to trivialize the differences between judges and the rest of us, then the psychology of judging is, simply, psychology. What we can learn about the psychology of human cognition, human reasoning, human perception, and human decision making will accordingly serve us well, with few modifications, in describing, predicting, and understanding the psychology of judging. But if the Realists are wrong, then what the existing research tells us about how ordinary people use analogy will tell us little about how judges decide according to precedent, what the existing research tells us about how people make decisions will tell us little about how judges make decisions according to rules, and what the existing research tells us about the inputs into human decision making will tell us little about how judges make decisions by following the dictates of even those authoritative sources with which they disagree.

At the very least, the contrast between the traditional and Realist accounts of legal reasoning suggests that a research agenda could be aimed at answering the precise question of the extent to which, if at all, judges actually do engage in second-order reasoning and actually do refrain from reaching what they believe to be the correct outcome in this case because of the perceived (or actual) constraints of precedent, rule, or authoritative source. Moreover, such a research agenda need not be limited to examining the hypothesis that judges engage in second-order reasoning. It could also usefully test the hypothesis that judicial second-order reasoning is substantially different from, more frequent than, or more effective than the second-order reasoning of nonjudge decision makers, even assuming that nonjudge decision makers engage in second-order reasoning at all.

Even the foregoing sketch of a research program is far too crude. In addition to attempting to control for intelligence, education, motivation, and other attributes that judges likely possess to a greater degree than the population at large, such a program would attempt to disaggregate the components of second-order legal reasoning in order to determine whether there was a gap between judges and lay decision makers for each of those components. When judges are expected to make a decision consistent with a previous decision with which they disagree—the central case of decision according to precedent—will they follow precedent and reach what they think is the wrong result more often than ordinary people assigned the same task? If judges are told that the only sources on which they may rely are part of an artificially constricted array of sources that in this instance might support an erroneous result (Schauer, 2004c), will they limit their attention to this suboptimizing and error-producing (from their lights) array to a greater extent than the nonjudges? If commanded to follow a bad rule or a good rule which in this instance produces an unfortunate outcome, will judges more than others simply follow the rule and swallow the unfortunate outcome? And if instructed to refrain from doing the right thing because doing the right thing is in someone else's jurisdiction or is someone else's responsibility,[27] will judges more than others remain passive in the face of an opportunity to do the right thing, or will they, like most others, treat jurisdictional and similar limitations as inconsequential?[28]

Even if such research were to indicate that judges really *were* different from lay people for some or all of these tasks, additional research would still be necessary to determine whether it was simply legal training that produced the difference, or whether it was something about the role of judge as judge. We can imagine a research design that might, for example, assign similar tasks to judges, practicing lawyers, and law students, in order to determine whether an identified difference between judges and lay people was explained by some difference between judges and lawyers, or was explained instead by a difference between judges and lawyers and (advanced) law students, on the one hand, and those without legal training, on the other. And even more fine grained research could attempt to locate differences even among classes of judges, as for example in the differences between elected and appointed judges, or between trial and appellate judges, or among judges with different varieties of prejudge backgrounds.

Other hypotheses and research possibilities abound, but like the ones just sketched they would identify a task other than fact-finding or verdict-rendering, and then seek to determine whether for this task judges were genuinely different, either in outcome or in method, from some relevant nonjudge class. An affirmative answer to this question would not, of course, exclude the likelihood of relevant similarities existing alongside the genuine differences. And that is why the existing research showing that judges are susceptible to many well-discussed cognitive failings and biases—anchoring and availability, for example—is highly important. Even though important, however, this research is incomplete. Even if judges when acting as finders of fact or when reaching verdicts are prone to all or most of these familiar reasoning failures,[29] the question remains entirely open whether there are also areas in which judges think quite differently, even supposing that with respect to *those* areas judges would be similarly afflicted with the same or analogous cognitive deficiencies. The existing research tells us little about whether there are such areas of differential thinking, and, if so, what they look like, but until we can answer this question we cannot know whether the conclusions of Legal Realism are correct, and whether the hidden Legal Realist premises of the existing psychological research on judging are sound. Much of the existing research on the psychology of judging takes the Realist view of judging as axiomatic, but that conclusion is hardly inevitable and hardly based on systematic research directed precisely at that question.

The Question of Expertise

Although a substantial psychological literature explores the nature of expertise and the differences between expert reasoning and that of novices,[30] surprisingly little of that literature is especially relevant to the question whether, if at all, judges reason differently from ordinary folk. And that is because the psychological literature on expertise tends to be focused on the question of comparative expertise within a single area of knowledge rather than on the hypothesized cognitive differences across different areas of knowledge. The existing research examines what experts at x do that novices at x do not, but almost none of it looks at whether people who know how to x, whether experts or novices or somewhere in between, tackle problems and make decisions differently from people who do not know how to x at all, or from people who know only how to y, again regardless of whether they are expert or not.

Yet although little research addresses this question of cross-domain expertise—what we might call specialization rather than expertise—this question is central to examining the psychology of judging. We *could* determine what expert fact-finders do that novice fact-finders do not, just as we could ask what expert judges do that novice judges do not. But if we are interested in testing the hypothesis that there is a psychology of judging that differs from the psychology of decision making *simpliciter*, then we want to see whether there are some tasks that judges perform differently just because they are judges. We know from the existing research on judging that in some tasks—many aspects of fact-finding, principally—judges do differ less from nonjudges and non-lawyers than the conventional wisdom has appeared to suppose. But to take these findings, important as they are, as answering the central question about the psychology of judging is like imagining that because auto mechanics approach the finances of their own small business in the same way that psychiatrists approach the finances of *their* own small businesses that auto mechanics are importantly similar to psychiatrists. That the two are similar with respect to accounting says nothing about whether they are similar with respect to fixing cars and fixing heads, and similarly the discovery that judges and jurors (or people generally) are similar with respect to fact-finding skirts the question whether there is something else that judges do for which their training and expertise might actually produce important differences.

If I am right that an important component of judging is something other than fact-finding—arguably true for trial judges and self-evident for appellate judges—then we can understand the importance of focusing on law-finding, law-applying, law-interpreting, and, yes, law-making, for these are a large part of the judicial task. But when judges perform these tasks, do they perform them in the same way that those without legal or judicial training or experience would approach them, which is what many of the Realists argued, or do they employ a different skill set, to use an infelicitous and fashionable but not inappropriate term from contemporary management-speak? When it comes to tasks other than fact-finding, do judges think like human beings, or like lawyers, or like judges? Addressing this question should be one of the central items on a research agenda for the psychology of judging, but it is, surprisingly, an item that up to now has been almost completely absent.

Conclusion

Jerome Frank understood the traditional claim about legal reasoning, but he argued that judges were psychologically unable to do what the traditional theory demanded.[31] Frank is treated nowadays as a bit idiosyncratic, but the psychological lens through which he viewed judging points to the importance of distinguishing three questions about second-order reasoning. The first, the answer to which is embodied in Frank's own point of view, is whether people are naturally particularistic. When engaged in decision-making tasks, do people just because of the makeup of the human mind think in terms of *this* task, thus being psychologically averse to making the wrong decision on this occasion in the service of larger or more distant goals?

In insisting on a deep human proclivity toward the particular, Frank may well have been wrong. After all, delayed gratification is hardly beyond the capacities of most people, and there is more than a remote possibility that Frank's speculations—and they were hardly more than that—about the raw material of human psychology were guided less by psychological fact than by Frank's own normative views about what lawyers and judges *ought* to be doing.

Even assuming that Frank was right about what humans start with, he may nevertheless have been unduly pessimistic about the possibility that these antecedent particularistic instincts could be changed. So even if humans are temperamentally, physiologically, or genetically averse to second-order reasoning, there is little reason to believe that this aversion is so hard-wired as to be incapable of change. Perhaps one form of education, including one form of moral education, is aimed, at least in part, at fostering various forms of second-order reasoning, and to the extent that such education is at times successful Frank and his compatriots may have given up too quickly on the possibility that anyone—and not just judges—can both grasp and perform the basic skills of reasoning from rules, making decisions constrained by precedent,[32] and taking the commands of an authority as providing reasons for action. To the extent that humans in general can be taught to engage in such reasoning, then there would be reason to believe that lawyers and judges could be trained to do the same thing, to do it more often, and to do it better. Implicit in the traditional picture of the artificial reason of the law, therefore, is a story about the possibility that this artificial reason can be inculcated in and internalized by even those humans for which it would initially seem artificial.

Because Frank believed that human particularism was so hard-wired as to be unchangeable, however, he was never forced to reach the normative question. If we assume that the basic tools of second-order reasoning are learnable, we then face the question whether it would be good for lawyers and judges to learn them. Weber sneered at his (erroneous, as a matter of Islamic law) image of the *q'adi*, making the best decision all things considered for each case. But as some voices in contemporary philosophy (Dancy, 1993) feminist theory (Bartlett, 1990), and legal theory (Sunstein, 1999) have insisted, making decisions for the particular case—deciding things one case at a time—is supported by influential arguments, and has much to recommend it, even for those of us (Schauer, 2003) who in the final analysis see fewer virtues in particularism than others. But the point here is not to rehearse these familiar debates. It is instead to emphasize that an inquiry into the possibility of judicial second-order reasoning—an inquiry into a central but understudied dimension of the psychology of judging—is important not only as description and explanation of how judges behave and decide, but also as the precursor to a normative inquiry into how judges *should* behave and decide. Such inquiries dominate legal scholarship, often to unfortunate exclusion of almost everything else, but they are hardly without import. But before we can intelligently decide what judges *should* do, we need to see both what they are doing and what they can do. This inquiry can be usefully informed by serious empirical inquiry into the psychology of judging, but little progress will be made even on this dimension until the research agenda begins to take seriously the possibility that there might actually *be* a psychology of judging, a possibility that is surprisingly absent from almost all of the existing literature.

Notes

An earlier version of this chapter was presented at the Workshop on the Psychology of Judging, University of Virginia, Charlottesville, Virginia, March 29–31, 2007. I am grateful for the comments of the participants on that occasion, for thoughtful and challenging written comments from Barbara A. Spellman and Dan Simon, and for research support from the Harvard Law School and the Joan Shorenstein Center on the Press, Politics and Public Policy, Harvard University.

1. For a useful analysis of the research that is genuinely focused on judges and judging, see (Robinson & Spellman, 2005).
2. There are numerous logistical and ethical impediments to research using real judges as experimental subjects, and thus the conclusion that nonjudge and nonlawyer research subjects are representative of judges is facilitated by the ease of locating the former and the obstacles to doing serious experimental work on the latter.
3. Fact-finding is not to be confused with fact-locating or fact-discovering. Fact-finding is the legal term of art for determining what actually happened based solely on the evidence presented in court by the parties.
4. Indeed, the preoccupation with the jury in much of the psychological research is itself curious in light of the fact that the institution of the jury does not much exist in civil law countries, is not used outside of criminal cases (with the occasional exception of libel trials) in any common law country other than the United States, and is a rapidly declining institution even for criminal cases in the United States and elsewhere (Guthrie, Rachlinski, & Wistrich, 2001; Schauer, 2006b).
5. On the implications for social science research of the distinction between the tasks typically performed by trial judges and those typically performed by appellate judges, see (Rowland & Carp, 1996).
6. The statement in the text is not intended to express even the slightest sympathy with the hoary but misguided cavil that experiments on university under-graduates are of limited value in learning about the behavior of people who are not undergraduates. In the absence of identifiable and germane differences between undergraduates and people in general, there is no good reason to doubt the generalizability of findings about undergraduates to conclusions about people as a whole. But when we are drawing conclusions about the decision-making characteristics of individuals who are in theory specially trained to make decisions of a certain kind—as are judges—it is far more appropriate to question whether research using people without that special

training can tell us much about the way in which people with special training make the very decisions for which they are supposedly specially trained and for which they are specially selected by virtue of possessing the requisite training and skills.

7. The man on the Clapham omnibus being the quaint British equivalent of the American "reasonable man" (*Hall v. Brooklands Racing Club*).

8. Those who become lawyers may self-select, or may be selected, on the basis of their possession of attributes that are relatively rare in the general population but that are not only germane to success as a lawyer, but are also germane to success as a judge even among the class of lawyers.

9. Or it may be that the causal mechanism operates in a different direction, with lawyers being selected for the judiciary, or self-selecting into the judiciary, because they possess skills or proclivities to forms of reasoning and decision making that are different from those of the mine-run of practicing lawyers.

10. This says nothing about the respective abilities or intelligence of judges, dentists, and plumbers. One need not be smarter (or dumber) than the average of humanity in order to engage in a cognitively specialized task.

11. It is worth emphasizing that nothing I say here denies that judges share some or perhaps even many decision making psychological characteristics with ordinary people (Simon, 1998, 2002, 2004), and that many of those shared characteristics are useful in understanding what judges do. My concern is that by focusing so heavily on the shared characteristics, researchers have slighted the nonshared characteristics to the detriment of a fuller understanding of what judges do. Tiger Woods and I both play golf, and I am reasonably sure that Woods and I share some number of decision making pathologies on the golf course, such as exaggerating the probability of making (for our skill level) low probability shots, or taking the most recent (and thus most cognitively available) shots as more representative of the array of outcomes on shots of that variety than they in fact are. But to focus only on these shared characteristics and to ignore the numerous ways in which Woods and I differ as golfers, mentally as well as physically, is to ignore something seemingly quite important. Without investigating the ways in which judges might be able to do things that lay people cannot, we run the risk of overgeneralizing from the ways in which judges assuredly have decision-making characteristics they share with lay people.

12. Outside of North America, the study of law takes place largely at the under-graduate level, although additional and postgraduate law study is common. A potentially valuable research project, although not my focus here, would be to examine whether studying law from the age of eighteen or nineteen, and in place of some other undergraduate specialization, produces a significant difference in reasoning and decision making from that which exists in those who do not commence the serious study of law until at least the age of twenty-two, and who already have as undergraduates studied another field.

13. And if they do, they shouldn't.

14. To forestall a potential objection, I signal here (and address at somewhat greater length below, and see also Schauer, 2007) that I do not take the use of analogy and the constraints of precedent as being especially similar. Lawyers use analogy frequently, but so do other professionals and most lay people. Feeling obligated to follow a previous decision that one believes to be erroneous, however, is arguably far less prevalent outside of law than in, and may thus comprise part of

the array of reasoning and decision-making modalities that collectively can be thought of as legal reasoning.

15. For skeptical views about the alleged distinctiveness of analogical reasoning, see Alexander (1996), Posner (2006), and Schauer (2008).

16. On the use of analogy in numerous occupations and endeavors, see Blanchette & Dunbar (2001a, 2001b).

17. There is scant connection between the question-centered methods of teaching employed by Socrates in the Platonic dialogues and the type of questioning that has traditionally taken place in the law school classroom. Even apart from the enormous advantage that Plato had over the rest of us in being able to write the answers as well as the questions, Socrates' goal was to extract from his interlocutors some latent but nonspecialized insight, rather than to inculcate in them a specialized skill that they hitherto did not possess. Now it may be that the ability to engage in just this kind of second-order reasoning is latent in everyone, but if it is sufficiently latent that it takes law professors and three years of law school to extract it for most people, then there is no difference of consequence between an inculcation and an extraction model of legal education, for in either case that student develops the ability actually to *do* something she could not do before.

18. A common mistake is to assume that legal argument is about persuasion, and that in seeking to persuade lawyers act similarly to politicians, editorialists, teachers, clergymen, and countless other persuaders. But legal argument under the traditional account is persuasion of a special kind precisely because it is parasitic on how the judge will make *her* decision. So if the traditional account of legal reasoning is sound—and it may not be—the lawyer is *not* attempting to persuade the judge that such-and-such is a good outcome *simpliciter*, but is instead trying to convince the judge that some good outcome is not precluded by contrary precedents, or that precedent commands a result without regard to the precedent-independent desirability of that result.

19. On the use of hypothetical cases to ensure principled decision making in just this way, see (Christie, 1969).

20. The "looking backward" aspect of law "makes judges think at least as much about conformity to an announced principle as about the right and justice and social utility of the case they are about to decide" (Ulman, 1933).

21. "[I]n most matters it is more important that the applicable rule of law be settled than that it be settled right," (*Burnet v. Coronado Oil & Gas. Co.*, Brandeis, dissenting; see also Alexander, 1989; Alexander & Sherwin, 2001; Schauer, 1987).

22. For earlier works articulating the traditional account even more boldly (and, perhaps, crudely) than the various sources cited in the previous section, see Black (1912), Cross & Harris (1990), and Wambaugh (1894).

23. Or, sometimes, American Legal Realism, not only in acknowledgment of its provenance, but also to distinguish it from the largely unrelated Scandinavian Realism of, for example Hägerström (1953), Olivecrona (1971), and Ross (1958).

24. On Legal Realism generally, see Kalman (1986), Leiter (2004), and Rumble (1968). There are competing conceptions of what ideas lay at the core of Realism, but I disclaim the role of arbiter among the multiple views of what Legal Realism was "really" all about. So although various Realists and their

fellow travelers advanced a cluster of different claims all in the name of Legal Realism, it is uncontroversial that the particular part of Realism I stress in the text is at least among the positions advocated by some of the more prominent Realists.

25. It is fashionable these days to marginalize Frank's contribution to Realism because of his belief that the judge's personal idiosyncrasies were a significant determinant of judicial outcomes (Dagan, 2007; Leiter, 1997). But although Frank's (and Hutcheson's) views about the *source* of the judge's decision may be unrepresentative of so-called mainstream Realism, he remains a seminal figure for the view that the judge's determination of the right outcome precedes the judge's consultation of formal legal doctrinal sources, and also for the view that judicial decision is substantially particularistic, both being central tenets of the broad Realist program.

26. For a modern and sophisticated version of this form of Realism, see Kennedy (1986).

27. See *Blanchflower v. Blanchflower* (2003), concluding that same-sex adultery ought to constitute grounds for at-fault divorce, but that such a change was for the legislature and not the courts.

28. Consider the question of federalism. Although lawyers and judges spend much time wrestling with the respective jurisdictional competences of the federal government and the states, there is little indication that either the public or the political world that caters to that public takes the principles of federalism as constituting an independent second-order constraint on either the states' or the federal government's adopting what the public believes to be a desirable first-order policy.

29. I bracket here the important debates about whether patterns of reasoning falling short of optimal or perfect rationality are better understood as desirable adaptive strategies (Gigerenzer, 2000; Gigerenzer & Selten, 2001) or instead as potentially correctable errors whose correction would, in general, be desirable (Kahneman & Tversky, 1981, 1984; Kahneman, Slovic, & Tversky, 1982).

30. For an introduction to the psychological literature, see Ericsson et al. (2006) and Chi, Farr, & Glaser (1998).

31. It is interesting that when Frank became a federal judge, a role he occupied from 1941 until his death in 1957, he wrote opinions that hardly differed in style from those of other judges. Much better examples of Realist judging can be found in the opinions of Justice William O. Douglas.

32. This is a good place to point out the important difference, off-hand remarks in the psychology analogy literature notwithstanding, between analogical reasoning and the legal constraint of precedent. When people, including lawyers (Levi, 1948; Weinreb, 2005), seek to persuade others, or seek guidance in making a decision, they often rely on analogies. They think it is good to take some action now because it is similar to some action in the past that has worked out successfully, or they think it wise to avoid some decision because the circumstances resemble circumstances of the past. But in such cases the decision-maker is using the analogy (Spellman & Holyoak, 1996) to help reach the right decision now. The analogy is a tool, and in theory a friend. The constraint of precedent in law, however, which is not coextensive with lawyers' use of analogical reasoning, is more foe than friend. Having concluded that the right thing to do now is ϕ, the lawyer or judge will sometimes find that ϕ is precluded

by some previous decision, often a decision that the present judge thinks mistaken. But insofar as the constraint of precedent actually constrains (which it likely does outside of hard Supreme Court cases far more than it does in the Supreme Court (Segal & Spaeth, 1996, 2002), then the judge is not looking for the analogy that helps, but instead seeking, often unsuccessfully, to avoid the analogy that hurts. Whether such constraint by precedent is desirable is itself debatable, as is the empirical question about its frequency in legal decision making. But the importance of these questions should not lead us to think that being bound by a similar but erroneous decision from the past is similar to choosing to be guided or persuaded by analogous circumstances from an earlier time (Schauer, 2008).

8

Features of Judicial Reasoning

Emily Sherwin

Adjudication of legal disputes depends inevitably on human decision making. It is not surprising, therefore, that legal scholars sometimes turn to psychology for help in understanding law. Importation of psychological insights to law leads naturally to the question whether certain aspects of human psychology are special to, or especially prominent in, legal decision making. From a psychological point of view, does legal decision making, and particularly judicial decision making, differ from decision making in nonlegal contexts?

Larry Alexander and I (2008) have argued at length that the methods of reasoning judges use to decide cases are no different from the methods of reasoning used by nonjudicial decision makers. Nevertheless, certain aspects of the psychology of decision making have special importance in law because of the role they play in the process of adjudication. In this sense, there is a psychology of judging, although there is no reason why it should not be informed by psychological research performed in other settings. My conclusions on this point are consistent with the conclusions Frederick Schauer reaches in his contribution to this book (ch. 7).

In this brief essay, I examine the various and sometimes conflicting psychological tasks our legal system assigns to judges. I begin with first-order judicial decision making, meaning reasoning about how particular disputes should be resolved in the absence of authoritative rules. I then turn to what Schauer usefully describes as second-order judicial decision making, meaning decisions judges must make about the bearing of authoritative rules on their own process of decision. From a psychological point of view, the most interesting feature of second-order judicial decision making is that law often requires judges to suppress reason in order to give authoritative effect to rules. How judges can achieve the mental state necessary for this purpose—a mental state consisting of abstinence from reasoning—is one of the great psychological mysteries of law.

What I say in this essay is nothing new. In particular, the analysis of rule-based decision making I provide is much indebted to Schauer's excellent work on the subject. Nor do I provide independent psychological insights: I write as a legal theorist without expertise in the field of cognitive science.

"First-Order" Reasoning About Legal Disputes

When judges decide cases, their immediate task is to decide what outcome is best in a particular, concrete dispute. For the moment, I shall set aside the problem of legal rules and assume that the dispute in question is a "case of first impression," not governed by existing law. In the absence of governing law, identifying the best outcome of a dispute involves empirical observation, induction, and moral reasoning.

Empirical and inductive reasoning generate the factual premises for adjudication.[1] Research in the field of cognitive science indicates that these forms of reasoning are subject to various types of bias: human reasoners rely on mental shortcuts that normally are useful but can distort their judgment about facts, and especially about probabilities (Tversky & Kahneman, 1982; Plous, 1993; Gilovich, Griffin, & Kahneman, 2002; Symposium, 2005). For example, they respond to irrelevant cues when making quantitative estimates, they overlook the effects of hindsight (Rachlinski, 1998; Guthrie, Rachlinski, & Wistrich, 2001), and they assume that vivid or emotion-provoking facts are more typical than they are of the statistical classes to which they belong. Work by Chris Guthrie, Jeffrey Rachlinski, and Andrew Wistrich (2001) confirms that judges are susceptible to these biases, although experienced judges may be somewhat better at controlling their effects than the population at large.

Given a set of facts (and assuming still that no law applies), judges must engage in moral reasoning to determine how the state should to respond to the parties' dispute. Philosophers commonly equate moral reasoning with reasoning to reflective equilibrium.[2] To achieve reflective equilibrium, the reasoner constructs a tentative moral principle applicable to the problem at hand, then tests the principle against moral intuitions about particular instances within the principle's scope and against background theories about the world at large. The reasoner then adjusts the principle, the reasoner's moral judgments, or both, until conflicts are satisfactorily resolved. The principle that emerges in equilibrium provides the answer to the problem case. As a method of justifying action or decisions, reasoning to wide reflective equilibrium is open to some devastating logical criticisms (Haslett, 1987), yet it may be the only method practically available.

Moral reasoning by the method of reflective equilibrium raises interesting questions about the nature of moral intuition (see Guthrie, Rachlinski, & Wistrich, 2007a). The process of constructing moral principles may also be affected by cognitive biases, particularly those that make salient examples appear more representative than they are. Biases come into play because moral principles necessarily are generalizations; meanwhile, the reasoner's objective is to resolve a particular problem. As a result, the specific facts that generated the reasoner's problem (in the case of a judge, the facts of a legal dispute) may loom large in the reasoner's mind and obscure other consequences of the moral principle the reasoner hopes to test.

Neither moral reasoning nor empirical and inductive reasoning, however, is peculiar to, or specially salient in, law. They operate in adjudication just as they operate in any decision-making context. The important psychological questions for law are about the extent to which judges can resist or counteract the biases that affect ordinary reasoners.

"Second-Order" Reasoning About Legal Disputes

In his essay in this volume, Schauer points out that judges make not only first-order judgments about the outcomes of disputes but also "second-order" judgments about the rules that govern their first-order decisions. Second-order reasoning of this kind is not limited to judges; moral decision making of any kind involves the application of general principles. Yet the nature of legal decisions as both sources of authority and products of authority makes second-order reasoning about rules a particularly important feature of law.

Judges engage in two kinds of second-order reasoning, which involve quite different mental tasks. First, judges must consider what authoritative rules their decisions will generate. In doing so, they must consider the probable future consequences of different decisional rules in cases not now before them. Second, and perhaps more interestingly from a psychological point of view, judges must submit to the authority of preexisting legal rules. At least according to traditional conceptions of adjudication, judicial decisions are constrained both by legislative rules and by rules announced by past courts. This means that if a rule applies, the judge must decide as the rule requires even if, by the judge's own assessment of relevant reasons for decision, the result the rule requires is wrong. Thus, to give authoritative effect to legal rules, judges must suppress either their normal reasoning processes or substantive conclusions they have already reached by means of normal reasoning. The mental feat of suspending reason in order to follow authority is not unique to law, but, at least according to one understanding of law and legal decision making, it is vital to an effective system of law. In this sense, it presents a psychological problem of special concern to the legal domain.

Rule Making

One prominent institutional circumstance of judicial decision making is that judges make rules of law as they adjudicate disputes. Judges may decide cases fairly narrowly, but in a legal system such as ours, in which judges commonly explain their decisions in opinions, some degree of generalization is unavoidable and generality leads to rules.[3] Moreover, in a system in which the outcomes of adjudication are accessible to the public, judicial decisions are studied by an audience of potential actors, who naturally generalize from past decisions to probable legal treatment of their own activities.

One might imagine a system in which judges say nothing about their decisions and the conclusions they reach are understood to have no precedential effect. Only legislative rules would have implications for future decisions. In our own legal system, however, this is not the case. The public expects a fairly high degree of consistency in judicial decision making over time and judges respond to this expectation by recognizing, to some extent, the authority of prior decisions. Moreover, the public's expectation of consistency has social value, because it enables the members of society to coordinate their actions and to treat controversies as settled (Postema, 1982, pp. 172–186; Raz, 1986, pp. 49–50; Hurd, 1999, pp. 214–221).

Thus, implicitly or explicitly, judges announce rules of decision as they decide cases. It follows that the complete set of reasons for or against a particular decision includes the future effects of the decisional rules on which it rests. To reach a fully reasoned decision in any case, the judge must generalize from the specific problem at hand to the class of problems governed by the operative decisional rule.

Research on cognitive bias, as described above, is pertinent to this aspect of second-order reasoning. Assessing the future effects of a decisional rule typically requires a calculation of statistical probability over a range of possible cases, some of which may be remote from the case before the court. At the same time, the judge must attend to the immediate task of achieving a fair outcome for the parties to the current dispute. These simultaneous demands on the judge's attention implicate at least two of the biases documented in cognitive studies: the availability bias and the affect bias, which lead reasoners to err in assessing probabilities when their attention is focused on salient or emotionally charged facts (Devins & Meese, 2005; Rachlinski, 2006; Schauer, 2006a). As a consequence of these biases, the facts of current cases are likely to appear more representative than they are of the class of cases covered by a proposed decision rule, causing judges to miscalculate the overall effects of rules.[4]

Rule Following

Following rules is more complicated analytically, and perhaps psychologically as well. Suppose a judge is called on to decide a case that falls indisputably within the terms of a rule announced by a prior court. One possible approach for the judge is what Schauer (1991) has termed "rule-sensitive particularism." Simple particularism is the process of deciding what outcome is best in a particular case, all things considered. The reasoning involved is ordinary reasoning (empirical observation, induction, and moral reasoning), applied to the problem at hand. When a rule applies, simple particularism is inadequate because it fails to consider what secondary consequences might result from following (or ignoring) the rule. Rule-sensitive particularism describes a process of decision making that takes account not only of the good or bad results the rule will bring about if applied to the case at hand, but also of the benefits that follow from compliance with an established rule (Schauer, 1991, pp. 94–100). A rule-sensitive particularist seeks the outcome that is best (or least bad), given the existence of a rule.

Much has been written about the benefits of rules (e.g., Raz, 1986; Schauer, 1991; Alexander & Sherwin, 2001). Rules settle controversy (Eisenberg, 1988, pp. 4–7; Raz, 1994, pp. 187–192). They support coordination among actors whose reasons for action depend on the actions of others: if most actors follow the rules, each can predict what others are likely to do. Rules designed by experts also can reduce error by individual actors, and procedural rules can allocate decisional authority or rule-making authority to experts. Each of these potential benefits, however, depends on regular compliance with the terms of the rules. A decision to disregard a rule in a particular case may have negative effects on the future effectiveness of the rule and, consequently, the social benefits that follow from an effective rule.

The process of reasoning entailed by rule-sensitive particularism is similar to the process of reasoning required to assess the future consequences of a proposed rule, although it adds some complications. A rule-sensitive particularist judge deciding a rule-governed dispute must first determine what outcome is best between parties. If the outcome the judge selects is contrary to the rule, the judge must make several further calculations. Specifically, the judge must determine how likely it is that his own judgment is wrong and what effect a decision to depart from the rule will have on other judges or private actors (whether or not the judge is wrong).

These are not easy calculations. At a minimum, judges acting as rule-sensitive particularists must determine the likelihood that others will observe their own defections; the extent to which others who observe their defections will discount the benefits of the rule; and the likelihood that others who observe their defections, discount the benefits of the rule, and consequently decide to defect themselves, will err in their own calculations of the relative costs and benefits of following the rule. Yet, despite the difficulty of the calculation, the reasoning involved is ordinary inductive reasoning, subject to the same psychological impediments that affect all inductive reasoning. Specifically, facts that are in the forefront of the reasoner's mind, and facts that evoke emotional responses in the reasoner, are likely to appear more representative than they are and thus to distort the reasoner's assessment of probabilities. As I have noted, this is a particularly serious problem for judges because judges take up the question of whether to follow a rule with the facts of particular cases outstanding in their minds.

Rule-sensitive particularism is a rational approach to rule-governed decision making. From the point of view of a legal rulemaker, however, it is not the ideal judicial response to rules. This may seem odd: rules are blunt, and as a consequence are likely to require the wrong result in some of the cases they cover. In a world of perfect reasoners, therefore, it might be best if rule-followers were rule-sensitive particularists who sometimes decided not to follow applicable rules. Judges, however, are not perfect reasoners: they lack the perfect information required for perfect reasoning[5] and, as noted, they are subject to cognitive biases that may cause them to systematically undervalue the long-term costs of deviating from rules. Consequently, rule-sensitive particularists will sometimes deviate from rules when they should not. In a community of rule-sensitive particularists, each judge will anticipate that some other judges will miscalculate in this way, and accordingly will discount the benefits of the rule. Each such discount, by each rule-sensitive particularist judge, means a corresponding decrease in the judge's estimate of the harm that will result from a decision to defect from the rule. Ultimately, the rule has no value at all, and rule-sensitive particularism collapses into simple particularism.[6]

Rule sensitive particularism may be more meaningful when some judges consistently follow rules. Yet it is still less than ideal from the rule maker's point of view. Imagine that within a given legal system, some judges are rule-sensitive particularists and others are rule followers. In this situation, a decision to deviate from a rule has adverse consequences that the rule-sensitive particularist must take into account. Specifically, other judges who observe the deviation will know that not all judges are consistent rule-followers. As a result, rule-followers may change their attitude, and rule-sensitive particularists may discount the benefits of the rule. These possibilities give the decision maker a reason to be cautious about deviating from the rule. Nevertheless, although rule-sensitive particularist judges now have some reason to follow the rule when it produces an outcome they believe to be wrong, they may still err in calculating the balance of harms, and, because of cognitive bias, their errors will tend systematically to favor deviation from the rule.

Because rule-sensitive particularism is unstable in this way, a rational legal rule maker would prefer that judges follow rules according to their terms. A well-designed rule, consistently applied, will prevent errors of judgment more often than it generates errors of overinclusion.[7] From the point of view of rule makers, therefore, a rule applied without reflection is preferable to case-by-case judicial reasoning, even if judges are sensitive to the value of rules. At the same time, when a judge believes that, in a particular case, the harm to substantive values from following the rule is greater than the harm to rule-based values from disregarding the rule, the only rational course is to disregard the rule. The result is a logically unbridgeable gap between the way in which rational rule makers would want judges to approach rules and the approach that is rational for judges.[8]

This leads to the second possible judicial response to rules, which is to follow them without further reflection about the justification, or lack of justification, for the particular results they require. Legal rules, on this approach, operate as the exclusive reasons for judicial decision in cases to which they apply (Raz, 1979, 1986).[9] If the terms of the rule call for a certain result, that result is correct.

In ordinary life, rules appear to function in this way, at least at times. For example, we may set schedules for ourselves to fend off procrastination, although the schedules will never control our actions if we pause to think about whether the time designated for each action is in fact the best time to act (Fumerton, 1990, pp. 178–188). Somehow, we manage not to think, and thus to follow the schedule. Judicial rule-following, in the manner necessary to avoid the pitfalls of rule-sensitive particularism, is similar in nature. Judges may in fact follow rules, but they can do so only by abstaining from thought about what is best, all things considered.

Thus, rule-following in the true sense presents a psychological enigma: in what circumstances, and by what processes, do human decision makers suspend their powers of reason and instead defer to authority?[10] This is not a phenomenon unique to adjudication: it occurs in daily life when people follow nonlegal rules, and it occurs whenever nonjudges follow legal rules. Nor is it something judges are especially likely to be good at: there is no reason to think that selection (or self-selection) as a judge corresponds to a heightened capacity to suspend reason. Yet, if in fact there are psychological mechanisms that permit blind rule-following, they have special social significance in the context of law because they enable judges to give serious effect to legal rules.

A further point is that when judges follow rules without reflection, they must suspend reason in a special way. Judges typically do not decide legal questions in the abstract; they resolve live disputes and enter judgments that penalize or impose liability on the losing parties. This means that when a rule calls for a result that the judge deems to be wrong in the case before the court, the judge not only must decide the case against his best judgment, but also must impose a penalty on a party he believes has acted correctly and does not deserve to suffer harm (Hurd, 1992, 1999, pp. 253–293; Alexander & Sherwin, 2001, pp. 78–86). Even when the judge believes the result of the rule is correct, enforcing the rule may sometimes entail penalizing a party who did not act culpably, but simply misjudged. Thus, following rules according to their terms requires judges to suppress both reason and moral censorship of their own actions toward others. This aspect of adjudication adds to the significance of the normative questions about rule following. We have reason to prefer that judges enforce legal rules as written, but we also have reason to question the morality of full enforcement of rules.

Assuming that blind rule-following is at least sometimes desirable from a social point of view, a further psychological question is whether the capacity to suppress reason can be taught or cultivated. Research indicates that to some extent, reasoners can learn to curb some forms of cognitive bias. The studies conducted by Guthrie, Rachlinski, and Wistrich (2001) confirm that this holds true for judges: certain common types of cognitive bias are less pronounced in experienced judges addressing legal problems. It seems unlikely, however, that *absence* of reason is a mental state that reasoners could develop deliberately in themselves. By definition, abstaining from reasoning is an unthinking, if not unconscious, process. It is possible that reasoners could become accustomed by force of habit to reaching decisions without reflection, but it is difficult to see how a propensity to decide without reflection could be instilled in a reasoner with the reasoner's conscious assent.

Rule Making and Rule Following

I have mentioned two "second order" judicial tasks that play an important part in the psychology of judging. First, judges must formulate rules of decision and calculate the effects of those rules will have when applied to future cases. In making this calculation, judges are subject to cognitive biases that can lead them to undervalue statistical probabilities. Second, judges are expected to treat established legal rules as authoritative. To give authoritative effect to rules, judges must decide cases mechanically, without reflecting on the relationship between the outcomes the rules require and the values the rules are supposed to promote.

The states of mind necessary to perform these two judicial tasks effectively are quite different. Designing sound rules is a highly deliberative process involving empirical observation, induction, and moral reasoning. Judges engaged in rule making must, among other things, remain alert to background probabilities and guard against the biases that might prevent them from accurately assessing the future effects of potential rules. Thus, for the purpose of rule making, the more judges know about their own psychological proclivities the better they will do. When judges are called on to follow rules, the opposite is true. To follow rules consistently, they must suppress their own judgment about the outcomes of the cases before them. The more judges reflect on the process of decision, the more difficult this will be.

The tasks of rule making and rule following are distinct. Judicial rule making, and the empirical and inductive reasoning it entails, come into play when no rule applies. Rule following, of course, is reserved for cases governed by rules. Accordingly, there is ordinarily no need to perform both these functions at once. Yet, judges must frequently shift from one mode of decision making to the other from case to case, or even in the course of a single litigation. This will not be easy: rationality and self-awareness, which conduce to good rule making, are naturally at odds with a habit of unreflective obedience that will enable judges to follow rules.

A further complication is that if a legal system hopes both to maintain effective rules and to command public respect, it must provide some relief from rules. Rules may be misconceived, and even well-conceived rules may become obsolete as conditions change. Legislatures can intervene to repeal unsound rules, but for various reasons they may fail to respond. When this occurs, the only avenue of relief is judges' own power to overrule judicial rules.

In our own legal system, the power of judges to overrule precedent rules established in prior judicial decisions is widely recognized. Ideally, however, judges should overrule rules only when the rules are unjustified *as rules.*[11] Rules are justified as rules if their benefits (settlement, coordination, and preemption of faulty judgment) outweigh their costs (errors of overinclusion) over the range of cases to which they apply. When a rule passes this test, it is best, from a societal perspective, that judges leave the rule in place and enforce it according to its terms, even when they believe that a particular outcome of the rule is a mistake. When a rule does not pass the test of net benefit over the full range of its applications, it should be overruled.

The difficulty is that when rules are justified, judges must combine the two types of mental tasks I have described to solve a single legal problem. To determine whether a rule is justified as a rule, the judge must calculate the future consequences of the rule. This requires both careful reasoning and attention to cognitive biases that may make a current bad outcome appear more representative than it is (Schauer, 2006a, 906–912). Then, if the balance of error favors the rule, the same judge must cease reasoning and follow the rule, whether or not the judge believes the outcome is correct. This is a difficult psychological feat.

Conclusion

The authoritative nature of law generates some psychological puzzles that, although not limited to law, take on special social importance in the context of adjudication. One set of questions relates to the rule-making role of judges: what sorts of errors are judges prone to make in designing or evaluating rules of common law and what mechanisms, if any, can a legal system use to control their errors? A second set of questions relates to judicial compliance with rules: do judges follow legal rules against their own best judgment, and if so, how do they disengage from the process of deliberating about the relationship between purposes and outcomes of rules? The mystery deepens when the functions of rule making and rule following are closely juxtaposed.

Of course, theoretical analysis of the type presented here can at best provide a map of the problem. As Schauer observes, the challenge is to find some means of empirical access to legal reasoning. Judicial opinions provide an immense source of information, but as Legal Realists are happy to point out, they are written after their authors reach decisions. Opinions also may be products of negotiation that do not reflect any single individual's process of decision. Experiments involving judges may be more promising, but they require heroic efforts and even then it may be difficult to recreate the moral pressures of adjudication in an experimental setting.

Notes

Thanks to Jeffrey J. Rachlinski and Frederick Schauer for helpful comments.

1. For present purposes, I am adopting a broad definition of empirical reasoning as the process of reaching conclusions about the world through observation or experiment. A cautionary point is that empirical observations may incorporate elements of induction, and both empirical and inductive judgments may be intertwined with normative judgment. There is no perfect line of demarcation between judgments of fact and judgments of law or between empirical and moral reasoning.
2. For explanations of the method of reasoning to wide reflective equilibrium, see Rawls (1971, pp. 14–21, 43–53, 578–582) and Daniels (1979).
3. For discussion of the generality of rules, see Schauer (1991, pp. 17–34).
4. Studies focusing specifically on judges, while they do not address the particular problem of rule making, confirm that judges are not immune to these biases. See Guthrie, Rachlinski, and Wistrich (2001, pp. 807–811) .
5. Part of the problem is lack of coordination: even a very wise judge cannot know with certainty what other, less wise, judges will decide and how many errors they will make.
6. For extended analysis of this problem, see Alexander and Sherwin (2001, pp. 61–68).
7. Of course, rule makers can also make mistakes, and judicial rule makers are susceptible to mistakes for the reasons mentioned above. My analysis, however, assumes sound rules. Overruling unsound rules is a separate, although not unrelated, question.
8. Larry Alexander and I have written in considerable detail about this gap, concluding that it cannot be reasoned away. See Alexander and Sherwin (2001, pp. 56–95). For similar analyses, see Alexander (1991); Schauer (1991, pp. 128–134).
9. For an analytical (as opposed to psychological) argument against the view that rules have an exclusionary effect, see Hurd (1999, pp. 62–94).
10. Stanley Milgram's (1974) famous experiments demonstrate that people certainly are capable of obeying authority, either contrary to reason or without engaging in reason. Interestingly, there are indications that Milgram's subjects did not follow authority thoughtlessly, but rather struggled with the problem (Milgram, 1974, pp. 41–43).
11. For extended discussion of this point, see Alexander & Sherwin (2008, pp. 61–63, 115).

9

In Praise of Pedantic Eclecticism: Pitfalls and Opportunities in the Psychology of Judging

Dan Simon

Though not always acknowledged, the subject matter of psychology—namely, human cognition and behavior—has long played a role in important jurisprudential debates. How do judges make decisions (e.g., Cardozo, 1921; Holmes, 1881; Posner, 2008)? Are judicial decisions determined by the law or are they driven by judges' predispositions (e.g., Edwards, 1998; Frank, 1930)? Are assertions of judicial constraint genuine (e.g., Altman, 1990; Kennedy, 1986)? Are judges better fact finders than jurors (e.g., Kalven & Zeisel, 1966)? How do judges weigh the numerous incommensurable and conflicting considerations involved in their decisions (e.g., Cardozo, 1921; Llewellyn, 1960)? Yet, as a discipline, psychology is rarely recognized in the debate. Though hardly a nascent field (see, Frank, 1930; Schroeder, 1918), the psychology of judging remains an underdeveloped body of research.

The reluctance to apply psychological research to the domain of judicial decision making can be understood to be based on at least two concerns.[1] First, unlike other disciplines that have successfully influenced legal discourse—most notably, philosophy and economics—psychological insights tend not to be deduced from overarching concepts or axiomatic characterizations of human behavior. The multidetermined nature of human behavior defies parsimony and makes experimental psychology a rather messy field. Psychological findings are made piecemeal, one finding at a time. Properly presented, psychological claims ought to be narrowed to certain experimental circumstances, and qualified by boundary conditions and counter influences.

A second, and more familiar, concern stems from the fact that psychological findings are generated mostly in the highly controlled environment of the laboratory, which are starkly different from worldly human practices in real life. The concern pertains to the *external validity* of experimental findings, that is, their generalizability to settings outside the laboratory. Psychologists, who are ever so sensitive to situational effects on human behavior (e.g., Lewin, 1935; Ross & Nisbett, 1991), are the first to acknowledge that results obtained in any given study could have come out quite differently under different variations of their experimental design. It is not hard to see why critics question the relevance of findings obtained by testing a relatively small group of lay subjects (say, sixty psychology undergraduates at a midwestern university), performing hypothetical tasks, with limited knowledge, and under specific instructions.

Psychological studies have been criticized for the nonrepresentativeness of the subject samples, the artificiality of the experimental setting, the disconnectedness from institutional contexts, the glossing over of individual differences, the lack of appropriate incentives, the inconsequentiality of the tasks, and more (e.g., Konecni & Ebbesen, 1986; Mitchell, 2002; Sears, 1986; Yuille & Cutshall, 1986). These reservations warrant a healthy dose of skepticism toward even cautious applications of experimental findings to real world situations (see Mitchell, 2003). This concern seems doubly warranted when applying the findings to specialized domains such as judicial decision making.

Concerns over the external validity of psychological research appear to have animated Fred Schauer's discerning and provocative essay in this volume (ch. 7). The core of his essay is a call for a unique and genuine psychology of judging. The proposal starts with an appealing proposition that a psychology of judging ought to be what it claims to be—an examination *of judging*, as performed *by judges*. Explanations that rely on cognitive processes that are performed also by nonjudges and in nonjudicial domains might make for an interesting application of psychological research, but they do not "constitute a discrete area of inquiry." Merely applying basic findings to the work of dentists and plumbers is "a long way from saying that there is a psychology *of* dentistry or plumbing."

Schauer proposes to distinguish decision making by judges from decision making by other people, even lawyers, for the same reason that one ought not to equate the mathematical reasoning of a Harvard mathematics professor with that of ordinary folks balancing their checkbooks. He contends also that the field ought to concentrate on decision making in domains that are unique to judging, such as finding, interpreting, and making law. Even if auto mechanics and psychiatrists approach the finances of their small business in similar fashions, it does not follow that they do the same when they fix cars or provide psychiatric care. The underlying intuition is that judicial training, acculturation, experience, and role may lead to deep cognitive effects that "generate process- and not just content-based differences between the cognitive mechanisms of judges and those of nonjudge humanity."

Schauer's proposal is constructive in that it actually suggests an experimental project to test his proposition. The central hypothesis focuses on the role of *second-order reasoning* in judicial decision making. Second-order reasoning stands for higher order decision rules that are supposed to trump reasons that would otherwise provide a sufficient basis for a decision. Second-order reasoning is deemed central to the judicial function in that it forces judges to abide by a hierarchy of reasons, and specifically, to yield to higher order considerations even when they feel that doing so leads to suboptimal or unwise outcomes for the case at hand. Schauer intuits that judges engage in second-order reasoning differently, more effectively, and with greater fidelity than nonjudges. Specifically, the studies would test whether judges are more inclined to follow a precedent or rule with which they disagree, and to limit their attention to a narrow range of permissible sources even when other sources lead to what they consider to be superior results. The studies are designed to compare judicial decisions with decisions made by lawyers and law students, and to compare decisions made by different classes of judges, such as elected and appointed judges, trial and appellate judges, and judges with different personal backgrounds. Undoubtedly cognizant of the complexity of the issues involved, Schauer emphasizes the tentative and exploratory nature of his proposal, characterizing it as a set of hypotheses, an invitation to consider a possible line of research.[2]

Schauer's proposal also has a distinctive critical component. He addresses extant research that tests real judges in a variety of experimental tasks that have previously been tested with lay subjects. These studies tend to demonstrate that judges are indeed prone to most of the same biases and errors as people in general (Guthrie, Rachlinski, & Wistrich, 2001; Wistrich, Guthrie, & Rachlinski, 2005). Schauer considers this research to be of marginal interest to his project because it focuses on the fact-finding and verdict-rendering dimensions of the judicial role, which are performed also by lay jurors. Because the studied tasks are not performed exclusively by judges, this research fails to meet the proposed standard of uniqueness. Schauer is far more critical of the literature that applies basic psychology to judging.[3] This research fails on both dimensions of the proposed uniqueness in that it uses ordinary people as subjects in the performance nonjudicial decisions. In other words, the external validity gap is seen to render this work invalid. Schauer briskly dismisses the application of this work for being axiomatic, unargued, and unresearched.[4]

Schauer's chapter provides a fortuitous opportunity to closely examine the concerns over external validity that hamper application of psychological research to legal theory. This chapter will focus on both the prescriptive and critical approaches of his approach. First, it suggests that the design of psychological experiments can be far more complex and subtle an endeavor than it appears. Along these lines, it should be appreciated that the intuitively appealing proposal to run experiments with judges is burdened by methodological pitfalls. External validity is just one piece of a larger set of validity issues, which tend to be intricately intertwined. Attempting to fix one aspect can be overwhelmed by greater compromises elsewhere, thus resulting in a net loss in validity. To prevent this, one needs to adopt a pedantic approach to the design of the study.

At the same time, the concern with external validity should not be exaggerated. The discrepancy between the experimental environment and real world settings does not automatically bar all applications of findings from the former to the latter. It does, however, require cautious work and oftentimes also more data. When experimental findings meet the heightened demands of external validity, they can be applied safely to real world domains, including specialized ones. This possibility opens up the field of judging to a wide range of methodological approaches and thus offers the benefit of insights originating from eclectic perspectives. To demonstrate the possibilities in this regard, the discussion will center on the application of a particular body of research—coherence based reasoning—to judging.

In Praise of Pedantry

Before expending the limited experimental resources on the proposed studies (there is no abundance of judge-subjects), one ought to ensure that the studies are capable of providing the insights they aim to discern. In this vein, a brief methodological detour would be helpful.[5] It is imperative to acknowledge that external validity does not exhaust the validity challenges facing experimental research. The foremost criterion of the validity of any psychological experiment is that it be *internally valid*, which stands for the degree to which the experimental treatment explains the observed results. Studies are said to be internally valid when they demonstrate that the variables that were set up or manipulated by the experimenter ("independent variables") were indeed the cause of variation in the focal point of the hypothesis (the "dependent variables"). Internal validity rests heavily on the researcher's ability to design the study so that it provides maximal control over the experimental environment. Control is necessary for the restraining of unintended factors that might affect the dependent variable.[6] There seems no reason to believe that Schauer's proposal would be lacking in internal validity. A finding of differences in decisions made by judges and nonjudges in a well-controlled environment could be fairly understood to be related to differences in the manner in which the respective groups make decisions.

Detecting differences, however, can be a far cry from understanding their underlying mechanisms at work. To bridge this explanatory gap, studies need to be shown to have *construct validity*, which stands for the degree to which one can correctly identify and explain the operative psychological constructs. This important and somewhat neglected facet of validity stands for the degree to which studies accurately operationalize their theoretical constructs, which is essential for the correct explanation of the relationship between the experimental treatment and the observed phenomena. Absent this validity, one cannot draw reliable inferences from the observed results.[7]

It should be acknowledged that the various forms of validity are often in tension with one another. Notably, the high levels of experimental control that are essential for ensuring internal and construct validity cut against the generalizability of the findings. Likewise, tests that are designed to have a large degree of external validity, such as archival research and field studies, typically lack important aspects of control, most notably, random assignment of subjects to the various conditions. Herein lies the tension in Schauer's proposal. Recall that the proposed research seeks to discern differences in the underlying cognitive processes between judges and nonjudges. This aspiration can be problematic, especially since such deep constructs are most difficult to study. Even if the proposed studies yielded the expected results—namely, that judges' decisions were better aligned with second-order principles than decisions by nonjudges—the underlying operative mechanism would remain unknown. A finding that judges show greater deference to a precedent might or might not be indicative of superior second-order reasoning. It could also be due to the fact that lay people lack a sense of the judicial conventions and practices involved in assessing case similarity, distinguishing precedents, and more. By the same token, a finding that judges display a heightened respect for jurisdictional limitations need not stand for the proposition that judges engage in different cognitive processes. It could be readily interpreted as standing for the proposition that lay people lack familiarity with the constitutional principles that underlie the rules of federalism,[8] lack the nuanced knowledge of how to weight them against competing considerations, and the like.[9] Lay people are bound to be unfamiliar with the profession's conceptions of the hierarchy of reasons, the reputational damage of being overturned, and the personal commitment to the judicial role.[10]

One plausible alternative explanation for hypothesized findings of judicial superiority is that judges are experts at judging, whereas lay people are novices. Psychological research on expertise shows that experts perform differently—in certain ways, better—than novices (Chi, 2006; Ericsson & Ward, 2007). The possibility that judges have a better grasp of the conventions and practices of the judicial role, and are better in weighting and trading off the competing rules is consistent with the advantages of expertise.[11] Moreover, the determinants of judicial uniqueness noted by Schauer— namely, selection, training, and experience—closely resemble the factors that have been found to develop expertise (Feltovich, Prietula, & Ericsson, 2006).[12] While Schauer explicitly rejects the explanation based on expertise,[13] the proposed studies do not seem to provide a way to discriminate between the two explanations.[14]

Underlying the proposed hypothesis is the belief that judges are considerably superior to lay people in following second-order rules. Schauer is skeptical of lay people's ability to abide by second-order rules, and goes so far as to suggest that they might not know how to engage in this form of reasoning at all.[15] The explanation offered for lay people's low capabilities is that they have little experience making decisions of this kind. Yet, there is reason to doubt whether second-order reasoning is rare or undeveloped in nonjudicial settings. People engage in some form of second-order reasoning every time they walk by a store window displaying a coveted item that exceeds their budget. Dentists oblige their patients' requests even when they might condone a different course of treatment. Plumbers heed the building code and the architect's plans even when a different solution seems to them to be more effective. Second-order reasoning plays a central role in other nonjudicial walks of like.[16]

While it is clear that judges do indeed engage in a considerable amount of second-order reasoning, there is reason to suspect that their fidelity is less than perfect. A substantial and growing body of quantitative analyses of judicial behavior shows that judicial decisions are systematically biased by judges' personal attitudes (Klein, 2002; Segal & Spaeth, 1993, 2002), the composition of panels (Cross & Tiller, 1998), personal prestige (Klein & Morrisroe, 1999), and more.[17] These observations suggest either that judges do not fully adhere to the second-order reasons, or that they interpret and apply those reasons in a biased manner that effectively undermines the rules' normative import.[18] It should be noted that one experiment that tested judicial adherence to second-order rules revealed a rather lackluster level of compliance. In this study, the judges' decisions tended to be influenced by information which they themselves ruled to be inadmissible (Wistrich et al., 2005).[19]

Moreover, it is worth noting that judicial experience might actually make judges feel less bound by second-order rules than one might otherwise believe. To a large extent, judging requires deciding not only which rules and precedents ought to be followed, but also which ones ought *not* to be followed. In most complex cases, judges are faced with multitudes of powerful reasons (Schauer, 1988b), some of which are likely to pose a conflict between two or more second-order rules. When such a conflict occurs, the judicial dilemma requires a determination as to which second-order principle ought to be followed and which one ought to be rejected. In such situations, the fidelity to second-order rules necessarily entails a rejection of (other) second-order rules, as indicated in Karl Llewellyn's conception of "dueling canons."[20] It appears, then, that finding acceptable ways to ignore, dismiss, or interpret away second-order rules is yet another facet of judicial expertise.

In Praise of Eclecticism

This brings us back to the ubiquitous concerns over the external validity of basic psychological research. With so many degrees of freedom separating the laboratory environment from real world contexts of human action, one might wonder how experimental research can ever be deemed to bear any practical relevance to real life. Yet, an array of experimental findings are notably present outside the confines of the laboratory. As it turns out, the gathering of intelligence by the CIA in preparation for the Iraq War[21] bears an eerie similarity to various forms of biased reasoning generated in the laboratory (e.g., Frey, 1986; Klayman, 1995; Kunda, 1990; Nickerson, 1998). The behavior of nations and ethnic groups entangled in real conflicts corresponds closely to the behavior of arbitrarily formed groups in the laboratory (e.g., Brewer, 1979). Marketers and political consultants routinely exploit human judgment processes gleaned from the laboratory (e.g., Rozin & Royzman, 2001; Nisbett & Wilson, 1977). Prejudicial behavior by employers (Bertrand & Mullainathan, 2004) mirrors behavior observed in experimental settings (e.g., Dovidio, Kawakami, Johnson, Johnson, & Howard, 1997). Likewise, jury decisions to send convicted inmates to their death (Eisenberg, Garvey, & Wells, 2001) appear to be influenced by the same attitudes that affect mock jurors' decisions in hypothetical cases (Thompson, Cowan, Ellsworth, & Harrington, 1984). A meta-analysis of experimentation is social psychology has shown a rather strong correspondence between findings obtained in the laboratory and in the field.[22]

Thus, it seems that applying psychological research to capture real world phenomena is a complicated feat, which can be neither accomplished nor controverted offhandedly. As discussed below, subject to a careful and methodical examination, psychological research can be safely applied to some real life situations, but not to others. Applications to the stylized domain of judicial decision making require a heightened level of scrutiny.

For the research to be deemed useful outside the confines of the controlled laboratory setting, it must first be shown that the observed phenomenon is not an artifact of the specific experiment. One important way to allay this concern is by replicating the finding under similar and different experimental settings. Validity increases when the same finding is observed using different populations of subjects, stimulus materials, instructions, and tasks. It increases also if replications are conducted in different laboratories. Validity is further increased by the robustness of the finding, that is, its recurrence under various manipulations, across wide ranges of values, and in the presence of counterforces.[23]

Still, external validity does not guarantee that the findings apply equally to every domain of human behavior. To be deemed applicable to a particular real world practice, the finding must not be trumped, weakened, or distorted by particular features of the domain, as these were not present in the experimental setting and their potential influence on the finding is unknown to the experimenter. This last link in the applicability chain has been coined *contextual attentiveness* (Arlen & Talley 2008), which stands for the degree to which the experimental findings map onto the rich context of the real world. Contextual attentiveness can be deemed an additional layer of external validity. A threshold criterion for establishing contextual attentiveness is the facial similarity between the behavior captured by the laboratory finding and the behavior observed in real life. It is enhanced by the extent to which the psychological theory that underlies the phenomenon is deemed germane to the domain, particularly in the absence of competing theories. Strong support can be derived from corroborative evidence derived from sources other than the experiment itself, such as when archival or field data reveal behaviors that are consistent with the experimentally observed phenomenon. Finally, one might also look, with caution, to self-reports by people working in the domain, particularly to those who are considered to be introspective.

It is important to note that there is no established gold standard for determining external validity. None of the abovementioned features can carry the day by itself, nor can any body of research be expected to fit them all. The guiding principle is convergent validity: the more of the noted features that converge toward validity, the more reliable the conclusion.

With these methodological guidelines in mind, we can return to assess Schauer's objection to the application of basic psychological findings to judging. It is beyond the scope of this chapter to examine the merits of this charge with respect to the various bodies of work Schauer mentions (in which he candidly includes his own previous work, Schauer, 2006a, 2006b; see also Arlen, 1998; Hanson & Yosifon, 2004). It is, however, feasible to assess the objection as it pertains to the applicability of one of the bodies of work, *coherence based reasoning.*[24] To do so, it would be helpful first to review this line of research.

Coherence based reasoning seeks to explain an enigmatic, yet prevalent mode of reasoning in judicial opinions. Even the casual reader of judicial opinions is likely familiar with the experience of being strongly persuaded by an opinion, with all of its components converging to provide overwhelming support for the outcome. The facts of the case, authoritative texts, governing precedents, legal principles, public policies, as well as sheer logic and common sense, all come together in a coherent whole to make for the inevitable and undeniably correct result. The sense of correctness is bolstered by the dearth or absence of arguments to the contrary. By the culmination of the opinion, one might wonder how the decision could be considered to have been anything but obvious in the first place. This sense of obviousness, however, quickly dissolves upon turning to the opinion of the dissenting judges. Dissenting opinions too tend to be strongly coherent and persuasive in defending their conclusion, which is invariably antithetical to the majority's conclusion. Thus, while the opinions are exceedingly coherent internally, they are radically inconsistent with a slew of seemingly plausible arguments contained in the opposing opinion. The divergence between opposing judges' views of a case can lead them to stake remarkable positions. For example, when interpreting statutes, it is not unusual for judges to deny outright that the there is any ambiguity in the statutory text, notwithstanding the fact that similarly positioned judges read the text to mean the very opposite.[25] This mode of reasoning is apparent in almost every appellate case.

As a matter of legal policy, this phenomenon has mixed effects that exceed the scope of this chapter.[26] As a theoretical matter, it offers an opportunity to peer into the judicial decision-making process and better understand the extent to which it is constrained by the law, as judges routinely claim it to be. If indeed the coalitions of reasons mustered by judges accurately represent the state of the law, one ought to infer that judicial decision making is indeed tightly constrained by the law, and more importantly, that the law is determinative of single right answers. If, however, we find an alternative explanation for this mode of reasoning, one might call into question the professed constraint and, by implication, the binding nature of the legal materials.

There are good reasons to suspect that the legal materials are considerably less determinant than they are portrayed in judicial opinions. For one, most cases decided by appellate courts are truly complicated and difficult, as they contain sound arguments supporting each side of the issue (Schauer, 1988b). The suspicion intensifies once opinions are dissected and stripped down to their constitutive arguments. Relatively short U.S. Supreme Court opinions typically contain a handful of core issues, each of which is supported by an array of arguments, which can easily total fifty arguments or more.[27] A notable feature of the opinions is that virtually every one of the dozens of arguments supports the corresponding conclusion and contradicts the opposite one.[28] This perfect alignment of reasons is plainly implausible. Assuming that the soundness of the opposing arguments are roughly similar, the mathematical probability that each of the fifty or more arguments line up perfectly is astronomically minute. This observation suggests that the overall conclusion of the case plays a role in determining which arguments are endorsed and which are rejected. While judicial decisions are most likely affected by their underlying reasons, there appears also to be an effect in the opposite direction, by which decisions affect the reasons that are claimed to support them. This calls into question the avowed unidirectional relationship between reasons and conclusions, namely that the former should affect the latter, but not the other way round. Judicial reasoning, it would seem, operates bidirectionally, from reasons to decisions, and back in reverse.[29]

This feature of judicial reasoning cannot be explained by the conventional theories of decision making (e.g., von Neumann & Morgenstern, 1944; Edwards & Newman, 1982), which seem ill suited to handle complex decisions of the kind that judges face—where the variables are numerous, conflicting, ambiguous, and incommensurable. The phenomenon could, however, be consistent with a body of psychological research that shows that certain cognitive tasks are driven by coherence-maximizing processes.[30] This line of research follows the tradition of cognitive consistency theories— notably balance theory (Abelson & Rosenberg, 1958; Heider, 1946, 1958) and cognitive dissonance theory (Festinger, 1957)—which are based, in turn, on Gestalt psychology (Wertheimer, 1923/1938). Cognitive consistency theories were animated by principles of structural dynamics, which posit that relevant cognitive processes are determined holistically, rather than elementally. The holistic structural properties are deemed to be dynamic, so that interrelatedness of the elements generates forces that determine the configuration of the structure. Some things "go together," that is, they are related by cohesive forces, whereas other things tend to disperse. These forces determine the stability of the structure and drive it toward a state of equilibrium, or Gestalt. Perhaps most importantly, the dynamic forces that occur at the structural level involve changes, or "reconstructions" of the cognitive elements (Rosenberg and Abelson, 1960), that is, by "distorting the state of affairs" (Asch, 1940, p. 454).

A series of experiments conducted by Keith Holyoak, Stephen Read, and myself was designed to explore the possibility that a theory of coherence-maximization would apply also to the domain of decision making, in particular to complex decisions like the ones judges make. To understand the concept of coherence based reasoning, it would be helpful to briefly describe the common design of the studies. In the first study, participants were first presented with a pretest that contained a number of apparently unrelated vignettes, that were followed by a statement or two that could be inferred from them. Participants were asked to rate their agreement with the total of twelve such inferences. Some vignettes involved factual judgments, and some involved more abstract issues such as analogies and issues of social policy. In a separate phase of the experiment, participants were asked to play the role of a young judge, assigned to decide a civil case in which Quest, a software company, filed a libel lawsuit against one of its shareholders, Jack Smith. The company alleged that Smith posted a libelous statement about the company that caused it to go bankrupt. The case revolved around six core points of dispute, with each party making an argument on each of the six issues. The key feature in the design was that the case was constructed from all of the vignettes that were used in the first phase of the experiment, and the litigants' arguments were virtually identical to the inferences that followed those vignettes. Participants were asked to render a verdict and to report their confidence in the verdict. They were also asked to rate their agreement with the twelve arguments made by the parties.

The central finding in these studies is derived from the comparison between the ratings on the virtually identical items obtained at the two different phases of the study. Consistent with the prediction from coherence based reasoning, participants were found to have made confident decisions despite the complexity and difficulty of the case. In comparison to the moderate and noisy ratings given in the first phase of the study, at the point of decision, the ratings manifested polarized states of coherence: participants who voted for Smith reported strong agreement with the arguments that supported his case and disagreement with the arguments that supported Quest's position, while opposite ratings were reported by participants who decided for Quest (Holyoak & Simon, 1999).

The findings from this and other studies support the conclusion that complex decisions are driven by coherence-maximizing processes, by which people's perceptions of the tasks shift during the decision-making process from an initial state of conflict to a final state of steadfast coherence. By the culmination of the process, the arguments involved in the task have shifted and spread apart into two or more coherent subsets, one providing overwhelming support for the emerging decision, and the other providing depressed support for the rejected decision choice. This process is understood to be adaptive in that it enables people to make decisions and conduct their affairs even in the face of stifling complexity. It follows, then, that the state of coherence is not a property of the arguments themselves, but rather an artificial cognitive state imposed by the decision-making process. In other words, attaining a state of coherence entails a certain distortion of the factors involved in the decision.

Though inspired by judicial decision making, these experimental findings were borne by a basic-psychological research program, and thus cannot automatically be said to pertain to the domain of judging. To support the claim of applicability, the research must be shown to withstand the test of external validity.[31] Coherence effects have been replicated repeatedly, without fail, in a wide range of studies (Simon, Krawczyk, & Holyoak, 2004; Simon, Krawczyk, Bleicher, & Holyoak, 2008; Simon, Pham, Le, & Holyoak, 2001; Simon, Snow, & Read, 2004. For reviews, see Simon, 2002, 2004). The studies have been replicated also by other researchers in the United States, Canada, and Europe. One study replicated the findings using the same materials as used in the original research (Glöckner, 2007), while others tested a variety of different tasks including financial auditing decisions (Lundberg, 2004, 2007; Phillips, 2002), judgment and decision making (Glöckner, Betsch, & Schindler, under review), legal-economic behavior (Landeo, under review), and evidence evaluation (Lundberg, 2004). Across the various studies, the subjects have role-played young judges, jurors, arbitrators, auditors, and job applicants, while other studies involved no role-playing at all. In all, the studies have been tested with some 3,000 subjects, including undergraduate students, graduate business students, a general sample of Internet users, and experienced professional auditors.[32] The studies have tested a wide range of reasoning tasks, including high level inferences, analogies, rule application, policy decisions, factual judgments, social judgments, probability assessments, and personal preferences. The robustness of coherence effects is further bolstered by the fact that they have been manipulated in numerous ways, always yielding the hypothesized results.[33]

Recall that to apply a body of research to the real world, it must be shown also that the research is contextually attentive to the particular domain. Support for the applicability of coherence based reasoning to judging is derived from the close resemblance between the coherence that is present in judicial opinions and the coherence that is found in the laboratory: complex and taxing decision tasks are resolved successfully, resulting in lopsided and coherent sets of arguments, accompanied by high levels of confidence.[34] The theory underlying the laboratory results—namely, that the cognitive system imposes coherence to facilitate choice—is consistent with the judicial function of producing compelling decisions even for the most close and contested of cases. It is noteworthy that key components of coherence based reasoning appear in the theorizing of the some of the notable commentators on the judicial practice, including Holmes (1881, 1897), Cardozo (1921), and Llewellyn (1960).[35] Furthermore, the effect of coherence based reasoning on appellate judging has been supported by a study that examined data from actual court decisions (Beebe, 2006).

There are three additional ways in which the research on coherence based reasoning maps onto judicial decision making. First, the research shows that coherence-maximizing processing operates mostly at a low level of awareness. People do not consciously manipulate their mental representation of the task. Their views of the task shift toward coherent states spontaneously and imperceptibly.[36] This lack of awareness offers a plausible retort to the Realist charge that judges consciously misrepresent the law by stacking their opinions with whichever arguments support their preferred choices. The research indicates rather that the excessive coherence is a natural by-product of the decision-making process.[37]

Another overlap with judging emanates from a recent study that shows that coherence can dissipate soon after the decision has been completed (Simon et al., 2008). Coherence seems to be an ad hoc construct that appears around the time of making the choice but does not linger on to limit the decision maker in future cases where the constellation of variables will not necessarily align in the same manner. Thus, while coherence tends to be very strong within each decision, it can be rather weak across cases. This finding suggests that people are capable of applying a particular rule or principle in one case, and not following it in the next. This observation is consistent with the view that judges apply different—even opposing—rules, policies, and interpretive principles from case to case (Llewellyn, 1950, 1960; cf. Schauer, 2007).

The research also seems to provide insight into the enduring question of freedom and constraint in judicial decision making, that is, why critics view the law as replete with indeterminacy and room for judicial discretion, while judges persistently describe the legal materials as constraining. Coherence based reasoning indicates that even though the legal materials in hard legal cases are not constraining, they can be experienced as such once the judge's cognitive system has imposed coherence on them and shifted the vying conclusions apart. Thus, the judicial characterization of constraint is best understood not as a reflection of the legal materials, but as an artifact of the cognitive process that people employ in the making of complex decisions, judicial and otherwise.

In conclusion, Schauer is of course correct in objecting to facile applications of basic research to judicial decision making. Yet, there seems good reason to conclude that coherence based reasoning meets the requisite standards of applicability. Whether one is persuaded by it or not, this application ought not to be regarded as unargued, axiomatic, or unresearched. Moreover, given the difficulties involved in understanding the judicial process, one ought not rush to discard a body of valid and pertinent basic-psychological research. Rather, what is needed is an eclectic stance, based on any valid and informative research. An illustrative example can be borrowed from the application of psychology to medicine, specifically, the growing field of medical decision making. This field employs a variety of methodological approaches, including testing of physicians (e.g., Leblanc, Brooks, & Norman, 2002; Wallsten, 1981), applying basic-psychological findings (Croskerry, 2002; Graber, Franklin, & Gordon, 2005; Pines, 2005; Redelmeier, 2005), and more. The reliance on generic psychological research in this highly specialized field manifests a belief that any type of valid psychological research ought to be brought to bear to better understand how medical decisions are made and how they can be made better (Groopman, 2007). This prioritization of the usefulness of the research over its uniqueness could likewise benefit the study of judicial decision making.

Conclusion

The psychology of judging is poised to benefit much from a call for more experimentation, especially when it comes from a scholar of Schauer's stature. Schauer's essay provides a good opportunity to force people working in the field to think hard about the strengths and limitations of their methodological choices. Hopefully, it will also attract others to engage these issues and contribute to the development of the field.

Still, the specifics of Schauer's critiques and the proposed research are not free of objections. The attempt to increase the external validity of the experimentation does not come without costs. The insistence on uniqueness ends up compromising the proposed studies' construct validity, and thus muddies up the conclusions that could be drawn from them. Methodological tradeoffs of this kind hound experimental psychologists on a regular basis.[38] It is possible also that like many other important aspects of human behavior, the hypotheses posed by Schauer simply do not lend themselves to experimental testing. The insistence on uniqueness might also undermine the contributions from nonunique research, especially basic psychology. Instead of uniqueness, the field has most to gain from a pedantic attention to the experimental design coupled with open-mindedness to the range of useful methodologies.

The answer to the question posed in the title of Schauer's essay ought to be: yes, there is a psychology of judging. Admittedly, it is underdeveloped. To foster its growth, the field should be guided by the understanding that the practice of adjudication comprises a wide and diverse range of decision-making processes. In some facets of their work, judges exert judicial expertise, in others they behave just like ordinary people, and it is possible that in some facets they engage in processes that are unique to them. Researchers should opportunistically employ whichever methods are best suited for the subject of inquiry. Looking forward, the field stands to be enriched by carefully validated findings from all strands of psychology: basic psychology, applied psychology, the psychology of expertise, and perhaps also by a unique psychology of judging.

Notes

1. In this chapter, the term "psychological research" refers to research based on experimental studies.
2. Note that the proposal bridges two ingredients of external validity, namely, the population of participants and the type of decision tested. It does not bridge other aspects, such as realism, consequentialism, and the like.
3. *Basic psychology* focuses on phenomena that are relatively generalizable across people, situations, tasks, and contexts. Basic psychologists research phenomena like memory, reasoning, and persuasion. *Applied psychology* research focuses on testing psychological phenomena as they are performed in particular contexts. For example, applied psychology tests memory performance in the context of witness testimony, reasoning in police investigations, and persuasion in political campaigning.
4. Specifically, the essay states that the premise underlying this literature is an "undocumented and unargued premise" that lurks in the background (p. 2). It is described as something that researchers merely assume (p. 2); an "unexpressed" and "typically unresearched" outlook (p. 14); and a viewpoint that is taken as "axiomatic" but "hardly based on systematic research directed precisely at that question" (p. 20).
5. For useful discussions on methodological aspects of experimental psychology, see Aronson, Wilson, and Brewer (1998) and Mitchell and Jolley (2007).
6. In the following examples, imagine a jury simulation that is intended to test the effect of gruesome photographs from the crime scene on verdicts in the murder trial. The hypothesis in this example is that the exposure of the fact finders to the photographs will result in an arousal of negative emotion, which will increase their tendency to convict.

   A typical violation of internal validity is the failure to control for alternative potential causal effects, also known as confounds. In this example, assume a comparison between one group that receives a case that contains gory photographs and another group that receives a different case that does not contain photographs. Given the discrepant stimuli, different rates of conviction (if obtained) could not be explained as driven necessarily by the exposure to the gory photographs. They could readily be explained by the fact that the two groups received different cases. The evidence in the former case might have been more incriminating.

7. In the abovementioned example of the study testing the effect of gruesome photographs on jury verdicts, observing the heightened conviction rates in the presence of gruesome evidence does not in itself provide a satisfactory understanding of the effect. While it is possible that the effect was driven by the arousal of emotion (the hypothesized cause), it is also possible that it was driven by the fact that the photographs contained incriminating information that tied the defendant to the crime.

   Construct validity is needed, first, to overcome the fact that human cognition is notoriously multidetermined. Thus, to reliably interpret experimental findings, studies need to be able to isolate the hypothesized mechanism and rule out alternative explanations. Studies designed to have this capability are said to have *discriminant validity*. Second, the experimental design needs also to overcome the fact that psychological phenomena are generally not directly observable. To attain construct validity, the design needs to be able to identify the psychological mechanisms that drive the observations. Studies designed to be capable of identifying the correct construct are said to have *content validity*. Content validity is enhanced also by the extent to which the construct fits into a broader underlying theory. Theories are particularly useful when they are capable of explaining other related constructs. The content validity in the study testing the effect of gruesome photographs could be enhanced by showing that the finding can be explained by a theory that explains other effects of emotional arousal, such as in judgments of tort liability (Lerner, Goldberg, & Tetlock, 1998) and aggressive behavior (Bushman, 1995).

8. Schauer actually discusses the potential problem with lay understandings of the concepts of federalism and jurisdictions (fn. 29), but does not treat it as a potential methodological problem with the study.

9. For an insightful demonstration of evaluating and weighting judicial goals see Robbennolt, MacCoun, and Darley (this volume, ch. 2).

10. A tempting solution to these difficulties would be to provide lay subjects with special training about these matters in preparation for the experiment. To the extent that the training would be feasible and effective, it could jeopardize the study's internal validity. For example, lay subjects might interpret the instruction as a cue for a desired decision.

11. It must be noted, however, that expertise is also characterized by subpar functioning. Experts tend to display overconfidence, fail to notice details, and are less agile in adapting to change. Expertise is also no guarantee against the effects of bias (Chi, 2006; Koehler, Brenner, & Griffin, 2002). It is also important to note that expertise is typically narrow in scope. While experts perform differently on one type of task, the do not necessarily perform differently on adjacent tasks, even within the domain of their expertise.

12. The expertise explanation would also explain the examples Schauer uses to illustrate the uniqueness of judging: the difference in the mathematical skills of a Harvard professor of mathematics and lay people, and differences between a psychiatrist and a mechanic when it comes to providing psychiatric care or to fixing cars.

13. See section 4, "The Question of Expertise."

14. The proposed comparison of judges to nonjudges parallels what researchers in the field of expertise call the *relative* line of inquiry. A different type of research takes an *objective* approach, namely, focusing on how well the experts' performance stacks up against predetermined measures of excellence (Chi, 2006). By adopting the former approach, the proposed studies will, at best, indicate that judges are somewhat better at some aspects of judicial decisions than lay people. But that finding falls short of answering what is arguably the crucial questions: whether judges are good enough relative to some objective expectation, and whether they fulfill their constitutional role satisfactorily.

15. Referring to second order reasoning, Schauer characterizes judges as "people who know how to x" and contrasts them with lay people "who do not know how to x at all" (p. 20).

16. For example, human resource personnel are habitually confronted with considerations such as employment laws, company policies, maintaining consistency with prior cases, and setting an example for future ones. It should be noted that the article by Sunstein and Ullman-Margalit (1999) cited by Schauer pertains to second-order decisions made in nonjudicial contexts.

17. This body of research is a good example of the productive use of cross-disciplinary research. While the constructs underlying these findings are psychological, much of this research has been performed by political scientists, in nonexperimental settings.

18. A recent experiment conducted with law students demonstrated how second-order rules are distorted by the ideology of the participants. See Furgeson, J. R., Babcock,. L., and Shane, P. M. 2008a), Behind the mask of method: Political orientation and constitutional interpretive preferences. *Law & Human Behavior.*

19. True, the tasks involved in these studies were more akin to fact-finding and rendering of verdicts, but there is no obvious reason to believe that the performance would be better in appellate-like decision making.

20. Llewellyn, K. N. (1950), Remarks on the theory of appellate decision and the rules or canons about how statutes are to be construed. *Vanderbilt Law Review, 3,* 395.

21. See Senate Report 108-301. Report of the Select Committee on Intelligence on the U.S. Intelligence Community's Prewar Intelligence Assessments on Iraq. July 7, 2004 (http://intelligence.senate.gov/pub108thcongress.html).

22. The correlate coefficient of the findings was found to be about 0.73. See Anderson, A. A., Lindsay, J. L., and Bushman, B. J. (1999), Research in the psychological laboratory: Truth or triviality? *Current Directions in Psychological Science, 8,* 3–9. The similarity between laboratory findings and field findings does not ensure that the findings are applicable to real world applications, but it does allay some of the concerns about the artificiality of the laboratory setting.

    Another aspect of validity is ecological validity, which captures the similarity between the experimental setting and the real life domain. It is undeniable that the bulk of basic psychological research has little ecological validity with respect to the practice of judging, or to any other real world practice for that matter. Still, external validity ought not be confused with ecological validity. High ecological validity naturally increases external validity, but the latter is not dependent on the former.

23. To follow the abovementioned example, the external validity of the study of the effect of gruesome photographs will be increased by showing that the same effect is observed in other experimental variations, such as using different photographs, media, populations, factual patterns, judicial instructions, and the like.

24. Schauer criticizes the application of coherence based reasoning to judging (Simon, 1998, 2002, 2004), and also singles out some of the underlying empirical work, namely Holyoak and Simon (1999) and Simon, Krawczyk, and Holyoak (2004).

25. See Simon (1998), p. 71.

26. While it can be said to increase the acceptability of the opinions, this mode of argument can be deemed detrimental to adjudication in that it obscures the complexity of the issues involved, blunts the thoroughness of judicial analysis, and unduly devoids the validity of the losing side. For a discussion, see Simon (1998), pp. 129–134.

27. There is of course more than one way to break down a case and to enumerate its components. Alternative ways will always be possible, though the differences should not bear on the substantive conclusions of the analysis.

28. This form of inquiry was first demonstrated in the analysis of *Ratzlaf v. United States*, 510 U.S. 135 (1994), a relatively mundane case chosen almost at random. See Simon (1998, pp. 61–72, and 73–102 *passim*). For another example, analyzing *Rogers v. Tennessee*, 532 U.S. 451 (2001), see Simon (2002). The *Bush v. Gore* case provides a more familiar manifestation of the phenomenon (draft on file with author).

29. One explanation for the excessive coherence of judicial reasoning is that the strong alignment of arguments is a product of "padding" of opinions (Posner, 1995a). The concept of padding implies that not all reasons play the same role in the decision, as some are deemed to actually exert power on the decision maker, whereas others merely serve as ex post justifications. This seems true, though it is doubtful that padding could fully account for the observed coherence (see Simon, 1998, pp. 35–36). To illustrate, even if all but the handful of core issues served as mere justifications, one would still need to explain how the handful of core arguments lined up to cohere with the decision. For example, in the Ratzlaf case there were six core issues. Assuming that they were about equally plausible, the probability of all six lining up to support the respective conclusion is one in sixty-four. A precise assessment of likelihoods would depend on the degree to which the issues and arguments are independent of one another.

30. The processes include vision (McClelland & Rumelhart, 1981), social reasoning (Read & Miller, 1998; Read, Vanman, & Miller, 1997), analogical reasoning (Holyoak & Thagard, 1989; Spellman & Holyoak, 1992), relational inference (Hummel & Holyoak, 2003), text comprehension (Kintsch, 1988), and more. These strands of research are based on a connectionist architecture, and are resolved via Parallel Constraint Satisfaction Mechanisms (Holyoak & Thagard, 1989; Read, Vanman, & Miller, 1997).

31. The studies' internal validity and construct validity are beyond the scope of this chapter. Concerns over internal validity can be put to rest in light of their salience in the extensive peer review that the studies have undergone.

32. The professional auditors were tested performing an actuarial task (Lundberg, 2007).

33. Manipulations can be found in Holyoak and Simon (1999), studies 1, 3; Simon et al. (2001), studies 1, 2, 3; Simon et al. (2004a), study 1; Simon et al. (2004b,) studies 1, 2, 3, 4.

34. See Simon (1998), pp. 61–102.

35. See Simon (1998), pp. 102–121.

36. Holyoak and Simon (1999), study 2. This lack of awareness further enables the endurance of this type of reasoning in the judicial practice (Wilson & Brekke, 1994).

37. See Simon (1998), pp. 134–137.

38. A key to the success of research projects is the critical examination that takes place in lab meetings at the early stages of experimental design. Of the many seemingly good ideas proposed at these meetings, only a small fraction make it to the phase of experimentation, not to mention onto the pages of scientific journals.

10

Judges, Expertise, and Analogy

Barbara A. Spellman

One appellate case, three courts—and seven disparate opinions. Clearly, different judges reach different decisions based on the same facts and same legal doctrine. Why? Political scientists have shown that one can anticipate how a judge will decide a case more often than chance, or a reading of the facts, might allow. Using various predictors—party affiliation, party of appointment, the judge's own decisions on earlier similar cases—regression analyses can demonstrate that judges are behaving in a manner consistent with their explicit prior beliefs (e.g., Segal & Spaeth, 1993, 2002). The simplest explanation for such behavior is that judges first decide what they want the outcome of the case to be, then go back to find the precedents that justify their opinions.[1] The more complicated claim that I want to make is this: people (and judges) may choose relevant analogies (or precedents) as better or worse, applicable or inapplicable, not because of any particular desired outcome but rather because of their own preexisting knowledge. The influence of such knowledge on the decision process may be entirely unconscious; therefore, judges may, in fact, be following the idealized decision-making process to the letter, and be unmotivated toward finding a particular result, yet may usually still reach the predicted result.

To understand this argument, I first present an overview of the analogical reasoning research done by cognitive psychologists. Next I address the question of whether judges are experts at analogical reasoning. If they are experts, then the large body of empirical analogy research conducted with nonexpert subjects might not be relevant to judges' analogical reasoning. However, I conclude that although judges might be expert at many things, analogical reasoning is not likely to be one of them. Accordingly, I turn to other research—including some from analogy and some from other areas relevant to analogy like similarity and categorization—to show how nonattitudinal and nonteleological factors (especially preexisting knowledge) can affect analogy use. Finally, I link these arguments back to the initial question: whether judges, or anyone, can be making "predictable" decisions while still following an idealized analogical reasoning process.

Overview of Analogical Reasoning

Analogical reasoning is a core component of intelligence. Most intelligence tests, not to mention general standardized tests like the GREs and LSATs, incorporate some kind of analogical reasoning tasks. Performance on analogical reasoning tasks correlates very highly with performance on almost all other components of IQ tests (Salthouse, 2005; Snow, Kyllonen, & Marshalek, 1984).

On those tests, analogical reasoning often consists of verbal four-term problems (like lawyer:client :: doctor:?) and geometric versions of such problems. Although those simple tasks have been studied in the laboratory, research using more complicated real world analogy materials has proven more informative.

Analogical reasoning involves taking a situation that is well understood (the "source") and using it to help explicate a situation that is less well understood (the "target"). Two important distinctions are *(1)* between the processes of retrieval and mapping, and *(2)* between the attributes and relations within analogs.

Steps in Using Analogies

Analogical reasoning typically involves several steps including retrieval and mapping. To illustrate: Suppose you are a lawyer and a potential client comes to you wanting to know whether she has a good negligence claim against a cruise line. She had been asleep in her locked cabin when someone reached through a window and stole her handbag including $500 in cash.

To figure out whether she has a good claim, you first need to retrieve—find potentially analogous source cases in memory (or by doing some legal research). First, you recall a case in which a businessman was asleep on a train berth in an open sleeping car and had his expensive cell phone stolen from the pocket of the coat he was using as a blanket. Second, you recall a case in which a man in a resort hotel had his wallet stolen from his room while he slept. Third, you recall a case in which a woman on a cruise ship was hit by another woman on the ship who used her handbag as a weapon.

The next step is to create a mapping—find a set of appropriate correspondences between elements of the source and target. You might think of your client as the business traveler, the cruise ship as the train, and handbag as the cell phone. Alternatively, you might think of your client as the man on vacation, the ship as the hotel, and the handbag as the wallet.

If you think your case is most like that of businessman on the train (who lost), you will expect the same outcome as in that case; if you think it is most like that of the vacationing man in the hotel (who won), you will expect that result. But despite the fact that the third case involves a woman, a cruise ship, and a handbag—just like your own—it probably doesn't seem very similar to your case because the objects that are the same don't stand in the same relations to each other—and relations are the key to analogy.

Similarity in Using Analogies

The second important distinction is between attributes and relations within the analogs (Gentner, 1983; Holyoak & Thagard, 1989). Attributes are objects or qualities of objects (or events or people); they are one-place predicates like: is-a-planet or is-valuable. Relations are two (or more) place predicates. Relations may link objects, for example: is-bigger-than, revolves-around, owns, has-a-duty-of-care-toward. But relations may also link other relations, for example, the relation "cause" is important in linking propositions like: *(1)* The sun is bigger than the earth and (causes) *(2)* the earth revolves around the sun. Or: *(1)* An innkeeper has a duty of care toward those who rent rooms (plus some other stuff) and (causes) *(2)* the innkeeper is liable for the theft.

Note that attributes are often referred to as "surface" or "superficial" features because they are usually physically visible or explicitly described, whereas relations must often be inferred.[2]

The difference between attribute and relational features is illustrated wonderfully in an experiment in which subjects were asked to find similarities between pairs of pictures (Markman & Gentner, 1993). In one pair, the top picture showed a tow truck towing a car to the left along a road; the bottom picture showed a (very similar looking) car pulling a motorboat to the right along a road. Subjects were asked which object from the top picture "matched" the car from the bottom picture. There are two obvious answers. Subjects who had to answer the question quickly were more like to match the car on the bottom to the car on the top because those two objects were very similar in looks; that is an attribute match. Subjects who had more time were more likely to match the car on the bottom to the tow truck on the top because those two objects filled the same role (i.e., of pulling something else that could not move over the road on its own); that is a relational match.

Attribute similarities between the source and the target play a greater role in the retrieval of analogs, whereas relational similarities play a greater role in mapping (Gentner, 1993; Holyoak & Koh, 1987). When people are asked to judge the "goodness" or similarity of analogies, the depth and structure of the relational similarities matters much more than the attribute similarities (Gentner & Kurtz, 2006; Gentner, Ratterman, & Forbus, 1993).

Note that the difference between attribute and relational similarity is key in the use of analogical reasoning in the law. A useful precedent is not usually one in which the parties themselves (or the property in question) are similar but rather one in which similar (legal) relations hold between the relevant parties or property.

So, in the earlier example of the theft on the ship, the relevant similarities are not whether the victim was a woman or man, whether it was a business or pleasure trip, or what was stolen;[3] rather what matters is the relation between the victim and the owner of the ship, train, or hotel. And although most people believe that a ship is more similar to a train than to a hotel, the court in *Adams v. New Jersey Steamboat Company* (1896) ruled that for liability purposes a ship's cabin is more like a hotel room, where there is an expectation of privacy and protection, than like an open berth in a sleeping car, where there is not.

Developing expertise in law is (at least in part) learning to ignore irrelevant attribute similarities, learning what counts as a relational similarity, and understanding which relational similarities are likely to matter in a given case.

Analogy and Expertise

What would it mean to say that judges are experts at analogical reasoning? Because analogical reasoning is a core component of IQ, and because judges are likely to be a more intelligent group than a random collection of folks, judges are more likely to be better than average at analogical reasoning. But are they experts? And why is it important?

What Is an Expert?

Due to study, training, and practice—often in addition to talent and motivation—experts are better than nonexperts in some domain of performance. Expert chess and golf and bridge players routinely beat nonexperts; expert surgeons perform difficult surgeries more successfully than nonexperts; expert violinists create truer sounds and make fewer mistakes than nonexperts.

One clear characteristic of expertise is that it is quite limited in domain. Expert golf players are not experts at all sports or even all sports requiring a swing or a ball. Expert neurosurgeons are not expert cardiac surgeons nor are expert violinists expert cellists. Much expertise involves being good at a procedure that involves a very specific content.

Within their domain of expertise, experts tend to be faster and more accurate than novices, tend to have superior short-term and long-term memories for information, see deeper relations in the structure of information, use less cognitive effort, and have more accurate monitoring skills

(Chi, 2006; Glaser & Chi, 1998). These qualities are thought to reflect not just that experts have more knowledge but also that experts have a "qualitatively different representation and organization of knowledge" (Ericsson, 2006).

A potentially important characteristic of experts for the law is that, in a variety of domains, being an expert means seeing past attribute similarities to underlying relational similarities. For example, when shown index cards depicting different physics problems and asked to sort them into piles, novice physics students sort them based on the type of objects involved in the problems (e.g., pulleys, inclined planes) whereas expert physicists sort them based on the underlying principles involved (e.g., conservation of momentum) (Chi, Feltovich, & Glaser, 1981). When using analogies, experts are more able to retrieve previous analogs based on structural similarity and avoid interference by those exhibiting only surface similarity (Novick, 1988).[4] Thus, someone who is legally trained is less likely to be distracted by the hit-by-a-handbag-on-a-cruise-ship case than someone who is not.

Another general characteristic of expertise is that it only develops given specific conditions. One is that the person spends a lot of time at it—but, of course, time itself is not sufficient. We all know people who have played golf or bridge for years, and who seem to enjoy it, but who aren't any better than they were years ago. More important than just the amount of time is how that time is spent: expertise develops out of a process called "deliberate practice" which involves thousands of hours of specific types of practice and training. Deliberate practice requires focused programmatic study with appropriate feedback about performance. It includes identifying errors and working on procedures to eliminate them (Ericsson, 2006; Horn & Masunaga, 2006).

Why Is Expertise Important

In his essay in this volume (ch. 7), Schauer poses the question: "Is there a psychology of judging?" His answer is essentially "no." He states that so far all the experimental evidence shows that judges demonstrate the same cognitive failings as mere mortals. But he correctly points out that psychologists have not (often) studied what judges do when they are doing what judges often do. He argues that it is there—in their domain of expertise—where a psychology of judging would exist. Of course that is true of other experts—"special performance" is only found within the domain of expertise; thus it is ironic that Schauer perfunctorily dismisses most research on expertise as being irrelevant to his conjecture.

In the "first generation" of theories of expertise (Holyoak, 1991), psychologists believed that experts in any particular cognitive skill should be experts at general reasoning and, therefore, should be experts at other reasoning tasks. But the next wave of research consistently found that experts, despite specialized skills and virtuoso performances, made the same errors as nonexperts on all sorts of general reasoning tasks; their expertise was limited to their domain of detailed knowledge. However, no one found that judges made those particular errors—because hardly anyone studied judges.[5] And now they have (e.g., Guthrie et al., 2001; Wistrich et al., 2005).

Some people seemed surprised that judges show the standard errors and biases on the standard cannon of reasoning tasks; however, for those of us who believed the findings that doctors and Indian chiefs were not special with regard to all kinds of reasoning tasks, and were only special with regard to tasks related to their expertise, the fact that lawyers and judges are not special with regard to those tasks is not the least bit surprising (or interesting).

However, as Schauer argues, if we can define what judges' expertise is, we can *(1)* begin a smarter inquiry into the psychology of judging and *(2)* argue that within their limited domain(s) of expertise, judges should show the kinds of enhanced performance of experts and should not fall prey to the errors that nonexperts would generate. Clearly, one candidate for judges' expertise is analogical reasoning.

Are Judges Experts at Analogical Reasoning?

Elsewhere others and I have argued that judges are *not* experts in several tasks that might be viewed as components of judging. For example, it could be argued that judges are neither expert fact-finders (Robinson & Spellman, 2005) nor expert at appropriately weighting evidence (Spellman, 2007). One reason for the theorized lack of expertise is that although (some) judges may often do those tasks, they are not trained to do them with extensive supervision and feedback.

In contrast, law school does train students (whether explicitly or implicitly) to reason analogically. In law school we had the pleasure of years of reading cases, abstracting rules and similarities, drawing analogies to other cases or hypotheticals, and being given corrective feedback about our analyses.[6] And, in fact, law schools often (explicitly or implicitly) use techniques in teaching that have been shown to improve analogical reasoning in the laboratory. Thus, it seems as though the conditions for developing expertise at analogical reasoning might be met.

Law School Techniques and the Possibilities of Improving Analogical Reasoning

Although the psychology literature is fairly glum about people's ability to take what they have learned in one domain and use analogy to transfer that knowledge to another domain (see Barnett & Ceci, 2002, for a review), there are, in fact, ways to improve people's performance on analogical reasoning tasks. In the laboratory, bad performance on analogical reasoning tasks is often to due a failure to retrieve—subjects trying to solve a problem do not find relevant analogs in memory; however, once they are told that a prior experience might be relevant, they are good at mapping.

In a basic laboratory procedure for studying analogical reasoning, subjects first learn about a way of solving a hypothetical problem. For example, a general wants to attack a well-guarded fortress but if he sends his entire army down one road, land mines will explode and significantly deplete his forces. A better plan is to send smaller groups of soldiers down different roads toward the fortress simultaneously. This divide-spread-and-converge approach is called the "convergence solution" (e.g., Gick & Holyoak, 1980, 1983; Holyoak & Koh, 1987).

Time passes and subjects are later asked to solve an analogous problem, typically Duncker's Radiation Problem (Duncker, 1945). A man has an inoperable tumor in his stomach. A type of radiation can destroy the tumor but if it is used at sufficiently high strength to destroy the tumor it will destroy the healthy tissue that it passes through and the man will die. What can be done?

There is a convergence solution to the radiation problem: use many less-powerful rays simultaneously from many different angles. About 10% of subjects will come up with that solution—and that is the same percentage whether or not they have previous read the fortress problem. Why doesn't having seen the obvious analogy help?

The main obstacle to using the earlier solution is that people do not think of it—that is, they fail to retrieve it from memory. However, if people are reminded of it—for example, if the experimenter tells them to think back to something they did earlier in the study—then most will think of the source analog, easily draw the mapping, and solve the radiation problem. Without explicit reminding (or expertise), however, people are only likely to think of superficially similar source analogs (Holyoak & Koh, 1987).

Laboratory studies that demonstrate ways to increase or improve the use of analogical reasoning therefore tend to address the accessibility of source analogs. But, of course, the source analog is a given; how can it be made more accessible? Although the analog is fixed, people's mental representations of the analog can differ. For example, rather than storing the fortress problem in memory as a "story about a general attacking a fortress," people could store it more abstractly, as a story about how a too-strong force can be split up into smaller forces and then converge to accomplish a goal. Later, when a new target situation comes along that has a similar abstract relational structure, the abstract version of the source analog is more likely to be retrieved because the two analogs seem more potentially related (e.g., if they are both about "converging forces" rather than one being about an army and the other about radiation).

Note that in some ways this characterizes the task of the law student, lawyer, or judge searching for relevant precedent—when facing a new fact pattern to find good analogous cases in memory. However, the legal task is also different. For one thing, in the legal arena people know that they should be trying to find an analogous case. For another, except for law students on an exam, the search for such cases is not just a search through memory but rather a search through a database or through cases presented as relevant in legal briefs.

Below I describe three techniques that were designed to improve reminding in the laboratory but are similar to techniques used in law school pedagogy. They are also what is needed for developing expert knowledge within a content area—making important similarities more obvious—in particular, making relational features as obvious—and as "superficial"—to experts as attribute features are to novices.

Creating More Abstract Source Representations Indirectly by Comparing Analogs

One way to improve analogical reasoning in the laboratory is to have subjects compare and abstract from multiple analogs. For example, subjects who read both the fortress story and a story about firefighters (who used many small hoses simultaneously from different directions) before trying to solve the radiation problem were more than twice as likely to come up with the convergence solution as subjects who had read only one source analog. In addition, if subjects are asked to explicitly compare the two analogs to each other, those who abstract the convergence solution from the comparison are more likely to use it later than subjects who do not have a good representation of the relational similarities between the stories (Catrambone & Holyoak, 1989; Gick & Holyoak, 1983). This compare-and-abstract technique has been shown to benefit business school students in negotiation classes who, like law students, participate in case-based learning (Loewenstein, Thompson, & Gentner, 1999). In law school, hypotheticals may provide the grist for comparing analogs.

Training People to Abstract Principles from Single Analogs

Another way to improve analogical reasoning is to train people to represent single source analogs at an abstract level. Mandler and Orlich (1993) had subjects read the fortress story and then describe the story at one of three different levels of abstraction: summarizing the story details; summarizing the main points by stating the general's goal, dilemma, and solution; or abstracting a general solution principle. When subjects later tried to solve the radiation problem, those who had produced a good abstract solution were much more likely to use the convergence solution and solve the radiation problem than subjects who had not. (Note, however, that very few subjects actually succeeded in creating a good abstract summary, suggesting that such a representation is hard to create without either training or practice.) In law school, students learning to extract abstract rules from single cases.

Teaching the Names of Relations

A third way to improve analogical reasoning is to use consistent relational labels when people learn the analogs. Although the laboratory data with adults is sparse, the idea is consistent with various kinds of developmental and anecdotal evidence. People tend to use the same labels for objects (e.g., car, tow truck) but different labels for verbs and relations (e.g., pulls, tows, drags)—making it easier to use objects/attributes in retrieval and also making relations more difficult to learn (Gentner & Kurtz, 2007; Gentner & Loewenstein, 2002). Relational categories seemed to be learned by "progressive alignment"—by first comparing examples that are similar, then comparing more distant ones (Gentner & Kurtz, 2007).

Law students learn the names of many legal relations: contracts, torts, negligence, standing, jurisdiction—all are about the relations between parties and/or actions that create legal rights or obligations. Certainly, there are some legal categories that are "attribute-based": there are laws that apply only to people over 18 years old and there are laws that apply only to ships. However, much of law school is about learning, by contrasting many examples, the requirements and limits of legal relations.

But Does a Law Student's Analogical Reasoning Actually Improve?

In effect, all of the above techniques—comparing multiple analogs, abstracting from single analogs, learning the names of legal relations—are techniques used in law school to teach the content of the law. Psychologists, however, do not have any measures that demonstrate that law school improves general analogical reasoning. In a study of the effects of graduate training on reasoning, law students, medical students, and graduate students in psychology and chemistry took tests involving statistical, methodological, conditional, and verbal reasoning during the first and third years in the programs (Lehman, Lempert, & Nisbett, 1988). The verbal reasoning test included verbal analogical reasoning (as on the GRE or LSAT). The first-year law students had higher initial verbal reasoning scores than the other groups—suggesting self- (or law school) selection. However, after three years of schooling, the law students improved only about 5 percent on average (a statistically nonsignificant difference) in verbal reasoning; all of the other groups' average scores improved more.

Granted, these data showing no improvement in analogical reasoning are not the best—among other flaws they only include law students (at the University of Michigan) after three years of training rather than experienced judges and, of course, the verbal reasoning tasks are not the same as the type of full-blown analogical reasoning done when reasoning about cases. However, these data are consistent with a wide variety of other data showing limitations on both the transfer of training and the generalization of expertise.

Expertise and the Process/Content Interaction

The best way to think of what judges may have developed is that it depends on both process and content: it is using analogy in a domain in which they have specialized knowledge—knowledge that enables them to quickly understand which features of a case are the relevant ones for analogical mapping. Thus, within the legal context (or, more likely, within a subset of that context), judges are experts at using analogy; however, when reasoning outside their knowledge base, although they may be more fond of using analogy than most people (because of practice or precocity), they will not be any better than equally intelligent and informed others.

To return to the cruise ship example, probably no one who was legally trained would think that the sex of the victim, the nature of the trip, or the particular items that were stolen would matter in that case; even if those features bring to mind similar cases, those that do not have an underlying structural similarity (e.g., the women being hit by the handbag on the cruise ship) would be easily rejected as irrelevant. And those who are legally trained should be less flustered by the surface similarity that boats and trains move whereas hotels do not. Rather, those who know that the law protects those who are justified in expecting privacy and security— whether passengers or hotel guests—would be more likely to recall, recognize, and use the analogy between the obligation of a ship to a passenger in a private cabin and the obligation of a hotel to a guest in a private room.

Nonattitudinal (Unintentional) Factors Affecting Analogy Selection and Use

To the extent that judges are not any different at analogical reasoning from nonjudges, their use of analogical reasoning should be affected by similar extra-logical influences. Below I describe several factors that influence the selection and interpretation of analogies that are *not* driven by a conscious motivation to find one analog more relevant or persuasive than others. I focus here on knowledge and representation; that is, how what someone knows, and the relations they consider between the things they know, affects analogy use. However, there are other cognitive factors that might also work to make the choice of precedent seem teleologically motivated.[7]

Knowledge and Unconscious Reminding

People may show unconscious influences of irrelevant parts of the source analog on selecting and using analogies. (Of course, that assumes that people are familiar with the source analog.) For example, when subjects read about a hypothetical political crisis and were asked whether they thought the United States should intervene, those who read a version with several superficial reminders of World War II (e.g., a briefing in Winston

Churchill Hall) made more interventionist recommendations than those who read a version with superficial reminders of Vietnam (e.g., a briefing in Dean Rusk Hall). Thus, the superficial features (unconsciously) affected the retrieval of similar analogs and those (unconsciously) influenced the interpretation of the target analog. Interestingly, however, when the subjects were later asked to explicitly rate how similar the hypothetical crisis was to both World War II and to Vietnam, the differences in superficial details had no effect (Gilovich, 1981).

Knowledge and Interests

A person's knowledge or interests can unconsciously influence which of several equally good analogical mappings will be chosen. For example, subjects read a science fiction story describing two different planets (Spellman & Holyoak, 1996). Planet 1 had three countries: Afflu was economically strong and gave economic aid to Barebrute; Barebrute was economically weak but militarily strong and gave military aid to Compak; Compak was militarily weak. Planet 2 had four countries: Grainwell was economically strong and gave economic aid to the economically weak Hungerall; Millpower was militarily strong and gave military aid to the militarily weak Mightless.

Subjects first made military or economic recommendations for each country. Then they matched the countries of Planet 2 to the countries of Planet 1. Which country was like Afflu? Easy, Grainwell. Like Compak? Also easy, Mightless. But which was like Barebrute? There are reasons to pick both Hungerall and Millpower.

Subjects' mapping choices depended on the recommendations they made. Subjects who made military recommendations saw Barebrute as more like the militarily strong Millpower; in contrast, subjects who made economic recommendations saw Barebrute as more like the economically weak Hungerall.

Thus, knowledge or interests may drive mappings within an ambiguous analogy.

Planet 1:
Afflu	→ aids →	Barebrute	→ aids →	Compak
(economically strong)		(economically weak; militarily strong)		(militarily weak)

Planet 2:
Grainwell	→ aids →	Hungerall	Millpower → aids → Mightless
(economically strong)		(economically weak)	(militarily strong) (militarily weak)

Figure 10.1 Representation of materials from Spellman and Holyoak, 1996.

Incorporating Structure in Levels of Abstraction

Which (of many potential) analogs one regards as best may depend on how much of the abstract analogical structure one incorporates (Hofstadter & Mitchell, 1994). Consider the following question:

If the string of letters *abc* is changed to *abd*, how would you change *kji* in the same way?

This question is, in effect, a four-term analogy question (like lawyer: client :: doctor:patient): find the relations in the first pair of letter strings, map *abc* to *kji*, and then apply the relations to create the fourth term.

The following two solutions are based on superficial features and are very literal—and people find them very unsatisfying: *kji* could be turned into *abd* or into *kjd*. The first ignores all internal properties of both *abc* and *kji* (and ignores how *kji* might be similar to *abc*); the rule is: turn any letter string into *abd*. The second also ignores all internal properties of *kji* but does consider the relation between *abc* and *abd*; the rule is: change the rightmost letter to *d*.

A less literal solution is to turn *kji* into *kjj*. That solution means considering the relation between *abc* and *abd* and also understanding that *c* is part of an alphabetical sequence and that *d* is one step lower in the sequence; the rule is: change the rightmost letter one step lower.

People generally prefer the two analogical solutions that incorporate the internal relational structure of the letter strings. Generating the answer *kjh* means seeing that *abc* is a downward sequence from which the rightmost letter is moved one more step down; however, *kji* is an upward sequence, therefore, the rule is: move rightmost letter one step more in the direction of the sequence. Generating the answer *lji* also means seeing that *abc* is a downward sequence and *kji* is an upward one. Then *abd* means changing the lowest (rightmost) letter down one; *lji* means changing the lowest (leftmost) letter down one.

One of the fascinating things about the Hofstadter letter-string analogies is how many different ones can be sensibly generated from such seemingly simple stimuli. Legal cases are similarly complicated in that they may contain relations that are or are not incorporated into the litigants' arguments and that analogies may be drawn at very literal or abstract levels. For example, the same case may be viewed as being about "the right to engage in homosexual sodomy" or "the right to be let alone" (*Bowers v. Hardwick*, 1986).

Coherence

The selection of a particular analog, or relevant precedent, might also (unintentionally) emerge out of a general pressure for cognitive coherence—that is, the tendency for people to be consistent in their reasoning. As a consequence, people's views of the applicability of a source analog change in line with other changes in their opinions (for overviews of this research see Simon, 2004; Simon & Holyoak, 2002). In the basic study (Holyoak & Simon, 1999), subjects (undergraduates) read a semifictional legal case. The plaintiff, a software company named Quest, sued Jack Smith, an investor in the company, for libel. Smith had posted a negative message about the company on an electronic bulletin board directed at investors, and soon after the stock's price dropped drastically and the company went bankrupt.

Before reading the case, subjects were asked whether they thought messages posted on electronic bulletin boards should be treated like items published in newspapers or like messages sent over a telephone network. Later, as part of the case, subjects learned that defamatory messages published in a newspaper could give rise to a cause of action for libel whereas those transmitted by telephone could not.

Subjects were about equally divided in verdicts. But whereas *before* reading the case, subjects found the newspaper and telephone analogies equally compelling, *after* rendering their verdicts, they widely diverged. Those who found for Quest believed that the newspaper analogy was much better than the telephone analogy; the opposite was true for those who found for Smith. Thus, belief in the quality of an analogy shifted coherently along with other beliefs that led them to their decision.

Legal Knowledge

An experiment comparing law students to undergraduates demonstrates how legal knowledge can affect analogical reasoning (Braman & Nelson, 2007, Exp. 2). Subjects (96 undergraduates and 77 law students) read an article summarizing the target case facts (but not the result) of *Wazereud-Din v. Goodwill Homes and Mission, Inc.* (1999) in which the plaintiff, an Islamic man, was denied admission to a Christian-administered drug treatment program. They also read about a potentially relevant previously decided case. The precedent case varied in its similarity to the target case and involved one of three different plaintiffs: Islamic man, gay man, or black man; one of three different types of defendant: religious treatment program, community service organization, or insurance company; and one of two holdings: discrimination or not. Subjects rated how similar the precedent was to the target case. They had also previously been asked whether they agreed that faith-based organizations should have the right to exclude people who did not share their beliefs from receiving their services.

Several findings demonstrate the effects of legal knowledge: *(1)* overall, undergraduates rated the precedents as more similar to the target case than did the law students, and *(2)* undergraduates treated precedents involving Islamic and gay plaintiffs similarly whereas law students tended to treat precedents involving Islamic and black plaintiffs similarly. These results suggest that the law students were using their prior knowledge—of the difference between "strict scrutiny" and "rational basis" tests—in their judgments.[8]

But Braman and Nelson (2007) want to go further than merely stating that *knowledge* matters to analogy use; they argue that there was (sometimes) evidence that subjects' prior *beliefs* mattered: in general, those who opposed exclusion based on religion were more likely to rate the target case as similar to the precedent when the holding was that there was discrimination, but those who favored exclusion were more likely to rate the target case as similar to the precedent when the holding was that there was no discrimination. This pattern was stronger and more consistent for the law students.

Therefore, Braman and Nelson (2007) also conclude in favor of "motivated reasoning"—that people's policy preferences (e.g., regarding exclusion) "influence legal decision making" (p. 954). However, the causal conclusion that preferences *influence* reasoning, and, especially, that it might have influenced reasoning in a consciously motivated way, is not justified. Subjects are not randomly assigned to favor or oppose exclusion—thus, subjects who start out holding different beliefs may differ from each other in other systematic ways (creating a so-called "third variable" problem). For example, subjects who are more tolerant of different groups and less likely to see differences between them might both *(1)* be more likely to oppose exclusion and *(2)* more likely to see similarities between the cases. Other types of preexisting knowledge—not necessarily directly related to the case—could have similar effects.

Note that the authors "hasten to add that nothing we have found suggests a *conscious* effort to twist the law to serve one's preferences" (Braman & Nelson, 2007, p. 954). It is easy to see how these results could emerge simply from different knowledge and from the (unconscious) pressure for coherence in reasoning.

Judges and Analogy

What can we conclude? Judges have had lots of practice using analogy; yet, they might not actually be "experts" because just as there is no real generalized expertise in "problem solving" it is not clear that there can be a generalized expertise in analogy use. More important, however, judges (like laypeople) know that when using analogies it is important to look for relational similarities and—because of their specialized training in legal content—they know which relational similarities matter within their domains of expertise.

Many of the limitations on using analogies described above have to do with "finding" or retrieving the proper analogs to use. Judges don't have to try to retrieve from memory—they have briefs and law clerks to find the relevant sources. Yet, as the WWII/Vietnam study shows, unconscious remindings of known analogs that are not present can affect judgments even though, when made explicit, the analogs are not viewed as any better or worse than other ones. In addition to this automatic retrieval of analogies, judges' knowledge and interests may influence how they mentally represent and use different analogs. When judges know more about some issues than others, or, in the past, have drawn analogies to one kind of outcome, they might be more likely to unintentionally find in a direction consistent with past judgments—in part because of what they see as more (or less) similar, in part because of the level of abstraction (i.e., how deep the relations) they use, and in part because of an effort to maintain coherence in their beliefs.

Thus, although judges might decide consistently with predictions, it is possible that they do so not for any of the intentional (and sometimes seemingly "nefarious") reasons suggested by legal realism. Regression analyses can reveal *that* it happens but understanding how analogical reasoning works, and how judges might use it, is necessary for understanding *why* it might happen.

Notes

1. This position is the most extreme version of the "legal realist" view. A more nuanced view is that they are sensitive to both attitudinal and jurisprudential concerns (Lindquist & Klein, 2006).
2. The terms "surface" and "superficial" are often mixed both within and across articles.
3. Note that although irrelevant in this case, such factors could be relevant in other types of cases.
4. When acquiring analogical skills, children parallel this development (Ratterman & Gentner, 1998).
5. But see Lawrence (1988) for an early study of how Australian magistrates impose sentences; and, Dhami (2003), with a larger data set showing that British judges' bail decisions can be well described by a simple heuristic model.
6. In a sense, when lawyers write briefs, and when judges read and rule on them, they are engaged in a similar activity. Of course, the kind of "feedback" that lawyers and, especially, judges get is much more erratic and sporadic than that of the law student.
7. Other potential factors include context effects (see Hunter, 2001); whether people set out to look for similarities or differences between cases (see Gentner & Markman, 1994; and Medin, Goldstone, & Gentner, 1990); and beliefs about the causal structure of relevant legal categories (see Kim & Ahn, 2002).
8. Under current constitutional doctrine, actions that treat people differently based on race and religion merit strict scrutiny, whereas those based on sexual orientation do not.

11

Thresholds for Action in Judicial Decisions

Len Dalgleish, James Shanteau, and April Park

Many decisions that people are called on to make can be thought of as involving thresholds for action. Should one buy a new computer, attempt a left turn into oncoming traffic, excuse a late submission from a student? In each case, we can understand the decision maker to be answering two questions: *(1)* How strong are the arguments in favor of taking this action? *(2)* How strong must the arguments be in order for me to take the action?

Decision makers in court cases, whether judges or jurors, are commonly required to make this kind of decision. Take a hypothetical, but fairly typical, drug trafficking case in a U.S. court, where the police uncovered one piece of evidence by stopping the defendant on the street for questioning, subjecting him to pat-down search, and finding a bulky packet of marijuana in his coat pocket. In one of several motions to the judge, the defendant's lawyer argues that the marijuana should not be allowed into the trial as evidence because the search was unconstitutional. The judge must decide, among other things, whether the police reasonably suspected that the defendant was, at the time of the search, "armed and presently dangerous."[1] Her decision will depend on both her assessment of the evidence available to the police at the time and her understanding of "reasonable suspicion." At the end of the trial, the jury (or judge, if a jury trial has been waived) must decide whether the prosecution proved the defendant's guilt "beyond a reasonable doubt." Again, the decision will require judgments about both the evidence itself and the threshold the evidence needs to cross.

These are just two examples of a great many. Appellate judges may have to decide whether a decision made by a trial judge constitutes an "abuse of discretion" or, in another case, whether a trial judge's mistake is "harmless." Judges at either level may have to decide whether an administrative agency has taken an "arbitrary and capricious" action or whether a state law is "narrowly tailored" to serve a "compelling" governmental interest. This list could be extended for pages.

The aim of this chapter is to set out a framework for analyzing decisions to take action in a judicial context. We begin by outlining a general model, continue with a description of several studies of mock-juror decision making, and conclude with implications for studying judges.

Model for Assessing Situations and Deciding to Take Action

The key to the model is a distinction between *(1)* the forming of an assessment given the evidence available to the decision maker and *(2)* the decision to take action or not, given that assessment. Consider a motion hearing, in which a judge hears the arguments, reads the submissions, and makes a decision. It is assumed that all the information presented to or available to the judge is combined to form an opinion or an assessment about the strength of evidence favoring approval along a continuum from low to high. An assessment is formed through a psychological process of integrating the information.

This assessment is then turned into a decision about action to deny the motion or not by a decision rule. It is assumed that on this continuum the judge has a personal threshold for action and this is in place before the judge forms an assessment of the amount of evidence. The threshold is an internal cutoff level for taking action. The decision rule is this: If the assessment is above the threshold the judge approves the motion. This model formalizes the question: "Is the evidence sufficient to grant the motion?" The threshold is the minimal amount of "evidence" a judge requires to grant the motion. Although it may feel like the assessment and the decision occur at the same time and can't be separated, it is useful to distinguish them since different factors influence the assessment and the decision (Dalgleish, 2003).

The left hand side of the model in Figure 11.1 shows that the factors affecting the formation of the assessment of strength of evidence are from information in the current situation presented to the judge. The right hand side of the model shows that factors from the experiences and history of the judge influence the placement of the threshold. These factors are not from the current case, and the threshold is in place before the current situation is assessed. For example, a judge may have a reputation for being "tough" in that he requires a lot of evidence before granting a motion. Another may have the reputation for being "easy to convince."[2] Of course, a judge's knowledge and experience influence the assessment. For example, their experience may have

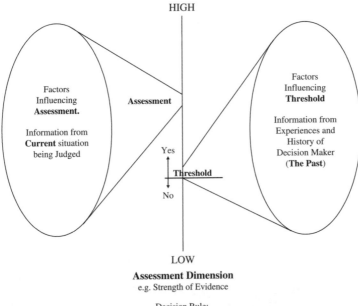

HIGH

Factors
Influencing
Assessment.

Assessment

Factors
Influencing
Threshold

Information from
Current situation
being Judged

Yes

Information from
Experiences and
History of
Decision Maker
(The Past)

Threshold

No

LOW

Assessment Dimension
e.g. Strength of Evidence

Decision Rule:
If the **Assessment** of the current situation is *above* the **threshold**, decide **Yes**.
If the **Assessment** of the current situation is *below* the **threshold**, decide **No**.

Figure 11.1 A general model for assessment and decision making (GADM).

taught them to give more weight to certain types of evidence than others. The case factors and to some extent their weight are reasonably easy to articulate. Cooksey (1996) reviews how to elicit and analyze the factors influencing the assessment. This chapter focuses on how to make explicit the factors influencing threshold placement. Since they are not case or situation factors, they are less easy to articulate.

An implication of the model is that it points to two different explanations for why different people when presented with the same evidence come to different decisions. Consider two judges presented with the same information in a motion hearing, where one chooses to grant the motion and the other denies it. According to the model, the difference in outcomes might come from differences in the assessment of the strength of evidence, but it may also arise from divergent thresholds for action, or from both causes combined. This chapter focuses on the implications of variation across people in their personal thresholds for action.

The left hand side of the model derives from Signal Detection Theory (SDT) (McNicol, 2004), which has had wide influence beyond its initial development for the interpretation of sensory processes in the 1950s. In the example above, the judge's task is to discriminate between two states: the motion should be granted and the motion should be denied. For a juror in a

Table 11.1 The Four Categories of Response in the Context of Juror Decision Making in Criminal Trials

	Should have convicted because defendant is truly guilty	Should have acquitted because defendant is truly innocent
You decide to convict	Correct Conviction (Hit)	Wrongful Conviction (False Alarm)
You decide to acquit	Wrongful Acquittal (Miss)	Correct Acquittal (Correct No)

criminal case, the task is to discriminate between two states: the defendant is guilty and the defendant is innocent. The "signal" the juror has to detect is the guilt of the defendant. This decision is made under uncertainty. Hammond (1996) argued that in all decision making there is irreducible uncertainty. This means that no matter what decision is made, deny or grant, convict or acquit, there is always the possibility of an error. The fourfold table makes explicit that there are two types of error. Table 11.1 illustrates this for the juror's task. The two types of error are Wrongful Acquittals, or misses, where the juror has missed the "signal," and Wrongful Convictions, or false alarms. For the judge's motion hearing example, the two types of error are "wrongful denial of the motion" and "wrongful granting."

There has been much interest in the relationship between the two types of errors. Volokh (1997) demonstrated that people have expressed a great many opinions about what the ratio of Wrongful Acquittals to Wrongful Convictions is or should be. One of those opinions is by the English jurist William Blackstone, who said, "Better that ten guilty persons escape than that one innocent suffer" (cited in Volokh, 1997). The ratio 10:1 has become known as the Blackstone Ratio (BR).

There has been considerable debate on the meaning of the numbers in the BR (Dekay, 1996). One view is that the numbers in the BR indicate frequencies in a population of cases. Assuming that jurors assess the likelihood of guilt as a probability, the numbers in the BR can be used to establish a "beyond reasonable doubt" probability against which they compare their assessed likelihood of guilt. Another view of the BR is that it captures the worth, utility, or value of one person's being wrongly convicted. Signal Detection Theory (SDT) combines these two views. In SDT, the decision maker is assumed to maximize the percentage of correct decisions and to maximize the utility of the decision. Using Bayes' theorem and Subjective Expected Utility theory, Coombs, Dawes, and Tversky (1970) give the formula for threshold placement in terms of the prevalence of "signals" and the utilities for the four possible outcomes in Table 11.1.

Dekay (1996), in the context of juror decision making, points out that the merit of SDT is that it separates two aspects of decision performance. These are the ability of the person to discriminate between the two states in Table 11.1 and the person's willingness to take action, their threshold placement. It can be equally helpful in analyzing judges' decisions on which side to err in considering a motion.

Studying Thresholds and Decisions to Take Action

In this section, we demonstrate studies designed to tap the factors influencing the threshold placement. Although the studies reported below use undergraduate students in simulated jury decision making, they could be adapted to use with judges making decisions such as motion decisions or any other decision able to be modeled by the GADM approach. The studies indicate that thresholds and the factors influencing them can be measured. This is important both theoretically and practically. The GADM model provides a theoretical account of disagreement between decision makers and provides a methodology for making the locus of the disagreement explicit. Practically, procedures can be developed to reduce the amount of disagreement and to make explicit the importance of values in the setting of thresholds for action.

Identifying Thresholds

The first study to be discussed was designed to test whether giving different definitions of the standard of proof shifted the threshold for beyond reasonable doubt, but we ignore that element of the study here.[3] Participants were given general information about a particular murder trial from South Australia, *Pfennig v. The Queen* (1995). This case was chosen because it was largely based on circumstantial evidence and was appealed through to the High Court of Australia. Table 11.2 gives a brief summary of the case.

Table 11.2 General Description of the Pfennig Case

Briefly, *Pfennig v The Queen* involved Peter Pfennig being charged with the murder of a 10-year-old boy named Michael Black. At trial, the Crown prosecutor argued that Pfennig had abducted Michael for sexual purposes and then killed him. Michael's body was never found. The Crown presented the court with much circumstantial evidence, including evidence of Pfennig talking to Michael at the last place that Michael was seen alive. The Crown also provided evidence that Pfennig had pleaded guilty to abducting and raping a 13-year-old boy almost one year after Michael disappeared. In that case Pfennig had placed his victim's belongings at the top of a cliff to encourage speculation that the victim had accidentally fallen. Similarly, Michael's belongings were found arranged neatly beside a river so as to suggest an accidental drowning.

Our approach to measuring thresholds was to present participants with 100 cases based on the Pfennig case. The hypothetical cases showed different combinations of seven different types of evidence that varied in amount. That is, each case was one way in which the evidence could have been. The types of evidence in the case were elicited from a group of lawyers who reviewed the trial and appeal transcripts. Figure 11.2 shows an example case. The cases were constructed so that there were two types of case that had overlapping distributions of strength of evidence. One set of 50 cases had an average of a high amount of evidence, 60 out of 100, and the other set had a low average amount of evidence, 40 out of 100.

Those with the high average were arbitrarily designated as "guilty," the signal, and those in the other set as "innocent." This is accord with the assumption that "if the legal process works at all, truly guilty defendants will, on average, appear more guilty than truly innocent defendants" (DeKay, 1996, p. 101). This procedure is analogous to studies on auditory signal

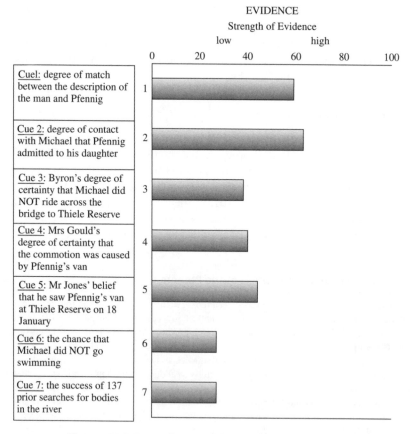

Figure 11.2 Example case vignette used in Study 1.

detection where the experimenter defines which stimuli are the "signals" and which are "no-signals" (Ryder, Pike, & Dalgleish, 1974). The important thing about this procedure is that it enables measurement of the threshold.

Three groups of 10 students from the University of Queensland participated as part of their course requirements. All participants were registered on the electoral roll as required by s.4 of the Jury Act 1995 (Queensland).

Each participant received information on the general case, definitions of the evidence cues, and practice cases. Each also received one of three different definitions of reasonable doubt. For each of the 100 hypothetical cases they made a judgment of the overall strength of evidence on a nine-point rating scale and made a decision whether to convict or acquit.

Table 11.3 shows a cross tabulation of the decisions made by two participants, chosen because they were given the same definition of reasonable doubt and their evaluations of the strength of evidence in different cases were quite similar. Despite these similarities, Juror C made 79 convict decisions whereas Juror A made 25 convict decisions. Their rates of Wrongful Convictions and Wrongful Acquittals differ considerably. Juror C is a "Convictor" because for a given case they need little evidence before they convict. On the other hand Juror A is an "Acquitter" and for a case needs much more evidence before they convict. Calculations from a Signal Detection Theory (SDT) analysis, Stainslaw and Todorov (1999), indicate that the index of threshold placement, $\ln(\beta)$, is -1.5 for Juror C and 1.2 for Juror A. Note that $\ln(\beta)$ is the natural logarithm of the threshold (or response criterion, to use SDT terminology). This index is useful because it is symmetrical around zero and is independent of the accuracy of the decision maker. It is negative when the participant has a decision tendency toward convicting. The differences in the decisions of these two

Table 11.3 Results for Two Participants

	Juror C		Juror A	
	"True State"		"True State"	
	Guilty	Innocent	Guilty	Innocent
Actual Decision: YES Convict	Hit	False Alarm (WC) 31	Hit	False Alarm (WC) 3
	48 96%	62%	22 44%	6%
Actual Decision: NO Acquit	Miss (WA) 2 4%	Correct No 19 38%	Miss (WA) 28 56%	Correct No 47 94%

participants are due to threshold differences, that is, differences in their threshold for beyond reasonable doubt.

Although these differences are particularly striking, we found considerable variation in willingness to convict among the participants. This is consistent with early experiments by Simon and Mahan (1971) showing a large variance in the way jurors interpret the phrase "beyond a reasonable doubt."

Judges could participate in a similar study. The instruction condition could be dropped and a relevant case to the sample of judges used and developed into a set of hypothetical cases. Of interest is the degree of variability in threshold across judges. An advantage of this methodology is that sufficient data is collected from each judge to enable the regularities in their decisions to be estimated (Cooksey, 1996). From the analysis of each judge's data their threshold and its standard error is estimated for each judge. Thus, a direct comparison of threshold placement between any two judges is available.

Exploring Differences in Thresholds

Consider Jurors A and C making a decision about the same case. Assume that they have worked hard on agreeing on the evidence in the case and they both assess the strength of evidence as "middling" on the overall strength of evidence scale, $J_A = J_B$. Figure 11.3 illustrates how differences in threshold, T_A and T_B, explain why Juror C decides to convict and Juror A decides to acquit.

SDT offers suggestions for accessing the locus of this variability. In SDT the threshold is determined by the base-rate or prevalence of the "signal" and the utilities for the outcomes in the fourfold table. In judicial decision making the "true" prevalence is not known. For example, in decisions about motions the proportion of motions that "should be denied" is not known and cannot

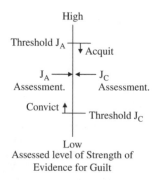

Figure 11.3 Conflict in decision making when there is agreement on the evidence.

be known. For the criminal trial, the proportion of "truly guilty" defendants is also not known. However, decision makers have beliefs about these proportions based on their experiences and history either directly or vicariously gained. That is, they have in mind a perceived prevalence that is their prior beliefs about the need to take action. This influence on the threshold is in place before the decision maker has any information about the current case or situation. Let $p(N_a)$ be the proportion of cases for which the decision maker believes they need to take action for a particular type of decision. If a decision maker has a high $p(N_a)$ then given the knowledge that they are about to see a case, they need less strength of evidence to decide yes than someone with a low $p(N_a)$.

The second theoretical influence on the threshold is a function of the utilities the decision maker has for each outcome in the fourfold table, Table 11.1. These utilities are subjective in that each decision maker has their own set of utilities and these derive from their experiences and history either directly or vicariously gained. If a decision maker wishes to avoid misses (Wrongful Acquittals), then they need less strength of evidence to decide yes than someone who wants to avoid False Alarms (Wrongful Convictions). In SDT both these influences are combined mathematically and captured in an index of threshold placement, $\ln(\beta)$.

In the next three studies to be briefly reported we attempt to measure the relative utilities and beliefs about the need to take action directly by eliciting people's prior beliefs about the prevalence of guilt. One view of the Blackstone Ratio is that it reflects the value people put on a Wrongful Acquittal compared to a Wrongful Conviction, that is, 10:1. We wanted to find out how people replied when we asked them for their own version of the BR directly and to look for variation in the elicited BR.

Thirty-six undergraduate Psychology students at Kansas State University participated. They were randomly assigned to three groups that received different labels for the standard of proof. Each participant was given a careful instruction individually. Participants were asked to imagine themselves on a jury, given a case to read, shown in Table 11.4, and asked to make a decision about whether to convict or acquit.

Table 11.4 Case Used in Study 2

A 32-year-old, Paul, was shot to death in his car outside Brooklyn, New York, at 11:30 pm on November 15, 2005.

The witness saw a man wearing black clothing who walked up to Paul and shot him several times as he was entering his car.

Paul was a restaurant manager. According to colleagues, he was friendly and successful.

However, he had financial problems with his ex-wife's boyfriend, John.

Police accused John of the murder, and a shoeprint matching one of John's shoes was found near the crime scene.

However, John said he was in bed with Paul's ex-wife at the time, and she confirms the fact.

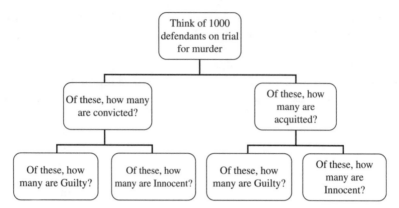

Figure 11.4 Diagram to elicit prior beliefs about guilt.

They were then asked to think about murder cases *in general* and asked this question to elicit their Blackstone Ratio, "**HOW MANY** truly guilty defendants charged with murder do you believe should be acquitted to avoid **ONE** truly innocent defendant being convicted?" To elicit their prior beliefs about guilt, they were asked to think about 1000 defendants before the court charged with murder. They filled out the boxes in Figure 11.4 by first thinking how many of the 1000 were convicted or acquitted. For those that were convicted they were asked to state how many did they think were truly guilty and how many were truly innocent. They did the same for those they thought were acquitted.

Results and Discussion

To calculate the participant's prior beliefs about guilt, the numbers in the first and third boxes from the left in Figure 11.4 were added and divided by 1000. There was large variability in the prior beliefs. The mean was .62 with a standard deviation of .19. The range was from .23 to .96. The interpretation is that when thinking generally about murder cases participants on average believed that 620 out of 1000 would be guilty. More worrying is the range with values of .80 or above for 7 participants and .40 or below for 5 participants. That is, without any evidence some participants had a strong tendency to convict whereas other had a strong tendency to acquit. The implication from the GADM model is that a sample of these participants serving on a jury would show decisional conflict as illustrated in Figure 11.3.

Table 11.5 presents the frequencies for the elicited Blackstone Ratio. The findings are quite variable with only 3 participants having a Blackstone ratio of 10 to 1 or greater. What is interesting is the fact that participants wanted no guilty defendants to be acquitted to avoid one wrongful conviction and that just over half the participants gave this as their answer. That is, most

Table 11.5 The Number of Wrongful Acquittals to Avoid One Wrongful Conviction

	Elicited Blackstone Ratios						
	0:1	1:1	2:1	3:1	4:1	10:1	100:1
Frequency	19	9	2	2	1	2	1
Percentage	53	25	5.6	5.6	2.8	5.6	2.8

participants wanted no truly guilty people to go free. It may also indicate that they do not understand the trade-off between Wrongful Acquittal and Wrongful Conviction. This may be because our participants probably had no experience with judicial processes. It would be very interesting to replicate this study with both judges and lawyers since they have directly experienced the judicial process. Of interest would be the variation in elicited prior beliefs about the prevalence of guilt within lawyers and judges as well as their elicited BR. We would expect that their elicited BR would be closer to spirit of the BR and have a high proportion of ratios greater than or larger than 10:1.

One difficulty with the design of this study is that participants did read a case and this may have contaminated the eliciting of prior beliefs about the prevalence of guilt and the Blackstone Ratio. In a third study, we elicited prior beliefs about the prevalence of guilt and the Blackstone ratio from participants without presenting any case material (or vignette). SDT suggests that the value of the consequences of Wrongful Acquittal compared to those for Wrongful Conviction influences the threshold for beyond reasonable doubt. That is, we wanted to know how potential jurors responded to the explicit tradeoff between Wrongful Acquittal and Wrongful Conviction and answer the question of how they value the two types of error.

Thirty-four students from an intermediate-level forensic psychology course in 2006 at Kansas State University participated. We elicited prior beliefs using the method from Study 2, Figure 11.4. The fourfold table for jury decision making was presented and explained in the context of irreducible uncertainty (Hammond, 1996). They were asked to write down on a sheet of paper in two columns the consequences of a Wrongful Conviction (defendant was convicted but was really innocent) and a Wrongful Acquittal (defendant was acquitted but was really guilty). They were asked the question: "Given that you can't avoid the possibility of an error, which error do you want to avoid the most?" This taps the relative utility of the two types of error. We then elicited their Blackstone Ratio as in Study 2.

Prior beliefs of guilt were distributed very similarly to those in Study 2, with a mean prior belief of .69, standard deviation of .15 and a range from .34 to .94. Seventy-nine percent (27/34) wanted to avoid Wrongful Convictions; but this means that 21% wanted to avoid Wrongful Acquittals, contrary to Blackstone. The results from the elicited Blackstone Ratio are similar to those

Table 11.6 The Number of Wrongful Acquittals to Avoid One Wrongful Conviction from Study 3

	Elicited Blackstone Ratios				
	0:1	1:1	2–7:1	10:1	10:1
Frequency	10	4	10	4	4
Percentage	31	12.5	31	12.5	12.5

from Study 2 with a sizable percentage not wanting to let any guilty people to go free, see Table 11.6. As in the other studies, there is wide variability.

The key message from a Blackstone Ratio of 10:1 is that the interests of the defendant are paramount. However, Volokh (1997, p. 211) cites the story of a Chinese law professor listening to a British lawyer state "it is better that 99 guilty men go free than that one innocent man be executed." The Chinese professor asked "Better for whom?" This may help with an explanation for the number of participants who wanted no guilty men to go free and the participants who wanted to avoid a Wrongful Acquittal. It may be that some participants have the defendant's interests as paramount but others may focus on the interests of society. Study 4 explores this explanation.

Consider the situation of a judge deciding to grant or deny a motion. For a particular type of motion, perhaps a frequently encountered type of motion, they will have beliefs about the prevalence with which such a type of motion should be granted. They will also have beliefs similar to those expressed in the BR. For example, how many motions should be wrongfully granted to avoid one wrongfully denied motion? Further, apart from the two adversaries before the judge, there are other stakeholders in the decision to grant or deny a motion, for example, the judge, society, and the "law."

There are many stakeholders in the criminal court, for example, the defendant, the lawyers, the judge, the jury members, the victims and their families, and society, to name some of them. The decisions made in court will have different consequences for different stakeholders. We think that when participants focus on the defendant as stakeholder, more will want to avoid Wrongful Convictions and that when focusing on society as stakeholder more will want to avoid Wrongful Acquittals. This could explain some of the variability in our studies reported so far. Further, using the idea that people with a conservative approach to justice would focus on the society as the main stakeholders and that those with a liberal approach would focus on the defendant as the main stakeholder, (Tetlock & Mitchell, 1993), we suggest that those who want to avoid Wrongful Convictions would identify themselves as more liberal.

Thirty-four students from an intermediate-level forensic psychology course in 2007 at Kansas State University participated. Prior beliefs were elicited as in Studies 2 and 3. The fourfold table was explained as in Study 3, and participants were asked to think about the defendant as stakeholder and write out the consequences for the two types of error. They were then asked to think about society as the stakeholder and wrote out the consequences for the two types of error, Wrongful Acquittal and Wrongful Conviction. Following this, we asked them which error they wanted to avoid the most with the defendant as stakeholder and then with society as stakeholder. They were also asked which stakeholder they thought was more important. We asked them to place their political views on a scale from 1 to 100 labeled "liberal" at the low end and "conservative" at the high end of the scale. We then elicited their Blackstone ratio as in Studies 2 and 3.

The results for prior beliefs for guilt were very similar to those from Studies 2 and 3. The mean was .623 with a standard deviation of .18 and a range from .13 to .91. This range does not seem to be a function of being an undergraduate student because it matched the range of prior beliefs elicited from seminar attendees at seminars given by Dalgleish for faculty and graduate students at some universities in the United States and the UK.

Table 11.7 presents the frequency with which participants wanted to avoid the two types of error by stakeholder. When considering the defendant, 76% wanted to avoid a Wrongful Conviction, whereas 26% wanted this when considering society. These two proportions are different using a McNemar's test, $\chi(1) = 73.5$, $p < 0.001$. Thus, the consideration of different stakeholders matters. The most important stakeholder was society for 21/34 (64%) of participants. The majority, 18/34 (53%), wanted to avoid Wrongful Convictions when considering the defendant and avoid Wrongful Acquittals when considering society.

What is the relationship between self-reported political views and the value placed on the consequences for different stakeholders? There were some weak relationships but all were in the expected directions. When thinking of the defendant as stakeholder those that wanted to avoid WCs had a more liberal political view ($N = 8$, $M = 52.2$) than those who wanted to avoid WAs

Table 11.7 Frequency of Desire to Avoid the Two Types of Error Depending on Stakeholder

		Society as Stakeholder		
		Wrongful Convictions	Wrongful Acquittals	Total
Defendant as stakeholder	Wrongful Convictions	8	18	26
				76
	Wrongful Acquittals	1	7	8
	Total	9	25	34
		26		

$(N = 26, M = 62.3)$, $t(30) = 1.42$, one-tail $p = .08$. This test has low statistical power because the sample sizes are small and the measure of political views was a simple one-item scale. It would be interesting to see if this effect is stronger if better measures of political views were used, such as those developed by Evans, Heath, and Lalljee (1996) and Mehrabian (1996). Those participants who said the defendant was more important had more liberal views, $(M = 50.2$ versus $M = 55.2$, $t(32) = 1.07$, one-tail $p = .15)$ but, while in the expected direction, this difference was not statistically significant.

The pattern for Blackstone's Ratio is similar to those for Studies 2 and 3. However, it is useful to tabulate the elicited BRs by which stakeholder was considered more important. Table 11.8 does this. There were 5 participants who stated their BR as not wanting any guilty defendants being free. We believe this category is separate from BRs that state that the participant wants at least one guilty defendant to go free. The participants with a BR of 0:1 may not have understood the question eliciting the BR or they have a particular interpretation of WA or WC or they really wanted no guilty defendants free. We calculated the mean political view for these 5 participants $(M = 72.3, SD = 21.8)$ and tested it against the mean for those 25 who said they wanted at least one guilty defendant free, $(M = 48.24, SD = 23.26)$. This difference is statistically significant, $t(29) = 2.36$, $p = .025$) showing that those who had a 0:1 BR rated themselves as more politically conservative. Combined over our 2nd, 3rd and 4th studies, 35 out of the 100 participants had an elicited BR of 0:1. The implication is that these people would be more conservative in their political views. Another implication is that in future research, the BR should be elicited using a different question that allows participants to state the ratio of WC to WA. For some of the participants who stated a 0:1 BR, their BR elicited using a different question may have been 1:10 or some ratio opposite to the direction of the ratio stated by Blackstone.

Excluding the 0:1 group, there were no differences in political view for those participants whose BR were <10:1 and for those with BRs ≥ 10:1. However, for those 10 participants with BRs ≥10:1 seven of them (70%) stated that the defendant was more important while for those that favored

Table 11.8 The Number of Wrongful Acquittals to Avoid One Wrongful Conviction from Study 4 by the Most Important Stakeholder

Most important stakeholder	Elicited Blackstone Ratios				
	0:1	1:1	2–7:1	10:1	>10:1
Defendant	2	1	2	5	2
Society	3	2	9	4	1
Equal	1	0	0	0	0
Total (N = 32)	6	3	11	9	3
Percentage	18.8	9.4	34.4	28.1	9.4

society 5/16 (31.3%) had BRs ≥10:1. These proportions were close to being significantly different, $\chi^2(1) = 3.72$, p = .054.

So when participants consider either the defendant or society, this influences their threshold since the relative costs of WC and WA change. However, which stakeholder is more important is not related to prior beliefs but is related to their Blackstone Ratio. From these results we could infer that the BR is more about values of consequences than about frequency (prior beliefs) (cf., Dekay, 1996).

From the GADM model there is the prediction that if two members of a jury have different thresholds, for example, one considers the defendant as a more important stakeholder and the other favors society, and they assess the strength of evidence as being the same in the case, then they will disagree about the verdict. Going back to the case evidence will not resolve this disagreement. There is a further implication of the GADM model from these findings. Consider a person from the group who wanted to avoid WC when considering the defendant and wanted to avoid WA when considering the society as stakeholder (the majority of participants). Let us assume one of them has a prior belief of guilt of 0.50 (neutral) and let them consider a case that does not have clear-cut evidence of guilt. Figure 11.5 illustrates this example with two possible thresholds for this juror. When considering the defendant the threshold is T_{def} and the assessment of the evidence is not sufficient to convict. When considering the society the threshold is $T_{society}$ and the evidence is sufficient to convict. This juror would be in a state of "internal decisional conflict" and would vacillate while trying to reach a verdict. This may be seen as indecision but searching the evidence is not going to resolve this internal conflict. The person needs to go with the stakeholder they evaluate as the most important and use the threshold for that stakeholder.

What are the implications of these findings for judges ruling on motions or other judicial decisions? The link between judicial decisions and political orientation, given the tentative evidence from Study 4, seems to lie not with

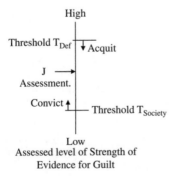

Figure 11.5 Internal decisional conflict within a juror.

the assessment of the evidence but with the relative importance of different stakeholders and the relative values of Wrongful Convictions and Wrongful Acquittals to the judge. The relative influence of the assessment of the evidence and prior beliefs about prevalence, the values of the two types of errors and the importance of the different stakeholders could be tested using a vignette study similar to our Study 1 together with the elicitation of the other factors developed for Studies 2, 3 and 4. More robust measures of political orientation would need to be used.

Conclusion

The data from the four studies indicates a tremendous amount of variation in *(1)* measured thresholds, and *(2)* measures of the influences on threshold. These were the prior beliefs about guilt and the error they wanted to avoid the most. Further there was considerable variation in the elicited Blackstone Ratios. Some of this variation was related to which stakeholder they thought most important or were considering and their self-reported political views. From the GADM model this variation in threshold for guilt, implies that, within jury trials, there will be considerable differences in verdicts reached that are not due to differences in the interpretation and assessment of the evidence.

While the data presented in this chapter has been with undergraduate students in simulated jury decision making, the aim has been to show that the methods could be generalized to judicial decision making. Whether the results of our studies generalize to other judicial decision making tasks is an empirical question. Throughout this chapter we have drawn parallels between the judicial task of deciding to deny or grant a motion and the jury task of deciding whether to convict or acquit a defendant. Further, we have suggested that our convict/acquit decision tasks could be used with judges and lawyers. The aim of these proposed studies would be to investigate the amount and variability in their thresholds for beyond reasonable doubt and in the theoretical influences on thresholds among judges and among lawyers and between judges and lawyers.

Similarly, the aim of the proposed studies on the judicial decision to deny or grant motions would be to investigate and document variation in the thresholds for action. If, for example, both trial judges and appellate judges did the same tasks, we could compare thresholds between pairs of judges. What are the implications of this? Let us consider a trial judge who has a tendency to deny motions of a particular type. Let us assume that some of the decisions are contentious enough to provide grounds for appeal. Now consider an appellate judge who reads the original submissions and decides against the original decision. Within the GADM model approach to the assessment of the original submissions and the decision to take action, the trial judge and the appellate judge may differ in their assessment or in their thresholds or both. It is important to isolate whether such differences in decisions are due to differences in the interpretation of the law or to differences in the values attached to the consequence of the decisions or to the judges' prior beliefs about the need to take action. In addition to the studies reported in this chapter, there seems anecdotal evidence, for example on websites such as "Decision of the Day"[4] that such differences of opinion exist. Investigating whether there is variation in the influences on the threshold is important because making such influences explicit to people enables discussion about them and provides ways of devising training to reduce the effects of decisional conflict. One of our studies found links between the relative importance of different stakeholders and political orientation and if such effects were found among judges and lawyers, it may inform and extend debate on the role of political orientation and judicial decision making. The GADM model and its associated methodologies provide a way to empirically study such issues.

Notes

Preparation of this chapter was supported by funds provided by the Scottish Funding Council to HealthQWest; A research consortium for the West of Scotland.

1. *U.S. v. Terry*, 392 U.S. 1 (1968).
2. Similarly, in applying the GADM model to verdicts, it is assumed that an assessment of the strength of evidence is made and a decision to convict is made if the assessment exceeds their threshold for action. This threshold depends on the level of proof needed to convict; for example, beyond reasonable doubt would be higher than the preponderance of the evidence.
3. Anna Rickard (1998) completed the study as an honors project at the University of Queensland.
4. http://www.enotes.com/blogs/decision-blog/

12

Every Jury Trial Is a Bench Trial: Judicial Engineering of Jury Disputes

C. K. Rowland, Tina Traficanti, and Erin Vernon

For decades virtually every scholarly work on civil trial courts and trial judges began by lamenting the unfortunate tendency of students of judicial behavior to concentrate almost exclusively on appellate courts generally and on the U.S. Supreme Court in particular. Fortunately, although this imbalance is still present to a degree, a nascent body of research has ameliorated the disparity and enhanced greatly our understanding of civil trial courts, trial judges, and the psychology of trial judging over the last decade.

This growth in attention to trial courts has, of course, included traditional legal analysis and over 25 years of sophisticated, multidisciplinary attention to all levels of criminal courts (Jacob, 1983; Gibson, 1980); however, studies of civil trial judges' behavior have, generally speaking, either pursued a political track, which studied trial judges as political actors by reference to appellate judicial behavior (Baum, 2007), or a "juror" track marked by explicit or implicit comparisons with juror behavior (Robbennolt, 2005).

Political studies, especially judicial comparisons have, not surprisingly, been primarily (but not exclusively) conducted by political scientists, and have borrowed heavily from the study of appellate judicial behavior and the influence of extralegal factors on that behavior (Rowland & Carp, 1996; Buchman, 2007). Relying almost exclusively on federal trial judges' published opinions (but see Rowland & Carp, chap. 4 re unpublished opinions), judicial scholars have found that for politically salient issues, such as abortion-related disputes, federal trial judges' published decisions can be predicted to an impressive degree by extralegal factors, such as the appointing president

(Carp & Rowland, 1983; Buchman, 2007). Moreover, these appointment effects tend to be most pronounced for ideologically relevant categories of cases that were important to the appointing president and served as "litmus test" appointment criteria (Carp & Rowland, 1983). Although still subject to appropriate criticisms regarding theories and methods (see below), the consistency of these findings is impressive, suggesting a value-based exercise of judicial discretion that may reflect intentional or unintentional bias in trial judging when the dispute involves ideological issues important to the judge and the appointing president.

Juror comparisons, most of which have been conducted by attorneys, law-school professors, and psychologists working in the law and psychology realm, have relied on a much wider variety of methodologies, ranging from archival analysis to surveys, to experimental designs to compare explicitly or implicitly the decisions of jurors and judges faced with similar decision stimuli and criteria (Blanck, 1991; Eisenberg et al., 2005; Robbennolt, 2005; Kalven & Zeisel, 1966). In the civil arena, this approach is exemplified by comparisons of judges' and jurors' willingness to award punitive damages (Eisenberg et al., 2002), ignore potentially biasing information (Landsman & Rakos, 1994), and the difficulty of ignoring inadmissible evidence (Wistrich et al., 2005). Although the results of these comparisons differ in their details, the key, consistent finding across multiple issues is that judicial decisions and juror decisions made under similar constraints are remarkably similar. Particularly interesting in this context is research that implicitly compares jurors and judges by focusing on judges' ability to understand complex evidence and/or apply legal standards that rely on scientific or statistical concepts. These studies are remarkably consistent in their finding that when faced with science-based standards (Gatowski et al., 2001), statistical evidence (Guthrie, et al., 2001), and other risk-assessment tasks, judges are susceptible to many of the same limits on objectivity and accuracy—for example, hindsight bias and framing effects—that plague jurors and all human decision makers faced with difficult judgments (Dhami, 2005).

Call for Synthesis and a Refocused Research Program

It is interesting and instructive to compare the political and juror tracks summarized above. Most striking is an obvious anomaly—the trial judges studied by political scientists turn out to resemble closely appellate judges and other political actors, but the trial judges studied by comparison with jurors turn out to behave much like jurors. This apparent anomaly is in large part the product of different research targets, methods, and theoretical perspectives (Baum, 2006; Braman, 2006b). It serves, however, as a reminder that the parallel research paths summarized above have left a large lacuna in our understanding of trial judges and trial-judge behavior, in part because one approach rarely acknowledges the contributions of the other (for a recent exception, see Buchman, 2007).

The political approach has done a good job of identifying variation among trial judges (at least federal trial judges) in "natural settings" and the extralegal correlates of that variation, but this approach has largely limited itself to atypical, politically relevant published decisions and has paid precious little attention to myriad unpublished decisions made by thousands of trial judges in thousands of trial courts—state and federal—every day (see Rowland & Carp, 1996, for an exception). Equally limiting has been the tendency of political studies to simply ignore or assume away the psychology under-lying the pattern of extralegal influences identified by their research. Juror comparisons, while they have done a much better job of addressing a wide variety of decisions that define everyday trial judging and are much more sophisticated regarding psychological theories of human judgment, have paid precious little attention to variation among judges in these decisions, especially to the legal and extralegal correlates of these decisions in natural settings.

The anomalous state of current research suggests that the time has come for synthesis—a research program that will, like the juror path, focus on decisions that define what most trial judges do most of the time and, like the judicial path, examine variation and the reasons for variation in these decisions in natural settings.

Trial Judges and Jury Trials

We believe that the most fertile ground for this synthesis is a research program aimed at understanding the behavior of trial judges in the context of jury disputes—that is, civil disputes in which one or both litigants exercise their constitutional right to a jury trial. In the remainder of this essay, we justify our call for a research program focused on jury disputes in natural settings and describe our expectations regarding what we will learn about judging and trial-judge behavior from the research.

Justification for Refocus on Jury Disputes

As suggested by the title of this essay, every civil trial is in important ways a bench trial, with evidence and, to some degree, outcomes "engineered" by the trial judge. Yet, with notable exceptions discussed below, most recent research has devoted little attention, especially in natural settings, to judicial participation in the resolution of civil disputes in which litigants demand a jury trial. Indeed, unlike students of the criminal justice process, who have for years focused on judges as participants in a "courtroom workgroup" whose members share an interest in efficient resolution of criminal disputes (Jacob, 1983), most students of civil trial judges and civil trial judging have explicitly or implicitly drawn a bright line between bench trials and "jury disputes," regardless of whether the dispute is ultimately resolved by a jury or resolved prior to a jury trial.

We believe that the current vacuum is ironic and unfortunate for several reasons. First, in thousands of disputes in thousands of trial courts every day, what the constitutional right to a jury trial actually guarantees citizens is the right to a trial in which a jury decides a dispute largely defined and engineered by the exercise of judicial discretion. These discretionary exercises of judicial judgment answer key questions—for example, what evidence the jury will hear and who among their fellow citizens will constitute their jury—and almost always favor one side or the other and greatly influence the likely resolution of the dispute. Because they favor one side or the other, judges' jury-dispute rulings define the likelihood of trial outcomes and are instrumental in determining whether a case will settle and, if so, which party gains the most favorable terms of settlement. Thus, the architecture of the right to a jury is in the constitution, but the engineering is left largely to the discretion of trial judges.

Second, resolving disputes in the context of an anticipated or actual jury trial is what most trial judges in state and federal district courts do much of the time, whether that resolution is via dismissal, settlement, or a jury verdict. This means that in the aggregate these decisions have a potential social importance that parallels their importance to individual litigants. Moreover, in the context of modern mass torts, where one trial judge may "manage" thousands of similar cases, judicial decisions in a crucial bellwether case engineer the legal and evidentiary context for thousands of potential jury trials. From a research perspective, the ubiquity of judicial engineering focuses inquiry in an unprecedented variety of legal and extralegal contexts, all of which serve as potentially important institutional constraints on behavior. Exemplar contextual variation includes differences in standards for cause strikes or admissibility of expert testimony, differences in how judges are selected, and differences in the extent to which the jurisdiction has been a target of tort reform and counter–tort reform campaigns.

Third, the study of judicial behavior in the context of a jury trial is important because most engineering judgments require judges to exercise a great deal of discretion, which maximizes the potential influence of subjective factors on those judgments and creates a unique opportunity to examine the interplay of legal and extralegal influences on trial-judge behavior. Moreover, the potential for extralegal factors to influence the exercise of engineering discretion is exacerbated by the fact that many engineering decisions—for example, rulings on motions for cause strikes—are reviewable only if there is evidence of judicial "abuse of discretion."

The scope of this discretion and the plethora of opportunities to exercise discretion in the course of a jury dispute make judicial engineering of jury disputes an ideal avenue for more insight into trial judges' behavior. Key individual variation includes, for example, whether the judge's pre-bench practice was primarily on behalf of civil plaintiffs, defendants, or neither, and the extent to which the judge's selection (whether via appointment or election) was supported by the plaintiffs' bar or by corporate defendants, or neither. (It is no exaggeration to say that, given the highly politicized nature of judicial selection in the federal and in many state systems, many federal and state trial judges would be struck for cause and most others would be subjected to a peremptory strike by one side or the other in many jury disputes.)

Finally, the evidence that trial judges are susceptible to biased assimilation (Lord et al., 1979, p. 119), hindsight bias (Guthrie, Rachlinski, & Wistrich, 2001), anchoring (Chapman & Bornstein, 1996) and other "cognitive illusions" (Robbennolt, 2005), suggests strongly that when faced with complex decisions and ambiguous evidence, trial judges will make decisions (whether consciously or not) that reflect the biases and motivations associated with their prebench experiences. A focus on trial judges' behavior in thousands of natural settings will not only let us test empirically the extent to which findings associated with atypical published decisions are replicated for more typical exercises of discretion but will also help us learn more about the utility of social science for explaining the exercise of everyday judicial discretion.

Specific Ways in Which Every Civil Jury Trial Is a Bench Trial

Experienced litigators accept as a truism that the exercise of judicial discretion can essentially obviate the distinction between jury trials and bench trials at every stage of the jury dispute, ranging from pretrial gate keeping, to rulings during trial, to posttrial modification of a jury verdict. However, it may be appropriate to specify for a social science audience several specific typical engineering decisions that create—indeed, require—the exercise of essentially unbridled judicial discretion. Jury disputes follow a predictable sequence requiring numerous judicial rulings on key issues ranging from jurisdiction and evidence to jury selection and posttrial modification of jury decisions. As reflected in the examples below, most of the opportunities for judicial engineering are issues hotly contested by the parties, and rulings tend to favor one side or the other. Key opportunities for judicial engineering and the exercise of judicial discretion include, but are not limited to, the following:

Pretrial

1. Jurisdiction. The trial judge's initial decisions regarding jurisdiction issues can exert a tremendous influence on likely outcomes, especially when the

choice to be exercised is between a federal and a state jurisdiction. Federal and state rules tend to be very different regarding key elements of a jury trial—for example, the conduct of voir dire—and federal jurisdictions tend to be larger and include more diversity of attitudes and demographics among jurors than do many state jurisdictions.

2. Discovery. The trial judge in a jury dispute can begin to shape the scope of the trial and the evidence jurors will hear from the outset of the discovery process by ruling, for example, on the number of depositions to be allowed; time limits for depositions and for the completion of discovery overall; whether to require further answers to written discovery or deposition responses; and whether access to medical records of the claimant is limited in any way.

3. Trial Date. Something seemingly as innocuous as the setting of the trial date can also benefit one side over the other, given, for example, issues with witnesses and party availability or the greater need of one party for more extensive discovery.

4. Pretrial Publicity and Change of Venue. Although disputes over pretrial publicity and motions for a change of venue are commonly associated with criminal disputes, these issues can be important in civil disputes as well. For example, local publicity in Houston regarding the Enron scandal generally and the treatment by Enron of its employees in particular raised the same publicity and venue issues in the civil claims brought by former Enron employees—most of whom had lost their life savings—as were raised by the defendants in the Enron criminal case.

5. Motions to Dismiss or for Summary Judgment. Perhaps the most obvious judicial intervention, at first blush, is the court's rulings on dispositive motions, such as Motions to Dismiss or Summary Judgment Motions. An extremely important component of this decision set is the decision to include or not include claims for punitive damages. Because the presence of punitive damages increases dramatically the defendant's potential exposure, this decision literally defines the "stakes" of the case. Moreover, it usually includes significant judicial discretion based on ambiguous standards, such as "malice" or willfulness and a projection of likely impact of evidence on a jury. Dismissal of some causes of action or partial grants of summary judgment also narrow the scope of the dispute in ways that typically favor one side or the other.

6. Motions in Limine. Motions in limine serve, by their nature, to narrow the scope of evidence presented at trial and may exclude key testimony or arguments, thus limiting what the jurors will hear and how they assess other evidence and witnesses. Many of these decisions are made on the eve (or morning) of trial and have a tremendous impact on the context and likely

outcome of the trial itself. Not surprisingly, many cases settle shortly after these rulings are made.

7. Motions regarding admissibility of expert witnesses and testimony. There are a multitude of preliminary decisions, leading up to the court's ultimate ruling, that can determine how the court will handle its "gate-keeping" function as it relates to expert testimony, all of which may dramatically alter the course of the trial. The judge has within his or her power to decide whether to hold a hearing at all, whether the hearing is evidentiary in nature and should include witness testimony, and which factors to employ in determining "reliability" of testimony. Because the motions are usually filed by defendants seeking to exclude plaintiffs' expert testimony, the rulings often define at an early stage which party has the higher evidentiary ground. Given the influence of these admissibility rulings for both parties, it is no accident that they are usually hotly contested, with extensive briefings and adversarial argumentation.

During Trial

1. Jury Selection. There can be little dispute that the demographics, background, education, experience and attitudinal bent of each individual juror is a critical component of how a jury dispute will eventually be resolved. The judge exercises great power and influence over the jury selection process, the ultimate makeup of the jury, and therefore, the verdict they will likely render by deciding: whether or not to strike jurors for cause; the number of peremptory challenges allowed to each side; the reasons accepted or rejected for hardship excuses; whether multiple plaintiffs or defendants are treated singly or as a group for peremptory challenges; how many strikes each side gets when the dispute involves multiple plaintiffs and/or defendants; whether a supplemental juror questionnaire is allowed, and, if so, what questions and what response options are permitted; whether attorneys can conduct their own voir dire or not; how much discretion is given to attorneys in conducting voir dire regarding scope of questions and latitude to introduce case themes and facts. These jury-selection judgments, virtually untouchable at the appellate level, define the right to a jury trial in practice perhaps more than any other exercise of judicial discretion.

2. Evidentiary Rulings. Evidentiary rulings do not stop once the trial begins. Interpretation of the rules of evidence and the amount of leeway given on issues like hearsay, laying proper evidentiary foundations, relevance, prejudicial effect, and to what extent, if at all, an expert witness can testify beyond the material contained in the four-corners of his/her report are judicial opportunities to impinge on the province of the jurors to decide a dispute, by limiting or expanding what it is those jurors will hear as evidence in the case.

3. Rulings on the Use of Demonstratives and Graphics. Another arena for judicial engineering is in the area of visual evidence: whether graphics or

demonstratives, including highly sophisticated animations, proffered by either side, depict accurately what it is they are purporting to demonstrate; when the attorney is permitted to introduce the demonstratives (opening statement?); limitations on which witnesses can use them to illustrate their testimony, and so forth, can color jurors' views of key evidence in the case. These rulings are especially important when, as in the case of many torts, one or both sides submit animations that essentially reify disputed events—for example, automobile accidents—in ways that significantly benefit one side or the other.

4. Rulings on Courtroom Etiquette. The form and content of objections, whether speaking objections are permitted, where attorneys must stand in the courtroom, whether they must use a podium to address the jury, and to what extent they can invade the "personal space" of the witness on the stand would, by all appearances, be neutral, and yet such procedural formalities may very well play to the strengths or weaknesses of the individual attorneys presenting the case for each side.

5. "Cues" from the Bench. There are myriad ways in which the trial judge, either consciously or unconsciously, can reveal his or her views or opinions of either side's witnesses, evidence, and arguments during the course of the trial. The manner of ruling on objections with each side's attorneys—tone of voice, facial expressions, sarcasm, and whether that manner is visited equally on each litigant's counsel; whether and to what extent the judge admonishes participants in the trial in front of the jury—witnesses and attorneys alike; whether and to what extent the judge visibly reacts to evidence presented— verbally or through facial expressions and/or other physical cues (body language) have the ability to influence juror reaction to those same witnesses, evidence or arguments. Moreover, most of the nonverbal cues are not recorded in the transcript and are, therefore, immune from appellate review (see Blanck et al., 1985).

6. Jury Instructions and Verdict Form. The language and content, emphasis, tone, and inflection of the trial judge when reading the jury instruction, the discretionary instructions that are utilized, and the Verdict Form itself— general versus special questions, the order of the questions—are all ruled on by the trial court and are critical to shaping the way in which jurors deliberate about the case and the verdict that they reach. At the risk of stating the obvious, even subtle differences in the questions the jury is asked to answer can go a long way toward determining the probable answer, again in ways that favor one side or the other.

7. Juror Deliberations. Once the jurors begin to deliberate, the trial court judge's influence does not end. The judge controls how long jurors deliberate, the schedule on which they are required to be in court, and how to respond to juror questions. Perhaps most importantly, the judge determines whether and when an Allen Charge, or other less incendiary alternatives suggested by the

American Bar Association, is warranted and can alter the language of the charge in subtle but important ways that determine the likelihood of a verdict or a mistrial.

Posttrial

Through posttrial motions—JNOV (Judgment Notwithstanding the Verdict), Motions for a New Trial, and Motions to Modify Damages—the trial court can nullify the jury's conclusion or alter it substantially—for example, by significantly reducing damages. At the extreme, such decisions have the potential to nullify not only the jury decision, but also to nullify the litigants' right to a jury trial.

It is obvious from this partial listing of discretion points that most of the decisions made in this context offer the trial judge a great deal of discretion to engineer process, content, and outcome probabilities with limited appellate guidance or threat of appellate reversal, a condition that maximizes the potential for variation in judge's behavior and the extralegal correlates of this behavior and demonstrates the importance of research that helps us understand judicial behavior in this context. We next propose a theoretical framework that we believe will most effectively guide inquiry into judicial engineering of jury trials.

Theoretical Framework

In this section we outline a proposed theoretical framework for a research program that focuses on the behavior of trial judges in jury disputes and the extralegal influences on that behavior. At first blush, one would expect our proposal to focus research on judicial behavior in natural settings to rely on theories of judicial behavior associated with political inquiry into extralegal influences on federal judges in natural settings. Unfortunately, with a few notable exceptions (Baum, 2006a; Rowland & Carp, 1996; Braman, 2006b), most of these studies have been either atheoretical or have relied rather uncritically on adaptation of preference-based theories and rational-choice models of strategic decision making (Epstein & Knight, 2000; Baum, 2006) developed in the context of appellate judicial behavior (Carp & Rowland, 1983; Buchman, 2007). Although political scholars have engaged in a healthy debate regarding the extent to which judges' "voting" their preferences may be bounded by institutional constraints (Baum, 2006; Epstein & Knight, 1998), their common assumption is that, to the extent possible under institutional constraints, judges are motivated by their policy preferences and their votes are strategic reflections of these preferences. Indeed, two of the leading scholars in the field have speculated that when judges explain their decisions by reference to legal reasoning, they may be "posturing" for the benefit of external audiences (Epstein & Knight, 1998).

It is, of course, one thing to say that judicial policy makers on the Supreme Court, who are expected to make policy for lower courts, are motivated by their policy preferences. It is quite another thing to assume that a state trial judge's jury-dispute rulings, many of which are reached in a context that affords the judge a great deal of discretion, are nothing more than the judge's expression of his/her preferred outcomes and personal biases. To do so in the context of fact-finding is quite literally to accuse a judge who has taken an oath against bias of violating his/her oath of office (Braman, 2006a; Rowland & Carp, 1996). Therefore, setting aside debate regarding the utility of preference-based models for the study of appellate courts and appellate judicial "votes," we believe that attempts to extend this paradigm to the study of extralegal influences on trial judge's decisions in jury disputes are fundamentally flawed and correctable only by abandoning the paradigm in favor of social psychological approaches that take seriously and respect the common insistence by trial judges that they are not biased in favor of their personal preferences (Edwards, 1998).

It is therefore incumbent on us to offer an alternative that takes seriously the judicial oath and the underlying psychology of human judgments but also accommodates the empirically based expectation that the exercise of judicial discretion in jury disputes will vary significantly among judges and that this variation will be correlated significantly with extralegal factors, many of which will be unacknowledged by the judge or the record.

Motivated Reasoning and Judicial Engineering

Rowland and Carp (1996) took a first step in this direction a decade ago. We started with the premise that any useful theory of trial judging had to reconcile the anomaly outlined above—that is, how trial judges' decisions, at least in their published opinions, could be predicted with remarkable accuracy by extralegal, ideology-driven variables when these same judges, including judges who acknowledged and were sensitive to their own policy predilections, insisted that their decisions were based on unbiased legal reasoning subject to the constraints imposed by the law and the facts before them (Baum, 1997). To accommodate this apparent anomaly, we turned to social psychology and adapted concepts from social cognition and social judgment theory to create an eclectic, rather primitive, general model of trial judging based on the assumption that trial judges, like jurors, are cognitive misers who, when faced with ambiguous decision criteria that exceed their cognitive capacity to resolve episodically, must process the evidence via existing schemata and rely on judgment heuristics—for example, the availability heuristic. Motives, according to this formulation, were essentially irrelevant in the context of judgment tasks whose complexity and ambiguity forced trial judges, like all human judges, to rely on cognitive shortcuts to make sense of otherwise unmanageable decision cues. The apparent anomaly, therefore, was theorized to be the product of what Robbennolt (2005) has appropriately labeled "cognitive illusions"—that is, unrecognized psychological biases such as anchoring or hindsight bias (Guthrie et al., 2001).

More recently, Eileen Braman (2006a; Braman & Nelson, 2007) has improved significantly on our initial effort by adapting a more refined social psychological model of "motivated reasoning" to judicial settings. Braman's work does not examine trial judging per se, but her adaptation of motivated reasoning; unlike the assumed preference-based motives in previous political studies, recognizes implicitly the complexity of the interface between motives and the kinds of engineering judgments required of trial judges in jury disputes. Moreover, a basic extension of motivated reasoning to judicial engineering of jury disputes is straightforward. As articulated succinctly by Kunda (1990) and Lodge and Taber, 2000) theories of Motivated Reasoning assume that human decision makers faced with complex, ambiguous judgment criteria are motivated by two sets of goals, both of which are potentially present when judges exercise judgment in the context of a jury dispute. On the one hand, human judges are motivated by "accuracy" goals—"to arrive at an accurate conclusion, whatever it may be" (Kunda, 1990). This goal set is, of course, consistent with the fact that trial judges share legal training, which includes training in legal reasoning and socialization to legal norms. Thus, when they participate in jury disputes, trial judges should be motivated in part by the shared legal constraints and norms that define their profession and are expressed in their oath of office—that is, they are committed to unbiased decisions that accurately reflect the evidence and law on which those decisions are based. A large body of research has demonstrated empirically the importance of accuracy goals in a variety of settings. Moreover, several characteristics of accuracy goals are particularly important for application of motivated reasoning models to jury disputes. For example:

- Accuracy goals tend to be most prominent in situations where subjects' judgments are made in public and/or subjects are expected to justify their judgments to others (Kunda, 1990). No matter how much discretion a trial judge has, his/her most important jury-dispute decisions are made and/or announced publicly and recorded in the court record; moreover, regardless of the standard for review, they must be justified to the litigants and their attorneys, and an appellate court must be convinced that the judge did not abuse his/her discretion.
- Decision makers whose judgments are public are less susceptible to biases and "cognitive illusions," such as priming (Tetlock, 1985); however, there is no indication that accuracy goals attenuate the effects of other, more fundamental "illusions," such

as hindsight bias or inappropriate reliance on the availability heuristic when decision criteria are complex and/or ambiguous (Kunda, 1990; Lodge & Taber, 2000). Thus, we have every reason to expect that trial judges will be motivated by accuracy goals, but that, no matter how committed they are to accuracy goals, trial judges in jury disputes will at the same time be susceptible to many of the same "cognitive illusions" identified in extant research. Moreover, these illusions are likely to be most apparent in the resolution of complex issues and the evaluation of ambiguous evidence.

- The influence of cognitive illusion is accentuated when subjects are required to make judgments under time pressures. As discussed more fully below, trial judges are *always* under formal or informal pressure to "move their docket" and dispose of disputes rather than clogging the system and creating backlogs. Thus, we would expect biases to potentially compromise accuracy goals and influence judgment more in courts with greater time pressures than in courts with less pressure.

Research associated with accuracy goals is certainly consistent with a view of trial judges as motivated to judge the relevant evidence and law as accurately as possible but limited in their ability to do so by circumstance and their propensity to cognitive illusion. However, models of Motivated Reasoning also assume that human decision makers are motivated by what Kunda calls "directional goals"—that is, "the motive to arrive at a particular, directional conclusion" (p. 480). Kunda points out that such goals are seldom unconstrained; rather, directionally motivated judges attempt to be rational and to construct a justification that "would persuade a dispassionate observer." (p. 483) They maintain an "illusion of [their own] objectivity" (Pyszczynski & Greenberg, 1987) by searching their memory for beliefs and rules that could support their desired conclusion. The illusion is maintained because subjects engaged in motivated reasoning, "do not realize that the process is biased by their own goals, that they are accessing only a subset of their relevant knowledge, that they would probably access different beliefs and rules in the presence of different directional goals, and that they might even be capable of justifying opposite conclusions on different occasions" (p. 483). Importantly for the research program proposed here, research has shown that directional goals may bias some of the judgments trial judges are called on to make in jury disputes. For example, directional motivation affects the evaluation of scientific evidence because, in Kunda's words, "people motivated to disbelieve evidence are less likely to believe it, and there is some evidence that this outcome is mediated by differential processing of the information" (Ginossar & Trope, 1987). This prediction is, of course, consistent with Buchman's (2007) finding that appointees of Republican presidents are more likely to rule in favor of defense motions to strike plaintiffs' scientific evidence and witnesses than are the appointees of Democratic presidents.

In sum, models of motivated reasoning predict that when human judges, with or without robes, are faced with difficult decisions and discretionary decision criteria, the interface between accuracy and directional goals, and cognitive illusion is complex and situational. Moreover, these goals and the interface between them should be especially salient where, as in the case of jury disputes, well-defined alternative accuracy and directional outcomes are often argued in briefs or motions and verbally in open court, as in "the court should do (directional) because (accuracy)." However, to maximize the utility of these models for trial judging in jury disputes, we propose an extension of motivated reasoning in trial judges to include a third potential set of goals and an elevated attention to the audiences associated with trial judges and trial judging.

Administrative Goals

As with many political actors, all trial judges are subjected to important time constraints on their discretion as gatekeepers and judicial engineers, and on their pursuit of accuracy goals. All are expected by their appellate and administrative principals to "manage their docket," and to achieve a case disposition rate that does not overburden their peers or deny a speedy trial to litigants. Indeed, since many states have adopted unified systems of judicial administration, federal and state judges' case disposition records are published and evaluated annually (Administrative Office, annual). The most important and obvious incentive created by administrative goals is the incentive to settle cases. Nothing wreaks more havoc with a trial judge's case backlog than a long jury trial, or series of jury trials, each of which is recorded at the end of the trial as one case resolution. Nothing alleviates this problem more than a settlement or dismissal, both of which are typically also recorded as one case disposition. Therefore, if models of Motivated Reasoning are adapted to studies of participation of trial judges in jury trials, we believe they should direct specific attention to the relative influence of administrative as well as accuracy and directional goals. Having said this, we recognize that administrative goals could in theory be accommodated by a judge's directional goal set—that is, rapid case disposition as desired direction. However, this is qualitatively different from motivation to arrive at a particular substantive conclusion. Moreover, as with plea bargaining in the criminal context, these administrative goals are, of course, shared by judges of diverse policy predispositions and may dominate other directional goals and accuracy goals, especially when judges are faced with external case-disposition pressures. These administrative goals may conflict with substantive directional goals because the desire to move his/her docket may conflict with a judge's desired substantive outcome, and with accuracy goals because the time necessary to maximize accuracy may cause unwanted delays. Therefore, for purposes of the research program proposed here, we believe that the assumption of administrative goals should be given independent status and introduced into the mix with directional and accuracy goals.

Audience

In our adaptation of motives to jury disputes, we expect that the trial judge involved in a jury dispute will have multiple motives, and that the absolute and relative salience of the three motive sets will vary significantly among jurisdictions, among judges within jurisdictions, and among dispute categories. Moreover, we believe that the relative saliency of each motive will be influenced by the relative importance of multiple "audiences" to the judge. Larry Baum has introduced this important concept of "audiences" to the general study of judicial behavior (Baum, 1997, 2006).

Borrowing heavily from psychological models of self-presentation, Baum assumes, axiomatically:

1. People want to be liked and respected by others who are important to them;
2. The desire to be liked and respected affects peoples' behavior;
3. In these respects, robes notwithstanding, judges are people.

For Baum, potentially important judicial audiences are numerous, ranging from appellate justices, to the general public, to members of the executive and legislative branches, to social and professional groups, to the media. Thus, some audiences, which we will label "task audiences," may be important for professional validation, while others, which we will call "expressive audiences," may be important for elevating the individual's self-esteem. For our purposes, audiences may be divided analytically into "accuracy," "administrative," and "directional" audiences. However, the distinction among these audience types is frequently blurred, and all three types of audiences may be important influences on judicial engineering of jury disputes.

Baum's adaptation of "a multiple audience perspective" to judicial settings is particularly helpful for inquiry into the behavior of trial judges in jury disputes. Because judicial decisions are a special case of "expressive choice" their decisions "link judges to particular values and to others who share those values. . . . By taking positions, judges align themselves implicitly with groups whose positions are consistent with theirs" (2006, p. 47). Moreover, trial judges at jury trials arguably have more potential audiences than do judges higher in the judicial hierarchy. Second, the importance of audience and audience approval may be more important for trial judges than for their appellate brethren. For example, the importance of audience is most apparent in jurisdictions where judges are elected, where the electorate and sources of campaign support are crucial audiences. Indeed, in the course of a jury trial, representatives from multiple audiences, including sources of electoral success or failure, are present in the courtroom and are eyewitnesses to many of the crucial *public* decisions that make a jury trial a bench trial. Finally, the context of jury disputes also enhances the potential importance of audience relative to appellate settings. Whether at pretrial hearings or during trial, the judge must make judgments and justify those judgments face-to-face with audiences—ranging from law-school classmates, to important donors, to officers in the state bar associations—whose success or failure may depend on those judgments.

In our adaptation of "audience" to judicial engineering of jury disputes, we expect that the trial judge involved in a jury dispute will have multiple audiences; that the quantity and qualitative importance of these audiences will vary significantly among jurisdictions, among judges within jurisdictions, and across disputes. We expect that this variation in audience will help explain variation in jury-dispute judgments, including the reasons given for these judgments, and we expect that variation in audiences will interact with variation among accuracy, directional, and administrative goals in ways that help us understand variation in judicial behavior in jury disputes.

Methodological Opportunities

Although the juror track has produced more methodological sophistication and variety than has the judicial/political approach to the study of judicial behavior, both tracks have relied almost exclusively on quantitative methods of analyzing their data, whatever the data's source. Indeed, this emphasis on quantification is an important part of what distinguishes social science scholarship in this area from traditional legal analysis. In this section we propose an extension of quantitative methods to the study of judicial engineering in jury disputes; however, we also outline some important opportunities created for a sophisticated application of underutilized qualitative methods.

Qualitative Methods

Applications of quantitative methods in current scholarship have established at high levels of confidence that, for disputes that are politically salient and offer judges' sufficient discretion, trial judges can vary significantly in their responses to similar disputes and that this variation correlates significantly with key value-based background variation, such as the judge and his/her appointing president's support for, or opposition to, a woman's right to choose. The most recent efforts in this area have included logistic regression models, which have helped us understand the relative influence of value-based variables and other variables, including institutional variables (Buchman, 2007). Scholars working in the law and psychology tradition have appropriately quantified findings ranging from descriptive analysis of survey responses (Gatowski et al., 2001) to aggregative comparison of judge-juror decision proclivities (Hersch & Viscusi, 2004), to multivariate analysis of data from experimental designs (Robbennolt, 2005). Each of these methodologies, including quantification of results, has obvious and potentially productive application to studies of judicial engineering of jury disputes. For example, one particularly intriguing possibility is an experimental design reversing aspects of judge-jury comparisons—for example, how do retired judges rule on *Daubert* motions when viewing alternative argumentation or offered alternative information regarding the identities of the parties. However, we believe that the research program proposed here also creates some important opportunities to benefit from underutilized qualitative approaches.

A research program that examines judicial behavior in the context of jury disputes, especially if framed in ways that respect judge's own descriptions of their judgments and the reasoning underlying those judgments, creates a rich set of unmined opportunities for harvesting insights available via qualitative analysis. Three exemplar avenues of opportunity are:

- *Content Analysis.* Many jury disputes produce a voluminous, publicly available written record of the dispute generally and of the opportunities for judicial engineering in particular. Depending on whether the dispute is resolved at a jury trial or how ripe the dispute was if resolved short of a jury verdict, this written record will include adversarial briefs interpreting facts and law in support of their position on key motions, trial transcripts of oral argument and verbal judicial response to key motions, and in some cases, the judge's written justification for his/her ruling on key motions. Analytical techniques available would, of course, vary from sophisticated, computerized content analysis to more traditional examination of legal and evidentiary content. However, each of these sources and techniques offers important opportunities to analyze qualitative variation, or the lack thereof, in aggregate patterns of behavior, and to identify specific examples of the presence or absence of "cognitive illusion" in judicial reasoning.
- *Interviews.* It is remarkable that with so much recent attention to trial judging, so little effort appears to have been made to interview judges and the parties to jury disputes engineered by trial judges. Traditional wisdom from the political perspective is that judges would be so unable or unwilling to acknowledge extralegal influences or even the possibility of cognitive illusion that such interviews would be unproductive and probably misleading.

However, this perspective derives in large part from the implicit assumption that judges are strategic actors, consciously driven by value-based preferences. If, as in our proposed theoretical framework, this assumption is dropped, a number of interview opportunities are apparent, ranging from identification of the judge's key audiences to questions asking the judge to recreate his/her rulings on key motions, perhaps by reference to these audiences. Moreover, addition of interview techniques to the methodological quiver also suggests the importance of interviewing not only judges but also the parties to a dispute and the authors of key briefs and arguments. These paired interviews would create a unique opportunity to, for example, reinforce the content analysis of motions and opinions by reference to each party's discussion of the evidence and law utilized in written reasons for the judge's ruling.

- *Case Studies.* Case studies have long been a mainstay of more traditional approaches to the study of courts and judging. As with most research in the judicial area, these studies have focused primarily on seminal Supreme Court cases—causes, consequences, and reasoning. Our proposed research program offers a unique opportunity to extend the case-study—whether the "case" is an individual judge, a single dispute, or combinations thereof—approach to judicial engineering of jury disputes. Specifically, it will be interesting to examine the consistency, or lack thereof, in judicial engineering for a single case. Do the judge's rulings consistently favor one party over the other? Does the judge consistently invoke the same or similar decision criteria, or is he/she less predictable? Are the judge's rulings consistent with accuracy, expressive or administrative goals? The case study methodologies will be particularly productive for mass torts—for example, asbestos, Vioxx, breast implants—in the context of Multi District Litigation (MDL) assignments in which a trial judge who administers the MDL may be called on to make important rulings that define the admissibility of evidence for literally thousands of cases and, perhaps more important, the likelihood that these cases will settle rather than go to trial and place thousands of burdens on case docket(s).

Exemplar Research Targets

Having called for a new research program, including new theoretical and methodological approaches, to study trial judges' behavior in the context of a jury dispute, we conclude this essay by suggesting two avenues of judicial engineering that we feel offer particularly fertile ground for examination of judicial behavior in the context of jury disputes: *(1)* judicial intervention in the jury selection arena, and *(2)* judicial decisions regarding the admissibility of expert testimony.

The exercise of jury-selection discretion is particularly appealing because it is a call to examine judgments that, while extremely important in defining the right to a jury trial, have been almost entirely ignored to date. Given the influence of jury composition on trial outcomes, this dearth of attention is puzzling and represents a major void in our understanding of key judicial behaviors and the implications of those behaviors for civil litigants' right to a jury trial. This puzzlement is buttressed by the fact that a judge's jury-selection decisions are virtually bullet proof, rarely the subject of appellate review unless the trial judge has violated the plain language of eligibility statutes or has demonstrably abused his or her exercise of discretion. Fortunately, jury-selection decisions are, for the most part, recorded in daily transcripts by court reporters and become part of the record for every jury trial presided over by a given judge; thus, the study of these engineering decisions can benefit from a rich combination of the methodological approach discussed above.

Having said that jury-selection decisions are appealing because they are virtually unexamined, the study of decisions regarding admissibility of expert testimony from the perspective proposed here is appealing precisely because it is the natural extension of productive recent efforts on both research fronts to understand trial judges' judgments regarding the admissibility of scientific expert testimony (Groscup, 2004; Buchman, 2007). Buchman's work offers a particularly inviting foundation because he has looked at federal district judges' published *Daubert* opinions and concluded that, at least for his sample of published decisions, judges' ideology influenced their decisions to grant or deny motions to admit or exclude expert testimony under the *Daubert* standards, and his work suggests implicitly numerous opportunities for expansion via the research program proposed here. Most obvious would be expanded attention to unpublished decisions generally and to state decisions regarding admissibility of scientific testimony in particular. This expansion could include reexamination of these decisions from the theoretical and methodological perspectives defining the research program proposed here—for example, examination of alternative motives and audiences, including donor groups in states that elect their judges, analyzing the briefs and arguments, and possibly interviewing a subset of judges and litigants. Less obvious is the possibility of synthesizing Buchman's political-science findings and Gatowski's findings (Gatowski et al., 2001) regarding the failure of most judges surveyed to understand most of the *Daubert* decision criteria outlined in the Supreme Court's *Daubert* decision. Moreover, the opportunities and incentives to expand this avenue of inquiry have been expanded by recent decisions that extend judicial gatekeeping and, therefore, judicial engineering to nonscientific expert testimony (Groscup, 2004).

Jury-selection and admissibility decisions notwithstanding, virtually every example of judicial engineering outlined in this proposal can be subjected to analysis that in the aggregate will help us understand not only how trial judges judge when they engineer the key elements of a jury trial, but also help us understand what the right to a jury trial means in a system where, constitutional architecture notwithstanding, judicial engineering defines that right in practice.

13

Searching for Constraint in Legal Decision Making

Eileen Braman

This essay is about constraint in legal decision making: how we should conceptualize it, how we should study it, and why psychological theory and methods provide such a promising avenue for doing so. I treat constraint as a "democratic good," necessary to justify the distributional decisions of unelected judges *and* as an empirical question: Does meaningful constraint exist? If so, where are we likely to find it? What are the potential sources of constraint in legal decision making? Asking these questions should lead to what I hope will be the next generation of empirical research on legal reasoning involving a wealth of theoretically based questions of interest to scholars in numerous disciplines.

Constraint itself is defined as "something that limits the freedom to act spontaneously; or some physical, moral or 'other' force that compels somebody to do something or limits their freedom of action." When legal types talk about constraint they are usually referring to professional norms and/or obligations that require judicial actors to use legal presumptions, rules and authority in reaching decisions.[1] Traditional legal approaches hold that the reasoned use of these tools will often compel particular outcomes.

The argument for requiring that decision makers use and cite accepted sources of authority is at least twofold. First, where judges use their training to apply the logic set forth in sources of legal reasoning, they are encouraged to think about specific disputes in light of generally applicable rules and larger societal values that legislative actors and other judges have deemed applicable in similar circumstances. In this way referencing legal considerations helps imbue judicial decisions with continuity and predictability. Second, judges utilizing tools of legal reasoning are prevented from calling on *their own* values, beliefs, and preferences in making decisions between adverse parties; the fact that judges are engaged in the seemingly objective task of legal analysis helps legitimate the distributive choices they make in our constitutional system.

The conception of law as a meaningful constraint on decision makers has taken a serious blow in the last century with the rise of legal realism in legal academia and studies of judicial behavior in the social sciences. The overwhelming weight of empirical evidence demonstrates that judges vote disproportionately for outcomes that are consistent with their political policy preferences. This casts significant doubt on the constraining force of legal authority jurists cite as determinative in their decision making.

These findings are extremely important from a normative perspective because attempts to justify judicial authority without reference to meaningful constraint are fundamentally flawed. As such, scholars in all disciplines, but particularly political science, should be deeply concerned with identifying constraint in legal decision making. If we come up empty in this search, or even empty in some types of cases we, as a discipline, will need to do some very serious rethinking about why judges are among the political officials that get to say "who gets what, where, and how."

How to Look for Constraint: Refining Our Empirical Approach

The search for constraint has been elusive in empirical studies. I think this is in part because scholars have inadequately conceptualized constraint in studies of judicial behavior. Empirical investigators commonly look for evidence of constraint in the wrong place (Segal & Spaeth, 1993, 2002) and they often use exceedingly hard or unrealistic tests of the concept (Brenner & Spaeth, 1995; Segal & Spaeth, 1996; Spaeth & Segal, 1999).[2]

Large-sample studies that correlate case votes with broad indicia of judicial preferences (like ideology, political party, or the party of a judge's appointing president) tend to treat law "in the abstract" as a constraining force. Critics of these studies argue they fail to take account of individual case facts and circumstances. Behavioral scholars counter that these differences "wash out" in the aggregate. Still, where results demonstrate the influence of attitudinal factors in legal decision making, we are left with debates about whether findings reveal the influence of attitudes and/or ideology "in the raw" or "ideologically influenced legal considerations" (Gillman, 2001).[3] Thus, for all our efforts we still know very little about *how* decisional norms and institutional context operate to constrain (or fail to constrain) judges that are the subject of our investigations.

Meaningful legal constraint may or may not exist; this is an empirical question that has yet to be adequately tested. Here I argue that constraint is not *undiscoverable*—and legal models of decision making are not unfalsifiable (cf., Segal & Spaeth, 1993, pp. 33–34). What we need are fair, theoretically based, tests of constraint.[4] Specifically, empirical scholars need to be more explicit about the competing goals and influences that act on judges in the process of decision making. Moreover, we need to consider how we investigate constraint; this means adopting (or at least being open to) appropriate methods and thinking more carefully about the decisions and legal decision makers we analyze in our investigations.

In formulating hypotheses researchers should ask the following questions: What are the sources of constraint in legal decision making? How do those sources operate to influence the choices of decision makers? How would a constrained decision look different from one where decision makers are acting in accordance with their personal preferences? What specific decision contexts allow us to observe behavior where the law and preferences are in conflict? Under what conditions should we expect decision makers to make choices consistent with the law? Under what conditions might preferences play more of a role?

This is where theory and findings from cognitive and social psychology have such great potential to inform our research. Here I identify various normative and contextual sources of constraint and discuss what psychological theory suggests about how we should approach studying these aspects of legal decision making. Knowledge of research on psychological topics like persuasion, group decision making, accountability, analogical reasoning, and the role of motives in the evaluation of evidence can significantly aid in our theory building about where judges are relatively free to make decisions and where they are constrained by norms of legal reasoning and/or the institutional context in which they act. Rather than perpetuate the all-or-nothing debate between legal and nonlegal determinants of behavior, we should not only consider, but allow for, the interaction of legal and nonlegal influences in our hypothesis testing.[5]

The concept of motivated reasoning is particularly useful for thinking about the interaction between legal and nonlegal factors in decision making (Kunda, 1990; MacCoun, 1998). Arguably, the theory has the potential to resolve the disconnect between empirical evidence of ideological influence in judges' outcome choices and their own subjective accounts of legal determinants of their own decisional behavior (Braman, 2006a; Braman & Nelson, 2007). As several other essays in this volume focus on judicial goals and motivations, I will not say much about motivated reasoning except that this line of literature can be particularly useful to empirical scholars in specifying our assumptions, operationalizations, and hypotheses. We should be thinking more about what decision makers are trying to achieve and how particular decision rules and institutional constraints facilitate and frustrate these decisional aspirations. Using motivated reasoning as an empirical framework can help us to be more explicit about all of this in theory building and hypothesis testing.

Although I am confident creative minds can think of ways to do this with regression analyses that judicial scholars have grown so comfortable with over the years, we should not be afraid of embracing methods cognitive psychologists have used to understand decision making processes. Indeed there already are studies employing content analyses (Tetlock, Bernzweig, & Gallant, 1985; Gruenfeld, 1995) and experiments (Guthrie, Rachlinski, & Wistrich, 2001; Braman, 2006a; Furgeson, Babcock, & Shane, 2008b; Braman & Nelson, 2007) to understand aspects of legal decision-making behavior.

Also, we may have to move away from analyzing final case votes toward discrete choices judges make in the process of legal reasoning in order to get a realistic idea of how and where constraint operates in their decision making. For instance, judges make many component decisions in the context of deciding a case: what issue is determinative? Does a particular statute govern? Is a cited precedent applicable or can it be distinguished from the current case? Understanding how the law shapes these discrete choices seems an important aspect of investigating how decision makers are or are not constrained by controlling authority.

Where to Look for Constraint: Potential Sources in Legal Decision Making

In thinking about the sources of constraint in legal decision making, two broad categories come to mind: *(1)* constraint imposed by legal authority and application of appropriate rules of decision making, and *(2)* constraint that results from the institutional context in which judges make decisions. I will refer to the first type of constraint as "normative constraint" and the second type as "contextual constraint." In describing each potential source of normative and contextual constraint I point to literature in cognitive and social psychology that should help our theorizing about how these constraints work (or fail to work) to limit individual discretion.

The list I propose is not exhaustive. Moreover, not all the sources of constraint I mention have easily identifiable correspondents in the psychological literature. It is meant as a *starting point* to help us think about where psychological theory can inform our research. In the spirit of hypothesis building, I suggest ways researchers may attempt to test the constraining force of norms and context when looking at these aspects of legal decision making.

Normative Sources of Constraint

Issues Related to Argumentation

In thinking about the normative sources of constraint we should start with what stylized norms of decision making require of judicial actors choosing between litigants in an adversarial context. One of the most basic assumptions in our legal system is that justiciable disputes meet criteria that make them appropriate for judicial resolution: there must be a "case or controversy" involving a plaintiff who has suffered an "injury in fact"; moreover, the conflict must be current and redressible by means of a judicial pronounce-ment. Where cases meet these criteria, judges are supposed to follow certain rules in the context of decision making.

We assume that as long as a dispute meets criteria demonstrating the necessary averseness, litigants will have the incentives to fight hard and bring the best legal arguments for their position to the attention of the court. As such, there is a norm that limits judges to the issues and arguments raised by litigants. In legal jargon the rule is that judges are not supposed to raise issues or arguments *sua sponte*. The rule is important to maintain fairness in decision making so litigants are not surprised by having cases decided on the basis of facts and/or arguments they have not briefed or considered in the context of their dispute. In this respect, judges are constrained by relevant case facts and arguments raised by the parties to litigation.

There is a lively debate in political science about the extent to which judges at the highest level of our judicial system comply with this norm, based on comparative content analyses of case briefs and opinions (McGuire & Palmer, 1995, 1996; Epstein, Segal, & Johnson, 1996). This is one area where research on normative constraint that has already caught the attention of empirically minded scholars may be aided by research methods and ideas from psychology. For instance one question that has *not* been adequately addressed in this literature is what motive(s) judges might serve by raising additional issues and arguments. One could image a range of potential motives ranging from the altruistic (e.g., to help litigants with inadequate representation) to the strategic (e.g., to aid a decision maker in reaching the ideological outcome the judge prefers).[6]

To get at this question, one might be able to create an experiment with different legal briefs related to an identical factual scenario that vary in terms of their comprehensiveness. If the norm is violated by decision makers there may be systematic differences in the pattern of results that help reveal their reasons for doing so. For instance, one could ask: are new issues or arguments more likely to be raised in conditions where legal argument is sparse (sug-gesting altruistic motives)? Or are they more likely to be raised by decision makers with certain ideological views or by decision makers who decide the case in a particular direction (suggesting more strategic motives)? Identifying why decision makers may violate this particular constraining norm may help us to sharpen our statistical analyses by identifying the class of cases where such behavior is most likely to occur.

Another issue related to argumentation has been raised by Stone Sweet (2002), who argues that we should reconceptualize our thinking about con-straint to encompass the range of *plausible arguments* adversaries could raise in litigation rather than the more narrow choice sets created by selected arguments. On this view, argumentative choices themselves represent an important part of the constraining influence of law. Framing literature from psychology and political psychology (Nelson & Kinder, 1996; Nelson, Oxley, & Clawson, 1997; Druckman, 2001) seems particularly relevant here.[7]

Also value pluralism models (Abelson, 1968; Tetlock, 1986), concerned with how individuals negotiate competing interests, have great potential to inform our research as we move from unidimensional models of decision making to more realistic models where multiple issues and arguments are present in light of complex, real-world fact patterns. After all, what is legal decision making but a competition between competing values and interests? As discussed in the chapter by Robbennolt, MacCoun, and Darley in this volume (ch. 2), the psychological literature on how people negotiate value conflict can help us move beyond the world of unidimensional theorizing toward a more realistic understanding of how judges operate where more than one issue is raised.

In a classic chapter on cognitive consistency, Abelson (1968) suggests four distinct strategies for dealing with value conflict: bolstering, denial, differentiation, and transcendence. Unfortunately not much has been done to investigate when decision makers use particular conflict reducing techniques since Ableson identified them. Kunda (1990, p. 480) points out that although researchers have been quite interested in the scenarios *that give rise to value conflict*, few have systematically explored specific strategies individuals use for *dealing with it*. Legal decision making provides fertile ground to undertake this inquiry. Content analysis strategies may be devised to investigate where judges ignore (deny) or emphasize (bolster) arguments made by litigants to get at these issues.

A final aspect of argumentation where we could benefit from psychological approaches to decision making is, of course, related to the ultimate goal of legal argument: persuasion. As there is an entire essay by Lawrence S. Wrightsman on the topic in this volume (ch. 4), I will not spend much time with it here, except to mention two points that seem especially relevant to the subject of this essay. First, among the accepted tools of decision making (legal text, statutory or constitutional intent, and precedent), there is what some consider a hierarchy of authoritative force—text is generally considered the most definitive statement of what the law is, and arguably the source that is least vulnerable to subjective interpretation (although admittedly text can be wrought with ambiguity). The interpretation of precedent and intent are considered by some to be somewhat more "suspect" because there is more subjectivity inherent in the endeavor (Bork, 1990); still each is an accepted source of legal analysis.

It would be interesting to know if the constraining force of one type of authority is stronger than the others. For instance, is a U.S. statute that declares a contested rule to apply in a certain class of cases more likely to constrain decision makers who disagree with the stated rule, than a controlling Supreme Court precedent declaring the same rule? It wouldn't be hard to create an experiment to test this. One might even find existing cases to analyze; for instance, you could measure compliance with a court decision in subsequent cases before and after it was codified by some legislative body. Related to this question is how decision makers act in the presence of competing types of authority. Does text trump conflicting precedent? Can overwhelming evidence of intent convince decision makers that a specific outcome should obtain notwithstanding contrary legal arguments? Howard and Segal (2002) have a piece on the use of originalism in Supreme Court jurisprudence that begins to investigate some of these interesting issues.

A final point related to persuasion and legal decision making is that several studies have evidence suggesting individual differences in how decision makers respond to constraining authority related to attitudinal/ideological traits of the decision maker (Braman, 2006a, findings suggesting differences in responses to controlling precedent; Randazzo, Waterman, & Fine, 2006, finding differences in responses to legislative authority). Until now legal scholars and political scientists have all assumed law constrained or (failed to constrain) uniformly across different types of decision makers. If findings of individual differences persist we will need to take this into account in our theorizing. Work in psychology and political psychology on individual differences in motivated reasoning (Jost et al., 2003) and motivated skepticism (Taber & Lodge, 2006) in evaluation of political arguments and evidence might be particularly helpful in this regard.

Issues Related to Decision Rules

A second sort of normative constraint involves the specific application of stylized rules of decision making in legal reasoning. Are individuals able to comply with norms concerning *how they should think* in the context of adversarial disputes? This is an especially interesting area of research as judges and legal academics often suggest anecdotally that decision makers are violating norms to reach decisions consistent with ideologically preferred outcomes. We can now bring our empirical skills to bear on important questions about the *process* of legal reasoning. How prevalent are violations of decision norms? Under what conditions are they most likely to occur? Do decision makers who are violating decision norms do so with self awareness? Or are unconscious mechanisms of influence at play in the process of complex decision making?

1. APPLICATION OF LEGAL PRESUMPTIONS.   In terms of empirical investigations researchers have been almost obsessively focused on outcomes. This ignores a potentially important source of constraint involving the ability of decision makers to apply required *presumptions* in their legal analyses. The ability to comply with rules about where reasoning should "start from" has important consequences for the administration of justice in our judicial system. One of the most important rules is, of course, the presumption of innocence in criminal trials. It is this presumption that creates a heavy burden of proof necessary for the state to take the freedom or lives of its citizens. If decision makers come to the table with preconceptions about the guilt of defendants the standard of evidence necessary for conviction is reduced. One could imagine that decision makers are more able to comply with this presumption in some types of cases (i.e., white collar vs. violent crime) or more skeptically, with regard to some type of individuals (class or race based differences in ability to apply the presumption). Experimental techniques might help us understand if decision makers fall short of making required assumptions and where they are especially likely to do so.

Prospect theory, especially as it relates to "status quo bias," can help us theorize about the application of presumptions in legal decision making.[8] Psychological research reveals that the price at which people are willing to sell things that already belong to them is typically higher than the price they would be willing to pay to acquire them. This "endowment effect" (Knetch, 2000) seems especially important to the aspect of constraint requiring decision makers to apply presumptions in the context of thinking about legal disputes. For instance, one of the most famous axioms in legal academia is the "Coase Theorem": in the absence of transaction costs it does not matter to whom a right is initially assigned because the parties will be able to bargain efficiently and it will wind up in the hands of whoever values it most (and is therefore willing to pay to get it). Introducing endowment effects may complicate matters significantly. If sellers attribute some unstated value to simply "possessing" an object—buyers who actually value that item more may not be able or willing to meet their terms to acquire it. This endowment effect is kind of a "surcharge" not adequately encompassed by the theory. Moreover, it is not clear if the endowment effect for owning some objects (for example, real property) is greater than the endowment effect for owning other objects (for example, cups and pens—which is what much of the experimental research on this topic has involved). One could hypothesize that the endowment effect could be more of an obstacle for some types of Coasean transactions than others.

Also, it is not clear whether there are third-party, "observer," endowment effects that might be relevant for judges adjudicating disputes concerning the allocation of rights and resources. Are judges able to do the mental acrobatics required of them if presumptions call for them to consider counterfactuals that are at odds with the status quo? How, if at all, does who *currently possesses* a right or resource influence their seemingly objective decision processes? For instance, law students commonly study water rights in Property classes. In western states, where water is scarce, a common presumption in this area of the law is "prior appropriation," the first person to use water from some natural source acquires "priority" rights to that source against later users. Often "junior" appropriators divert water from the beneficial use of land owners with superior right to a particular source for several years before such conflicts become the subject of litigation. How does the current state of affairs influence the decisions of judges and/or juries in such matters?

Finally, presumptions are especially important in motion practice. As discussed more fully in the essay by Rowland, Traficanti, and Vernon in this volume (ch. 12), motions represent a highly significant aspect of legal reasoning not often studied by empirical scholars. For instance, in deciding motions for summary judgment, where parties argue there is "no question of material fact," judges are required to decide the case as a matter of law, presuming all factual representations in the plaintiff's portrayal of the dispute are true. We do not have a good idea of whether judges are able to do this—or what role attitudinal factors play in deciding whether or not issues of material fact actually exist. It would also be good to know the relationship between factual and legal arguments in this sort of decision making. For example, if the law favors the person who files the motion, are decision makers hostile to that party's claim more likely to find some factual question precluding summary judgment than decision makers who are not hostile to the claim? Or are all decision makers constrained by interpretation of seemingly objective facts in the same way?

2. ISSUE "INDEPENDENCE" AND ORDER OF OPERATIONS.   One norm I have gotten some leverage on with the use of experimental methods involves the ability of legal decision makers to think independently about distinct issues in litigation where multiple issues are raised (Braman, 2006a) Specifically, I did this in the context of testing how decision makers decide a "threshold question" in light of their views on policy questions related to the merits of a politically charged case. I have used intuitions about separable preferences to theorize about these concerns, but there might be other theories that are equally (or more) appropriate.

There are certainly other aspects of legal decision making where the violation of this particular norm can have important implications. For instance, in bench (and jury) trials can decision makers separate their reasoning about liability (or guilt in criminal matters) from potential penalties defendants are facing? If this is a problem, does bifurcation help? Or would we do better to have separate decision makers at each stage? Recent work by Wistrich, Guthrie, and Rachlinski (2005) suggests that magistrate judges have trouble disregarding inadmissible information they may have been privy to in preconference discussions. The authors recommend that different judges handle distinct stages of litigation. Their study and recommendations demonstrate how psychological research can suggest relatively easy changes in our judicial system to make litigation more equitable.

Another very interesting question involving legal decision rules concerns the "order of operations" legal decision makers are supposed to follow when considering arguments and authority. Akin to mathematics, there is a logical sequence decision makers are supposed to follow when reasoning through cases where certain types of grounds are available for a decision. The rationale behind these rules (which are sometimes referred to as the *Ashwander* rules for a Supreme Court decision in 1936 that summarized them) is that judges should cause as little disruption to existing democratic forms as possible when deciding specific disputes. The most familiar rule is that decision makers should not "reach" constitutional issues unless absolutely necessary. This means if a matter can be determined on statutory (or other) grounds judges are required to do so without considering the constitutional questions that are potentially raised by the fact pattern.

Have judges been able to follow this norm? Do attitudinal factors come into play where judges reach different conclusions about the necessity of addressing constitutional concerns? An analysis of cases specifically citing *Ashwander* (1936) could help us answer some of these questions. Is it cited more often where judges choose to avoid or reach the constitutional issue? Where judges do find it necessary to address constitutional matters does it depend on the ideology of the judge(s) deciding the case in some respect? A study much like Spaeth's (1964) classic critiquing Justice Frankfurter's practice of "legislative deference" may be useful here. Looking at the actual grounds of decision in cases where *Ashwander* is cited might shed significant light on whether there are ideological factors at play in using this seemingly neutral decision rule.

3. LATITUDE IN APPLICATION OF ACCEPTED DECISION RULES.   Another issue regarding decision rules concerns the level of discretion decision makers have in the application of specific rules that are supposed to govern their analyses. Perhaps the most commonly discussed issue in this vein is whether and to what extent decision makers are constrained by the application of precedent (Sunstein, 1993, 1996; Sherwin, 1999; Simon, 2004). Much of the legal work on analogical reasoning in legal discourse borrows from disciplines like philosophy or linguistics. Psychological findings and theories of analogical reasoning (Holyoak & Thagard, 1995; Gentner, 1998) have been vastly under utilized in this discourse. The clear exception to this rule is Simon's work (with Holyoak and on his own) on the importance of coherence in similarity judgments (Simon, 2004, Holyoak & Simon, 1999); although others are starting to think carefully about applications in legal research (Spellman, this volume, ch. 10). Clearly there is much more to learn about how and whether decision makers are meaningfully constrained by precedential authority. Psychological research can greatly inform this important inquiry. Similarly, research on more general *categorization processes* may help us understand decisions about the applicability of statutes involving certain types of litigants and/or categories of behavior in the minds of judges.

A final question having to do with the differential constraining authority of decision rules has to do with the oft made distinctions between "rules" and "standards" in legal discourse. Conventional wisdom holds that "black-letter rules" confine decision makers to a greater extent than more flexible "legal standards" (see, for instance, Schauer, 1991; Schlag, 1985; Sullivan, 1992). This is actually an empirical question that has yet to be tested (Braman, 2006b). One could do this experimentally by giving decision makers an identical factual scenario and asking them to make the same decision with different decision criteria. One condition would involve a decision rule; the other a legal standard. Decisions across conditions could then be compared with respect to the degree of attitudinal influence and variance across decision makers. If conventional wisdom is right, decision makers in the rule condition should be less influenced by their attitudes and there should be less variance across decision makers within that condition.[9] Regardless of what the findings show, this sort of experiment would tell us something very interesting about the confining influence of different decision criteria that have been a subject of substantial interest in legal discourse.

Contextual Sources of Constraint

An essay on constraint in legal decision making would be remiss if it failed to mention contextual or "institutional" constraint on the ability of judges to decide cases as their preferences dictate (Gibson, 1980). Rather than go through an exhaustive list of contextual sources of constraint I will mention two where research from cognitive and social psychology seem particularly relevant: the group nature of appellate decision making and the requirement that judges justify and be held accountable for their decisions.

Issues Related to Group Decision Making

Political scientists generally attribute directional policy motivations to judges. Whether researchers take a "strategic" or "sincere" view of the role of preferences in decision making, the presence of others in the decision process acts as a constraint on the ability of judges to reach outcomes they most prefer. Neither strategic nor sincere accounts of attitudinal influence portray judges as open to reasoned arguments about why the decision should be different than they believe at the outset of discussions. One could argue that this is at odds with how decision makers themselves actually conceive of the process of appellate decision making. The democratic justifications for having judges decide cases in groups are to *(1)* avoid error and *(2)* reach the "best" resolution of legal questions by having several decision makers come to a compromised agreement about what outcome should obtain in particularized disputes. To the extent judges have internalized these justifications for group decision making, portrayals of them posturing to achieve predetermined policy goals in conference are taken as a personal affront.

Furthermore, much of the extant empirical research treats group processes as the sum of individual preferences, measuring for instance, how much traditionally liberal judges move "toward" conservative positions in the process of appellate decision making (Epstein & Knight, 1998; Collins & Martinek, 2007). This emphasis on discrete individuals in the group context is due, in part, to path dependence in the way political science operationalizations have evolved. Ideology is an individual trait; separate case votes are easy to count and analyze.

I would like to draw attention to another conception of group decision making that has been ignored by political scientists who assume directional policy motivations on behalf of judges, by raising a possibility more in line with legalistic conceptions of appellate decision making and more consistent with psychological research on group decision processes (see Morehead, 1998, for review; Gruenfeld & Hollingshead, 1993). This is the idea that group decision making is more appropriately conceptualized as a collective cognition process with its own unique properties. Research on sociocognition in groups (Gruenfeld & Hollingshead, 1993) tends to demonstrate that group outcomes are more than (and different from) the sum of individual views of group members.

When legal decision makers act in groups they are arguing about more than case votes; they are talking about doctrine and what the appropriate grounds of a decision should be. In this process decision makers likely come to a collective understanding of what the law requires in a particular case that is distinct from what any individual thought at the outset. Indeed group discussion may itself lead to insights and considerations that would not have come into play if several decision makers had not come together to discuss a particular matter.

Perhaps where decision makers write separate opinions traditional notions from political science are appropriate; there judges may refuse to accommodate beliefs or opinions. But when judges are part of majorities, I think political scientists should at least allow for the possibility that decisions result from group processes more akin to sincere compromise and reasoned accommodation than strategic interaction. Creative research minds might even be able to come up with a way to test these competing conceptions of appellate group dynamics. Simulations where researchers collect individual data before group discussion, then have decision makers come to some collective judgment—carefully observing group dynamics and outcomes— seem like the most promising avenue to "get at" these processes. Law students or retired judges who are familiar with stylized rules of decision making could be used as participants in simulations.

Finally, there are many psychological studies on related topics like social influence (Sherif, 1936; Asch, 1955), majority and minority influence (Moscovici, 1980), group polarization (Moscovici & Zavalloni, 1969), and groupthink (Janis, 1982) that could be relevant to appellate decision processes. Gruenfeld has done some very interesting work looking at the integrative complexity of majority versus separate opinions on the Supreme Court (Gruenfeld, 1995). I reference this work here to acknowledge that I have not dealt with the potential contribution of literature on group decision processes as fully as I might have in this chapter. I strongly believe, however, it is a literature we should be paying much more attention to in our theorizing.

Issues Related to Accountability

There is some excellent work on the psychology of accountability as a result of a research agenda of Tetlock and colleagues that spans a period of over 20 years (see Lerner & Tetlock, 1999, for a cogent review of findings). Here I will highlight findings that seem particularly relevant to the behavior of judicial decision makers required to account for decisions via written opinions that justify their choices in adversarial disputes. First, through a series of very clever pre- versus postjudgment experimental manipulations, Tetlock (1983b, 1985) and Tetlock, Skitka, and Boettger (1989) have shown that accountability concerns influence not only how decision makers justify their choices, *but how they think* about the decisions for which they may be held accountable. This is important and perhaps underappreciated in the judicial literature, where researchers sometimes talk as if judges are only concerned with coming up with explanations to satisfy (or perhaps pacify) external observers of court outputs (Epstein & Knight, 1998).

Although not all the effects of accountability on thought processes are positive,[10] generally decision makers who understand they will be accountable for their choices tend to engage in more in-depth processing than decision makers who do not expect to have to justify choices. Accountability tends to stimulate open-minded, self-critical thinking and attenuate biases under specific conditions including those where an audience *(1)* is interested in accuracy, *(2)* is reasonably well informed, and *(3)* has a legitimate reason for inquiring into the reasons behind particular judgments (Lerner & Tetlock, 1999, p. 259). Put another way, accountability tends to heighten accuracy motivations. When we know others are watching we want to "get things right" and we also strive to use appropriate decision criteria to avoid criticisms that may be raised down the line. One could argue judicial decision makers operate under these conditions and, as such, accountability concerns should heighten their motivation to comply with norms of appropriate decision making.

A second, but equally relevant, point is that *whom* decision makers are accounting to is important. Judges have multiple audiences including litigants, attorneys, legal academics, other judges, and members of ideological groups (Baum, 2006). A judge's desire to court, appease, or satisfy any one of these audiences can act as a real constraint on their decisional behavior.[11] Here a second strand of the value pluralism literature mentioned previously regarding "self-categorization" processes may help understand how judges think about themselves in light of multiple possible identities (Tajfel & Turner, 1985; see also, Brewer, 1991). Also, as we come to realize judicial actors are human and potentially concerned with issues like self-presentation (Baum, 2006), value pluralism models can help us understand when they are likely to "court" certain constituencies and when their desire to do so may be a real limit on their decisional behavior.

Conclusion

This is an exciting time in the development of our knowledge of legal decision making and the constraints that act on judges engaged in the task. Part of this excitement is because of the important implications these findings have for democratic notions of expert legitimacy and for how we must accommodate our theories to recognize what we know and have yet to learn about how judicial actors decide cases in our constitutional system. More of the enthusiasm I feel is based on what *we all* have to gain from the endeavor. I hope I have made a convincing argument that understanding constraint in decision making will greatly contribute to our mutual understanding of legal decision making behavior.

Notes

1. There are, of course, also contextual sources of constraint in our legal system including the group nature of appellate review and accountability mechanisms. I will deal with these more fully later in the essay.
2. See Braman and Nelson (2007) for a detailed critique of extant operationalizations of the constraining influence of precedent:

   > For a variety of reasons, the Supreme Court is perhaps the least likely place to detect the powerful gravitational pull of cited authority. Because the Supreme Court sits atop our judicial hierarchy, justices are not subject to the constant threat of review that may serve to heighten accuracy goals for lower court judges. Moreover, the Supreme Court has the ability to overrule itself. Lower court judges must follow binding authority without explicit license to change or ignore higher court rulings. Many of the justices on the Supreme Court see themselves as high-profile representatives of a specific jurisprudential approach (Baum 2006), and are thus unlikely to back away from public statements about how the law should be applied in prior dissenting or concurring opinions. Thus, tests of constraint that have been applied to the Supreme Court set an exceedingly high bar, and may not be appropriate to assess the influence of precedent more generally.

3. See Braman (2004, pp. 45–52) Braman and Nelson (2007, p. 942) regarding "top down" versus "bottom up" theories of attitudinal influence in legal decision making on why this is important distinction. See also Bartels (this volume, ch. 3) "Top-Down and Bottom-Up Models of Judicial Reasoning."
4. Gillman (2001) writes, "[I]f some contemporary positivists are willing to make empirical claims about the determinate influence of rules, then it is not unreasonable for scholars such as Spaeth and Segal to ask them to formulate those claims in ways that allow for hypothesis testing" (Gillman 2001, p. 486). That is what I attempt to do here.
5. I do not mean to imply that empirical studies have been blind to the influence of legal factors in models of decision making (Segal, 1984 [search and seizure]; Songer & Haire, 1992 [obscenity cases]; Gryski, Main, & Dixon, 1986 [sex discrimination]) but where such factors are treated as control variables that improve our attitudinal predictions (i.e., Segal & Spaeth, 1993) their influence tends to be obscured.

6. Significantly, altruism (as I have defined it) may be less of a motivating factor at the Supreme Court, where researchers have actually looked at this question—especially if one assumes that litigants who get to our highest court are likely to be relatively well represented.

7. See also, Nelson, Maruska, and Braman (2002) for an analysis of how alternative argument frames can influence lay perceptions of important issues in litigation.

8. The challenge Kahneman and Tversky's (1979) theory of decision under risk poses to purely rational models of decision making has been realized and acknowledged across multiple disciplines. Legal scholars have shown through their own experimental techniques that magistrate judges, like ordinary people, can be subject to framing effects in choosing between settlement options (Guthrie, Rachlinski, & Wistrich, 2001).

9. I have yet to come up with a psychological theory to express this expectation that seems almost intuitive to legally trained individuals. It might be an example of the kind of decision domain where there is no psychological theory that neatly corresponds with conventional legal wisdom.

10. For instance, decision makers who will be held accountable tend to overemphasize the importance of irrelevant information; this is commonly referred to as the "dilution effect."

11. Moreover, where judges have a prior record of deciding cases in a certain way, memorialized in written opinions accounting for prior decisions, consistency motives (Abelson et al., 1968) are likely to kick in and act as a further constraint on decisional behavior.

Part III

EVALUATING AND IMPROVING JUDGING

14

Evaluating Judges

Gregory Mitchell

Much of the interest in empirical studies of judges lies in the comparison of actual to ideal behavior. When we ask what makes a good judge or whether a judge rightly decided a case, we implicitly compare the judge's decisions to a normative standard. In some instances, the content of the normative standard is uncontroversial and its application straightforward. Hence, a trial judge who sentences African American defendants to longer terms of imprisonment than white defendants, all other things being equal, departs from the normative ideal that application of criminal laws should be color-blind (e.g., Blair et al., 2004; Pruitt & Wilson, 1983). Or the circuit court judge who votes to uphold a state law banning abortions on grounds that *Roe v. Wade* was wrongly decided departs from the normative ideal that inferior court judges should follow the Supreme Court's constitutional decisions (for evidence on how circuit judges view their obligations within the legal hierarchy, see Klein, 2002).

In many instances, however, the content of the normative standard chosen for comparison purposes proves controversial or hard to delimit and its application unclear. Is the judge who applies a rule of evidence according to its plain language a "better" judge than one who applies the rule to achieve its purpose when following the text would contravene the purpose? Is the judge who deviates from the law to correct a disparate impact that the law is having on minorities, say, in sentencing, a bad judge? Is the circuit judge who narrowly construes the Supreme Court's abortion cases a better judge than the circuit judge who broadly construes this precedent? Does it matter if the former judge favors this minimalist approach because of pragmatic commitments rather than political preferences? Is there even a neutral approach to construal of Supreme Court precedent that can be labeled the way of the ideal judge?

We may decompose any empirical study that attempts to address the competence of judges or the quality of judging into three basic components: *(1)* the specification of a normative benchmark; *(2)* the conversion of the benchmark into testable form and judicial behavior into measurable units; *(3)* the interpretation of the results of any comparison to draw appropriate conclusions about the descriptive-normative gap.[1] In this chapter, I consider complications at each stage in the comparison process, with illustrations from existing studies of judicial competence and studies from psychology that examine the gap between behavior and norms of rational judgment and decision making.

I contend that we presently know very little about the degree to which judges depart from normative ideals because political scientists focus too much on the Supreme Court and often employ flawed benchmarks, psychologists focus too much on juries, and legal scholars focus too much on the normative side of the descriptive-normative comparison. I discuss seven different conceptual approaches to the evaluative study of judging: benchmarking based on social, moral, legal, coherence (or internal consistency), and efficacy (or correspondence to an external criterion) norms; evaluations based on notions of good judicial character; and evaluations based on relative performance in judicial tournaments. In the process, I consider the benefits that may be achieved by embracing a more diverse set of benchmarks for judicial evaluations. I predict that greater diversity in normative perspectives will lead to a greater appreciation of the importance of legal structure relative to personal characteristics in judicial behavior and lead to new views about the contours of the descriptive-normative gap.[2]

Why Study Judicial Competence?

Knowledge about the descriptive-normative gap in judicial behavior is important for what it may reveal about the lawfulness of particular cases and the predictability of courts, but more generally for what the size and contours of this gap may reveal about the legitimacy of the legal system and the meaning of the rule of law. Describing judicial behavior in relation to norms of good judging holds an important place within debates about the proper role and power of the federal judiciary relative to other branches of the federal government and relative to state governments. As Sherry (2005) argues, the rise of the view of federal judges as just another political actor within the government likely contributes to elite, and perhaps popular (Scheb & Lyons, 2001), discontent with judicial review and provides cover for those elites seeking to change the balance of power (see Sisk & Heise, 2005). Characterizing judges as unaccountable yet political actors rather than experts in the administration of law takes the sting out of arguments to limit judicial review and give greater power to the legislature and executive. Likewise, to the extent that the legitimacy of the courts and their ability to motivate voluntary compliance with the law derives from the popular view of the courts as detached from ordinary political processes (Tyler & Mitchell, 1994), evidence that judges are just political actors in robes should undercut the legitimacy of the courts. However, these arguments should lose steam if existing studies into the descriptive-normative gap are far from compelling, as I contend they are.

From a prescriptive perspective, reliable knowledge about the descriptive-normative gap is needed to understand where judicial incompetence exists so that we may attempt to correct it.[3] If judicial behavior systematically deviates from legal norms in some domains, then steps may need to be taken to rein in this predictably unlawful behavior. If judicial behavior commonly, but randomly, deviates from legal norms in other domains, then steps may need to be taken to eliminate chance influences in these domains.[4] If judicial behavior proves unresponsive to prescriptive interventions in these domains, then the legal norm, or the task to which the norm is to be applied, should be reconsidered on grounds that "ought" implies "can." If some types of judges perform better than others under consensual norms, then we can evaluate whether our preconceptions of the personal qualities and training associated with competent judging are correct and gain valuable information about whether the judicial selection process should be altered.

By suggesting the many different standards that may be used to examine judicial competence and by suggesting the limits of the usual comparison focused on law versus politics (between "attitudinal-type" models and simple legal models of judicial behavior[5]), I hope to encourage the debate to move beyond characterizations of judges as driven primarily by ideology or law (for a more comprehensive effort in this regard, see Baum, 2006). At all levels of the judiciary, judges' political attitudes undoubtedly play some role in their judgments and decisions, but many other aspects of a judge's psychological make-up and of the social-psychological setting in which a judge acts will be influential as well, with some of these influences pushing the judge toward idealized normative behavior and some pushing the judge away from judicial ideals. Gaining a more sophisticated understanding of when and why judges deviate from various judicial norms should provide a better understanding of potential sources of judicial legitimacy or illegitimacy and aid in the important task of developing prescriptive models of judicial behavior.

The Limits of Our Present Knowledge on the Descriptive-Normative Gap

One need not endorse a skeptical view of the limits of social scientific knowledge to endorse the view that we presently know little about the size and contours of the descriptive-normative gap in judicial behavior. Political scientists, who by far have conducted the greatest number of empirical studies of judicial behavior, focus a disproportionate amount of their efforts on appellate courts and the U.S. Supreme Court in particular (see Friedman, 2006; Klein, 2002; Maveety, 2003). Even if the strongest claims of the "attitudinalists" and "quasi-attitudinalists" (Baum, 2006, p. 7) are true about the role of personal policy preferences and strategic preference-maximization behavior in shaping the decisions of Supreme Court justices, there is little reason to believe that any strong version of the attitudinal model generalizes to judges on inferior courts (see Gerber & Park, 1997). Although lower courts are studied much less commonly, existing empirical evidence indicates that legal norms influence judges on lower courts to a greater extent than on the Supreme Court (Cross, 2007; Klein, 2002; Rowland & Carp, 1996), and many social psychologists would argue that the situation of the judge will often exert greater influence on judicial behavior than preexisting preferences. From this perspective, studies of supreme courts have limited external validity: one cannot assume that judicial actors in very different situations (especially those who do not control their docket in the way the Supreme Court does) will act the same; equivalence must be empirically demonstrated rather than assumed.

Psychologists, for their part, simply have not conducted many empirical studies of judicial behavior. Whereas mock jury studies make up a high percentage of all law and psychology empirical studies, studies of judicial behavior are infrequent. Consider, for instance, that the chapter on "Psychology and Law" in the most recent edition of the *Handbook of Social Psychology* contains no discussion devoted specifically to studies of judicial decision-making (Ellsworth & Mauro, 1998). Thus, while psychology may have much to offer the study of judging (Wrightsman, 1999), psychologists have had little to say about judges.

Legal scholars, for their part, spend enormous amounts of time telling the courts how they should decide cases—indeed, normativity seems almost a prerequisite to publishing in law reviews (Rubin, 1997)—but relatively little time studying empirically what, beyond the reasons given in opinions, motivates judges and whether courts can in fact follow the norms that legal scholars recommend to them. When legal scholars do consider the descriptive side of the descriptive-normative comparison, they tend to favor qualitative studies that identify descriptive-normative gaps in particular cases (e.g., Barnett, 2005; Vermeule, 2006) or lines of cases (e.g., Barnett, 2004). While qualitative studies can generate important hypotheses for future testing and rich stories about how judges do or do not comply with legal norms, such studies can provide only limited evidence about the systematicity of this behavior and cannot test competing causal hypotheses due to sample restrictions (Büthe, 2002; King et al., 1994).

A variation on the last point is worth emphasizing: beware of vivid anecdotal evidence of alleged judicial misbehavior (of the kind found, for instance, in Boot, 1998) or alleged theory-confirming judicial decisions. Segal and Spaeth (2002) begin the revised edition of *The Supreme Court and the Attitudinal Model* with discussion of the Supreme Court's decision in *Bush v. Gore*, which they take to be a recent example of judicial policymaking. Baum (1997), on the other hand, begins his review of judicial behavior research with anecdotes about conservative Supreme Courts deciding *Roe v. Wade* and then affirming *Roe* in *Planned Parenthood v. Casey* to suggest that judicial attitudes cannot do the explanatory work often assigned to them.[6] Neither book bases its main conclusions on anecdotal evidence; rather, each understandably uses anecdotes for narrative purposes. But the contrast illustrates the point: empirical debates cannot be decided with anecdotal evidence, as each side will be able to find a seemingly endless supply of supportive stories. That is not to say that exemplary judges or exemplary cases cannot be important sources of information about the characteristics and behavior of good (and bad) judges and the institutional features that promote or inhibit good judging. But reaching consensus on exemplary behavior returns us to the original problems of identifying the norms to use for evaluating judges and measuring the exemplary qualities.

Alternative Normative Perspectives on Judging

Normative standards derive from analytical frameworks that enjoy authoritative status, either by general acceptance because the framework seems to work well or because it has been justified or promulgated by a source to whom deference is widely given (Baron, 2004). Some frameworks impose order, such as the rules of arithmetic; other frameworks are supposed to promote desired goals efficiently, reliably, or accurately, such as expected utility theory for the maximization of utility or scientific principles for the development of accurate and reliable empirical knowledge. Some normative systems, including systems of social and legal norms, are not easily reducible to a single clear, consensual goal or function (Elster, 1989), and some normative systems remain quite controversial, as with the debate over the propriety of norms of rationality for evaluating human judgment and choice behavior (e.g., Cohen, 1981). For the most part, empirical legal researchers take norms as identified by others (usually philosophers, statisticians, game theorists, or legal scholars) and apply them to actual judgment and decision-making behavior without wading into the foundational normative disputes.

The potential norms for evaluating judicial behavior may be divided into five categories: social, moral, legal, coherence, and efficacy norms.[7] Social norms, in this context, involve interjudge or intercourt comparisons: Did Judge X behave as the median judge behaves in such a case? Are the judges of the Ninth Circuit outliers in their treatment of Establishment Clause cases? Although some judicial studies do discuss social norms within courts, few treat deviation from judicial social norms as a reason in and of itself for criticizing a judge's behavior.[8]

Moral norms, as I use the term here, encompass any norm derived from a theory of justice or ethical obligations. Legal scholars often use moral norms to evaluate individual judicial decisions (see Posner, 1999), but these studies typically dispute the normative status of the law by recourse to moral arguments rather than describe judicial behavior. Several empirical studies examine the degree to which parties or citizens in general perceive judges and the courts to be acting justly or to be allocating outcomes justly (e.g., Tyler & Huo, 2002; Tyler & Mitchell, 1994). Procedural justice norms are an important source for evaluation, but they typically are used in connection with efficacy norms as discussed below. Other than procedural and distributive justice norms, few empirical studies of judging evaluate judges against moral norms as defined here (except with respect to selected decisions).

Legal norms for present purposes are norms established by an authoritative governmental body, including constitutional, statutory, and administrative law and judge-made common law, to bind public and private institutions and the persons running and governed by these institutions. The power of courts to clarify, establish, or alter legal norms complicates matters from an empirical perspective, for it means that in some instances it is legitimate for a court to ignore, alter, or invalidate one norm to resolve conflict with another norm (as may occur through judicial review or common law development) or to embellish a norm (as may occur through legislative or constitutional interpretation). Uncertainty about what counts as law or binding legal norms likewise complicates matters (e.g., Hart, 1961), as we have seen with recent disputes about the role of foreign law in U.S. courts (e.g., Rahdert, 2007; see generally Shapiro, 2007).

Accordingly, a secondary set of legal norms has developed to govern interpretive practices and to establish a hierarchy of precedent and deference to guide superior and inferior courts, future panels of the same court, and branches of the government as they sort out the content of legal norms and the obligatory status of these norms. For instance, the norm of rationality review within constitutional law provides that a legislative act with some conceivable purpose behind it should be upheld by the courts.[9] It is often this secondary set of interpretive and role norms that serve as the primary legal norms in comparisons of actual to ideal judicial behavior (e.g., Segal & Spaeth, 2002, operationalize the "legal model" of judicial behavior as requiring fidelity to the plain meaning of statutory or constitutional text, to the legislative or constitutional drafters' intent, and to precedent).

Coherence norms, including norms of rationality, require logical consistency and coherence in the formation and ordering of beliefs and preferences, whatever those beliefs or preferences may be:

> technical discussions of rationality generally adopt a *logical* conception, in which an individual's beliefs and preferences are said

to be rational if they obey a set of formal rules such as complementarity of probabilities, the sure-thing principle or independence of irrelevant alternatives. In the laissez-faire spirit of modern economics and decision theory, the content of beliefs and of preferences is not a criterion of rationality—only internal coherence matters. (Kahneman, 1997, pp. 105–106)

"The goal of this coherence metatheory of judgment is to describe and explain the process by which a person's judgments achieve logical, or mathematical, or statistical *rationality*" (Hammond, 2000a, p. 53).[10]

Rationality as coherence requires that judgments exhibit *(1)* resistance to logically irrelevant features of the situation (e.g., post hoc judgments about the reasonableness of a course of conduct should be immune to whether the course of conduct caused no harm or severe harm, given that this information was unavailable when the conduct was undertaken), and *(2)* appropriate sensitivity to logically relevant features of the situation (e.g., base rate information should be properly assimilated into a Bayesian calculation) (Kahneman, 1991). Furthermore, *(3)* judgments should lead to a coherent and consistent web of beliefs (i.e., a change in one belief may require that other related beliefs be altered) (Tversky & Kahneman, 1982).

Coherence norms evaluate behavior solely in terms of coherence and consistency, with no necessary connection to real world success or empirical accuracy:

It may come as a surprise to the reader that rationality does not directly imply accuracy and vice versa, but brief reflection shows that this is the case. Rationality always operates in a closed system; given the premises, certain conclusions follow *if* a rational reasoning process is followed. When the reasoning process satisfies a logical test, the system is termed coherent, and that is all it is and all it claims to be. (Hammond, 2000a, p. 53)

This does not mean that behavior within a coherence metatheory is purposeless, nor that goals or beliefs are irrelevant to rationality in this system. It means only that goals and beliefs are to be defined by the individual, and then behavior is examined to determine whether it is logically consistent and coherent in light of these goals and beliefs and whether beliefs are appropriately updated in response to new evidence.

In contrast, what may be called efficacy norms test judgments and decisions against empirical reality. The most common efficacy norm used in psychological research on judgment and decision-making is a correspondence norm: "The goal of a correspondence metatheory is to describe and explain the process by which a person's judgments achieve *empirical accuracy*" (Hammond, 2000a, p. 53). Thus, whereas psychologists applying a coherence norm may examine whether causal attributions seem to follow norms for unbiased testing of causal hypotheses—with no attempt being made to assess the accuracy of these attributions—psychologists applying a correspondence norm examine the circumstances under which causal attributions tend to be more or less accurate (Funder, 1999). Correspondence norms, in theory, provide the simplest source of comparison standards because they provide an objective baseline for comparison and hold obvious attraction for evaluating the decisions of judges. Of course, in many instances, reality is not easily measured (e.g., truth is a correspondence norm for judging the outcome in criminal trials, but it is often very hard to determine truth in criminal trials).

Efficacy norms focus on the outputs of a system to test whether the system is functioning as it is supposed to according to a functional analysis or a division of labor, whereas coherence norms focus on fidelity to the rules prescribed to govern the system. Thus, if our perceptual system leads to effective navigation in our environment, then the perceptual system receives high marks under efficacy norms despite evidence of systematic perceptual illusions (Funder, 1999; Hammond, 2000b).

A variety of possible efficacy norms for judicial evaluation exist, most obviously norms of accuracy and error avoidance: how accurate are a judge's fact-based rulings and empirical predictions and how does a judge resolve evidential ambiguities: does she err in the direction desired by the system (e.g., significantly more Type II than Type I errors in verdicts in criminal cases and slightly more Type II than Type I errors in verdicts in civil cases—where the null hypothesis is not guilty or not liable—or substantially more Type II errors on threshold rulings in civil cases, such as rulings on motions for failure to state a claim)? Or we may ask whether judges succeed at obtaining compliance with the law in their adjudications, however that goal is achieved. Or the related question of whether parties are subjectively satisfied with a judge's rulings.

Note that these efficacy norms derive from analytical frameworks developed independent of what happens in actual cases. That is, the norms derive from some theory or observable consensus about what makes judgment and decision-making behavior good or bad or about what goals judges should strive to achieve. Alternatively, one could reason backward from cases where, say, litigants (or others) express low and high levels of satisfaction to search for patterns of judicial behavior associated with those reactions and try to discern what norms, if any, the judges tend to follow or what cognitive and motivational qualities these judges tend to possess. Such an empirics-based approach to norms of good judgment has not, to my knowledge, ever been undertaken in a formal or systematic fashion with respect to judicial behavior, but historical and anthropological studies of courts contain elements of this approach (e.g., Philips, 1998).[11]

Many evaluative studies of judicial behavior begin with one of these norms of good judgment and compare specific judicial behaviors to that norm, but that is not the only way to approach the descriptive-normative gap. One increasingly popular alternative is to conduct a tournament of judges (see, e.g., Choi & Gulati, 2004a, 2004b), in which judges compete on one or more measurable criterion variables and the tournament produces a relative ranking of judicial performance on these variables. The impetus behind such tournaments is, in part, recognition of the contested nature of specific norms of good judging and the desire to emphasize objective measures of performance in judicial evaluations.[12] Another popular alternative is to proceed from a dispositional or character-based theory of good judging, which posits that the possession of certain traits or qualities is sufficient for judicial competence (e.g., Solum, 2003). According to these theories, judges should be evaluated for good character rather than good decisions. Because these last two alternatives present unique issues, I consider the particulars of each after first considering complications that arise with more standard empirical approaches to the descriptive-normative gap.

General Complications

The process of choosing a normative standard and applying it to judicial behavior presents predictable complications, some more difficult than others. First, the researcher must decide whether to take an internal or external normative perspective. From an internal perspective, the researcher asks the judge (or otherwise determines, perhaps through the judge's opinions) what goal he or she was trying to achieve, selects the proper evaluative norm given that goal, and compares behavior to the norm to measure degree of success or compliance with the norm.[13] An external perspective asks what goal the judge should be trying to achieve and applies norms proper to those goals; no effort is made to gain judicial input on proper normative standards. An external perspective may be justified from a metatheoretical stance about the proper role of judges within the legal hierarchy or from the perspective of interested parties subject to the authority or influence of the courts (e.g., litigants may hope that judges' decisions are legal, just, and accurate). Or the external perspective may be chosen simply to test some theory about the degree to which judicial behavior, whether intentionally or not, accords with particular normative standards.

The choice of norms is crucial, because different norms will often point to different conclusions about competence. A judge presented with inadequate evidence at trial may irrationally convict the truly guilty defendant, while another judge presented with this inadequate evidence may rationally acquit the truly guilty defendant. The first judge did a good job under the correspondence standard but a poor job under the coherence standard, and conversely with respect to the competence of the second judge. Hence, the choice of normative criteria controls the assessment of the judge's competence on particular tasks.

It may be that the judge was capable of providing the normative response the researcher is testing for, but the judge had different values or concerns than the researcher assumed or intended and these other concerns overwhelmed the judge's interest in applying the norm of the researcher's choice. In such a case, it is not that the judge has misunderstood her task or role nor that biases drove the judge's behavior, but rather that there is a mismatch between the task or role as the researcher perceives it and as the judge perceives it. In some instances, being perceived as logical, consistent, legally principled, or fair-minded may be less important to the judge than achieving some other goal (e.g., moral and public policy concerns may override base rate information in determining liability[14]), and, in other instances, the researcher may have mistaken beliefs about the judge's goals or beliefs in light of the larger social setting. In these latter cases, where the researcher simply misconstrues the judge's beliefs or goals but the judge's behavior is logical in light of her true goals or beliefs, then we cannot say that the behavior is irrational under a coherence standard if that is our normative perspective of choice.

"Unifunctionalist tunnel vision blinds the research community to empirical and normative boundary conditions on basic effects. Inconvenient though it is, people are multifunctional entities that demand cumbersomely complex explanations" (Tetlock, 2002, p. 469).[15] Even within the confines of a theory of the role of a judge, much room exists for different conceptions of the judge's proper functions. Thus, a narrow view of behavior may reveal departures from the coherence definition of rationality, but a broader view of the same behavior may reveal a larger purpose that makes this lack of coherence look instrumentally rational and that confounds conclusions that the irrationality was due to cognitive bias.[16]

Existing discussions of judicial competence typically employ externally determined measures of competence, rather than internally determined measures based on the judge's self-chosen goals or norms. Because we are usually interested in how judges fulfill their roles within the larger legal-institutional setting, it is fair to impose values and goals on the judge that he or she might not endorse or that might even be contrary to the judge's own goals or values—although sharp disparities between internal and external normative perspectives should be rare if the judge deems her legal system legitimate and the researcher accurately perceives the goals of the legal system.[17] Nevertheless, a finding of external incompetence does not necessarily mean that the judge was incompetent from an internal perspective; it only means that the judge failed to meet an externally imposed normative standard. Indeed, a judge may be judged externally incompetent precisely because the judge is quite competent at achieving a goal that is internally desirable but undesirable from an institutional, external standpoint.

Second, because there may be dispute about the goals that should be served by certain tasks or because the judge may need to serve multiple goals, the researcher may need to employ multiple, possibly conflicting normative criteria or justify her choice of some normative criteria to the exclusion of others (for more on this topic, see the chapter by Robbennolt, MacCoun, & Darley in this volume).[18] Otherwise, the research may be dismissed as irrelevant or be disputed on grounds of incompleteness.[19] Absent an agreed ranking of values and norms, however, contending factions may exalt or impugn judicial competence simply by invoking selectively those norms against which judges fare better or worse.

Third, we come to what may be the single most difficult problem in attempting to study compliance with legal norms (and which explains in part the preference for the two alternative conceptions of judicial competence that I discuss below): even if there is no dispute over the proper norms, there may be dispute over, or uncertainty about, how to operationalize these norms for testing purposes. If efficacy norms of accuracy and party satisfaction are employed, for example, then the researcher must of course devise a measure of accuracy and outcome satisfaction. Experiments provide a particularly attractive setting for addressing this problem, because they allow the researcher to vary the dimensions of hypothetical or staged cases to examine whether fact-finder behavior conforms to different formulations of the norms and allows the specification of true and false results (as, for example, in tests of false-confession detection).

In some cases, it may be impossible to formulate workable tests of goals, which may result in the selection of a second-best goal. Indeed, we might prefer that truth be the ultimate touchstone in fact-finding, but we may have to settle for a coherence measure of competence over a correspondence measure because we lack a reliable measure of truth in many real cases. Of course, while many of the rules of evidence can be seen as rules designed to lead to accurate decision-making (or risk-of-error allocations, per Stein, 2005), other rules endorse values other than truth and prevent the introduction of evidence that might improve accuracy. We may thus favor a coherence standard that asks whether judges follow the rules of evidence because we believe that these rules are the most feasible and manageable means to truth approximation in light of epistemic constraints and because of the other values contrary to truth detection that the trial process must serve. Which brings us to a more detailed discussion of legal norms.

Legal Norms

Many empirical studies of judicial competence employ "perfect lawfulness" as the normative standard: Do extralegal factors affect judicial decisions that ideally should turn solely on what the law and legally relevant facts of the case dictate? The numerous studies by political scientists into the correlation of Supreme Court justices' political attitudes with the direction of case votes on judicial decisions employ this normative standard (e.g., Unah & Hancock, 2006). Most prominently, Segal and Spaeth (2002) contrast their attitudinal model of Supreme Court judicial decision-making with what they call the "legal model," which is supposed to represent how a law-bound ruling would be made (through fidelity to text, drafter's intent, or existing precedent), and they find that justices' political attitudes relate significantly to patterns of votes on cases.[20] They conclude that "the legal model and its components serve only to rationalize the Court's decisions and to cloak the reality of the Court's decision-making process" (Segal & Spaeth, 2002, p. 53).

There are considerable limitations to the use of perfect lawfulness as the normative standard. First, the norm is typically just "in the air" and does not serve as a source for direct comparison. In these studies, the normative position of perfect lawfulness at best serves as the null hypothesis, and any measured extralegal variable that is statistically related to case outcomes leads to a rejection of the null hypothesis. In Segal and Spaeth's (2002) main tests of the attitudinal model of judicial decision making, there is no direct comparison between judicial decisions and the predictions of any specific instantiation of the "legal model." Rather, Segal and Spaeth, after finding that ideology can explain some significant percentage of variance in judicial decisions, simply assume that this finding contradicts what a legal model would predict.

Of course, to the extent a legal model would predict absolutely no influence of justices' attitudes, then the legal model is contradicted, but I am aware of no legal model that would predict that liberals and conservatives would perfectly agree on the controlling legal norm in all Supreme Court cases. Indeed, I am aware of no single legal model or set of coherent legal norms that all conservative scholars and judges would agree on as the correct approach, nor that liberal elites would similarly agree on, and I suspect that many politically conservative and politically liberal elites would disagree over the proper outcome in many Supreme Court cases from even a narrowly self-interested, purely political perspective.[21] In other words, Segal and Spaeth's support for the attitudinal model certainly casts into doubt "perfect lawfulness" as an accurate description of judicial behavior, but the degree of deviation from this vague standard goes unspecified, and, given competition over what perfect lawfulness requires across cases, interpretations of a particular outcome as reflecting inappropriate policy preferences or principled disagreements between liberals and conservatives as to what the law requires in particular cases will often be contestable.[22]

This last point is not a minor quibble with political science studies of the Supreme Court. If a conservative judge can choose among legally principled courses C1, C2, and C3 to reach the conservative result that he politically prefers, but if the judge feels constrained by legal norms to choose C1 over the other two options, then this constraint is significant if writing the opinion pursuant to C1, as opposed to pursuant to C2 or C3, has effects on the lower courts and later Supreme Court decisions (see Richards & Kritzer, 2002; see also Friedman, 2006; Hansford & Spriggs, 2006).

Second, because these studies almost invariably test for an extralegal influence rather than compliance with a legal norm, a finding that the variable of interest is not significantly related to judicial behavior tells us little about judicial competence other than that this variable, in this study, did not exert any influence. It may be the case that judges were acting pursuant to the normative standard, that the wrong extralegal influences were investigated, or that some other norm or feature of the institution or situation other than the

particular law of the case dampened individual differences in voting inclina-
tions (as Fischman, 2008, argues with respect to the norm of consensus).[23]

Third, dependent variables (i.e., the judicial behavior of interest in
extralegal influence studies, such as votes to grant certiorari or votes on the
merits of a case) are often operationalized in categorical terms that may be too
crude to capture the influence of extralegal factors or, if a significant influence
is found, may obscure the real nature of this influence (as Maveety, 2003,
notes, this is a long-standing criticism of political scientists' judicial studies).
For instance, judicial outcomes may reflect a wide range of political positions,
from very liberal to very conservative, but Segal and Spaeth (2002, ch. 8)
categorize Supreme Court decisions as liberal or conservative, and the decisions
these researchers make regarding what constitutes a liberal or conservative
decision reflect particularized versions of liberalism and conservatism (e.g.,
pro-federal-government rulings are generally deemed conservative, but of
course some varieties of conservatism would probably not uniformly endorse
such rulings). That is not to say that dichotomous dependent measures are
not appropriate for testing some deviations from legal or other norms—just
that one needs to be sensitive to the loss of sensitivity that accompanies such
choices.

Fourth, many legal norms are process norms as opposed to substantive,
or outcome, norms (e.g., rules of procedure and evidence at the trial level,
or interpretive norms for statutory and constitutional construction and
standards of review at the appellate level). Process norms specify the range of
permissible considerations and at best forbid some categories of outcomes
that could be reached only through reliance on certain sorts of impermissible
evidence or considerations, such as using lotteries or coin flips to assign
responsibility for torts; process norms narrow the range of permissible outcomes but do not compel particular outcomes. Unless one takes the position
that it is impossible to test compliance with process norms (a proposition that
psychological studies of the rules of evidence have falsified, see, e.g., Wistrich
et al., 2005) or that process norms have no important constraining force (an
empirical claim itself), then the overwhelming focus of political science
studies on case outcomes as opposed to decision processes greatly limits the
utility of these studies of the descriptive-normative gap in judicial behavior
(Richards & Kritzer, 2002).[24]

A related problem is the requirement that a legal norm lead, a priori, to
definitive predictions for empirical testing purposes. This requirement is, of
course, reasonable from an empirical perspective, but its implementation has
been problematic. As Segal and Spaeth (2002, p. 59) correctly point out, a
legal norm that cannot tell a judge how to act in a particular case cannot be the
subject of empirical testing (nor can it have normative force) (see also Segal &
Spaeth, 1994), but a legal norm need not compel a particular decision on the
merits to have some constraining force (stated counterfactually, would the
same evidence have been considered, would the same rulings on all issues
have been made, or would the decision have been written in the same way had

the legal norm not existed?). How an opinion is written may have more lasting influence on the behavior of other courts as well as that of lawyers and parties than the particular outcome of a case (Hansford & Spriggs, 2006); so it is no small matter if norms constrain opinions without altering outcomes (Richards & Kritzer, 2002). Whereas legal scholars may give too much explanatory weight to the reasons stated in opinions, the tendency to ignore the reasons stated and focus on case outcomes and external motives greatly restricts the usefulness and acceptance of empirical judicial studies by judges and lawyers.

Stated another way, if one of the goals of empirical judicial studies is to predict how judges will act and rule under specified conditions rather than assess normative compliance (see Leiter, 1997), then disregard of the text of statutes and cases constitutes a curious omission unless the prediction game is confined only to how a particular court—most notably the Supreme Court—will rule on a case once the judges hearing the case are known. Attorneys cannot play the prediction game in that truncated manner because they must often advise clients before the ideology of the whole series of judges who may ultimately hear a case is known. Accordingly, attorneys must look to existing case law and the text of statutes and regulations to predict how a generic judge would rule and advise their clients accordingly. Until studies demonstrate convincingly that looking to these documentary sources of the law is pointless to predict judicial behavior outside the Supreme Court, attorneys will continue to do so for lack of any better guidance on predicting how the law will be applied. Furthermore, when the prediction game is really a multilevel prediction game with tremendous uncertainty (trial judge A will rule this way, but appellate judges X, Y, & Z are likely to rule that way assuming X, Y, & Z are assigned to the case...), it is unclear whether any rational attorney, ex ante, should look more to judicial ideology than the law to advise her client.

Additional Distinctions for Legal Norms as Benchmarks

These concerns suggest that it may be wise to look for alternatives to treating perfect lawfulness as the null hypothesis and then declaring the legal model invalid when significant deviations from the null are found. In general, direct tests for compliance with legal norms, rather than indirect tests using the "perfect lawfulness" standard, will provide the information we are most interested in from an evaluative perspective. The nature of the direct test depends on the nature of the legal norm being tested. One way (and surely not the only way) to classify legal norms for purposes of testing is with respect to their injunctive content: *(1)* proscription norms: certain kinds of considerations must not be taken into account or certain processes or outcomes cannot be chosen under specified conditions; *(2)* permission norms: certain kinds of considerations may be taken into account or certain processes or outcomes may be chosen under specified conditions; *(3)* prescription norms: certain kinds of considerations must be taken into account or certain processes or outcomes must be chosen under specified conditions; *(4)* ordering norms: if multiple considerations or outcomes are prescribed or permissible, prioritize the considerations or outcomes in a particular way; *(5)* decision norms: decide a case in a particular way in light of permissive and prescriptive considerations.

Proscription norm tests will look very much like many of the extralegal influence studies found within psychology that examine whether juries (and occasionally judges) can disregard inadmissible evidence as required by the rules of evidence (e.g., Wistrich et al., 2005). Proscription norms can be found, of course, at the appellate level as well (e.g., rules about the record on appeal). The difference from the generic perfect lawfulness test is that the improper extralegal influence is specifically defined by the specific proscription norm, and the norm typically specifies the conditions under which a particular consideration/outcome/process is not appropriate.

Permission norms vest judges with discretion to decide the propriety of certain outcomes or considerations with broad guidance as to the range of acceptable discretion, and, as such, these norms pose difficult testing problems for they require an empirical measure of acceptable discretion. One way to test for compliance with permission norms is to test whether discretion is exercised in a biased fashion. Thus, if judges with sentencing discretion impose higher sentences to black than white defendants, all else being equal, then the judges exercise their discretion in a biased way. These tests require, however, another norm to resolve whether the bias is itself nonnormative, as with a proscription norm against taking race into account in sentencing. If younger judges appointed by Democrats grant summary judgment more frequently than older judges appointed by Republicans in sexual harassment cases (e.g., Kulik et al., 2003), all else being equal, then it appears that one set of judges is using its discretion in a biased way, but it is not clear which direction constitutes the nonnormative response. Another approach to tests of permission norms would be to have experts agree on the appropriate range of permissive outcomes in a set of cases and test judges against these benchmarks.

Prescription norms allow point-specific tests of normative compliance. This category of tests includes testing for enforcement of bright-line rules, particularly those triggered by objective conditions such as deadlines. Because tests of prescription norms will typically yield clear results (assuming the prescription norm can be operationalized and compliance with it measured without much controversy), detection of deviation from these norms should be straightforward.

Ordering norms also allow for straightforward tests in many instances. Lower court obedience to Supreme Court precedent rather than contrary circuit precedent and preference orderings for types of evidence in certain types of disputes (e.g., statutory interpretation cases) will often yield clear results (of course, there may be dispute about whether the proper ordering norm is being applied). In other instances, such as implementation of the

Chevron norm of deference to administrative agency interpretations of statutes where the interpretation is reasonable, will prove more difficult because implementation of the ordering rule is based on subjective determinations about a case (on the politics of applying *Chevron*, see Miles & Sunstein, 2006). In such instances, we must revert to looking for systematic disparities (tied to types of cases/values at stake, types of parties, or other situational or judge-specific factors) or deviations from expert orderings.

Decision norms specify particular outcomes when triggering conditions are met. The more objective the trigger and the conditions for determining whether the trigger is pulled, the easier the decision norm will be to test. Some decision norms function as constraints on the authority of the judge, such as minimalist or incrementalist norms about case law development or constitutional interpretation, and the focus will be on testing whether judges abide by such constraints. In tests of norms such as these, the key will be ranking possible decision outcomes in terms of restraint to monitor for compliance (or ranking for allegiance to text, intent, or purpose depending on the nature of the decision norm being tested).

From a psychological perspective, we should expect the greatest deviation to occur with permission norms (that assign discretion to judges and thus invite individual differences in application), where triggering conditions for norms are most ambiguous (and possibility of detection of norm violation lowest),[25] and where accountability is the least (e.g., with supreme courts reviewing constitutional issues). If the deviation appears to be in one direction across judges, then we should look for problems with how the norm is presented to judges (e.g., perhaps the text of a rule contains an unnoticed confusion) or for some systematic situational influence driving behavior in that direction. If the deviation appears bimodal (or some other systematic but not unidirectional pattern), then it is likely that an individual difference variable or some covarying situational influence is driving the deviations. If the deviation appears to be random, then it may be that the norm is difficult to apply in some subset of cases, this subset of cases is randomly distributed across judges, and, for this subset, some irrelevant situational or individual difference variable is having an influence that it does not outside this subset of cases. Random deviation may also represent the operation of a norm that is hard to implement for some reason (e.g., some complex rules of evidence may be difficult to implement consistently under the time demands of making real-time rulings on motions at trial).

Coherence Norms

There are, of course, many coherence norms other than legal norms that we may want judges to follow. Axioms of rational choice, rules of logic and probability, hypothesis-testing rules, and Bayes' formula for updating beliefs are the most common coherence norms employed in behavioral decision theory studies.[26] Many legal norms, such as interpretive rules and the rules of evidence, clearly allow room for other coherence norms to operate. In general, the more closely a judge follows norms of rationality, logic, and probability, the more consistent and predictable her behavior should be and the more likely the judge will maximize the values she deems most important.

In the abstract, the notion that judges and jurors should act rationally when evaluating the law and evidence in a case is uncontroversial, and therefore proof from psychology of apparently rampant irrationality understandably commands the attention of legal scholars (as Saks & Kidd, 1980, noted many years ago). In some ways, this evidence should be more troubling to positive political theorists and others who advocate rational choice models of judicial decision-making as explanatory models of actual judicial behavior (e.g., Epstein & Knight, 1998; Schanzenbach & Tiller, 2006) than to scholars examining judicial behavior for the size of the descriptive-normative gap. For there are a host of other norms that we may care equally about from an external perspective that do not require strict compliance with norms of rationality. Indeed, to the extent that systematic deviations from rationality are caused by cognitive and motivational mechanisms that have evolved or are used to serve alternative goals than those served within the closed rationality system under observation (e.g., efficiency in processing at acceptable levels of accuracy [Hammond, 2000b] or attributing greater causal responsibility to persons than rationally justified to encourage care and deter excuse-making [Tetlock, 2000]), then we should expect deviations from rationality to accompany satisfactory performance under alternative normative standards.

Nevertheless, whether judges, given their experience, training, and the decision aids available to them, comply with norms of causal hypothesis testing, probability and rationality is of interest from an external normative perspective because this information may lead to prescriptive models of judging. We now know that several predictable judgmental biases can be debiased (Heath et al., 1998; Larrick, 2004), and we know that the structure of some environments ameliorates or exacerbates some biases (see Mitchell, 2002b, 2003b). We also know that there are individual differences in rationality, a topic addressed in other chapters in this volume (see generally Mitchell, 2003b; Stanovich, 1999). Identifying the norms that judges have the greatest difficulty following and identifying the characteristics of more and less rational judges may lead to feasible prescriptive models for legal reform.

Tests of norms of rationality and probability will look like many of the tests of legal norms, because all are coherence norms. Thus, if a norm of rationality directs the judge to ignore outcomes and focus only on ex ante information available to the parties to assess their behavior, we will test whether the judge can ignore these improper influences (see Rachlinski, 1998). Where the norm directs that certain information should be considered, such as base rate evidence in assessing the probative value of evidence, we will test whether the judge properly uses this information. Experimental tests allow the cleanest tests of judges' abilities to engage in analytical thought and comply with norms of rationality, but testing judges outside their natural environments may lead us to worry more than we should about the harms associated with laboratory normative deviations (Gigerenzer, 2006). Thus, experimental tests should be seen as providing an important first step toward understanding the rationality of judges and identifying possible normative deviations, but that step should be followed by studies assessing how institutions and individual judges adapt, if at all, to correct for such deviations.

Efficacy Norms

If one is interested in judges primarily as one among several interdependent actors within the governmental division of labor, then efficacy norms may be of particular interest for evaluative purposes. For instance, if a key role of judges within the larger institution of government is to induce voluntary compliance with the law to ease pressure on executive enforcement of the law, then testing judges for their ability to persuade parties to accept legal decisions and voluntarily obey the law become important efficacy norms for evaluative purposes (hence the popularity of measuring perceptions of procedural justice and its relation to perceptions of the legitimacy of the legal system and voluntary compliance with the law; Gibson, 2006; Tyler & Huo, 2002). Likewise, the function posited for constitutional adjudication by the Supreme Court will determine the efficacy norm one would choose to evaluate constitutional decisions.

The empirical and theoretical importance of efficacy norms is that they take the focus away from whether the law can constrain judges from turning their own preferences into law and refocuses attention on how effective judges are at achieving whatever goal is sought, by whatever means. Thus, a judge who possesses preternatural lie detection skills (see O'Sullivan & Ekman, 2005) and employed those skills to achieve highly accurate results in trials, while completely ignoring the rules of evidence, would be an excellent judge under a correspondence norm. The results one obtains from an efficacy norm study will only be as compelling as the argument one advances for the propriety of that norm, but, given agreement on the norms, efficacy norms arguably provide the most important information of any of the evaluative comparisons that can be conducted because such tests directly link performance to desired outcomes.

Once one satisfies oneself that the efficacy norm chosen is defensible and worth studying, then one confronts the task of devising a criterion measure. Once outside experimental settings, where the experimenter controls how the comparison to the norm will be conducted and measured (e.g., asking judges to rate known true and false confessions for truthfulness; cf. Kassin et al., 2005), a "backward" or known-outcomes approach for testing compliance with correspondence norms in trial settings may be wisest. In this approach one identifies cases where the values of the output variable of interest are known (e.g., innocence or guilt as determined with a high level of certainty based on DNA evidence or corroborated confessions by others [e.g., Garrett, 2008], or the outcomes of predictions made previously by judges), and then one examines the conditions under which judges made accurate or otherwise efficacious decisions. One must take into account, of course, that legal norms may constrain judges from giving certain types of evidence, at certain stages of a case, the weight the evidence might deserve under a strict correspondence test. Thus, such studies may reveal places where correspondence and coherence norms work at cross-purposes.

Efficacy norms have been relatively neglected compared to coherence norms and legal coherence norms in particular. Yet getting things empirically right is what we often care most about in courts, and at times there will be objective (or at least intersubjectively reliable) measures of efficacy. Appellate judges often make predictions about the empirical consequences of choosing one legal interpretation over another, and the most dire predictions are typically found in dissents, which makes their predictions testable in some instances (we should expect dissenters whose parades of horribles never materialize to claim that conditions changed, making predictions no longer applicable; Tetlock, 2005). For instance, Albiston and Nielsen (2007) tested the Supreme Court's empirical prediction that rejection of the catalyst theory of fee awards in civil rights cases would not discourage the filing of suits by surveying public interest organizations, and their findings cast doubt on the accuracy of the Court's prediction. Or we can treat judicial decisions as natural experiments and examine the effects of these decisions on other courts, other institutions, and the pattern of lawsuit filings (e.g., examining the effects changes in the standards for admitting expert evidence; see Vickers, 2005). The tournament approach to judicial competence, with its emphasis on objective comparisons, may be particularly well suited to testing compliance with efficacy norms.

Judicial Tournaments and Judicial Character

Recently, researchers have shown interest in going beyond examinations in which correlations between party affiliation and voting patterns play a central role, as is so often the case in political science studies of judicial behavior. The two leading alternative approaches, already mentioned above, involve judicial tournaments that emphasize multiple performance measures and theories of good judging that emphasize judicial character rather than judicial performance in particular cases. These two very different approaches present their own difficulties, but each has the potential to push research in new and important directions.

Choi and Gulati (2004a, 2004b; Gulati & Choi, 2007) recently popularized the judicial tournament approach as part of a proposal to reform the Supreme Court appointment process (for discussion of variants on the judicial tournament idea, see Goldberg, 2005; WERL, 2004). Traditional judicial studies, which examine justices for ideological voting and typically contrast behavior to perfect legality (or rather a norm of no ideological voting), often have data that can be reported in tournament format (e.g., Segal & Spaeth, 2002, report the relative influence of values on different justices' votes), but the emphasis is on testing for deviations from a specified norm or finding confirmation that some extralegal factor influences judicial behavior. The emphasis in judicial tournaments is on the relative ranking itself and, at least in Choi and Gulati's judicial tournaments, on relative rankings derived from objectively measurable variables. This emphasis on relative performance gives rise to a fundamental criticism of the tournament approach: a relative ranking of judges fails to provide compelling evidence of judicial competence absent some independent normative benchmark (e.g., Solum, 2005a): the winner may simply be the best judge in a tournament of bad judges.

The skeptical response to this criticism is that relative standing on weakly diagnostic objective measures of performance is the best we can do given the contested nature of the concept of good judging and given the difficulties of translating judicial votes and opinions into data. Under this view, any eva-luative study of judges yields at best a relative ranking of judges according to the researcher's flawed theory or methodology, and hence we avoid at least the problems of subjective judgment by employing objectively determined rankings.

The ecumenical response is that relative standing yields useful information about judicial competence along dimensions that may hold relevance for a variety of conceptions of good judging, and perhaps provides definitive information for some norms. A well-theorized selection of objective measures can provide good, if imperfect, proxies for testing abstract norms of judicial competence (e.g., some of Solum's [2003, 2005a] "thin" judicial virtues may be captured roughly by objective measures of ethics compliance, opinion clarity, educational achievement, and productivity), and a number of objective measures may approximate widely accepted conceptions of good judging (e.g., most theorists would place a judge who writes her own opinions above one who does not; Choi & Gulati, 2005). When the tourney's results converge across multiple measures designed to get at the same qualities, then we should have confidence that the tournament meaningfully and reliably assesses qualities related to differential effort or ability at judging.

Furthermore, understanding how judges compare on objective measures moves debate away from the mechanics of operationalizing independent and dependent variables to a debate about the relevance of these and other measures to notions of judicial competence (Choi and Gulati's tournaments certainly motivated much fruitful debate in this regard; see Gey & Rossi, 2005). When objective measures identify sets of judges as high versus low achievers, and alternative approaches to judicial competence yield different outcomes, then understanding why the divergence occurs can only improve theorizing about what constitutes good judging and how to identify it (e.g., Farber, 2005; Goldberg, 2005; WERL, 2004). For instance, on what objective dimensions do Democrats and Republicans agree, and is such agreement consistent with the attitudinal model of judges? Along what objective dimensions other than voting behavior are liberal and conservative judges predicted to act in an ideological fashion, and do they behave as predicted (for one example along these lines, see Law, 2005)? And of course, the judicial tournament need not involve only objective measures. Many states systematically collect data on judicial performance, including attorney and juror surveys of judicial demeanor and performance, and this wealth of data, if made available to empiricists, could be readily adapted for academic research and judicial tournaments in particular (see Kourlis & Singer, 2007, on judicial performance evaluation programs).

The relative ranking approach to judicial competence may also proceed in an atheoretical fashion to explore courts and areas of law for unexpected patterns. For instance, are there consistent sets of characteristics associated with judges on particular courts who perform well versus poorly on mundane measures of productivity, influence, or reversal rates? Judicial tournaments can identify the high and low achievers on such measures, who can then be systematically studied for similarities and dissimilarities in their backgrounds and situational settings that may account for these differences. Areas of law that provide objectively determinable outcomes allow for the use of judicial tournaments based on a correspondence norm: for instance, courts that randomly assign criminal cases, and hence provide a natural control on factual differences across cases, and that collect data on probation and parole violations provide a setting for a judicial tournament involving the ability of judges to discriminate between good and bad risks.

The judicial tournament, in short, presents a host of research opportunities and should be seen as a necessary, but not sufficient, part of the judicial competence research repertoire. The relative ease of conducting tournaments based on objective measures compared to labor-intensive and debatable coding of opinions and outcomes makes this tool a particularly valuable one as judicial researchers seek to expand knowledge about judicial competence beyond the U.S. Supreme Court.

The second popular alternative to traditional political science studies of judicial competence is to focus on the possession of certain traits or qualities rather than particular behaviors to determine judicial competence (e.g., Farber & Sherry, this volume, ch. 18). This dispositional approach risks converting intuition into unproven tautology: wise judges will issue wise decisions (because the desirable trait of wisdom means acting wisely). To move beyond tautology, some justification needs to be provided for giving a dispositional theory normative weight. Normative authority could arise from agreement, as with a "thin theory of judicial virtue," in which only uncontroversial traits that are desired in all judges are chosen (Solum, 2003). Or its normative status could arise from showing that the dispositional theory of judging derives from another theory that already enjoys normative status (e.g., Solum derives his virtue-centered theory of judging from virtue ethics), or from empirical studies showing that other types of judges with particular characteristics perform better and worse on various normative tests (for a discussion of the concept of expertise and its application to judicial studies, see the chapter in this volume by Shanteau & Dalgleish, ch. 16). Or the theory could be justified through empirical observation (which appears to be the basis for Sherry's [2005, 2006] views on the traits and experiences that appellate judges should have or should not have; namely, in this last respect, experience as an academic): if empirical observation reveals that judges who possess qualities X, Y, and Z reliably produce excellent decisions, then these qualities should be favored. The problem with this last approach is that it simply moves the normative question to another point in the equation: we will need justified normative standards for deciding whether the decisions of these judges were indeed excellent.[27]

One interesting feature of character-based approaches to evaluating judges is that, if one accepts the character traits chosen, then the evaluative focus shifts to whether judges possess these traits and away from performance. The task becomes measuring the traits of existing and potential judges to evaluate them for good and bad judicial character.

From an empirical perspective, the measurement problems associated with dispositional approaches to judicial evaluation are severe for judicial traits of the kind Solum advances (abstract virtues and vices),[28] but much less so for judicial traits of the kind Sherry advances (at least for the experience-based factors she argues for as proxies for the more abstract character traits she ultimately favors). Consider a popular judicial trait within some dispositional approaches: good judgment, which may go by a variety of labels, such as wisdom or pragmatism (see Sherry, 2003).[29] There is no single theory of judicial pragmatism or judicial wisdom, and certainly no well-validated measure of pragmatism or judicial wisdom. It may be difficult to distinguish a pragmatic from a textualist outcome in a particular case (because, as Posner [2005] notes, at times the pragmatic judge will adopt the textualist outcome), but it will be near to impossible to distinguish a pragmatist from a textualist from biographical material about judges (though Solum [2005b] disputes this with respect to his proposed virtues and vices) (and, in any event, "clinical" assessments of character are considerably less reliable than those based on validated assessment tools, none of which exist for pragmatism). If a judge's opinions serve as the source for making determinations about the judge's pragmatic character, then we return to our tautology problem.[30]

Another interesting feature of these theories, and the most problematic feature from a social-psychological perspective, is the assumption that judges with ideal "judicial character" are more likely to follow the law strictly, wisely interpret and apply the law, or, perhaps, do justice (whatever those terms imply) than those without this character. While it is certainly the case that individuals differ in important ways that may relate to judicial behavior (e.g., Tetlock et al., 1985), it is also the case that these individual difference variables interact with situational variables (such as being in the majority or minority; Gruenfeld, 1995) to produce judicial outcomes. Neither a strong personality-based nor a strong "situationist" view of judging (or of behavior in general) can be supported by the evidence from the long debate about the primacy of the situation versus the person; rather, interactionism is the proper view (see Funder, 1999, 2001). A salutary by-product of empirical tests of dispositional theories of good judging might well be a greater appreciation for the role of interactions between personality and situational variables in achieving normative compliance.

Thus, while I am optimistic that a dispositional approach to evaluating judges will lead to new insights because researchers taking this approach will likely ask different questions than those posed in standard norm-based evaluative approaches (or at least employ new and different norms), I am not optimistic that, ultimately, dispositional approaches to good judging will avoid the usual problems encountered in attempts to study the descriptive-normative gap. For if tests of judicial character remain unmoored from actual decisions, critics will eventually dismiss the dispositional claims as irrelevant or invalid. In the end, we evaluate judges to learn how well they are doing their jobs, however "doing their jobs" may be defined, and so we must focus on what judges actually do in relation to what we wish they would do.

Conclusion

Empirical evaluative studies of judges have historically been dominated by a focus on the U.S. Supreme Court and a narrow debate about the degree to which Supreme Court justices allow their personal preferences or political values to influence their decisions. I have argued that these studies fail to provide compelling evidence on the law versus politics debate as applied to the Supreme Court, much less other courts, and these studies distract attention from a host of other possible normative comparisons that judicial scholars should care about, and from alternative empirical approaches that may be more easily, or at least less controversially, implemented.

A diverse and robust literature on the normative-descriptive gap in judgment and decision-making exists within psychology, and this literature contains much healthy debate about the size, contours, and meaning of this gap (see, e.g., Krueger & Funder, 2004). The insights and methods of this literature are just starting to filter into empirical studies of judicial competence, and by explicating some of the norms utilized in this literature and some of the methodological issues that evaluative studies present, this chapter is meant to accelerate the rate of interdisciplinary exchange and encourage diversification in evaluative studies. Trite though it now is to suggest that judicial researchers should let a thousand empirical flowers bloom (given the long history of invocation of this dictum within judicial studies; Maveety, 2003), this recommendation may have no more apt application within the field than to studies of judicial competence. If the attitudinalist orientation to judicial studies continues to dominate empirical research in this field, then outside interest in the field will likely remain limited and a host of important dimensions of judicial competence with possible prescriptive implications will continue to be unexplored.

Notes

1. I use the term "competence" to refer to a judge's (degree of) compliance with a normative standard (see Stein, 1996, for a similar usage). The term is meant to have the same meaning here as the terms "rational" or "irrational" do in psychological studies of the concordance of actual judgment and choice with norms of rationality.
2. My primary and modest goal is to provide a framework for organizing empirical questions about judicial competence, but I do venture some predictions and offer some critical assessments of existing evaluative studies. For an extended discussion of the difficulty in operationalizing good judgment for assessing the quality of real world judgments, see chapter 1 in Tetlock (2005).
3. Within psychology, prescriptive models are distinguished from normative and descriptive models of judgment and decision making. Normative models supply the standards or rules for evaluating judgments; descriptive models compare judgments to the normative models; prescriptive models specify the conditions under which judgments can be brought more into line with the normative models (see Baron, 2004).
4. These random deviations constitute mere performance errors, whereas systematic deviations would suggest an underlying incompetence (Stein, 1996). Both may need attention, but likely different sorts of attention.
5. Of course, not all political scientists embrace the strict attitudinalist view and very few legal scholars embrace a strict legalistic view. Segal and Spaeth's influential framing of the debate in this way, however, surely has framed the larger debate, for better or worse, and their strongly worded skeptical view of the power of the law to constrain (e.g., Segal & Spaeth, 2002), or the modified strategic view in which other political institutions but not the law constrain judges (e.g., Epstein & Knight, 1998), now regularly serves as the starting position within empirical quantitative studies of judicial behavior.
6. Segal and Spaeth (2002, pp. 289–292) assimilate *Casey* to their attitudinal model and thus do not treat it as dissonant evidence.
7. Others may parse the norms differently; this particular categorization is used for organizational purposes only and holds no special importance in the chapter.
8. The few works that do evaluate judges in relation to social norms usually involve norms of secrecy and civility (e.g., Gaffney, 1994). Baum (2006) argues for greater attention to collegiality as an important judicial motive, which might lead to a greater emphasis on social norms and the degree to which judges comply with them. Fischman (2008) presents interesting evidence that a norm of consensus may significantly moderate individual judges' policy preferences. For further discussion of collegiality as an important influence on appellate judges' behavior, see the chapter by Martinek in this volume (ch. 5).

9. See, e.g., *FCC v. Beach Communications, Inc.*, 508 U.S. 307, 315 (1993): "On rational-basis review, a classification in a statute such as the Cable Act comes to us bearing a strong presumption of validity, and those attacking the rationality of the legislative classification have the burden 'to negative every conceivable basis which might support it.' Moreover, because we never require a legislature to articulate its reasons for enacting a statute, it is entirely irrelevant for constitutional purposes whether the conceived reason for the challenged distinction actually motivated the legislature" (citations omitted). Whether rationality review actually operates in this minimal, deferential form is the subject of debate (see Farrell, 1999), but the standard does serve as a normative baseline.

10. Technically, legal norms are a subcategory of coherence norms because they constitute a closed system of rules to be followed without regard to some independent measure of the quality of system outputs. The goals are determined by the body that promulgates the legal norms, and the legal norms are designed to produce outputs in line with the desired goals. Legal norms are thus analogous to scientific norms: scientific principles for conducting empirical research, if followed, should lead to reliable empirical knowledge; the scientific status of research is determined by its fidelity to scientific principles rather than the reliability or truth of the knowledge produced (Kitcher, 1993). Likewise, fidelity to legal norms should lead to the kinds of outcomes lawmakers desire. I treat legal norms separately from other coherence norms because of their special importance for judicial evaluations.

11. Alexander George (1980) and Irving Janis (1982) developed their important models of good political decision-making through historical studies of flawed and successful executive decision making.

12. In addition to moving selection away from political litmus tests and irresolvable debates about merit, Choi and Gulati (2004b) also hypothesize that tournaments with implications for selections for higher courts may provide positive incentives to judges.

13. We may question the sincerity of judges' stated goals, and the possibility of insincerity does complicate the interpretation of results obtained from an internal perspective: if empirical tests reveal a large gap between actual and ideal behavior under the judge-chosen norm, then the gap may be due to insincerity or incompetence.

14. Windschitl and Wells make this argument:

> Consider . . . the general implication of a system of justice that could find people liable, based on the balance of probability that derives merely from membership in a group or class. Would it be good social or legal policy, for instance, to consider a man to have harassed female coworkers merely because he is a member of a corporate organization in which 80% of the males have harassed female coworkers. Our point is that it would be inappropriate to use such base rates for these types of judgments. (Windschitl & Wells, 1996, p. 41)

15. As an alternative way to understand the possible problem of confounding between seemingly biased behavior and underlying values and beliefs, consider how the interplay between cognitive bias and different aversions to the types of verdict errors may play out at trial. Imagine a criminal case with Judge 1 who

considers conviction of an innocent person to be a mortal error that must be avoided at all costs and Judge 2 who has aversions of equal magnitude to the errors of convicting an innocent person and failing to convict a guilty person. Imagine further that Judge 1 rationally processes all evidence but, at the end of the trial, Judge 1's judgment of the probability that the defendant committed the crime does not reach the high level of subjective certainty needed by this judge to convict. Judge 2, on the other hand, irrationally processes the evidence and acquits due to this biased processing of evidence. A focus only on the end result—two votes for not guilty—will obscure the very different thought processes and error aversions or values that led to the same votes.

16. With surprising frequency within behavioral decision theory, researchers simply assume that study participants would endorse a particular goal with a particular set of normative standards, without justifying this external normative perspective. Which may lead to premature judgments of incompetence:

> Even when people appear to be making systematically biased judgments or irrational decisions, it is likely that they are trying to solve some problem or achieve some goal to the best of their abilities. The behavioral researcher is well advised to look carefully at his or her research participant's behavior, beliefs, and goals to discern "the method in the apparent madness. (Hastie, 2001, p. 659)

17. If the judge takes, that is, something like Hart's (1961) "internal point of view" and feels obliged to obey and uphold the law. That does not mean the judge will do so with complete success, given psychological limitations as well as evidential and normative ambiguities, but the judge internalizes the legal system's rules and tries to follow them.

18. Or it may be that different legal systems embrace different goals, and it may be impracticable to consider all of the different goals within a single study if each goal requires a variation in design to test for competence.

19. For instance, Feigenson (2003) criticized the Sunstein et al. (2002) study of punitive damage awards (mock jurors served as the primary subjects, but one study in the collection examined judges) for its emphasis on optimal deterrence as the goal of punitive damages to the exclusion of a retribution as a goal.

20. Given the public policy issues often at stake in appellate cases, particularly constitutional cases, the emphasis within political science studies of judging on personal policy preferences as a likely motivating factor in how cases are decided is quite understandable. But political ideology or attitudinal orientation, as presently measured by political scientists (typically from the party of the president or the senators in whose state the judicial vacancy is being filled; see Sisk & Heise, 2005) is unlikely to capture other important, enduring extralegal influences. Basic assumptions about human behavior and the role of internal and external forces in determining behavior, about the ability of the market to correct inequalities and errors of judgment and choice, and about the harm of different types of errors may exert much more pervasive influence on judicial decisions than policy attitudes (see Tetlock & Mitchell, Forthcoming), though no doubt there will be a correlation between conservatism-liberalism and various assumptions about human behavior and the power of markets. From a political psychology standpoint, we should focus not simply on political values but also causal beliefs as determinants of public policy positions, not to

mention a host of more mundane motives and influences (see Baum, 2006; Schauer, 2000). Of course, how to measure these other extralegal factors can create large new problems.

21. To the extent that ideology and normative perspectives are confounded (e.g., if conservatism is positively correlated with acceptance of textualism as a legal process norm and liberalism is positively correlated with purposivism as a legal process norm), the correlation between outcomes and ideology does not compel the conclusion that legal norms fail to constrain decisions. Correlation cannot establish causation: the conservative may conveniently favor textualism to advance desired policy ends, or the conservative may endorse textualism as part of a sincere set of beliefs about the proper role of the judiciary; partial correlations can suggest the proper causal model but cannot establish that ideology causes a strategic choice of normative perspectives.

22. A direct comparison would compare actual votes to the votes predicted by a legal norm. Very few studies undertake this direct comparison, perhaps because "it is very difficult to operationalize a quantitative empirical test with legal variables" (Cross, 2004, p. 31). For instance, Spaeth and Segal (1999) have only directly tested compliance with the "follow precedent" norm within their simplified legal model.

23. As I discuss below, when testing legal proscription norms, which forbid consideration of some specific factor(s), a finding of no influence from these factors may vindicate the judge's conduct relative to the legal norm. But tests for extralegal influences will often *not* provide a direct test of compliance with other types of norms, as I discuss below.

24. In some domains, process norms dominate legal scholars' normative discussions. For instance, process norms dominate discussions of constitutional interpretation (i.e., norms for how to make constitutional decisions rather than norms about the specific decisions that should be made), making their relative neglect within empirical studies all the more unfortunate given the great interest in constitutional cases within judicial behavior studies.

25. Arguably the central mediating variable in studies of extralegal influences is the degree of discretion or subjectivity permitted or perceived with respect to any given judgment or decision, yet this variable typically goes unmeasured in judicial studies.

26. Although probability and hypothesis-testing rules ultimately serve the purpose of making accurate and reliable judgments, they are still types of coherence rather than correspondence norms, just like the rules of logic or rationality, because they do not guarantee correspondence to reality. If one complies with rules of probability and hypothesis testing, one is more likely to reach reliable conclusions about probabilistic and causal relations, but compliance is measured by fidelity to the rules rather than the correspondence of judgments with reality.

27. Or we might ask what kinds of judges seem to act in ways that are contrary to existing normative theories, using the character of these judges as negative evidence. For instance, the attitudinal model research would suggest that judges who hold less extreme ideological views should rule very differently than ideologues, and, if moderates are more constrained by the law (i.e., if their decisions are less predicted by ideology), then political moderation should be favored to the extent legal constraint is desired.

28. Solum accepts that virtues of the kind he advocates are not easily quantified (Solum, 2005a). He offers templates of the judicial qualities to look for (Solum, 1988, 2003) and offers some specific ideas on how to screen out those with judicial vices (Solum, 2005a). But on the more abstract judicial virtues, Solum offers little specific guidance on how exactly to identify these qualities in particular judicial candidates and is largely content to rely on recommendations of persons who know the judges, with those recommendations proceeding from vague standards.

29. Posner (1995b) provides one of the more explicit defenses of pragmatism, even if the content remains somewhat vague, though Posner seems to argue less that some are predisposed to be pragmatic judges and more that all judges should strive to be pragmatists.

30. The point here is not that looking to opinions to find pragmatic judges is wrongheaded; the point is that the character of pragmatism is, at this point, doing no independent work except serving as a label for how this judge ruled. It will be impossible to identify pragmatic judges and predict their rulings if we can only identify pragmatic judges from their rulings. In this approach, pragmatism may be seen as a proper norm for judging judicial acts, but it is now just another of our normative standards rather than part of some character-based theory of good judging. Of course, this may be the sense most advocates of pragmatic judging intend; few scholars advance as explicitly as Solum does a dispositional theory of good judging.

15

Defining Good Judging

Andrew J. Wistrich

When Supreme Court Justice Oliver Wendell Holmes Jr. was quite old, he took a trip by train. During the trip, a conductor asked him for his ticket. After unsuccessfully searching through one pocket after another, Holmes became flustered. The conductor recognized the famous jurist and tried to reassure him: "You don't need to find your ticket now, Mr. Holmes. I'm sure you bought one. Just send it to the railroad office when it turns up." Holmes replied with impatience: "The problem is not that I can't find my ticket, the problem is I don't know where I'm going!"[1]

Some have suggested that we must define good judging before we begin studying, evaluating, and reforming judicial decision making.[2] That plausible suggestion flows from the same intuition as the one expressed in the story about Holmes; that is, before we embark on a journey, it would be nice to know where we are going. While I agree that it might be nice, I am not sure that it is possible, or necessary, or even that it would be helpful. Therefore, when we are thinking about what research should be done concerning judges and judicial decision making during the next decade, and what improvements to our justice system might result from that research, perhaps what seems like the most logical place to start is actually not the best place to start. In fact, beginning by trying to define good judging might delay our departure and lead us in the wrong direction.

Attempts to Define Good Judging

What is good judging? Attempts to formulate a definition have been pursued for millennia. Since ancient times, philosophers, theologians, judges, lawyers, politicians, social scientists, law professors, bar associations, and judicial nominating commissions have wrestled with the question of what makes a judge good. Many of their definitions have been intriguing, and some have been enlightening, but none has provided a fully satisfactory answer. Trying to formulate a meaningful definition of good judging is like trying to find the end of a rainbow; for all of our efforts, we never seem to get there. Reviewing just a few of the many attempts illustrates the point.

Early efforts are a convenient place to start. In about 1500 B.C., Pharaoh Thutmose III of Egypt issued the following instructions to Chief Justice Rekhmire:

> Mayest thou see to it for thyself, to do everything after that which is in accordance with law; to do everything according to the right thereof. . . .
>
> It is an abomination of the god to show partiality. This is the teaching: thou shalt do the like, shalt regard him who is known to thee like him who is unknown to thee, and him who is near. . . like him who is far. . . .
>
> Be not enraged toward a man unjustly, but be thou enraged concerning that about which one should be enraged. (quoted in Breasted, 2001, p. 269)

The Old Testament, dating back to the twelfth century B.C., teaches judges, "Thou shalt not wrest judgment; thou shalt not respect persons, neither take a gift: for a gift doth blind the eyes of the wise, and pervert the words of the righteous" (Deuteronomy 16:19).

Several hundred years later, the Greek philosopher Socrates said, "Four things belong to a judge: To hear courteously, to answer wisely, to consider soberly and to decide impartially"(Sampson, 2004). Writing at about the same time, and in the same place, Plato argued that "the good judge must not be young but old" (Plato, 2006, bk. 2 div. 409).

St. Augustine, who served not only as Bishop of Hippo, but also as a civil and ecclesiastical judge during the 4th and 5th centuries A.D. (Schaff, 1954), said that "[a] good judge does nothing according to his private opinion but pronounces sentence according to the law and the right."[3]

Not surprisingly, many definitions of good judging have been authored by judges. Often their definitions consist of a mixture of personal qualities a judge should possess and ways in which a judge should act or behave while doing his job.

In 1612, Sir Francis Bacon, philosopher, statesman, and Lord Chancellor of England, wrote: "Judges ought to be more learned than witty, more reverend than plausible, and more advised than confident. Above all things, integrity is their portion and proper virtue. . . . Let judges also remember that Solomon's throne was supported by lions on both sides: let them be lions, but yet lions under the throne" (Montagu, 1850, pp. 58–59).

An especially notable effort by a judge dates from the mid-1600s. It was authored by Sir Matthew Hale, Lord Chief Justice of England, and is remarkable for its detail and down-to-earth practicality:

LORD HALE'S RULES FOR HIS JUDICIAL GUIDANCE:
Things Necessary To Be Continually Had In Remembrance

. . .

4. That in the execution of justice I carefully lay aside my own passions, and not give way to them, however provoked.
5. That I be wholly intent upon the business I am about, remitting all other cares and thoughts as unseasonable, and interruptions.
6. That I suffer not myself to be prepossessed with any judgment at all, till the whole business and both parties be heard.
7. That I never engage myself in the beginning of a cause, but reserve myself unprejudiced till the whole be heard.
8. That in business capital, though my nature prompt me to pity, yet to consider there is also pity due to the country.
9. That I be not too rigid in matters purely conscientious, where all the harm is diversity of judgment.
10. That I be not biased with compassion to the poor or favor to the rich, in point of justice.
11. That popular or court applause, or distaste have no influence upon any thing I do, in point of distribution of justice.
12. Not to be solicitous what men will say or think, so long as I keep myself exactly according to the rules of justice.
13. If in criminals it be measuring cast, to incline to mercy and acquittal.
14. In criminals, that consist merely in words where no more harm ensues, moderation is no injustice.
15. In criminals of blood, if the fact be evident, severity is justice.
16. To abhor all private solicitations, of what kind whatsoever, and by whomever, in matters depending.

. . .

18. To be short and sparing at meals, that I may be fitter for business.[4]

In more recent times, several judges have compiled shorter lists of the qualities judges should attempt to display while doing their jobs. One thoughtful attempt offered ten commandments for new judges: *(1)* "be kind"; *(2)* "be patient"; *(3)* "be dignified"; *(4)* "don't take yourself too seriously"; *(5)* "a lazy judge is a poor judge"; *(6)* "don't fear reversal"; *(7)* "there are no unimportant cases"; *(8)* "be prompt"; *(9)* "common sense"; and *(10)* "pray for divine guidance" (Devitt, 1979).

Twenty years later, another judge offered his own ten-part definition of what it means to be a good judge:

1. Being a judge means having self-confidence without conceit, decisiveness without arrogance, and passion without pretension.
2. Being a judge means using common sense as well as the law to handle problems.
3. Being a judge means being temperate under circumstances that at times would try the patience of the most serene.
4. Being a judge means being civil to those who are uncivil.
5. Being a judge means using awesome judicial power sparingly and with restraint.
6. Being a judge means accepting criticism, justified or unjustified, without always being able to respond.
7. Being a judge means not being afraid to make mistakes.
8. Being a judge means having confidence in the system, that mistakes can be corrected, and that justice is attainable.
9. Being a judge means recognizing that the great principles upon which this country was founded and endures apply not just to the best of us, not just to the worst of us, but to all of us.
10. Being a judge means accepting the responsibility to represent the justice system at your very best —to exhibit patience, tolerance, and understanding (Nadeau, 2000, p. 35).

One judge approached the question from a different perspective. He essentially asked: What would a judge like to have written on her tombstone? His answer was: "An appropriate epitaph for a trial judge is this: this judge exercised common sense, was slow to anger, rich in courtesy and under-standing; unquestionably fair but firm; and steadfastly encouraged the search for truth" (Weber, 1979, p. 11).

Many of these lists of the qualities a good judge should possess or exhibit are aspirational. They sound more like the Boy Scout oath than a set of criteria that actually would be useful to reform-minded judges, law professors, and social scientists. They also set an unrealistically high bar against which to measure judicial performance.[5] No wonder one judge observed that "[w]e shall find the ideal judge if, as and when there is combined in a single person the strength of Samson, the patience of Job, the wisdom of Solomon, the statesmanship of Marshall, the economic foresight of Mansfield, the political acumen of Machiavelli, the trenchant pen of Holmes and the nervous system of William J. Bryan" (Dobbie, 1951, p. 477).

Not surprisingly, appellate judges trying to define good judging have focused on the qualities or behaviors good appellate judges should possess or display. One offered the following thoughts about the characteristics that distinguish good appellate judges from bad or mediocre ones: "[A]n ideal appellate judge should possess the following six characteristics: the quality of being fair, just and impartial; the twin qualities of devotion and decisive-ness; the quality of clarity of thought and expression; the quality of being professionally literate; the quality of institutional fidelity; and the quality of political responsibility" (Aldisert, 1982, p. 29).

Commenting on the especially weighty responsibility borne by Supreme Court justices relative to appellate court judges, Justice Felix Frankfurter said that in choosing the former, "what is essential is that you get men who bring to their task, first and foremost, humility and an understanding of the range of the problems and of their own inadequacy in dealing with them; disinterestedness, allegiance to nothing except the search, amid tangled words, amid limited insights, loyalty and allegiance to nothing except the effort to find their path through precedent, through policy, through history, through their own gifts of insight to the best judgment that poor fallible creatures can arrive at in that most difficult of all tasks, the adjudication between man and man, between man and state, through reason called law" (Frankfurter, 1953, p. 95).

Academics, especially law professors, also have tried their hand at the task. One law professor made the following perceptive observations:

> Most of the cases, and thus most of the judicial work, involve trials; either criminal prosecutions or civil disputes. There are a few important skills which are required of the judges dealing with such trials. First, and often overlooked, they must be good triers of fact. They must know how to conduct the trial efficiently but with respect and courtesy, so that the parties will have a sense that justice is being done. They must have the legal competence to identify the laws relevant to the facts and the basic ways of legal reasoning and interpretation. They must have a basic sense of justice and a measure of common sense which will check the applications of these norms. They must act, and seem to be acting, impartially and without bias or prejudice to either party. They must also act, and seem to be acting, in obedience to the laws of the land. They must have the ability to make decisions with caution and good judgment but without delay, so that legal justice will be as speedy as it can be, on the one hand, but that the parties will not feel that the judge came to the trial with a closed mind about the case, on the other hand. Finally, judges must know how to justify their decisions in a way that will be persuasive both to the parties and to the legal community. (Gavison, 1988, pp. 1623–1624)

Another law professor, now also a federal appellate judge, has suggested that good judging may best be defined as conformity to widely endorsed conceptions of the judicial role. In his view,

> To regard oneself and be regarded by others, especially one's peers as a good judge requires conformity to the accepted norms of judging. One cannot be regarded as a good judge if one takes bribes, decides cases by flipping a coin, falls asleep in the courtroom, ignores legal doctrine, cannot make up one's mind, bases decisions on the personal

attractiveness or unattractiveness of the litigants or their lawyers, or decides cases on the basis of "politics." (Posner, 2008, p. 61)

Some scholars have attempted to begin by defining bad judging, and then back into a definition of good judging. Professor Lawrence Solum (2003) has employed this strategy. He lists as judicial vices: *(1)* corruption; *(2)* civic cowardice; *(3)* bad temper; *(4)* incompetence; and *(5)* foolishness. He lists as judicial virtues: *(1)* judicial temperance; *(2)* judicial courage; *(3)* judicial temperament; *(4)* judicial intelligence; and *(5)* judicial wisdom. He then adds a sixth judicial virtue, justice, of which he identifies three aspects: *(1)* judicial impartiality; *(2)* judicial integrity; and *(3)* legal vision.[6]

Two law professors approached the problem from an unconventional point of view. Eschewing many of the typical criteria of good judging, they instead chose to emphasize "the human relationships constructed and implicated by the act of judgment" (Minow & Spelman, 1989, p. 59). Their definition contains the following elements:

(1) The judge should try to take the perspective of all parties before the court prior to reaching a decision.

(2) The judge should try to remain open to the newness of each case, even if it resembles previous ones, while also subjecting new understandings to scrutiny through comparison with past experiences.

(3) The judge should not disguise how he or she actually reached the decision, and should explain the decision not only through post-hoc justifications but also with reference to intuitions and reasons for selecting one principled justification over other possible ones.

(4) The judge should confront the difficulty of rejecting the arguments of a party by trying to develop reasons that would persuade that party or explain the result in terms that party would concede are fair.

(5) The judge should acknowledge what it feels like to have power over the lives of others in the act of judgment, and, if the judge does not experience such power, the judge should reflect on why, despite the actual effects of the decisions he or she will make, he or she experiences not having much power.

Codes of judicial ethics are a rich source of guidance about what constitutes good, or perhaps more accurately, bad, judging (e.g., Model Code of Jud. Conduct, 2007; Miller, 2004). Here is one early example from the ABA canons of Judicial Ethics:

In every particular his conduct should be above reproach. He should be conscientious, studious, thorough, courteous, patient, punctual, just, impartial, fearless of public clamor, regardless of public praise, and indifferent to private political or partisan influences; he should administer justice according to law, and deal with his appointments as a public trust; he should not allow other affairs or his private interests to interfere with the prompt and proper performance of his judicial duties, nor should he administer the office for the purpose of advancing his personal ambitions or increasing his popularity. (Dobie, 1951, p. 477)

More recently, the American Bar Association (2005) published a set of guidelines by which the performance of judges could be evaluated. Those guidelines, which are reproduced in the Appendix at the end of this chapter, are remarkable for their thoroughness. They identify 31 separate dimensions on which judicial performance might be measured. While portions of the ABA guidelines focus on adjudication and overlap with some of the earlier definitions described or quoted above, they also include several elements that earlier definitions do not. These include the precepts that a good judge "promote[s] public understanding of ... the courts," utilizes hiring and promotion practices that will ensure a diverse pool of applicants for court employment, and "ensure[s] that disabilities and linguistic and cultural differences do not limit access to the justice system" (sections 5-4.6, 5-5.9, 5-5.10). The ABA guidelines, then, extend the definition of good judging into an important but often neglected realm, albeit one that is only tangentially related to the judge's disposition of cases or behavior in court, namely, judicial administration. On the other hand, for all of their detail, even the ABA guidelines are somewhat vague, sometimes exhorting judges to be dignified, courteous, or patient, and often stating only that a judge should perform a particular task or pursue a particular goal "appropriately."

One scholar tried an empirical approach to defining a good judge (Rosenberg, 1966). He asked 144 trial judges of varying experience and backgrounds to answer the following question: "What qualities best equip a lawyer to become a trial judge?" He gave each judge a list of 23 possible attributes compiled from the preexisting literature on judicial qualifications and a variety of other sources, and then asked them to rate their importance. Those the judges rated as highest in importance were: "(1) moral courage; (2) decisiveness; (3) reputation for fairness and uprightness; (4) patience; (5) good health, physical and mental; (6) consideration for others." Those the judges rated as lowest in importance were: "(23) past honorable partisan political activity; (22) higher earnings in practice than as a judge; (21) active in civic and community affairs; (20) experience in supervision of subordinates; (19) well above average law school record; (18) active in professional associations and work."

Modern empirical researchers arguably are more sophisticated. They use computerized citation analysis to determine which appellate judges' opinions are cited most frequently and by which courts or by which scholars (Choi & Gulati, 2004a, 2004b; Gulati & Sanchez, 2002). This taps into a "market" reflecting how judges are viewed by their peers or by those who study judges. Good judges are defined as those whose opinions are cited most often or are included in the leading law school casebooks. In addition to measuring the quality of a judge's opinions, other criteria, such as the amount of effort a judge exerts in approaching her job and the willingness to decide cases impartially and independent of political ideology, are considered (Choi & Gulati, 2004b).

Whatever its value with respect to appellate judges, however, citation analysis is of little use with respect to trial judges. In most states, trial court decisions are not published. In the few states where they are published, or in the federal courts, published decisions by trial courts are usually of negligible importance as precedent (except as to issues that are rarely litigated on appeal), and most are seldom cited.

The results of these laudable efforts to define good judging make interesting reading. They also possess some practical value. Reviewing them occasionally can remind judges of the abstract ideals to which they should aspire. Some of the definitions conceivably could be used as a crude measuring stick to assess the quality of judicial performance. As the basis for scholarly research or judicial reform, however, they are inadequate (Frankel, 1976).

While a handful of traits have persisted over the centuries and appear to be universally accepted as desirable, no clear consensus has emerged regarding the criteria that should be employed to determine whether someone is a good judge or whether a particular decision embodies good judging (Fennell, 1999). Moreover, widely accepted criteria such as integrity, impartiality, dignity, and patience are subjective or immeasurable, making it difficult to determine whether a judge did or did not display them in making a particular decision (Minow & Spelman, 1989, p. 50).

Modern definitions of good judging are more detailed than their predecessors, and tend to emphasize more practical judicial qualities or goals. They also acknowledge that judges do more than simply decide cases, and that judges' ancillary responsibilities should be reflected in the definition of good judging as well. Although those newer definitions may be slightly more realistic when compared to the lofty and often superhuman standards of good judging emphasized in the past, they still contain many terms that are vague or subjective (Schaefer, 1960).

The failure of so many sincere efforts by so many capable people leads me to believe that defining good judging in the abstract is infeasible. Others have reached the same conclusion (e.g., Posner, 2008, p. 12; Champagne, 1986, pp. 104, 110; Farthing-Capowich, 1985, p. 23; Dubois, 1980, p. 17). Gregory Mitchell's understandable failure to offer such a definition in his fine essay on evaluating judges in this volume (ch. 14), coupled with his ingenious and exhaustive account of the difficulty and complexity of doing so, only confirms that attempting to define good judging in the abstract is a fool's errand.

Conceptual Difficulties

In addition to the difficulty of crafting a meaningful definition of good judging, attempting to do so creates conceptual problems. One such problem is that beginning with a definition of a good judge or good judging causes us to focus too much on the qualities or characteristics of judges, and not enough on the nature of the context or environment in which they make decisions. People systematically tend to give too much weight to the individual, and too little weight to the situation, when assessing causation or responsibility. Psychologists call this widespread phenomenon "the fundamental attribution error" (Plous, 1993, pp. 180–181). Attempts to define good judging exacerbate this tendency by encouraging us to give even more weight to judges as individuals, and even less weight to the situations in which judges act, than we ordinarily would. In fact, the emphasis on defining what makes a judge good may itself be a product of cognitive bias.

The context in which judges decide matters. As an example, courts depend on the adversary system. When it works well, the adversary system can help judges avoid mistakes and ensure that they are confronted with both sides of the story before issuing a ruling. But it is not always effective. Sometimes one lawyer misses something important. Occasionally both lawyers do a poor job, and an overworked judge fails to detect their mistake. When the lawyers slip, it is not just the litigants, but also the judge, who falls (Lasky, 1965, p. 680; Brandeis, 1916, p. 470). An important difference between a good judge and a bad judge might be that the former benefited from having better lawyers appear before him than did the latter. This insight—that actors operate within a system, and that errors often are the result of a confluence of factors of which the quality of the actors' personal performance is only one—is crucial to achieving meaningful reform (Bates & Gawande, 2000).

A second problem is that any single definition—assuming that a workable definition could ever be formulated—inevitably would foster the misguided notion that there can be a "one size fits all" standard of good judging. Not all judges do the same work. To take the simplest example, the role of appellate court judges is very different from the role of trial court judges. As Supreme Court Justice Stephen Breyer has observed, "they're simply different jobs."[7] Even within trial courts, the variety of judicial tasks is enormous. Some judges are generalists, while others are specialists assigned to hear only bankruptcy matters or family law cases. Some spend most of their time presiding over civil or criminal trials, while others devote the bulk of their attention to pretrial motions or case management. Still others serve in nontraditional collaborative or therapeutic courts (see Judicial Council of California, 2007; Williams, 2007), in which they perform functions foreign to the classical conception of the umpireal judge (Frankel, 1975), or even to the more modern conception of the managerial judge (Resnik, 1982). To adequately define good judging, then, we would have to come up with a different definition for trial court judges than for appellate court judges (Mott, 1948, p. 265), and we likely would have to distinguish among several different types of trial court assignments as well (Gavison, 1988, p. 1623). This would complicate the task enormously, but failing to draw those distinctions would be misleading. In today's courts, there is no "one size fits all" description of what judges do, and therefore no single, all-encompassing definition of what they should do.

The role of trial court judges in performing nontraditional tasks such as mediation and case management creates especially challenging problems of quality evaluation or measurement. What counts as bad judging in a mediation setting? Is it any behavior that either coerces or discourages settlement in the particular context presented? Or is it conducting a settlement conference in a manner that is more evaluative than transformative regardless of the outcome? Similarly, how should an error in case management be defined? Is it setting a schedule that is too strict, so that the facts cannot be developed adequately or the lawyers are severely stressed? Or is it setting a schedule that is too lax, so that a case languishes rather than being disposed of promptly and inexpensively? Might it also consist of sequencing motions in a way that gives one party an unfair tactical advantage over the other? Defining and measuring quality in these dimensions of judicial performance would be difficult indeed. Perhaps for that reason, few attempts have been made. Even the ABA's judicial performance guidelines, which go further than just about any definition of good judging in accounting for the varying roles that judges play, fail to address these sorts of questions in a meaningful way. Yet these sorts of decisions and actions comprise a large chunk of what many trial court judges do (see, e.g., Otis & Reiter, 2006; Parness, 2006).

The nature of judging in collaborative or nontraditional trial court contexts makes it especially difficult to evaluate quality in those contexts. For example, consider child custody determinations, the appropriate response to juvenile delinquency, or public law cases involving structural relief. As one scholar has noted, in these types of assignments,

> what is important is not to mete justice, but to help the parties design
> an arrangement which will be least destructive and vindictive,
> especially when children are involved. The prime commitment of the
> decision maker should not be justice or the application of (legal)
> norms, but a viable resolution of the dispute. For this commitment,
> legal education is neither necessary nor clearly desirable.
>
> Similarly, for cases in which intervention is needed to supervise
> a complex administrative agency structure, such as a company or a
> prison system, judges must have the skills to help them identify the
> right and the feasible arrangement, and design the supervision
> mechanism which might be most effective and least demanding of
> constant review. I know of no law school which seeks to provide its
> students with such skills, nor of a [judicial] selection criterion which
> reflects them. (Gavison, 1988, p. 1625)

A third problem is that attempting to formulate a definition of good judging encourages the misperception that the judicial role is fixed. Judges' jobs, however, evolve over time. The mix of tasks judges perform has changed during the past few decades (Parness, 2006, pp. 1892–1898), as has our perception of the relative importance of those tasks. For example, as the role of case management has waxed and the role of presiding over trials has waned (Galanter, 2004), our assessment of the skills judges should possess, as well as our vision of good judging, has begun to shift. As one law professor has pointed out,

> the claim that "the more dispositions, the better" raises difficult valuation tasks; decisionmaking must be assessed not only quantitatively, but also qualitatively. On any given day, are four judges who speak with parties to sixteen lawsuits and report that twelve of those cases ended without trial more "productive" than four judges who preside at four trials? (Resnik, 1982, p. 422)

Questions such as this, which no one would have thought to ask a few decades ago, must be addressed today.

Today, excellence at presiding over jury trials, which remains a valuable skill, arguably has become less important relative to excellence at the now far more common tasks of mediating, scheduling, and ruling on pretrial motions. While the personal qualities and skill sets that judges need to excel at the wide range of tasks they are assigned undoubtedly overlap, they are not congruent. Historical wish-lists of judicial qualities and guidelines for how judges should do their jobs need to be revised to take this into account. Any definition of good judging we develop today will have to be updated as judges' jobs continue to evolve. Thinking that we can settle on one—or even several—definitions of good judging that are capable of providing a stable platform for research over a decade or more is unrealistic.

Proceeding Without Definitions

Can we improve the justice system without first defining good judging? I believe we can. One need look no farther than the field of medicine for a striking example of what rigorous interdisciplinary analysis might do for law.

General anesthesia is risky. Some patients, who otherwise would have survived their surgeries, are killed or seriously harmed by the anesthesia itself. Not surprisingly, death from anesthesia initially was common. By the 1940s, however, the situation had improved to the point that there was only 1 death from anesthesia in every 2,500 operations. By the 1960s, the rate of death from anesthesia had dropped even lower, to merely 1 in every 5,000 operations.

Considering the substantial risks posed by anesthesia, that death rate seems relatively low.[8] Some anesthesiologists, however, regarded it as unacceptably high. They asked a young engineer named Jeffrey Cooper for help. In an exhaustive study of 359 anesthesia-related errors, Cooper and several colleagues researched the procedures followed by anesthesiologists, analyzed the design of anesthesia machines, and, in meticulous detail, reconstructed from interviews of the nurses and physicians involved exactly how and why each mishap occurred (Cooper et al., 1978; see also Cooper et al., 1984).

Based on Cooper's work, the American Society of Anesthesiologists brought together anesthesiologists, surgeons, nurses, human factors engineers, equipment manufacturers, and others at an international conference. The combination of a willingness to acknowledge mistakes, careful empirical study, and the consideration of interdisciplinary and cross-cultural perspectives proved fruitful. Sources of error were identified, and strategies to mitigate or eliminate them were implemented. Hours on duty for anesthesiology residents were shortened so that fewer slips or lapses would be caused by fatigue. Manufacturers redesigned their machines, standardizing dials to turn in a uniform direction, adding a mechanism to prevent the accidental administration of more than one type of anesthetic gas simultaneously, and changing controls so that oxygen delivery could not be turned off. Where an error could not be eliminated, methods for detecting it before irreparable harm was done to the patient were developed.

These efforts paid off. Within a decade, anesthesia-related deaths fell from 1 in every 5,000 operations to just 1 in every 200,000 operations.[9]

What does this inspiring story about anesthesiology have to do with judges? A lot. It suggests how judicial decision making might be improved if the justice system adopted a similar approach.

Law is different from medicine in a variety of respects, of course, so it may not be possible to replicate in the justice system the remarkable success achieved in anesthesiology. It may be easier to identify errors in medicine than in law, where the standards of correctness may be more subjective (Posner, 2008, p. 3). Also, physicians may be more accountable for poor performance than judges, because they can be sued for malpractice while judges generally are immune from civil liability or criminal prosecution for judicial acts.[10] There already is at least one example, however, of the use of empirical research in psychology to improve the quality of decisions in trial courts.

Psychologists have known for decades that the traditional way of conducting lineups — in which an eyewitness is shown six photographs or six people simultaneously under the supervision of a law enforcement officer involved in investigation — is likely to result in mistaken identifications (Behrman & Davey, 2001; Steblay et al., 2001). There is a much better technique that significantly reduces false positive identifications without significantly increasing false negative identifications, and without significantly increasing the cost of conducting lineups. That method is to show the eyewitness one person or photograph at a time, and to ask the eyewitness to make a decision about that individual before moving on to the next person or photograph. If the eyewitness wants to view a particular person or photograph again, he is allowed to do so, but only after he has first seen all of the individuals separately, and only after the order in which the individuals are presented has been reshuffled. In addition, the live or photographic lineup should be conducted by a law enforcement officer who does not know which individual is the suspect and which individuals are not.

These two changes improve the accuracy of identifications because research has shown that when confronted by a simultaneous array, witnesses tend to assume that the perpetrator is included, and then to compare the individuals in the array to determine which one best matches their recollection of the perpetrator. Also, having the lineup supervised by an officer who is not involved in the investigation reduces the danger that something might tip off the eyewitness as to who the suspect is.

Although the advantages of this new method of conducting lineups have been known for a long time, law enforcement agencies have been slow to adopt it. Recently, however, New Jersey decided to require that this new method of conducting lineups be used throughout its criminal justice system (Kolata & Peterson, 2001). Other jurisdictions are following suit.[11] This is a good example of how social science research can be used to improve the accuracy of the justice system by strengthening the quality of the evidence available to judges and juries. It also demonstrates that not all clearly beneficial changes to our justice system necessarily require expensive, unpalatable, or dramatic changes to existing procedures.

Improving Judging

Assuming that we want to follow in the footsteps of anesthesiologists, and skip or defer the step of defining good judging, how should we proceed? Probably by continuing some of the research we already are conducting, and by trying a few new tacks as well. One approach would be to begin with a few existing criteria of good judging we can all agree on (e.g., Klein, 2005; Farber & Sherry, this volume, ch. 18). For example, no one would argue that the length of a federal criminal sentence should be based on the race or gender of the defendant rather than the relevant factors specified by statute. Nor is that something that is likely to change over time, or even to vary depending on whether the sentence is a conventional one imposed by a traditional criminal court or a disposition implemented by an innovative collaborative court. One thing we could do without first defining good judging would be to determine whether judges have been imposing racially biased sentences by carefully analyzing past decisions. Several scholars already have done this. I discuss just one example, notable for its thoroughness and perceptiveness.

David Mustard (2001) examined the sentences imposed on 77,236 federal offenders during 1991–1994. His analysis revealed large disparities in the length of sentences based on race, gender, education, income, and citizenship. On average, white offenders received shorter sentences than black or Hispanic offenders, and female offenders received shorter sentences than male offenders. After controlling for a myriad of factors, the difference in sentence length amounted to about six months in both instances. Significantly, most of the difference occurred when the sentencing judge departed from the guidelines promulgated by the United States Sentencing Commission.

Mustard started with a criterion of good judging we can all agree on— judges should not determine sentences based on statutorily forbidden characteristics like the defendant's race or gender—and simply tested how well judges were doing. His research revealed that judicial discretion for individualizing—which seems desirable in the abstract—continued to create the risk of forbidden discrimination even under the then tighter control of the guidelines.[12] This suggests that, whatever their other shortcomings, tight sentencing guidelines may not be so bad after all.

Another approach is the one that Jeffrey Rachlinski, Chris Guthrie, and I have taken in our work.[13] We have tackled the problem experimentally rather than archivally. We began by examining the psychology literature to identify mistakes people commonly commit when making decisions. Assuming that judges should avoid cognitive error while ruling on cases, we then attempted to discern which of those mistakes plausibly might occur in situations in which judges work. Our next step was to test judges, eliciting from them responses to hypothetical cases or other sorts of problems to determine if, when faced with choices similar in content and structure to those they confront when doing their jobs, they would be vulnerable to the same sorts of cognitive biases or illusions that cause ordinary people to make mistakes in experiments conducted by psychologists.

This approach possesses some advantages. There is an extensive literature concerning flaws in judgment and decision making on which one can draw, rather than starting from scratch. That made it possible for us to start identifying nonobvious potential sources of error immediately. If judges are susceptible to committing particular types of errors, then we can think about the situations in which judges act and try to identify solutions. It is not necessary to have a comprehensive definition of good judging to know that judges should not consider evidence they themselves have correctly decided is inadmissible under the rules of evidence, be wildly influenced by an arbitrary number mentioned by a litigant, make rulings based on a litigant's attractiveness rather than the merits of the case, and so on. If it turns out that judges are not susceptible to a particular type of error across a range of situations, then we can cross that type of error off the list, at least provisionally, and move on to others on the list.

Of course, this approach is not perfect. There may be questions about its external validity,[14] and it may be that some of the problems in human decision making that have the most serious consequences for judges have not been identified or systematically studied by psychologists. Cognitive biases, however, are things we can identify, and in many instances, do something about, right now.

Careful study of reversals in the aggregate would be another way of identifying potential sources of error. There are many studies of reversals, of course, but most seem to focus on reversal rates, either overall or in particular categories of cases (e.g., Guthrie & George, 2005). Others explore the impact of reversals on subsequent trial court decisions (e.g., Gellis, 1985; Liberato & Rutter, 2003; Smith, 2005). There do not seem to be any, however, that attempt to determine—as Cooper did in his study of anesthesia mishaps— the types of errors lower courts are making. That is something that can, and should, be tried.[15]

Another criterion of performance could be developed from studying the appellate records of individual lower court judges. It is well known that the judgments of some judges are more frequently appealed than are judgments of others. It is likewise recognized that some lower courts conform more closely to the law as interpreted by the higher courts than do other lower courts. The extent to which a trial judge should attempt to conform to the opinions of her appellate court superiors may be debatable in some cases, but regardless of the side one takes in that debate, both the frequency of appeal and the frequency of reversal are objective criteria of judicial performance of considerable significance (Mott, 1948, p. 276).

Even if an appellate court finds that the trial court erred, it will only reverse the decision if it concludes that the error was not harmless. We should study cases in which error was found to be harmless very carefully. Not only may the error have affected the outcome—despite the appellate court's determination to the contrary—but if it did not that may have been a fortuity. Like the situation in which a doctor makes a mistake, but subsequently notices it and fixes it before it harms the patient, the error occurred and might have had injurious consequences in a different case, so we ought to figure out how to prevent it. These "near misses" could be a valuable source of information about needed reforms that may be overlooked by focusing only on reversals.

We also could go a step further and review a sample of cases that were not appealed to determine whether errors were made that escaped appellate review entirely. For example, a confidential peer review process could be implemented, in which respected judges would periodically visit other courts and study a few randomly selected cases in which no appeal was taken. The judges under study could be given feedback on their performance to help them improve. This would help us to determine whether the errors that are appealed are representative of those that are not appealed. It also would help us to ascertain whether errors that are likely to be harmful are escaping appellate review.

Of course, reversals provide noisy signals of error. Appeals are infrequent, particularly in civil cases, and reversals are rare (Guthrie & George, 2005, pp. 359–363). Some interim decisions are isolated from appellate review, and final judgments are reviewed deferentially. Further, some reversals result from disagreements over policy, or occur in cases that are extremely close. These arguably cannot be characterized as "errors" in any meaningful sense. Despite these shortcomings, however, studying the causes of reversal might be fruitful.

An even better place to begin might be exonerations based on postconviction determinations that a criminal defendant actually was innocent. We know that such wrongful convictions occur. By carefully studying cases in which that happened, we might be able to discern why our usually good justice went bad in those instances, and what might be done to prevent such miscarriages of justice in the future. Some have pursued this line of inquiry (Borchard, 1932; Christianson, 2004), but more remains to be done.

Conclusion

Like the talented and hard-working anesthesiologists, judges (and others, such as scholars and legislators) possess both the ability—and, I would argue, the responsibility—to try to reduce the frequency and the magnitude of error in trial court decision making. What we need is the dedication and the courage to do what anesthesiologists did: openly pursue a painstaking interdisciplinary inquiry into the question of how best to structure the process of judicial decision making, and then implement reforms based on what we learn. And we need to get started right away.

It is significant, I think, that anesthesiologists did not begin by trying to define a "good anesthesiologist" or "good anesthesiology." Instead, they rolled up their sleeves and collected data. Then, viewing the delivery of medical care as a system of which anesthesia and anesthesiologists were merely a part, they attacked the most common and serious problems, leaving the philosophizing for later. That is exactly what judicial reformers should do.

If, on the other hand, defining good judging is made a prerequisite to empirical research concerning judicial decision making, then I doubt we will progress very far anytime soon. We will have missed the opportunity to make rapid progress like the anesthesiologists did, and that would be a terrible shame.

My respectful disagreement with those who contend that we must begin our efforts to achieve judicial reform by defining good judging reminds me of a story about two clerics who were debating the finer points of theology. After they had been at it for awhile, one put his arm around the other's shoulders and said: "Brother, why do we argue? After all, we both serve God. You in your way, and I in His."

Appendix

American Bar Association Committee On Judicial Performance Evaluation, Black Letter Guidelines for the Evaluation of Judicial Performance with Commentary, 5-1 to 5-6 (2005)

Guideline 5-1. A judge should be evaluated on his or her legal ability, including the following criteria:

    1.1. Legal reasoning ability.

    1.2. Knowledge of substantive law.

    1.3. Knowledge of rules of procedure and evidence.

    1.4. Keeping current on developments in law, procedure, and evidence.

Guideline 5-2. A judge should be evaluated on his or her integrity and impartiality, including the following criteria:

    2.1. Avoidance of impropriety and the appearance of impropriety.

    2.2. Treating all people with dignity and respect.

    2.3. Absence of favor or disfavor toward anyone, including but not limited to favor or disfavor based upon race, sex, religion, national origin, disability, age, sexual orientation, or socioeconomic status.

    2.4. Acting fairly by giving people individual consideration.

    2.5. Consideration of both sides of an argument before rendering a decision.

    2.6. Basing decisions on the law and the facts without regard to the identity of the parties or counsel, and with an open mind in considering all issues.

    2.7. Ability to make difficult or unpopular decisions.

Guideline 5-3. A judge should be evaluated on his or her communication skills, including the following criteria:

    3.1. Clear and logical oral communication while in court.

    3.2. Clear and logical written decisions.

Guideline 5-4. A judge should be evaluated on his or her professionalism and temperament, including the following criteria:

    4.1. Acting in a dignified manner.

    4.2. Treating people with courtesy.

    4.3. Acting with patience and self-control.

    4.4. Dealing with pro se litigants and litigation fairly and effectively.

    4.5. Participating and providing leadership to an appropriate degree in professional development activities and in jurisdiction-wide and statewide court improvement and judicial education activities.

    4.6. Promoting public understanding of and confidence in the courts.

Guideline 5-5. A judge should be evaluated on his or her administrative capacity, including the following criteria:

    5.1. Punctuality and preparation for court.

    5.2. Maintaining control over the courtroom.

    5.3. Appropriate enforcement of court rules, orders, and deadlines.

    5.4. Making decisions and rulings in a prompt, timely manner.

    5.5. Managing his or her calendar efficiently.

    5.6. Using settlement conferences and alternative dispute resolution mechanisms as appropriate.

> 5.7. Demonstrating appropriate innovation in using technology to improve the administration of justice.
>
> 5.8. Fostering a productive work environment with other judges and court staff.
>
> 5.9. Utilizing recruitment, hiring, and promotion policies and practices to ensure that the pool of qualified applicants for court employment is broad and diverse.
>
> 5.10. Acting to ensure that disabilities and linguistic and cultural differences do not limit access to the justice system.

Guideline 5-6. Additional criteria should be developed reflective of jurisdiction (specialized versus general) and level of court (trial versus appellate).

> 6.1. A specialized court judge should be evaluated according to whether he or she demonstrates the knowledge and skills necessary.
>
> 6.2. An appellate court judge should be evaluated on the quality of his or her preparation for and participation in oral argument and on his or her effectiveness in working with other judges of the court.

Notes

1. Differing versions of this story have been recounted. See, for example, Reed (2005).
2. See Gregory Mitchell's essay in this volume and Schauer (1988b). See generally Dworkin (1986).
3. Quoted in St. Thomas Aquinas, *Summa Theologica*, pt. 2, question 67, art. 2, objection 4.
4. Reprinted in *In re Code of Judicial Conduct* (1994), 1037–38 n.2. See also Campbell (2005).
5. For a fine example of this, consider the following:

   > "I venture to believe that it is as important to a judge called upon to pass on a question of constitutional law, to have at least a bowing acquaintance with Acton and Maitland, with Thucydides, Gibbon and Carlyle, with Homer, Dante, Shakespeare and Milton, with Machiavelli, Montaigne and Rabelais, with Plato, Bacon, Hume and Kant, as with the books which have been specifically written on the subject. For in such matters everything turns upon the spirit in which he approaches the questions before him." (Hand, 1930, pp. 12–13)

6. See also Solum (2005a).
7. Stephen J. Breyer, quoted in "Toward 'Active Liberty': A Supreme Court Justice Offers a View from the Top," *Harvard Law Bulletin*, 57:14, 17 (Spring 2006).
8. To put these anesthesia-related death rates into perspective, consider the error rate in adjudication. Perhaps the best measure—albeit an imperfect one—of whether a decision is mistaken is whether it is reversed on direct appeal or set

aside on collateral review. In the federal courts, reversal rates in appeals terminated on the merits typically hover around 9 percent, or about 450 in every 5,000 appeals from civil and criminal trial court judgments. See 2006 Fed. Judiciary Ann. Rep. Director, Table B-5, available at http://www.uscourts.gov/judbususc/judbus.html. Arguably more relevant is the ratio of trial court decisions reversed on the merits to all trial court judgments whether appealed or unappealed. That would yield a reversal rate of approximately .7 percent, or about 35 in every 5,000 trial court judgments. (See Tables B-5, C, D.) Thus, the error rate appears to be higher for law than for anesthesia.

Death penalty cases offer another basis for comparison. There are about 300 death sentences imposed annually in the United States. Most are subjected to both direct appeal and collateral review, often in both state and federal courts. Approximately 68 percent of death sentences are overturned or materially altered because either the conviction or the sentence was wrong (Liebman, 2000). Therefore, the error rate in capital cases from 1973 to 1995, appears to be higher than the error rate in anesthesia during the 1960s.

9. This account of what anesthesiologists accomplished is based on the summary presented in Gawande (2000).
10. See, for example, *Mireles v. Waco*, 502 U.S. 9, 11-12 (1991) (per curiam). See generally Olowofoyeku (1993).
11. In 2007, eyewitness identification reform legislation was signed into law by the governors of Georgia, Maryland, North Carolina, Vermont, and West Virginia. Press Release, California Commission on the Fair Administration of Justice, Commission Chair John Van de Kamp Responds to Governor's Vetoes of Critical Criminal Justice Reform Bills Passed By California State Legislature (Oct. 18, 2007), available at http://ccfaj.org/news.html.
12. Initially, the federal sentencing guidelines were mandatory, but after the period Mustard studied, they were relaxed somewhat to allow for greater judicial discretion (Stith, 2008).
13. Guthrie, Rachlinski, and Wistrich (2001; 2002; 2007a; 2007b); Wistrich, Guthrie, and Rachlinski (2005); Rachlinski, Guthrie, and Wistrich (2009); Rachlinski, Johnson, Wistrich, and Guthrie (2009). Of course, we are neither the first nor the only researchers to have adopted this approach. See, for example, Landsman and Rakos (1994); and Solan, Rosenblatt, and Osherson (2008).
14. We have attempted to address these concerns in Guthrie, Rachlinski, and Wistrich (2001, pp. 819–821).
15. Of the studies of reversal, Gellis's (1985) article comes the nearest to doing this.

16

Expertise of Court Judges

James Shanteau and Len Dalgleish

Even a casual glance at papers on the expertise of court judges reveals widespread disagreement about the quality of judicial decisions. Consider the following recent articles:

"Playing Dice with Criminal Sentences," by Englich, Mussweiler, and Strack (2006)
"Judicial Decision Thresholds for Violence Risk Management," by Monahan and Silver (2003)
"Conditional Bail Decision Making in the Magistrates' Court" by Dhami (2004)

The first article implies a deficiency in judicial decision making, whereas the second implies competence. The position taken here is consistent with the third article: the expertise of court judges is tied to the particular domain in which judges are asked to make factual or probabilistic assessments in the face of uncertainty or ambiguity.

We believe that expert performance is not best understood and assessed in terms of general characteristics applying across all domains. Rather, it should be analyzed in the context of the specific tasks that experts in a particular domain are called on to accomplish. Drawing on a substantial line of research from psychology, we will argue that considerable empirical evidence supports this domain-specific view of expert competence, that there are reasons to believe this view holds with respect to court judges, and that, to be as fair and useful as possible, assessments of judicial performance should incorporate this view.

The paper is organized into five sections as follows. First, there is a review of the literature on expertise in general. Second, the implicit theory behind expert decision making (judges are either good or bad decision makers) is described. Third, the role that domain differences play in disagreement between experts across a wide variety of domains is considered. Fourth, an alternate theory of expertise is proposed that posits that decision quality depends on domain differences. Finally, the paper concludes with implications for judicial decision making and future research directions.

Background

Since the start of systematic analyses of skilled performance in the 1950's, investigators have expressed surprise and dismay at the extent to which experts make poor or inconsistent decisions. For example, if we ask two court judges to assess a court case, the expectation of most analysts is that they should come to the same conclusion. If they arrive at different conclusions, then we wonder whether they are as skilled as they claim to be.

In a seminal paper, Einhorn (1974) argued that *consensus* or between-expert reliability is a necessary condition for expertise.[1] He found, however, significant differences in diagnoses made by three expert medical pathologists. The average between-expert correlation (r) was .55 (where .0 is chance and 1.0 is perfect). In comparison, weather forecasters were reported to have high consensus values, $r = .95$, for short-term predictions (Stewart, Roebber, & Bosart, 1997). Thus there is widespread variability in the agreement of experts.

It is also possible to examine *internal consistency*, the extent to which an expert makes the same decision for the same case if repeated. For pathologists, Einhorn (1974) reported an average within-expert consistency r of .50. For weather forecasters, on the other hand, the average internal consistency is near perfect, r = .98 (Stewart, Roebber, & Bosart, 1997).

In a study of livestock judges, four professionals were asked to evaluate overall breeding quality of swine (Phelps, 1977). Despite a high level of internal consistency (average $r = .96$), the consensus agreement was much lower, $r = .50$. Apparently, livestock experts have internally consistent strategies, but they disagree with each other about what those strategies should be. Comparable results have been reported for other types of experts. For instance, grain inspectors were found to have a consensus value between judges of $r = .60$, with internal consistency of $r = .62$ (Trumbo, Adams, Milner, & Schipper, 1962).

In other domains, the correlations are often lower. For example, Hoffman, Slovic, and Rorer (1968) and Goldberg and Werts (1966) reported consensus values of less than .40 for judgments by professional stockbrokers and clinical psychologists. The internal consistency values were slightly higher, with correlations of just over .40.

Several studies have explored whether between-expert consensus increases with experience. Ettenson, Shanteau, and Krogstad (1987) found that between-auditor correlations increased from .66 to .76 to .83, for students, audit seniors (mid-level professionals), and full partners, respectively. Messier (1983) reported similar results—audit partners with more than 15 years experience had greater consensus than partners with less experience.

These results lead to three conclusions: First, experts in a variety of domains often disagree with each other; the consensus correlations range from .40 to .60. Second, some experts, such as weather forecasters, do show high levels of agreement, with r values up to .95. Finally, in nearly all domains, the internal consistency values are higher than the between-expert consensus values, that is, experts usually agree with themselves, even if they disagree with others.

Experts-Should-Be-Perfect Argument

The less-than-impressive results from most studies of expertise have led many analysts to question the abilities of experts in general. Following Einhorn's logic, these investigators assumed that agreement on the "correct answer" is a necessary condition for expertise. The lack of agreement, therefore, suggested that "experts are no damn good" (Gettys, personal communication, 1980). This interpretation apparently derives from an implicit five-part argument about experts:

(1) In expert domains, there is an assumed "gold standard" or unique "ground truth." If this truth is readily accessible, then we don't need experts—anyone can obtain it. In most cases, however, it requires an expert, such as court judges, to access truth. In these cases, the answer is outside the realm of common knowledge of most people. That is why we need experts.

(2) Because of their special skills and experience, the experts' job is to tell the rest of us about this "ground truth." That is because experts should be able to access answers that others cannot access. Put another way, experts should have a unique ability to "know the truth."

(3) Since by definition there can be only one "ground truth," all experts should arrive at the same (single) correct answer. The special abilities of experts thus allow them to arrive at the "ground truth" correct answer.

(4) If experts disagree, then someone is wrong. Since there is one and only one correct answer, some (or all) of them must not be "real experts." Thus, disagreement about the correct answer is a reflection of incompetence within the group of would-be experts.

(5) Since lay people do not know which of the so-called "experts" is correct, the only safe course of action is to distrust all (or at least

most) of the claimants. Thus, disagreement between experts implies that we should be suspicious of any claim of special abilities.

This argument, of course, is not a formal chain of logic. However, it is implicit in the way that many analysts have interpreted the meaning of disagreements between domain experts about correct answers. The bottom line: disagreements are a sign of likely incompetence.

Domain Differences

It is common knowledge that experts in different domains perform different tasks. Yet, many decision analysts persist in treating all fields of expertise alike, that is, the term "expert" is used generically. For instance, Kahneman (1991) concludes, "there is much evidence that experts (in general) are not immune to the cognitive illusions that affect other people" (parenthesis in the original). Of course, this may be true for some, or even many, domains. But there are domains, such as weather forecasting, where experts show little sign of biases or "cognitive illusions" (Lichtenstein, Fischhoff, & Phillips, 1982; Murphy & Winkler, 1977; Stewart, Roebber, & Bosart, 1997). Thus, despite the broad generalizations of incompetence drawn about experts, there are a number of exceptions to the rule.

In an effort to account for these domain differences, Shanteau (1992a, 1992b) constructed a table to differentiate those domains where experts do well from those where experts do not. Table 16.1 is an updated version based on a continuum from high to low competence. In the left column are those domains where experts make aided decisions using Decision Support Systems (DSS) or other computerized tools, for example, weather forecasters. The

Table 16.1 Progression of Domains from High to Low Performance

Highest Levels of Performance		Lowest Levels of Performance	
Aided Decisions	Competent	Restricted	Random
Weather Forecasters	Livestock Judges	Clinical Psychologists	Stockbrokers
Auditors	Grain Inspectors	Pathologists	Polygraphers
Test Pilots	Chess Masters	Parole Officers	Office Managers
Insurance Analysts	Photo Interpreters	Student Admissions	Parole Officers
Physicists	Soil Judges	Intelligence Analysts	Court Judges

Note: Each domain was classified based on analyses of expert performance reported in the literature.

next column contains domains where experts make skilled, but largely unaided decisions, for example, livestock judges. The third column lists domains where experts show limited competence, for example, clinical psychologists. The behavior of experts in the last column is close to random, for example, stockbrokers and, unfortunately, court judges.

It should be noted that assignment of domains within the table was based on our review of the conclusions of the authors of each study. That is, the level of competence is categorized from the assessments of the researchers who studied each domain.

There are many ways to describe the differences in this table (Shanteau, 1992a, 1992b). For present purposes, it is sufficient to observe that domains to the left (more competent) side involve stable (static) properties. That is, the stimuli and the problem "hold still" for experts to evaluate. The domains to the right (less competent) side involve more changeable (dynamic) properties. Thus, the stimuli and problem are less stable, more difficult to specify— more like "moving targets."

Another way to view this distinction is to note that most domains to the left side of the table involve physical or natural properties, whereas most domains to the right involve human or social behavior. This may reflect the fact that natural sciences in left-side domains have a longer history of development. In contrast, the domains to the right have relatively young social sciences. Given this difference, it makes sense that, as a general rule, expert competence will tend to be higher to the left side and lower to the right side.

The question remains whether this distinction between domains is predictive of different levels of agreement. To examine this proposition, Table 16.2 summarizes consensus values reported by the author(s) for a variety of domains. Two specialties are listed under each category, with the between-expert agreement (consensus) given as average correlations. As can be seen, the mean consensus r value for weather forecasters is .95, whereas the average value for livestock judges is .50. The consensus values for clinical psychologists, and stock forecasters are .40, and .32, respectively. Comparable results for other domains appear in the second line. The trend supports the prediction outlined

Table 16.2 Between-Expert (Consensus) Reliability Values

Highest Levels of Performance		Lowest Levels of Performance	
Aided Decisions	Competent	Restricted	Random
Weather Forecasters $r = .95$	Livestock Judges $r = .50$	Clinical Psychologists $r = .40$	Stockbrokers $r = .32$
Auditors $r = .76$	Grain Inspectors $r = .60$	Pathologists $r = .55$	Polygraphers $r = .33$

Note: The values cited in this table were drawn from the following studies (from left to right): Stewart, Roebber and Bosart (1997); Phelps and Shanteau (1978); Goldberg and Werts (1966); Slovic (1969); Kida (1980); Trumbo, Adams, Milner, and Schipper (1962); Einhorn (1974); and Lykken (1979).

Table 16.3 Within-Expert (Internal Consistency) Reliability Values

Highest Levels of Performance		Lowest Levels of Performance	
Aided Decisions	Competent	Restricted	Random
Weather Forecasters $r = .98$	**Livestock Judges** $r = .96$	**Clinical Psychologists** $r = .44$	**Stockbrokers** $r = <.40$
Auditors $r = .90$	Grain Inspectors $r = .62$	Pathologists $r = .50$	Polygraphers $r = .91$

Note: The values cited in this table were drawn from the following studies (from left to right): Stewart, Roebber and Bosart (1997); Phelps and Shanteau (1978); Goldberg and Werts (1966); Slovic (1969); Kida (1980); Trumbo, Adams, Milner, and Schipper (1962); Einhorn (1974); and Raskin and Podlesny (1979).

above—more-structured natural-science domains lead to high consensus values whereas less-structured social-science domains leading to lower consensus.

For comparison, the average within-expert reliability (consistency) correlations for these same domains are listed in Table 16.3. The trends are similar, with better-structured domains leading to higher internal consistency. As expected from psychometric theory (Nunnally, 1967), the consistency values are higher than the corresponding consensus values in Table 16.2 (except for pathologists). In two domains (livestock judges and polygraphers), there are notable discrepancies between consensus and consistency correlations. These apparently reflect the existence of different "schools of thought" as to how experts should do their jobs in these fields, that is, there are several approaches to evaluating polygraphs that reflect the training of the operators.

Analysts' View of Experts

Investigators in artificial intelligence, expert system design, cognitive science, systems analysis, and computer science have all concluded that experts are superior decision makers. That is why knowledge engineers design computer simulations around what experts know. Similarly, most domain-specific researchers (such as in medicine and weather forecasting) view experts as possessing unique information essential for making good decisions. In short, investigators in these disciplines see human expertise as an ultimate goal to be emulated.

In contrast, decision analysts have concluded that experts are typically flawed and prone to making simple errors (e.g., Kahneman, 1991). Moreover, experts and novices are viewed as sharing the same shortcomings. For instance, Tversky (quoted in Gardner, 1985, p. 360) states, "whenever there is a simple error that most laymen fall for, there is always a slightly more sophisticated version of the same problem that experts fall for."

Decision analysts have apparently overlooked the fact that there are important domain differences between areas of expertise. For instance, both weather forecasters and livestock judges are skilled professionals. Yet, there is a major difference for these two fields in the level of disagreement between experts. The former is based on a well-developed science, whereas the latter is based more on "informed judgment." It should not be surprising, therefore, to find livestock experts disagreeing more with each other about their judgments than weather forecasters.

Nonetheless, judgment and decision researchers continue to view experts as extensions of the flawed decision making typically seen in undergraduates (Kahneman, 1991). That is, the characteristics of flawed decision making associated with the biases and heuristics tradition are generalized to skilled professionals (Gigerenzer, 1993; Klein, Orasanu, Calderwood, & Zsambok, 1993; Yates, 1990).

Importance of Domains

The position taken here is that previous analysts have unknowingly adopted the *experts-should-be-perfect* view of expertise. As argued above, this view implies that disagreement between experts is taken as a sign that something is wrong. That in turn leads to the conclusion that experts are not as skilled or as competent as they claim. In this section, we propose an alternative perspective based on a domain-dependent view of expert performance. This perspective is based on a five-part argument:

(1) The primary job of an expert is not to make decisions but to help others reach a broadly defined target state. For example, the goal may be to help policy makers design better strategies to reduce recidivism or to increase the efficiency (i.e., reduce the cost) of the court system. These goals do not involve single answers, but instead require something more elaborate from the expert, such as strategic plans.

(2) To reach these goal states requires dealing with multiple, constantly changing, and dynamic factors. As noted by Klein et al. (1993), the situations faced by experts are different and more complex than the simplified situations considered by most analysts. Thus, experts work on problems that are much more complex than those studied in idealized settings with undergraduates making decisions.

(3) Using their knowledge and experience, the role of the expert is to recognize patterns and find consistencies in a dynamic problem space. The expert's job is to clarify the issues and to identify alternative approaches. In other words, the challenge for an expert is "to make sense out of chaos." This is certainly a description of what many court judges have to do.

(4) Based on their experience and insights into the nature of problems, experts try to help others (such as jury members) clarify their

thinking. Typically, an expert will identify various alternate paths to a desired goal state (arriving at a verdict). The expert's role is to lay out the options and the consequences in a clear and comprehensible fashion so that others may make the final decision.

(5) In the end, it is others, for example, a jury, not the expert judge who makes most decisions. The judge offers insights and observations, but it is up to others to make the final choice(s). In a jury trial, the ultimate responsibility for the decision rests on the jury, not the judge.

The view is nicely summarized by the management consultant Golde (1969: "We seem to expect too much and the wrong things of our experts." That is, experts generally act more like knowledgeable consultants. Rarely do they function as the "all-knowing, single-answer decision makers" envisioned by many analysts (who often see a parallel to economic/statistical theory).

When experts disagree, therefore, it is because they often see alternative paths to the goal state. In court settings, there are almost always multiple perspectives to any problem. Thus, disagreements between expert judges are not only expected, they are a necessary consequence of the situation in which judges find themselves.

Implications for Research

By relying on an inappropriate argument for expert decision making, many analysts have unknowingly adopted a distorted view that leads them to expect that experts should always agree on the "correct decision." The next section looks further at the research implications arising from this distortion.

By drawing a parallel to economic/statistical theory, decision analysts have adopted a "single correct answer" approach to assessing expertise. In most quantitative assessments, we expect to find one and only one answer to a question. When an expert (or anyone else) gives an answer different from the "correct answer," he/she is said to have a "bias" (Tversky & Kahneman, 1974). Moreover, when two or more experts give different answers, their claim of special competence is questioned (Einhorn, 1974).

The position here is that these analysts have relied on an inappropriate view of how experts function. For instance, the environment in which experts work is much different from that reflected in the idealized world envisioned by these analysts. The complex, changeable environment that experts actually operate in is considerably more complicated. In reality, problems rarely are simple enough to lead to single correct answers. Instead, there are almost always multiple answers (or at least multiple routes to answers). If so, it should not be surprising to find that experts, especially in domains involving human behavior, often take different approaches to finding solutions.

The underlying problem is that analysts misunderstand what experts do and what is expected of them. These investigators seem to think that experts see the world as they do—with simplifying assumptions and single-answer solutions. However, experts generally have a different worldview, with many complexities and contingencies, but with few optimal solutions. In addition, experts have a flexible approach to adaptation that helps them manage uncertainty (Shanteau, 1992a).

From the present perspective, therefore, disagreements between experts are expected. Although analysts view disagreements as evidence of incompetence, our view is that experts see disagreements as a more-or-less inevitable part of their job.

One explanation for these errors in judgment was offered by Gaeth and Shanteau (1984). They noted that irrelevant materials (e.g., excessive moisture) significantly impacted the decisions of soil judges. They also found that training to compensate for irrelevancies was successful in reducing the impact of these inappropriate factors. Another approach to improving expert judgment was developed for weather forecasting; Murphy and Winkler (1977) found that precipitation forecasts could be improved using a feedback system based on Brier scores (a quadratic lossfunction). Since the introduction of Brier scores, the accuracy of weather forecasts has increased dramatically (Stewart et al., 1997).

Thus, it appears that experts can perform reasonably well, although there is clearly room for improvement, for example, experts' judgments are not perfectly consistent. Moreover, there are sizable domain differences, that is, there is greater agreement between experts in some areas than others. Experts working in domains with better-defined properties, such as tax law, would be expected to show sizable agreement. In contrast, experts in domains with more subjective standards, such as sexual harassment, would be expected to perform less well.

Conclusion

Dawes (personal communication, 1987) offered an insightful observation about an earlier version of Table 16.1. The performance standards expected by clients are different for the left and right sides. Weather forecasters are allowed to make occasional mistakes. However, court judges and managers are expected to be correct almost all the time. That is, in the less predictable (right-side) domains, experts are held to higher standards of performance.

This is important for court judges, since with increased computerization and media coverage, there has been a shift in skills needed. Traditionally, a judge needed to be a jack-of-all-trades, with general skills in many areas. Today, modern courtrooms place more demand on cognitive (thinking) abilities. For example, with the trend toward more complex legal cases, there is a greater need for judges with management abilities. These are precisely the psychological skills associated with right side of the table (as opposed to the more technical skills on the left side).

As argued here, disagreements are a natural product of the various domains that experts work in. If disagreement between experts is not a critical issue, then what should be? Let us suggest four useful goals for future research on expertise. First, as argued above, the superiority of experts depends on their ability to distinguish between relevant and irrelevant information (Ettenson, Shanteau, & Krogstad, 1987; Jacavone & Dostal, 1992; Mosier, 1997; Schwartz & Griffin, 1986; Shanteau, 1992b). One goal in future research should be to discover how experts make these discriminations and to find ways to enhance the process (also see Wistrich, Guthrie, & Rachlinkski, 2005).

A second goal should be to understand the kinds of intellectual and physical tools expert judges use to enhance their decisions. Experts seldom, if ever, make unaided judgments of the sort emphasized in laboratory research. In fact, analysts regularly use the very tools denied their subjects. "The experimenters themselves, using tools and expertise, are able to perform (laboratory) tasks rather well" (Edwards, 1983, p. 511). The type of tools used by experts needs to be better understood. Perhaps it will be possible to borrow some of the tools used by left-side experts to assist those making decisions on the right side.

The third goal should be to develop insights into domain differences. As Edwards (1983, p. 512) argues, "we have no choice but to develop a taxonomy of intellectual tasks themselves. Only with the aid of such a taxonomy can we think with reasonable sophistication about how to identify among the myriad types of experts and the myriad types of tasks … just exactly what kinds of people and tasks deserve our attention." The analyses in Tables 16.1, 16.2, and 16.3 offer an initial start in building a taxonomy.

The final goal is to find better methods for assessing the expertise of individual experts in particular situations. As demonstrated here, expert performance varies both between individuals in a given situation and within individuals across various domains. The consensus and consistency correlations presented above capture some of this variation. What is needed, however, are measures that reflect both the difficulty of the domain and the skill of the judge. Dalgleish and Weiss (2007) are working on this measurement problem with hopeful progress.

Research on such goals will help broaden our understanding of expertise. In contrast, concern about the supposed incompetence of experts based on disagreements about correct answers offers little opportunity for expanding our insights about expertise in the court room. Instead, we should focus our efforts on analyses of relevance/irrelevance, tool usage, domain differences, and measurement methods.

Note

1. Preparation of this chapter was supported by funds provided by the Scottish Funding Council to HealthQWest; A research consortium for the West of Scotland.

17

Cognitive Style and Judging

Gregory Mitchell and Philip E. Tetlock

An important dimension of judicial decisions much discussed by legal scholars (e.g., Breyer, 2005; Molot, 2004; Peters, 2000; Sunstein, 1999, 2005), but little studied by social scientists, is the scope of a court's opinion. Traditional political science studies of judicial decisions emphasize the political valence of judicial opinions—as endorsing a liberal or conservative outcome—but do not address the scope with which commands or proclamations are issued. The valence of an opinion is, however, theoretically orthogonal to the scope of an opinion. The judge who writes opinions that curtail the use of affirmative action programs in education (e.g., Justice O'Connor in *Grutter v. Bollinger* (2003)) and the judge who writes opinions that would widely bar the use of affirmative action programs in education (e.g., Justice Thomas in *Grutter*) may both take politically conservative positions, but they do so in ways that may have significantly different implications for future cases and the development of the law (see Richards & Kritzer, 2002, on the importance of jurisprudential regimes). Thus, focusing only on the valence of decisions ignores an important dimension of judicial opinions.[1]

Case details and other situational features surely affect the nature and scope of judicial opinions, but differences in the manner in which opinions are written may also reflect deep differences in the ways that individual judges understand the causes of human behavior and their own ability to predict behavior and influence it through court action. These deep differences involve what psychologists broadly refer to as variations in "cognitive style," a psychological construct that has been operationalized in a variety of ways to refer to individuals' consistent ways of perceiving stimuli, processing information, and thinking about problems.[2] From a cognitive styles perspective, judges will naturally vary in the ways that they process case-relevant information and solve problems, and these stable *processes* of thought are likely to have important implications for the *content* of judges' thoughts and ultimately the content of their judicial opinions. For instance, integratively complex judges—judges who differentiate among many facets of a problem but also look for connections across these dimensions that can provide integrative solutions—are more likely to write opinions that take into account multiple sources of evidence and multiple, potentially conflicting legal rules and interests, whereas integratively simple judges are more likely to write opinions that focus on key pieces of evidence, see some arguments as clearly right and others as clearly wrong, and avoid trade-offs (see Tetlock et al., 1985; Gruenfeld, 1995).

One instantiation of the cognitive style construct that we believe holds particular relevance to judicial behavior is what Tetlock (2005) labels, after Berlin (1953), the hedgehog-fox cognitive-style continuum: persons toward the "hedgehog" pole on this continuum hold relatively simple theories about human nature, which they believe apply across many domains, and they have relatively high confidence in the long-run predictive success of these theories; persons toward the "fox" pole on this continuum exhibit skepticism about grand theories of human nature and deductive application of such theories, believing instead that behavior and outcomes are contextually dependent and subject to many random perturbations, and they have relatively low confidence in their forecasting abilities.[3] In a 15-year study of expert prediction of political and business events, Tetlock (2005) found that a seven-item measure of the hedgehog-fox cognitive style distinguished among his sample of experts in several important ways: "foxes" were better calibrated and more accurate in their predictions, particularly within their areas of expertise, were more rational in the updating of their beliefs following failed predictions, and were less likely to exhibit defensive maneuvers after predictive failures and "knew-it-all-along" effects after outcomes were known.

The results from Tetlock's (2005) prognostication tournament suggest that judicial foxes will more accurately predict future conditions, and be more humble in their concomitant predictions and ambitions, when acting as social engineers who must predict how their rulings will interact with future societal conditions (see, e.g., Albiston & Nielsen, 2007). Judicial hedgehogs, on the other hand, should be much more likely to see the world in deterministic and predictable terms and thus should issue more expansive and less contingent proclamations that will tend more often to be wrong factually. Extension of this distinction to judging finds support in legal discussions of judicial philosophy, particularly the work of Cass Sunstein on constitutional decision-making. Indeed, Gelman (2001) notes the striking similarity between Berlin's dichotomization of historical thinkers into hedgehogs and foxes and Sunstein's (1999) dichotomization of appellate judges into maximalists and minimalists. Judicial maximalists (i.e., hedgehogs) favor broad rulings that implement abstract theories about individual rights and institutional competencies, whereas judicial minimalists (i.e., foxes) do not apply broad theories deductively to particular cases but instead proceed incrementally, through analogy, and issue narrow rulings (see Sunstein, 1999). Cognitive style research suggests that the consistent differences that Sunstein identifies reflect judges' broad orientations to the world and their information-processing tendencies more than consciously chosen judicial philosophies (i.e., cognitive style likely leads to a preference for minimalist or maximalist approaches to judging).

The potential relevance of cognitive style research to judicial behavior extends beyond the formulation of opinions. Judicial foxes, who see much greater causal murkiness in the world, should exhibit greater humility in their choices to end cases without the aid of trial, where evidence can be more fully developed. Thus, at the appellate level, they should be more likely to remand cases for new trials rather than resolve the cases through review of the appellate record, and, at the trial level, they should be less likely to grant summary judgment motions and Rule 12(b)(6) motions on grounds of implausibility, per *Bell Atlantic v. Twombly* (2007).

Further, Tetlock (2005)'s finding that hedgehogs tend to be less corrigible and more protective of their preexisting views than foxes suggests also that the opinions of judicial hedgehogs should show less change over time in both their content and direction because of the greater rigidity of these judges' views, and their opinions should thus be more predictable and internally consistent than those of judicial foxes. And, given their certitude, judicial hedgehogs should be less prone to compromise in response to pleas from members of the same court, particularly pleas from judicial foxes who see issues so differently, and more prone to write separate opinions when the majority opinion is authored by a judicial hedgehog of a different ideology or by a judicial fox of any political type.

Tetlock (2005) found hedgehogs on both the left and the right in his study of experts, and legal scholarship suggests the same may be true of judicial hedgehogs (cf. Sunstein, 1999). If so, we should find liberal and conservative judicial hedgehogs looking more ideological and less sensitive to legal and case-specific variations—and thus more predictable—within political science studies of the role of attitudes in judicial decision-making (e.g., Segal & Spaeth, 2002), as compared to judicial foxes of either political bent. This hypothesis runs counter to theories of political ideology founded on a rigidity-of-the-right thesis, which associates conservatism with right-wing authoritarianism and a need for closure and associates liberalism with open-mindedness (e.g., Jost et al., 2003), but our hypothesis is consistent with the view that judicial activism is not the primary domain of liberal judges (Cross & Lindquist, 2007; Sunstein, 2005) but rather of ideologues generally (see Tetlock, 1986).

While Tetlock's (2005) results with respect to forecasting accuracy and learning, and our predictions about the relation of judicial hedgehoggishness to judicial activism, might suggest that judicial foxes should be favored over judicial hedgehogs (e.g., Farber & Sherry, this volume, ch. 18, advocate giving preference in judicial selections to foxes), the attractiveness of hedgehog-like or fox-like tendencies will depend on the interests of the audience. The judge who appears to some to be a wise judicial fox, deciding only what is necessary to resolve the case at hand, will appear to others as an unprincipled, timid judge who fails to provide necessary guidance to future legal actors (cf. Tetlock et al., 1993; Waldron, 2007).

Fox-like tendencies are likely to be especially valued in public law domains, which preoccupy many legal scholars, where the issues presented in cases often implicate many contentious trade-offs and implicate debates about the relative competency of courts versus legislatures versus executives to make these trade-offs. Thus, a humble, incremental approach will often be seen as the least likely to lock-in-place bad guesses about future conditions and unpopular resolutions of trade-offs (see, e.g., Sunstein, 2007). In the domain of private law, however, where parties can often contract around undesirable legal rules or choose from competing legal regimes, we suspect that judicial hedgehogs, with their more sweeping, definitive, and predictable approaches to cases, will fare much better in the eyes of the key attendant audiences—businesses and business lawyers.

If we are right that the hedgehog-fox cognitive style dimension can illuminate how judges go about their business, then researchers should naturally be concerned with issues of measurement and testing of our hypotheses on judges, for it is perilous to assume that findings from Tetlock's research on forecasting experts holds with respect to judges, who inhabit unique institutional positions and generally have similar educational backgrounds that may greatly affect the expression of individual differences in cognitive style. The most straightforward approach would be to recruit judges to complete Tetlock's (2005) hedgehog-fox scale and then examine these judges with respect to their opinion-writing and other behaviors consistent with the different cognitive styles.[4] Alternatively, observers may score a sample of judges' opinions for hedgehog- versus fox-like perspectives and examine the consistency of these tendencies across cases and the ability of these scores to predict other judicial behaviors. Unfortunately, no content-analytic protocol for the placement of writers on the hedgehog-fox continuum presently exists.

However, given the potential gains from cognitive styles research on judges, we believe that investments in the development of empirical tools to measure judicial cognitive styles would be well-rewarded. Because interest in the hedgehog-fox variable supplements rather than supplants traditional political-science interest in the judicial ideology variable, and offers a way to explain more of the non-law-related variance in judicial behavior, political scientists should find this research perspective congenial to prevailing attitudinal theories of judicial behavior. Because the hedgehog-fox distinction mirrors existing legal discussions of judicial philosophy, and offers a way to explain the bases for these philosophies and to focus on elements of judicial behavior largely ignored by political scientists, legal scholars should find this research perspective congenial to prevailing theories of legal interpretation and the development of the common law. We thus see cognitive style research as offering an empirical bridge between the political science and legal literatures. Most provocatively, cognitive style research may show that traditional, competing positions of the political scientist and the legal scholar are both correct, but only for subsets of judges: judicial hedgehogs may allow their personal beliefs and values to drive their legal decisions, thus supporting many political scientists' views of judging, but judicial foxes may be much more sensitive to the facts and law of particular cases and much less willing to inject their own beliefs and values into cases, thus supporting many legal scholars' views of judging.

Notes

1. Scope itself can be seen as multidimensional. For instance, Sunstein (1999) distinguishes between the width and depth of an opinion, with the former referring to the reach or breadth of the legal ruling announced and the latter referring to the nature of the doctrinal or theoretical foundations for the opinion.
2. In this brief discussion, we focus only on one area of cognitive style research. For reviews of this large body of research, see Kozhevnikov (2007), Suedfeld (2000), and Suedfeld & Tetlock (2001). We focus here on individual differences in cognitive style because of their potential for differentiating among judges and their opinions. There are, however, situational differences in cognitive style as well, and these situational differences may cause convergence across judges who otherwise would exhibit different individual styles (see Tetlock, 2005).
3. This distinction follows from Isaiah Berlin's now classic essay, *The Hedgehog and the Fox*, in which he describes the distinction as "one of the deepest differences which divide writers and thinkers, and it may be, human beings in general":

> For there exists a great chasm between those, on one side, who relate everything to a single central vision, one system less or more coherent or articulate, in terms of which they understand, think and feel—a single, universal, organizing principle in terms of which alone all that they are and say has significance—and, on the other side, those who pursue many ends, often unrelated and even contradictory, connected, if at all, only in some *de facto* way, for some psychological or physiological cause, related by no moral or aesthetic principle; these last lead lives, perform acts, and entertain ideas that are centrifugal rather than centripetal, their thought is scattered or diffused, moving on many levels, seizing upon the essence of a vast variety of experiences and objects for what they are in themselves, without, consciously or unconsciously, seeking to fit them into, or exclude them from, any one unchanging, all-embracing, sometimes

self-contradictory and incomplete, at times fanatical, unitary inner vision. The first kind of intellectual and artistic personality belongs to the hedgehogs, the second to the foxes; and without insisting on a rigid classification, we may, without too much fear of contradiction, say that, in this sense,... Dante belongs to the first category and Shakespeare to the second; Plato, Lucretius, Pascal, Hegel, Dostoyevsky, Nietzsche, Ibsen, and Proust are, in varying degrees, hedgehogs; Herodotus, Aristotle, Montaigne, Erasmus, Moliere, Goethe, Pushkin, Balzac, and Joyce are foxes (Berlin, 1953, pp. 1–2).

4. A few items in this scale will likely need substitution or revision for a judicial context, however (see Tetlock, 2005, p. 268).

18

Building a Better Judiciary

Daniel A. Farber and Suzanna Sherry

We have spent much of our academic careers arguing that judicial decision making—even in constitutional cases—is a specialized craft, not merely an exercise in politics (Farber & Sherry, 2002; Farber, 1992, 1995; Farber & Adams, 1999; Sherry, 2003, 2005, 2007). We have suggested that good judging requires both expertise and a certain set of dispositional traits, and that it can be enhanced or hindered by both personal traits and situational characteristics. In a recent book, we describe and defend our vision of the process of constitutional adjudication, provide examples of good and bad judicial opinions, and identify existing and proposed structural supports conducive to good constitutional decision making. (Farber & Sherry, 2008).

Our task in this essay is to translate our theorizing into concrete suggestions for further research. Anyone who has read this far in the current volume is probably persuaded that the task is hopeless. In constitutional cases, there seems to be no hope of reaching agreement on an appropriate normative standard. Certainly there is no consensus on outcome-based norms: If everyone agreed about the ultimate meaning of constitutional provisions, the Supreme Court would have no docket. Decisional norms fare no better, insofar as judges and scholars disagree about both the appropriate method of constitutional interpretation and the role of the judiciary in our constitutional democracy. As for our claim that certain dispositional traits can lead to better judging, the empirical testing of such a claim would prove difficult if not impossible.

Being legal academics as well as pragmatists, however, we remain undaunted by philosophical dilemmas and empirical gaps. The reader will have to judge whether our optimism is warranted. Mindful of the fate of Gaul, we nevertheless divide this essay into three parts: In the first part, we describe what judges do when they decide constitutional questions, concluding that they are primarily exercising the same legal expertise that judges and lawyers utilize in all of their professional decisions. In the second part we focus briefly on the personal and contextual characteristics that have been shown to produce or interfere with expert decision making in general. Finally, we turn to our main focus: the legal structures that might enhance the positive characteristics and minimize the negative ones.

Deciding Constitutional Questions

Constitutional decision making, like all legal decision making, is a process of constrained discretion. While there are rarely unequivocally correct answers, some answers are better than others—and some methods are more or less likely to produce better answers. Consider such run-of-the mill legal questions as how the parties to a contract would interpret an ambiguous provision, or whether a particular piece of evidence is likely to be more prejudicial than probative to a jury, or whether the efficacy of a safety regulation outweighs its cost. In each case, there is room for legitimate disagreement about the correct outcome. In other words, there is no formula for reaching the correct answer, and discretion is inevitable although not unlimited.

We suggest that the same standard can be used to evaluate judicial decisions. We can ask, essentially, whether the judge considered all of the appropriate legal and factual factors (and only those factors) and whether the conclusion is reasonable rather than arbitrary. This move does not eliminate discretion or provide certainty, since there will often be more than one reasonable outcome. And ultimately, knowing what is reasonable is a matter of judgment. But this standard does rule out both some arguments and some answers. It requires attention to precedent, constitutional history, and public values, and demands that judicial justification of the outcome meet a fairly high level of plausibility and coherence.

No formula can tell us what it means to provide "due process" or to afford everyone "equal protection of the laws," nor what constitutes an "establishment" of religion or "probable cause" for a search. (Easy constitutional questions do exist, but rarely reach the courts: No one is ever going to litigate the meaning of the requirement that one must be at least 35 years old to become president.) While some judges and scholars have tried to devise such formulas, their theories raise more questions than they answer, and do not in fact cabin discretion. Originalism, the most commonly invoked formulaic theory of interpretation, is a case in point. It merely transposes the question from the meaning of the ambiguous text into the equally unanswerable historical query of what the founding generation meant by that ambiguous text (Farber & Sherry 2002, pp. 10–28). Given that professional historians themselves disagree about such issues, and that judges are not trained in historical analysis, originalism cannot effectively constrain judicial discretion. Indeed, it is likely to prove less effective in constraining discretion than the common law method, with which judges have years of professional training and experience to guide them (Farber & Sherry, 2002, pp. 153–154).

So how *do* judges make decisions in constitutional and nonconstitutional cases? What distinguishes a reasonable answer from an unreasonable one, a legitimate decision from an illegitimate one? As we argue in our book, we can look to administrative law to help us answer these questions. Legislatures often delegate broad but not unlimited discretion to administrative agencies, and courts are frequently called on to review agency action to determine whether it is a legitimate exercise of the agency's discretion. In doing so, courts focus on two aspects of the agency's decision: They ask whether the agency considered all of the relevant factors and only the relevant factors, and they ask whether the decision was "arbitrary and capricious."[1]

Administrative decision making also helps us see how sound judgment and expertise can play a key role in decision making even in situations where politics and ideology matter. Clearly, it matters whether the administrator of EPA is appointed by a Republican or a Democrat. But science, law, and economic analysis also matter. Two good professional EPA administrators appointed by presidents of different parties (say, William Ruckelshaus and Carol Browner) have more in common with each other, and their decisions have more similarity, than either has with a political ideologue like Anne Burford. The exercise of discretion leaves room for a variety of factors, but not all of those factors are political. Good administrative decisions are also shaped by legal directives, prior practice, and rigorous analysis. So it is with constitutional interpretation.

When good judging is described in this way, it should be apparent that it is not very different from good decision making in other contexts. Expert decision making, judicial and otherwise, is the ability to identify and take into account all of the relevant information and then draw reasonable conclusions. Lawyers rely on this sort of expertise all this time: when advising a client about whether a proposed course of action is likely to lead to legal liability, when drafting a contract designed to have a certain legal effect, or when deciding whether a particular legal argument might persuade a court. Of course, lawyers do not always agree about the right answer, and these disagreements may relate in part to broader differences in personal experience and perspective, but there is a core of shared skills in these tasks. Interpreting the Constitution may have more political salience than interpreting a statute, a contract, or a body of precedents, but it is fundamentally analogous. Judicial expertise is simply legal expertise in a different context.

Once we conclude that judicial decision-making is the exercise of legal expertise, we can turn to the field of psychology and expert decision making more broadly to help us understand what personal and situational factors enhance decision making. In particular, we can look for characteristics that incline decision makers toward the careful consideration of all relevant factors, that increase the likelihood of reasonable and coherent decisions, and that allow individuals to overcome the cognitive biases to which humans are so prone.

Personal and Contextual Characteristics

As suggested by several essays in this section, especially that by Mitchell and Tetlock (ch. 17), numerous studies have pointed to a cluster of personal characteristics that tend to improve decision making by increasing the ability to overcome common cognitive biases. By reducing the effect of these biases, such characteristics are also likely to make judges better able to identify and rely on relevant factors and to process the information correctly.

The primary finding seems to be that foxes make better decisions than do hedgehogs. The more broadly a person is inclined to search, the better for both the reasoning process and the ultimate decision (Tetlock, 2005). This should be true for judges as well as for other decision makers. Moreover, to the extent that "foxiness" incorporates specific characteristics such as integrative complexity and open belief systems, it is especially important that *judges* be foxes rather than hedgehogs. Recall that our standard for good judging requires a willingness to consider carefully all relevant information. For the reasons identified at the outset of this essay, we cannot measure directly whether a judge has done so (except to the extent that the opinion reflects the judge's decision process) or whether a failure to do so has produced a worse decision. Instead, we must rely on a judge's dispositional preference for multiple perspectives over dogmatism. Focusing on these individual characteristics is most helpful at the stage of judicial selection.

Turning to situational characteristics, two seem to make the most difference: collegial decision making in a heterogeneous group (Sunstein, 2000), and accountability—especially accountability to persons whose views are unknown. This insight can be of use both in selecting judges and in designing the structure of the legal regime generally and the judiciary in particular.

Legal Characteristics

With these personal and situational characteristics in mind, we can now examine which aspects of the American legal landscape are likely to be conducive to good judicial decision-making, which might be in need of improvement, and what changes we might want to make.

Let us begin at the beginning, with legal education. A traditional legal education seems quite well suited to fostering a judicial disposition. Most law schools use the Socratic method: Teachers call on individual students and ask sequential questions that add new or different information and make the students think ever more deeply about an issue. This method forces students to confront arguments on all sides of an issue, and to consider an increasingly complex web of information. They will often be called on to identify the weak points in their own arguments or to make the strongest arguments on the other side. All of this helps students develop the professional judgment that they will need as lawyers and the fox-like disposition that makes good judges—especially since the discussion is usually focused on existing precedent, which does not allow students to run freely with any preconceived big ideas. Throw in the traditional emphasis on the incremental development of the common law and the careful attention to texts, and American legal education has the capacity to foster exactly the expertise that facilitates good judgment.

There are some flaws, of course. Most lie with individual teachers and scholars. The critical legal studies scholars and their heirs (including the popular constitutionalists, as we argue in our book) teach students that constitutional law is simply politics by another name, denying the possibility of expert judgment. Many conservative constitutional scholars want judges to be hedgehogs, urging a single overarching method of constitutional interpretation. Both of these schools of thought, to the extent that they seep into the classroom, undermine the efficacy of a legal education in producing good judgment as we have defined it. The problem is exacerbated by the lack of curricular requirements after the first year of law school: Students in their last two years of law school are free to choose the courses (and teachers) they prefer, and can thus avoid—inadvertently or deliberately—confronting uncomfortable intellectual challenges. The contemporary pedagogical philosophy that students are consumers and that education ought to be entertaining and "relevant" also makes it easier for students to escape some of the experiences that might make them better lawyers and judges. Despite these problems, however, legal education provides a good basis for development of legal judgment and legal expertise. But perhaps legal educators should be more knowledgeable about the ingredients of good judgment and more conscious of their role in fostering it.

Clinical education, properly conceived, can also cultivate important habits of thought. Good lawyering requires an ability to imagine opposing arguments and alternative perspectives on a case (Farber, 1994). It also requires an ability to think broadly about the interests and goals of a client, which may require consideration of a range of institutional and interpersonal factors as well as deliberation about the ethical factors that define the lawyer's role. Although clinical education can sometimes be no more than basic training in the rudiments of legal practice, it is also capable of inculcating important elements of good judgment.

What legal education begins, a life in law practice—especially private practice—hones. Professional judgment makes the difference between a successful lawyer and an unsuccessful one. Everything a lawyer does depends on his ability to accurately predict legal consequences. Like experts in all fields, then, good lawyers must develop the dispositional characteristics that are most conducive to good decision-making. The context of private practice also fosters good decision-making. Clients make sure that lawyers are accountable. And the practice of law is a collaborative enterprise, often (especially for young lawyers) with little or no choice of collaborators. The heterogeneous working groups that result further contribute to good decision making.

Two groups of lawyers, however, work in environments that may not provide such incentives to the exercise of good judgment. Long-time lawyers for a particular cause or client—whether it is the NRA, the ACLU, the prosecutor's office, or the public defender—are less often forced to confront multiple perspectives that differ from their own. While they do have to anticipate opposing arguments, the homogeneous environment tends to reinforce their own perspectives and denigrate the validity of any counterarguments. They are also less accountable, because their clients often lack the choice, control, or incentives of private paying clients. We might therefore expect that lawyers with only this type of legal experience are likely to make poorer judges than those who have a more diverse background. This will not always be true, particularly if the individual has played multiple roles, such as working as a prosecutor and later as a defense lawyer.

Legal academics are even less constrained by the realities of private practice, and indeed are often subject to exactly the wrong incentives (Farber & Sherry, 2008; George, 2001). Legal scholars generally work alone, and are (in their scholarship, at least) accountable to no one (at least after tenure!). Their own biases are often reinforced as they seek out like-minded colleagues. Unlike practicing lawyers, academics are free to ignore the legal world around them, and legal expertise can sometimes seem almost irrelevant, particularly for those whose work is the most theoretical. Moreover, the most highly valued scholarship is the most innovative; legal scholars are thus *encouraged* to flout common sense and exhibit poor legal judgment. Innovation is obviously a desirable trait, but what makes it treacherous in legal scholarship (as opposed to more empirically oriented social sciences) is the absence of a strong reality check.

All of these factors—as well as others we canvass in *Judgment Calls*—suggest that academics are among the least likely to internalize the dispositional traits conducive to good judicial decision making. We should note, however, that this depressing picture of legal academia is of relatively recent origin, and may be moderating somewhat—in addition, there are obviously a large number of exceptions to this generalization. (For instance, we ourselves have excellent judgment. Identifying the cognitive biases in the preceding sentence is left as an exercise to the reader.) Also, many legal academics have had other kinds of experiences, either prior to teaching or in the thankless tasks of academic administration, which may be more conducive to developing balanced judgment.

Identifying which professional experiences are most likely to produce good judges leads us to the next, and most problematic, topic: the judicial selection process. What we have already discussed suggests that we should prefer judges with private practice experience, and avoid most academics. But the selection process for federal judges is in need of even more improvement. Once upon a time, presidents generally nominated (and the Senate confirmed) experienced and competent moderates—usually, although not always, from the president's party. While a judge's overall political perspective was usually aligned with that of the nominating president, the difficult cases that reached appellate courts were resolved largely through legal expertise and good judgment. Being good lawyers rather than political animals, judges exercised independent judgment that sometimes surprised their nominating presidents. President Eisenhower, for example, was famously disappointed in Chief Justice Warren and Justice Brennan.

In recent years, however, some presidents have been much more determined to influence judicial decision making and avoid future surprises. They have substituted ideological litmus tests for professional competence in nominating judges. And in trying to ensure ideological purity and fidelity, they have deliberately sought nominees with an unyielding record of ideological commitment. Offices within the executive branch are now charged with the task of identifying true believers, and the slightest hint of ideological impurity will sink a candidate. Of course, some presidents are more committed to this strategy than others, but the trend is worrisome.

Whether or not this contemporary selection process means that federal judges decide cases based on political considerations (and we believe that most judges still do not, at least not consciously), it does diminish the likelihood of appointing foxes rather than hedgehogs. The stronger the commitment to a particular ideology, the less open a judge will be to other perspectives. Instead of focusing on ideological commitment, then, presidents and senators should be looking for evidence of the dispositional traits that have been shown to enhance judgment and good decision making (Sherry, 2003). We should be seeking an openness to other perspectives, a willingness to revise one's views in the face of new information, and a refusal to adopt a single approach to decision making. Hedgehogs should be shunned: A nominee who espouses an overarching grand theory of constitutional interpretation, of whatever ideology, should be immediately disqualified.

The selection of state judges is even worse. Most state judges are popularly elected or subject to popular reappointment or recall, and judicial elections—especially at the appellate level—are becoming ever more politicized. The same campaign strategies that are lamented in legislative races are now infecting judicial elections. Our constitutional commitment to free speech means that states cannot effectively limit judicial electioneering or organized smear campaigns. Here the cure is obvious: State judges, like federal judges, should be appointed rather than elected. The public has no way to evaluate a candidate's judgment or expertise, so it is no surprise that elected judges are only coincidentally good decision makers.

One further factor should guide the selection process. Since heterogeneity has been shown to improve collegial decision making, we should try to maintain a diversity of viewpoints on the bench. This often happens naturally, as presidents and senates with different perspectives have a chance to nominate and confirm new judges. But long periods of single-party rule, random fluctuations in the judicial vacancy rate, and particular commitments to ideological nominees can sometimes produce a largely homogeneous judiciary. When this seems likely, senators of both parties should take seriously our constitutional ideal of an independent judiciary, and insist on greater diversity. (We can dream, can't we?) To the extent that presidents focus on expertise and open-mindedness rather than ideology, of course, deliberately creating diversity will be less necessary.

Moving from individual character traits to the institutional context, a number of existing structural features enhance judicial decision making. The two most important are the collegial and hierarchical structure of the judiciary, and the tradition of issuing written opinions to explain judicial decisions. A less important but still significant factor is the influence of multiple nonjudicial actors on judicial decision making.

All American appellate courts make their decisions collegially, on multimember panels. Since virtually all important constitutional questions get to the appellate level, we need not be overly concerned about constitutional adjudication by single judges at the trial level. Additionally, all judges save the nine on the Supreme Court are subject to oversight by other judges. Thus all judges must persuade others in order to prevail, and all except the nine justices are directly or indirectly accountable to some other court. Both collegiality and accountability, the two most important situational characteristics for good decision making, are therefore already present.

The heterogeneous nature of the judiciary contributes two further benefits. First, collegial decision making by a heterogeneous group injects multiple perspectives and limits the problem of self-reinforcement within the members of the group. Second, because judges often know neither the identities nor the perspectives of those who will be reviewing their decisions, the beneficial effect of accountability is increased. This will always be true for decisions by trial court judges. It can also be true for judges on three-member federal appellate panels, whose decisions might be scrutinized by other members of their court via a petition for en banc review, by the Supreme Court, or by both. These judges may also be concerned about how their decisions will be received by colleagues in different circuits, who are not bound by their decisions and are free to criticize them.

Even more important is the fact that in the United States (as in most countries whose legal systems are primarily derived from the English common law regime), judges routinely issue written opinions explaining and justifying their decisions. Judicial decision making is therefore relatively transparent. This transparency enhances decision making by subjecting decisions to public scrutiny and thereby increasing accountability. It also forces judges to confront counterevidence and counterarguments. Many judges recount the experience of having reached a particular decision, only to have a change of heart after finding that the opinion "won't write." A judicial career spent deliberating with colleagues and writing opinions is also likely to lead to greater open-mindedness and critical thinking over time, further improving the quality of decision making in life-tenured judges. It is well-known that judges can "grow" on the bench, and the psychological literature on decision making may offer a partial explanation.

Unfortunately, opinion-writing is declining in the federal appellate courts, as more and more cases are decided by perfunctory unpublished decisions. The recent adoption of Fed. R. App. Proc. 32.1, which bars courts from prohibiting the citation of unpublished opinions, should help alleviate this problem; since most unpublished opinions are easily located through electronic databases, it was only the courts' prior ban on citation that allowed such decisions to escape scrutiny. Now that judges know that *all* their opinions are subject to citation, they are more likely to take them all seriously.

But the underlying problem is one of time and resources: As long as the federal appellate docket is overloaded, judges will not be able to devote sufficient time to each case. Increasing the number of courts or judges might help, but is not a panacea, because it could create more inter- and intracircuit conflicts. In the end, we have to decide which cases are most in need of federal judicial resources, and cut back on the others. Our own view is that Congress has been acting irresponsibly by increasing federal jurisdiction in diversity cases (which do not need federal adjudication in the first place) and by enacting too many federal criminal statutes that simply criminalize behavior that is already punishable under state law. In part, this trend is driven by a sense that federal judges are more capable of handling complex, major cases, but a better solution would be federal funding to help state courts develop this capacity. In any case, we cannot expect good decisions from judges whose dockets are bloated with cases unworthy of their attention.

Finally, although judges are ultimately responsible for their own decisions, they are subject to multiple influences and thus to multiple perspectives. The adversary system ensures that all interested parties will have a say. Most appellate judges have law clerks, whose short tenure and youthful perspective can complement the judge's experience. And to the extent that judicial opinions are subject to critical scrutiny by law professors, journalists, politicians, and the public, judges may have to refine their views over time.

We also have some improvements to suggest, especially at the Supreme Court level. First, the problem of insufficient attention to each case is not limited to the lower courts, although the problem is somewhat different in the Supreme Court. It is not that they have too many cases—indeed, we think they decide too few—but that they place unnecessary artificial limits on the amount of time for each case. Two small changes could have a great effect: Routinely allow more than one hour for oral argument, and permit cases to carry over into the next term if some number of justices think more time should be devoted to deliberation or to opinion writing.

Another problem is that the Court's focus on constitutional and other politically salient cases has a tendency to make its job seem more exceptional, and less like ordinary legal decision making. To the extent that the justices themselves believe this, it might interfere with their judgment. Again, two changes could help alleviate the problem by exposing the justices to a greater number of more routine (albeit legally difficult) cases. The Supreme Court's mandatory jurisdiction might be expanded, so that it is required to decide more cases: for example, cases in which the circuit courts disagree—in mid-twentieth century the Court tried to resolve almost all circuit splits, but now it ignores most of them. Another possibility would be to reinstate the justices' circuit-riding duties, requiring them to sit regularly with courts of appeals and hear the gamut of cases (Sherry, 2005). Some appellate judges, including Richard Posner on the Seventh Circuit and the late Chief Justice William Rehnquist, have voluntarily chosen to sit as trial judges, and we suspect the experience was good for them.

We also think that it is useful for judges to be exposed to other viewpoints. The problem is that most people with whom they associate have every reason to cater to their views—few lawyers will tell a sitting judge that his views are wrong, and lower courts judges are equally unlikely to provide challenges to the intellectual viewpoints of their reviewing courts. It is useful for high court judges to meet with their peers: state supreme court judges with colleagues in other states; U.S. Supreme Court justices with colleagues from foreign constitutional courts. To encourage this, Congress should provide funding to assist in meetings of state court judges and to finance travel to foreign conferences, as well as funding to hold conferences with foreign jurists on U.S. soil.

A final proposal would be to encourage peer review, especially at the Supreme Court level. A panel of eminent retired judges, lawyers, and academics might be created, on the understanding that subgroups of those with relevant expertise would be selected to give feedback on Supreme Court opinions before they are issued. A particularly noncontroversial form of this review would be to require the circulation of opinions to retired justices for comment. Playing this peer review role might make retirement more attractive to some justices, increasing turnover and therefore potentially diversity on the Court. Retired solicitors general and attorneys general might also be recruited with minimal controversy. A more modest, and less controversial, program would be to appoint a nonpartisan commission with the charge of issuing assessments of the Court's performance on a regular basis.

Considered individually, it is possible that none of these proposals would have a substantial effect. They might, however, have a significant cumulative impact. They might also have some effect on the recruitment and retention of judges, making the job more attractive to the kind of people we wish to have as judges: those who enjoy being exposed to different viewpoints and who like engaging in legal analysis rather than political rhetoric.

None of these existing or proposed structural features, of course, guarantees good decision making. A judge who is dogmatic and closed-minded or whose hedgehog-like devotion to certainty or to an abstract theory is unshakable will not be swayed by colleagues or critics nor dissuaded by the impossibility of writing a coherent opinion. In the end, then, it is the character traits that are most important. Former Attorney General Nicholas Katzenbach put it most eloquently when he told the Senate Judiciary Committee deliberating on the nomination of Robert Bork: "Were I in your position ... the central question I would be asking is this. Is Judge Bork a man of judgment? ... Is he a wise person?" (Lewis, 1987). It is our hope that the project begun with this book will eventually help us answer that question about future nominees.

Note

1. The leading case is *Citizens to Preserve Overton Park v. Volpe*, 401 U.S. 402 (1971).

References

Abelson, R. P. (1968). Psychological implications. In R. Abelson, E. Aronson. W. McGuire, T. Newcob, M. Rosenberg, & P. Tannenbaum (Eds.), *Theories of Cognitive Consistency: A Sourcebook*. Chicago: Rand McNally.

Abelson, R. P., & Rosenberg, M. (1958). Symbolic psycho-logic: A model of attitudinal cognition. *Behavioral Science, 3,* 1–8.

Abrams, D., Wetherill, M., Cochrane, S., Hogg, M. A., & Turner, J. C. (1990). Knowing what to think by knowing who you are: Self-categorization and the nature of norm formation, conformity and group polarization. *British Journal of Social Psychology, 29,* 91–119.

Ackerman, B. (1999). Taxation and the Constitution. *Columbia Law Review, 99,* 1.

Adams v. The New Jersey Steamboat Company, 151 N.Y. 163, 45 N.E. 369 (N.Y. Ct. of Appeals, 1896).

Ajzen, I., & Fishbein, M. (1980). *Understanding Attitudes and Predicting Social Behavior*. Englewood Cliffs, NJ: Prentice-Hall.

Albiston, C. R., & Nielsen, L. B. (2007). The procedural attack on civil rights: The empirical reality of Buckhannon for the private attorney general. *UCLA Law Review, 54,* 1087–1134.

Aldisert, R. J. (1982). What makes a good judge? *Pennsylvania Lawyer, 4,* 22.

Alexander, J. C. (1994). Judges' self-interest and procedural rules: Comment on Macey. *Journal of Legal Studies, 23,* 647.

Alexander, L. (1989). Constrained by precedent. *Southern California Law Review, 63,* 3.

Alexander, L. (1991). The gap. *Harvard Journal of Law and Public Policy, 14,* 695.

Alexander, L. (1996). Bad beginnings. *University of Pennsylvania Law Review, 145,* 57–87.

Alexander, L., & Sherwin, E. (2001). *The Rule of Rules: Morality, Rules, and the Dilemmas of Law*. Durham, NC: Duke University Press.

Alexander, L., & Sherwin, E. (2008). *Demystifying Legal Reasoning*. Cambridge, UK: Cambridge University Press.

Aliotta, J. M. (1988). Social backgrounds, social motives, and participation on the U.S. Supreme Court. *Political Behavior, 10,* 267–284.

Alpert, L., Atkins, B. M., & Ziller, R. C. (1979). Becoming a judge: The transition from advocate to arbiter. *Judicature, 62,* 325–335.

Altman, S. (1990). Beyond candor. *Michigan Law Review, 89,* 296.

American Bar Association Committee on Judicial Performance Evaluation. (2005). *Black Letter Guidelines for the Evaluation of Judicial Performance with Commentary.*

Anderson, A. A., Lindsay, J. L., and Bushman, B. J. (1999). Research in the psychological laboratory: Truth or triviality? *Current Directions in Psychological Science, 8,* 3–9

Anderson, M. C., & MacCoun, R. J. (1999). Goal conflict in juror assessments of compensatory and punitive damages. *Law & Human Behavior, 23,* 313.

Arlen, J. (1998). The future of behavioral economic analysis of law. *Vanderbilt Law Review, 51,* 1765–1788.

Arlen, J. H., & Talley, E. L. (in press). Introduction. In J. H. Arlen & E. L. Talley (Eds.), *Experimental Law and Economics,* pp. 1–56. Cheltenham, UK: Edward Elgar Publishing.

Aronson, E., Wilson, T. D., & Brewer, M. B. (1998). Experimentation in social psychology. In D. T. Gilbert, S. T. Fiske, & G. Lindzey (Eds.), *The Handbook of Social Psychology, Vol. 1* (4th ed.). New York: McGraw-Hill.

Arrow, H., McGrath, J. E., & Berdahl, H. L. (2000). *Small Groups as Complex Systems: Formation, Coordination, Development, and Adaptation.* Thousand Oaks, CA: Sage.

Asch, S. (1955). Opinions and social pressure. *Scientific American, 193*(5), 31–35.

Asch, S. (1956). Studies of independence and conformity: A minority of one against a unanimous majority. *Psychological Monographs, 70*(9), Whole Number 416.

Asch, S. E. (1940). Studies in the principles of judgments and attitudes: II. Determination of judgments by group and by ego standards. *The Journal of Social Psychology, 12,* 433–465.

Ashwander v. Tennessee Valley Authority, 297 U.S. 288 (1936).

Atkins, B. M., & Zavoina, W. (1974). Judicial leadership on the court of appeals: A probability analysis of panel assignment in race relations cases on the Fifth Circuit. *American Journal of Political Science, 18,* 701–711.

Austin, J. (2006). *Do the Supreme Court Justices' Questions during Oral Arguments Predict their Decisions?* Honors Thesis, Department of Psychology, University of Kansas, Lawrence.

Bainbridge, S. M., & Gulati, G. M. (2002). How do judges maximize? (The same way everyone else does—boundedly): Rules of thumb in securities fraud opinions. *Emory Law Journal, 51,* 83–151.

Bales, R. F. (1950). *Interaction Process Analysis.* Cambridge: Harvard University Press.

Bandstra, R. A. (2005). Looking toward Lansing: Could you be a lawyer-legislator? *Michigan Bar Journal, 89,* 28–29.

Barber, J. D. (1965). *The Lawmakers: Recruitment and Adaptation to Legislative Life.* New Haven, CT: Yale University Press.

Barberis, N., & Thaler, R. (2003). A survey of behavioral finance. In G. M. Constantinides, M. Harris, & R. M. Stulz (Eds.), *Handbook of the Economics of Finance.* Amsterdam: Elvesier.

Bargh, J. A., & Chartrand, T. L. (1999). The unbearable automaticity of being. *American Psychologist, 54,* 462–479.

Bargh, J. A., & Ferguson, M. L. (2000). Beyond behaviorism: On the automaticity of higher mental processes. *Psychological Bulletin, 126,* 925–945.

Bargh, J. A., Gollwitzer, P. M., Lee-Chai, A., Barndollar, K., & Trötschel, R. (2001). The automated will: Nonconscious activation and pursuit of behavioral goals. *Journal of Personality and Social Psychology, 81,* 1014–1027.

Barnett, R. E. (2004). Restoring the lost Constitution: The presumption of liberty. Princeton, NJ: Princeton University Press.

Barnett, R. E. (2005). Foreword: Limiting Raich. *Lewis & Clark Law Review, 9,* 743–750.

Barnett, S. M., & Ceci, S. J. (2002). When and where do we apply what we learn? A taxonomy for far transfer. *Psychological Bulletin, 128*(4), 612–637.

Baron, J. (2004). Normative models of judgment and decision making. In D. J. Koehler & N. Harvey (Eds.), *Blackwell Handbook of Judgment and Decision Making.* Malden, MA: Blackwell.

Baron, R. E., Byrne, D., & Branscomb, N. R. (2006). *Social Psychology* (11th ed.). New York: Pearson.

Bartels, B. L. (2005). *Heterogeneity in Supreme Court Decision-Making: How Case-Level Factors Alter Preference-Based Behavior.* Paper presented at the annual meeting of the Midwest Political Science Association, Chicago.

Bartels, B. L. (2006). *Heterogeneity in Supreme Court Decision Making: How Situational Factors Shape Preference-Based Behavior.* Unpublished doctoral dissertation, Ohio State University, Columbus.

Bartlett, K. (1990). Feminist legal methods. *Harvard Law Review, 103,* 829–888.

Bates, D. W., & Gawande, A. A. (2000). Error in medicine: what have we learned? *Annals of Internal Medicine, 132,* 763.

Baum, L. (1990). *American Courts: Process and Policy* (2nd ed.). Boston: Houghton-Mifflin.

Baum, L. (1994). What judges want: Judges' goals and judicial behavior. *Political Research Quarterly, 47,* 749–768.

Baum, L. (1997). *The Puzzle of Judicial Behavior.* Ann Arbor: University of Michigan Press.

Baum, L. (2006). *Judges and Their Audiences.* Princeton, NJ: Princeton University Press.

Baum, L. (2007). *The Supreme Court* (9th ed.). Washington, DC: CQ Press.

Baumeister, R. F., & Newman, L. S. (1994). Self-regulation of cognitive inference and decision processes. *Personality and Social Psychology Bulletin, 20,* 3–19.

Beck, R. C. (2000). *Motivation: Theories and Principles.* Upper Saddle River, NJ: Prentice-Hall.

Becker, G. (1969). Crime and punishment: An economic analysis. *Journal of Political Economy, 79,* 169.

BedRock Limited v. United States, 124 S.Ct. 1587 (2004).

Beebe, B. (2006). An empirical study of the multifactor tests for trademark infringement. *California Law Review, 94,* 1581–1654.

Behrman, B. W. & Davey, S. L. (2001). Eyewitness identification in actual criminal cases: An archival analysis. *Law & Human Behavior, 25,* 475.

Bell Atlantic Corp. v. Twombly, 27 S. Ct. 1955 (2007).

Bergara, M., Richman, B., & Spiller, P. T. (2003). Modeling Supreme Court strategic decision making: The congressional constraint. *Legislative Studies Quarterly, 28,* 247–280.

Berger, J., Fisek, M. H., Norman, R. Z., & Zelditch, M. Jr. (1977). *Status Characteristics in Social Interaction: An Expectation-States Approach.* New York: Elsevier.

Berger, J, Wagner, D. G., & Zelditch, M. Jr. (1985). Expectation states theory. In J.M. Berger & M. Zelditch (Eds.), *Status, Rewards, and Influence*. San Francisco: Jossey-Bass.

Berlin, I. (1953). *The Hedgehog and the Fox: An Essay on Tolstoy's View of History*. Chicago, IL: Ivan R. Dee.

Bertrand, M., & Mullainathan, S. (2004). Are Emily and Greg more employable than Lakisha and Jamal? A field experiment on labor market discrimination. *The American Economic Review, 94*, 991–1013.

Bickel, A. (1986). *The Least Dangerous Branch*. New Haven, CT: Yale University Press.

Biskupic, J. (2004, June 8). June is often the time of compromise in court. *USA Today*, p. 2A.

Biskupic, J. (2005). *Sandra Day O'Connor*. New York: HarperCollins.

Black, H. C. (1912). *Handbook on the Law of Judicial Precedents*. St. Paul, MN: West Publishing Co.

Blair, I. V., Judd, C. M., & Chalpeau, K. M. (2004). The influence of Afrocentric facial features in criminal sentencing. *Psychological Science, 15*, 674–679.

Blanchette, I., & Dunbar, K. N. (2001a). The inVivo/inVitro approach to cognition: The case of analogy. *Trends in Cognitive Science, 5*, 334–339.

Blanchette, I., & Dunbar, K. N. (2001b). Analogy use in naturalistic settings: The influence of audience, emotion, and goals. *Memory & Cognition, 29*, 730–735.

Blanchflower v. Blanchflower, 834 A.2d 1010 (N.H. 2003).

Blanck, P. D. (1991). What empirical research tells us: Studying judges' and juries' behavior. *American University Law Review, 40*, 775, 777.

Blanck, P. D., Rosenthal, R., & Cordell, L. H. (1985). The appearance of justice: Judges' verbal and nonverbal behavior in criminal jury trials. *Stanford Law Review, 38*, 89.

Boot, M. (1998). *Out of Order*. New York: Basic Books.

Borchard, E. M. (1932). *Convicting the Innocent: Sixty-five Actual Errors of Criminal Justice*. New Haven, CT: Yale University Press.

Bork, R. (1990). *The Tempting of America*. New York: Touchtone.

Bowen, T., & Scheb, J. M. (1993). Freshman opinion writing on the U.S. Supreme Court, 1921–1991. *Judicature, 79*, 239–243.

Bowers v. Hardwick, 478 U.S. 186 (1986).

Brace, P. R., & Hall, M. G. (1997). The interplay of preferences, case facts, context, and rules in the politics of judicial choice. *Journal of Politics, 59*, 1206.

Braman, E. (2004). *Motivated Reasoning in Legal Decision Making*. Doctoral dissertation, Ohio State University, Columbus.

Braman, E. (2006a). Reasoning on the threshold: Testing the separability of preferences in legal decision making. *Journal of Politics, 68*, 308–321.

Braman, E. (2006b, February 15). *Exploring discretion in legal decision making: An experimental approach*. Paper prepared for Presentation at Law & Society Workshop, University of Indiana University Law School.

Braman, E., & Nelson, T. E. (2007). Mechanism of motivated reasoning?: Analogical perception in discrimination disputes. *American Journal of Political Science, 51*(4), 940–956.

Brandeis, L. D. (1916). The living law. *Illinois Law Review, 10*, 461.

Breasted, J. H. (2001). *Ancient Records of Egypt: Volume Two. The Eighteenth Dynasty*. Urbana-Champaign: University of Illinois Press.

Brehm, S. S., & Brehm, J. W. (1981). *Psychological Reactance: A Theory of Freedom and Control*. New York: Academic Press.

Brenner, S., & Hagle, T. M. (1996). Opinion writing and acclimation effect. *Political Behavior, 18,* 235–261.

Breyer, S. (2005). *Active Liberty*. New York: Vintage Books.

Brenner, S., & Spaeth, H. J. (1995). *Stare Indecisis*. Cambridge, UK: Cambridge University Press.

Brewer, M. (1979). In-group bias in the minimal intergroup situation: A cognitive-motivational analysis. *Psychological Bulletin, 86,* 307–324.

Brewer, M. (1991). The social self: On being the same and different at the same time. *Personality and Social Psychology Bulletin, 17,* 475–482.

Brewer, S. (1996). Exemplary reasoning: Semantics, pragmatics, and the rational force of legal argument by analogy. *Harvard Law Review, 109,* 925–1028.

Bright, S. B., & Keenan, P. J. (1995). Judges and the politics of death: Deciding between the bill of rights and the next election in capital cases. *Boston University Law Review, 75,* 759.

Brooks, R. R. W., & Raphael, S. (2003). Life terms or death sentences: The uneasy relationship between judicial elections and capital punishment. *Journal of Criminal Law and Criminology, 92,* 609.

Brudney, J. J., & Ditslear, C. (2001). Designated diffidence: District court judges on the courts of appeals. *Law & Society Review, 35,* 565–606.

Brust, R. (2005, September). Balancing act. *American Bar Association Journal, 37.*

Buchman, J. (2007). The effects of ideology on federal district judges' decisions to admit expert testimony. *American Political Science Review, 35,* 671.

Burnet v. Coronado Oil & Gas Co., 285 U.S. 393 (1932).

Burton, S. (2005). *An Introduction to Law and Legal Reasoning* (3d ed.). Frederick, MD: Aspen Publishers.

Bush v. Vera, 517 U.S. 952 (1996).

Bushman, B. J. (1995). Moderating role of trait aggressiveness in the effects of violent media on aggression. *Journal of Personality and Social Psychology, 69,* 950–960.

Büthe, T. (2002). Taking temporality seriously: Modeling history and the use of narratives as evidence. *American Political Science Review, 96,* 481–494.

Byrne, M. D. (1995). The convergence of explanatory coherence and the story model: A case study in juror decisions. In J. D. Moore & J. F. Lehman (Eds.), *Proceedings of the 17th Annual Conference of the Cognitive Science Society*. Mahwah, NJ: Lawrence Erlbaum Associates.

Caldeira, G. A. (1977). Judicial incentives: Some evidence from urban trial courts. *Iusticia, 4*(2), 1–28.

Caldeira, G. A., & Wright, J. R. (1990). The discuss list: Agenda building in the Supreme Court. *Law & Society Review, 24,* 807–836.

California Supreme Court. (n.d.) *Internal Operating Practices and Procedures of the California Supreme Court*. Retrieved August 27, 2007, from http://www.courtinfo.ca.gov/courts/supreme/documents/sc082504.pdf

Callins v. Collins, 510 U.S. 1141 (1994).

Caminker, E. H. (1994). Why must inferior courts obey superior court precedents? *Stanford Law Review, 46,* 817–873.

Campbell, J. (2005). *The Lives of the Chief Justices of England: From the Norman Conquest Till the Death of Lord Mansfield*. London: Elibron Classics.

Cardozo, B. N. (1921). *The Nature of the Judicial Process*. New Haven, CT: Yale University Press.

Carp, R. A., & Rowland, C. K. (1983). *Policymaking and Politics in the Federal District Courts*. Knoxville: University of Tennessee Press.

Cartwright, D. (1968) The nature of group cohesiveness. In D. Cartwright & A. Zander (Eds.), *Group Dynamics: Research and Theory*(3d ed.). New York: Row, Peterson, & Co.

Cartwright, D., & Zander, A. (1968). Origins of group dynamics. In D. Cartwright & A. Zander (Eds.), *Group Dynamics: Research and Theory*(3d ed.). New York: Row, Peterson, & Co.

Catrambone, R., & Holyoak, K. J. (1989). Overcoming contextual limitations on problem-solving transfer. *Journal of Experimental Psychology: Learning, Memory, and Cognition, 15*, 1147–1156.

Cattell, R. B. (1963). Theory of fluid and crystallized intelligence: A critical experiment. *Journal of Education Psychology, 54*, 1–22.

Chaiken, S. (1980). Heuristic versus systematic information processing and the use of source versus message cues in persuasion. *Journal of Personality and Social Psychology, 39*, 752–766.

Chaiken, S., Giner-Sorolla, R., & Chen, S. (1996). Beyond accuracy: Defense and impression motives in heuristic and systematic information processing. In P. M. Gollwitzer & J. A. Bargh (Eds.), *The Psychology of Action: Linking Cognition and Motivation to Behavior*. New York: Guilford Press.

Chaiken, S., Liberman, A., & Eagly, A. H. (1989). Heuristic and systematic information processing within and beyond the persuasion context. In J. S. Uleman & J. A. Bargh (Eds.), *Unintended Thought*. New York: Guilford Press.

Chaiken, S., & Trope, Y. (Eds.). (1999). *Dual-Process Theories in Social Psychology*. New York: Guilford Press.

Champagne, A. (1986). The selection and retention of judges in Texas. *Southwestern Law Journal, 40*, 53.

Champagne, A. (2005). Tort reform and judicial selection. *Loyola of Los Angeles Law Review, 38*, 1483.

Chapman, G. B., & Bornstein, B. H. (1996). The more you ask for, the more you get: Anchoring in personal injury verdicts. *Applied Cognitive Psychology, 10*, 519, 527, 531.

Chapper, J. A., & Hanson, R. A. (1990). *Intermediate Appellate Courts: Improving Case Processing*. Williamsburg, VA: National Center for State Courts.

Chen, S., & Chaiken, S. (1999). The heuristic-systematic model in its broader context. In S. Chaiken & Y. Trope (Eds.), *Dual-Process Theories in Social Psychology*. New York: Guilford Press.

Chi, M. T. H. (2006). Two approaches to the study of experts' characteristics. In K. A. Ericsson, N. Charness, P. J. Feltovich, & R. R. Hoffman (Eds.), *The Cambridge Handbook of Expertise and Expert Performance*. Cambridge, UK: Cambridge University Press.

Chi, M. T. H., Farr, M. J., & Glaser, R. (Eds.). (1988). *The Nature of Expertise*. Hillsdale, NJ: Lawrence Erlbaum.

Chi, M. T. H., Feltovich, P. J., & Glaser, R. (1981). Categorization and representation of physics problems by experts and novices. *Cognitive Science, 5*, 121–152.

Choi, S. J., & Gulati, G. M. (2004a). Choosing the next supreme court justice: An empirical ranking of judge performance. *Southern California Law Review, 78*, 23–117.

Choi, S. J, & Gulati, G. M. (2004b). A tournament of judges? *California Law Review, 92,* 299–322.

Christianson, S. (2004). *Innocent: Inside Wrongful Conviction Cases.* New York: New York University Press.

Christie, G. C. (1969). Objectivity in law. *Yale Law Journal, 78,* 1311–1342.

Chutkow, D. M. (2007). The Executive Chief Justice: Appointments to the Judicial Conference committees, May 31, 2007. Available from Social Science Research Network. Web site: http://ssrn.com/abstract=990167

Citizens to Preserve Overton Park v. Volpe, 401 U.S. 402 (1971).

Clark, H. R. (1995). *Justice Brennan: The Great Conciliator.* New York: Birch Lane Press.

Clayton, C. W. (1999). The Supreme Court and political jurisprudence: New and old institutionalism. In C. W. Clayton & H. Gillman (Eds.), *Supreme Court Decision-Making.* Chicago: University of Chicago Press.

Clemen, R. T. (1999). *Does decision analysis work?* Unpublished manuscript.

Cohen, F. (1935). Transcendental nonsense and the functional approach. *Columbia Law Review, 35,* 809–845.

Cohen, J. M. (2002). *Inside Appellate Courts: The Impact of Court Organization on Judicial Decision Making in the United States Courts of Appeals.* Ann Arbor: University of Michigan Press.

Cohen, L. J. (1981). Can human irrationality be experimentally demonstrated? *Behavioral and Brain Sciences, 4,* 317–370.

Cohen, M. A. (1991). Explaining judicial behavior, or what's "unconstitutional" about the Sentencing Commission? *Journal of Law, Economics, and Organization, 7,* 183.

Coke, E. (1985). *Commentary upon Littleton* (18th ed., Charles Butler, Ed.) Legal Classics Library. Delran, NJ: Gryphon Books. (Original work published 1628).

Collins, P., and Martinek, W. L. (2007). The small group context: Designated district court judges on the United States Courts of Appeals. Paper presented at the meeting of the Southern Political Science Association.

Cooksey, R. W. (1996). *Judgment Analysis: Theory, Methods and Applications.* San Diego, CA: Academic Press.

Coombs, C. H., Dawes, R. M., & Tversky, A. (1970). *Mathematical Psychology: An Elementary Introduction.* Englewood Cliffs, NJ: Prentice-Hall.

Cooper, J. B., Newbower, R. S., & Kitz., R. J. (1984). An analysis of major errors and equipment failures in anesthesia management: Considerations for prevention and detection. *Anesthesiology, 60,* 34.

Cooper, J. B., Newbower, R. S., Long, C. D., & McPeek, B. (1978). Preventable anesthesia mishaps: A study of human factors. *Anesthesiology, 49,* 399.

Cooper, P. J. (1995). *Battles of the Bench: Conflict inside the Supreme Court.* Lawrence: University of Kansas Press.

Cooter, R. D., & Ulen, T. S. (2007). *Law and Economics* (5th ed.). Boston: Pearson/Addison Wesley.

The Court's uncompromising libertarian. (1975, November 24). *Time Magazine,* p. 69.

Craig v. Boren, 429 U.S. 190 (1976).

Croskerry, P. (2002). Achieving quality in clinical decision making: Cognitive strategies and detection of bias. *Academic Emergency Medicine, 9,* 1184–1204.

Cross, F. B. (1997). Political science and the new legal realism: A case of unfortunate interdisciplinary ignorance. *Northwestern University Law Review, 92,* 251.

Cross, F. B. (2003). Decisionmaking in the U.S. Courts of Appeals. *California Law Review, 91,* 1457–1515.

Cross, F. B. (2004). Explaining U.S. Circuit Court Decision Making. *Judicature, 88,* 31–35.

Cross, F. B. (2007). *Decision Making in the U.S. Courts of Appeals.* Stanford, CA: Stanford University Press.

Cross, F., & Tiller, E. (1998). Judicial partisanship and obedience to legal doctrine: Whistleblowing on the Federal Courts of Appeals. *Yale Law Journal, 107,* 2155–2176.

Cross, F. B., & Nelson, B. J. (2001). Strategic institutional effects on Supreme Court decisionmaking. *Northwestern University Law Review, 95,* 1437–1493.

Cross, F. B., & Lindquist, S. A. (2007). The scientific study of judicial activism. *Minnesota Law Review, 91,* 1752–1784.

Cross, R., & Harris, J. W. (1990). *Precedent in English Law* (4th ed.). Oxford: Clarendon Press.

Cushman, B. (2000). Formalism and realism in Commerce Clause jurisprudence. *University of Chicago Law Review, 67,* 1089.

Dagan, H. (2007). The realist conception of law. *University of Toronto Law Journal, 57,* 607–660.

Dalgleish, L. I. (2003). Risk, needs and consequences. In M.C. Calder (Ed.), *Assessments in Child Care: A comprehensive Guide to Frameworks and Their Use.* (pp. 86–99). Dorset, UK: Russell House Publishing.

Dalgleish, L., & Weiss, D. (2007). *Evidence-based expertise: A theoretical framework and some data.* Paper presented at the annual meeting of the Brunswik Society, Long Beach, CA.

Dancy, J. (1993). *Moral Reasons.* Oxford: Blackwell.

Danelski, D. J. (1960). The influence of the Chief Justice in the decisional process. In W. M. Murphy & C. H. Pritchett (Eds.), *Courts, Judges, and Politics.* New York: Random House.

Daniels, N. (1979). Wide reflective equilibrium and theory acceptance. *Journal of Philosophy, 76,* 256.

Darley, J. M. (2001). The dynamics of authority influence in organization and the unintended action consequences. In J. M. Darley, D. M. Messick, & T. R. Tyler (Eds.), *Social Influences on Ethical Behavior in Organizations.* Mahwah, NJ: L. Erlbaum.

Darley, J. M., Carlsmith, K. M., & Robinson, P. H. (2000). Incapacitation and just deserts as motives for punishment. *Law and Human Behavior, 24,* 659–683.

Darley, J. M., & Pittman, T. S. (2003). The psychology of compensatory and retributive justice. *Personality & Social Psychology Review, 7,* 324–336.

Daubert v. Merrell Dow Pharmaceuticals, 509 U.S. 579 (1993).

Dekay, M. L. (1996). The difference between Blackstone-like error ratios and probabilistic standards of proof. *Law & Social Inquiry, 21*(1), 95–132.

Denniston, L. (2005, November 27). Court to rule on military tribunals. Web site: http://www.scotusblog.com/movabletype/archives/2005/

Denzau, A., Riker, W., & Shepsle, K. (1985). Farquharson and Fenno: Sophisticated voting and home style. *American Political Science Review, 79,* 117–134.

Deutsch, M. (1975). Equity, equality, and need: What determines which value will be used as the basis of distributive justice. *Journal of Social Issues, 31,* 137.

Devins, N. (2004). The judicial safeguards of federalism. *Northwestern University Law Review, 99,* 131.

Devins, N., & Fisher, L. (2004). *The Democratic Constitution*. New York: Oxford University Press.

Devins, N., & Meese, A. (2005). Judicial review and non-generalizable cases. *Florida State University Law Review, 32*, 323.

Devitt, E. J. (1979). Ten commandments for the new judge. *American Bar Association Journal, 65*, 574.

Dhami, M. K. (2003). Psychological models of professional decision making. *Psychological Science, 14*, 175–180.

Dhami, M. K. (2004). Conditional bail decision making in the magistrates' court. *Howard Journal of Criminal Justice, 43*(1), 27–46.

Dhami, M. K. (2005) From discretion to disagreement: Explaining disparities in judges' pretrial decisions. *Behavioral Sciences & the Law, 23*(3), 367–386.

Dobie, A. M. (1951). A judge judges judges. *Washington University Law Quarterly, 1951*, 471.

Dorff, R. H., & Steiner, J. (1981). Political decision making in face-to-face groups: Theory, methods, and an empirical application in Switzerland. *American Political Science Review, 75*, 368–380.

Dovidio, J. F., Kawakami, K., Johnson, C., Johnson, B., & Howard, A. (1997). On the nature of prejudice: Automatic and controlled processes. *Journal of Experimental Social Psychology, 33*, 510–540.

Downs, A. (1957). *An Economic Theory of Democracy*. New York: Harper & Row.

Drahozal, C. R. (1998). Judicial incentives and the appeals process. *Southern Methodist Law Review, 51*, 469–503.

Druckman, J. (2001). The limits of framing effects: Who can frame. *Journal of Politics, 63*(4), 1041–66.

Dubois, P. L. (1980). *From Ballot to Bench: Judicial Elections and the Quest for Accountability*. Austin: University of Texas Press.

Duckworth, K. L., Bargh, J. A., Garcia, M., & Chaikin, S. (2002). The automatic evaluation of novel stimuli. *Psychological Science, 13*, 513–519.

Duncker, K. (1945). On problem-solving (L. S. Lees, Trans.). *Psychological Monographs, 58*(5), Whole No. 270.

Duxbury, N. (1995). *Patterns of American Jurisprudence*. New York: Oxford University Press.

Dworkin, R. (1986). *Law's Empire*. Cambridge, MA: Harvard University Press.

Eagly, A. H., & Chaiken, S. (1993). *The Psychology of Attitudes*. Fort Worth, TX: Harcourt Brace Jovanovich.

Edwards, H. T. (1985). Public misperceptions concerning the "politics" of judging: Dispelling some myths about the D.C. Circuit. *University of Colorado Law Review, 56*, 619.

Edwards, H. T. (1998). Collegiality and decision making on the D.C. Circuit. *Virginia Law Review, 83*, 1335–1370.

Edwards, H. T. (2003). The effects of collegiality on judicial decision making. *University of Pennsylvania Law Review, 151*, 1639–1689.

Edwards, W. (1983). Human cognitive capacities, representativeness, and ground rules for research. In P. Humphreys, O. Svenson, & A. Vari (Eds.), *Analyzing and Aiding Decision Processes*. Budapest, Hungary: Akademiai Kiado.

Edwards, W., & Newman, J. R. (1982). *Multiattribute Evaluation*. Beverly Hills, CA: Sage.

Einhorn, J. (1974). Expert judgment: Some necessary conditions and an example. *Journal of Applied Psychology, 59*, 562–571.

Eisenberg, M. A. (1988). *The Nature of the Common Law*. Cambridge, MA: Harvard University Press.

Eisenberg, T., Garvey, S. P., & Wells, M. T. (2001). Forecasting life and death: Juror race, religion, and attitude toward the death penalty. *The Journal of Legal Studies, 30*, 277–311.

Eisenberg, T., Hannaford-Agor, P. L., Hans, V. P., Waters, N. L.; Munsterman, G. T., Schwab, S. J., et al. (2005). Judge-jury agreement in criminal cases: A partial replication of Kalven and Zeisel's The American Jury. *Journal of Empirical Legal Studies, 2*(1), 171–207.

Eisenberg, T., LaFountain, N., Ostrom, B., Rottman, D., & Wells, M. T. (2002). Juries, judges, and punitive damages: An empirical study. *Cornell Law Review, 87*, 743, 747–749.

Eisenstadt v. Baird, 405 U.S. 438 (1972).

Eisler, K. I. (1993). *A Justice for All: William J. Brennan, Jr., and the Decisions That Transformed America*. New York: Simon & Schuster.

Ellsworth, P. C., & Mauro, R. (1998). Psychology and law. In D. T. Gilbert, S. T. Fiske & G. Lindzey (Eds.), *Handbook of Social Psychology* (4th ed., pp. 684–732). New York: McGraw-Hill.

Elster, J. (1989). *The Cement of Society*. Cambridge, UK: Cambridge University Press.

Enelow, J. M., & Hinch, M. (1990). *Advances in the Spatial Theory of Voting*. New York: Cambridge University Press.

Englich, B., Mussweiler, T., & Strack, F. (2006). Playing dice with criminal sentences: The influence of irrelevant anchors on experts' judicial decision making. *Personality and Social Psychology Bulletin, 32*(2), 188–200.

Epstein, L., & Jacobi, T. (2008). Super medians. *Stanford Law Review, 61*, 37.

Epstein, L., & Knight, J. (1998). *The Choices Justices Make*. Washington, DC: CQ Press.

Epstein, L., & Knight, J. (2000). Toward a strategic revolution in judicial politics: A look back, a look ahead. *Political Research Quarterly, 53*, 625–661.

Epstein, L., Knight, J., & Martin, A. (2003). The political (science) context of judging. *St. Louis University Law Journal, 47*, 783.

Epstein, L., Segal, J. A., & Johnson, T. (1996). The claim of issue creation on the U.S. Supreme Court. *American Political Science Review, 90*(4), 845–852.

Ericsson, K. A. (2006). The influence of experience and deliberate practice on the development of superior expert performance. In K. A. Ericsson, N. Charness, P. J. Feltovich, & R. R. Hoffman (Eds.), *The Cambridge Handbook of Expertise and Expert Performance*. New York: Cambridge University Press.

Ericsson, K. A., Charness, N., Feltovich, P. J., & Hoffman, R. R. (Eds.). (2006). *The Cambridge Handbook of Expertise and Expert Performance*. New York: Cambridge University Press.

Ericsson, K. A., & Ward, P. (2007). Capturing the naturally occurring superior performance of experts in the laboratory: Toward a science of expert and exceptional performance. *Current Directions in Psychological Science, 16*, 346–350.

Eskridge, W. N., Jr. (1991). Reneging on history? Playing the court/congress/president civil rights game. *California Law Review, 79*, 613–684.

Estrich, S. R., & Sullivan, K. M. (1989). Abortion politics: Writing for an audience of one. *University of Pennsylvania Law Review, 138*, 119.

Ettenson, R., Shanteau, J., & Krogstad, J. (1987). Expert judgment: Is more information better? *Psychological Reports, 60*, 227–238.

Evans, G., Heath, A., & Lalljee, M. (1996). Measuring left-right and libertarian-authoritarian values in the British electorate. *British Journal of Sociology*, *47*(1), 93–112.

Fabrigar, L. R., Wegener, D. T., MacCallum, R. C., & Strahan, E. J. (1999). Evaluating the use of exploratory factor analysis in psychological research. *Psychological Methods, 4*, 272–99.

Farber, D. A. (1992). The inevitability of practical reason: Statutes, formalism, and the rule of law. *Vanderbilt Law Review, 45*, 533–559.

Farber, D. A. (1994). Missing the "play of intelligence." *William & Mary Law Review, 36*, 147–171.

Farber, D. A. (1995). Reinventing Brandeis: Legal pragmatism for the 21st century. *University of Illinois Law Review, 1995*, 163–190.

Farber, D. A. (2005). Supreme Court selection and measures of past judicial performance. *Florida State University Law Review, 32*, 1175–96.

Farber, D. A, & Adams, E. (1999). Beyond the formalism debate: Expert reasoning, fuzzy logic, and complex statutes. *Vanderbilt Law Review, 52*, 1243–1340.

Farber, D. A., & Sherry, S. (2002). *Desperately Seeking Certainty: The Misguided Quest for Constitutional Foundations*. Chicago: University of Chicago Press.

Farber, D. A., & Sherry, S. (2008). *Judgment Calls: Principle and Politics in Constitutional Law*. New York: Oxford University Press.

Farrell, R. C. (1999). Successful rational basis claims in the Supreme Court from the 1971 term through Romer v. Evans. *Indiana Law Journal, 32*, 357.

Farthing-Capowich, D. P. (1985). Designing programs to evaluate judicial performance: Participation is key to success. *Supreme Court Journal, 9*, 22.

Fazio, R. H. (1986). "How do attitudes guide behavior?" In R. M. Sorrentino & E. T. Higgins (Eds.), *Handbook of Motivation and Cognition*. New York: Guilford Press.

Fazio, R. H. (1990). Multiple processes by which attitudes guide behavior: The MODE model as integrative framework. In M. P. Zanna (Ed.), *Advances in Experimental Social Psychology*. San Diego, CA: Academic Press.

Fazio, R. H. (1995). Attitudes as object-evaluation associations: determinants, consequences, and correlates of attitude accessibility. In R. E. Petty & J. A. Krosnick (Eds.), *Attitude Strength: Antecedents and Consequences*. Hillsdale, NJ: Erlbaum.

Fazio, R. H., Jackson, J. R., Dunton, B. C., & Williams, C. J. (1982). Attitude accessibility, attitude-behavior consistency, and the strength of the object-evaluation association. *Journal of Experimental Social Psychology, 18*, 339–357.

Fazio, R. H., & Towles-Schwen, T. (1999). The MODE model of attitude-behavior processes. In S. Chaiken & Y. Trope (Eds.), *Dual Process Theories in Social Psychology*. New York: Guilford Press.

Fazio, R. H., & Williams, C. J. (1986). Attitude accessibility as a moderator of the attitude-perception and attitude-behavior relations: An investigation of the 1984 presidential election. *Journal of Personality and Social Psychology, 51*, 505–514.

FCC v. Beach Communications, Inc., 508 U.S. 307, 315 (1993).

Feigenson, N. R. (2003). Can tort juries punish competently? *Chicago-Kent Law Review, 78*, 239.

Feltovich, P. J., Prietula, M. J., & Ericsson, K. A. (2006). Studies of expertise from psychological perspectives. In K. A. Ericsson, N. Charness, P. J. Feltovich, & R. R. Hoffman (Eds.), *The Cambridge Handbook of Expertise and Expert Performance*. New York: Cambridge University Press.

Fennell, L. A. (1999). Between monster and machine: Rethinking the judicial function. *Southern California Law Review, 51,* 183.

Fenno, R. M. (1973). *Congressmen in Committees.* Boston: Little, Brown.

Festinger, L. (1957). *A Theory of Cognitive Dissonance.* Evanston, IL: Row, Peterson.

Festinger, L. (1968). Informal social communication. In D. Cartwright & A. Zander (Eds.), *Group Dynamics: Research and Theory* (3d ed.). New York: Row, Peterson, & Co.

Festinger, L., Schacter, S., & Back, K. (1968). Operation of group standards. In D. Cartwright & A. Zander (Eds.), *Group Dynamics: Research and Theory* (3d ed.). New York: Row, Peterson, & Co.

Fiorina, M. P., & Plott, C. R. (1978). Committee decisions under majority rule: An experimental study. *American Political Science Review, 72,* 575–598.

Fischman, J. B. (2008). Decision-making under a norm of consensus: A structural analysis of three-judge panels. Unpublished manuscript.

Fishburn, P. C. (1991). Decision theory: The next 100 years? *Economic Journal, 101,* 27.

Fisher, W. W., III, Horwitz, M. J., & Reed, T.A. (Eds.). (1993). *American Legal Realism.* New York: Oxford University Press.

Fiske, S. T. (2003). Five core social motives, plus or minus five. In S. Spencer, S. Fein, M. P. Zanna, & J. M. Olson, *Motivated Social Perception.* Mahwah, NJ: Lawrence Erlbaum Associates.

Fiske, S. T., and Taylor, S. E. (1991). *Social Cognition.* New York: McGraw-Hill.

Fong, G. T., Krantz, D. H., & Nisbett, R. E. (1986). The effects of statistical training on thinking about everyday problems. *Cognitive Psychology, 18,* 253.

Forgas, J. P. (Ed.). (2000). *Feeling and Thinking: The Role of Affect in Social Cognition.* New York: Cambridge University Press.

Foroni, F. & Mayr, U. (2005). The power of a story: New, automatic associations from a single reading of a short scenario. *Psychonomic Bulletin* & *Review, 12,* 139–144.

Forsyth, D. R. (1999). *Group Dynamics* (3d ed.). Belmont, CA: Wadsworth.

Foucha v. Louisiana, 504 U.S. 71 (1992).

Frank, J. (1930). *Law and the Modern Mind.* New York: Brentano's.

Frankel, M. E. (1975). The search for truth: An umpireal view. *University of Pennsylvania Law Review, 123,* 1031.

Frankel, M. E. (1976). The adversary judge. *Texas Law Review, 54,* 465.

Frankfurter, F. (1953). Chief justices I have known. *Virginia Law Review, 39,* 83.

Frey, D. (1986). Recent research on selective exposure to information. In L. Berkowitz (Ed.), *Advances in Experimental Social Psychology* (vol. 19). New York: Academic Press.

Frickey, P. (1996). The fool on the hill: Congressional findings, constitutional adjudication, and United States v Lopez. *Case Western Law Review, 46,* 695.

Fried, C. (1981). The artificial reason of the law or: What lawyers know. *Texas Law Review, 60,* 35–58.

Friedman, B. (2006). Taking law seriously. *Perspectives on Politics, 4,* 261–276.

Friedman, L. (2002). The Rehnquist court: Some more or less historical comments. In M. Belky (Ed.), *The Rehnquist Court: A Retrospective.* New York: Oxford University Press.

Fumerton, R. A. (1990). *Reason and Morality.* Ithaca, NY: Cornell University Press.

Funder, D. C. (1999). *Personality Judgment: A Realistic Approach to Person Perception.* San Diego, CA: Academic Press.

Funder, D. C. (2001). *The Personality Puzzle.* New York: W.W. Norton & Company.

Furgeson, J. R., Babcock, L., & Shane, P. M. (2008a). Behind the mask of method: Political orientation and constitutional interpretive preferences. *Law and Human Behavior, 32*, 502–510.

Furgeson, J. R., Babcock, L., & Shane, P. M. (2008b). Do a law's policy implications affect beliefs about its constitutionality? An experimental test. *Law and Human Behavior, 32*, 219–27.

Gaeth, G. J., & Shanteau, J. (1984). Reducing the influence of irrelevant information on experienced decision makers. *Organizational Behavior and Human Performance, 33*, 263–282.

Gaffney, E. M., Jr. (1994). The importance of dissent and the imperative of judicial civility. *Valparaiso University Law Review, 28*, 583–646.

Galanter, M. (2004). The vanishing trial: An examination of trials and related matters in federal and state courts. *Journal of Empirical Legal Studies, 1*, 459.

Gardner, H. (1985). *The Mind's New Science: The History of the Cognitive Revolution.* New York: Basic Books.

Garrett, B. (2008). Judging innocence. *Columbia Law Review, 108*, 55–142.

Gatowski, S. I., Dobbin, S. A., Richardson, J. T., Ginsburg, G. P., Merlino, M. L., & Dahir, V. (2001). Asking the gatekeepers: A national survey of judges on judging expert evidence in a post-Daubert world. *Law and Human Behavior, 25*, 433, 442.

Gavison, R. (1988). The implications of jurisprudential theories for judicial election, selection, and accountability. *Southern California Law Review, 61*, 1617.

Gawande, A. (2000). When doctors make mistakes. In J. Gleick & J. Cohen (Eds.), *The Best American Science Writing 2000.* New York: HarperCollins.

Gellis, S. L. (1985). Reasons for case reversal in Texas. *St. Mary's Law Journal, 16*, 299.

Gelman, S. (2001). The hedgehog, the fox, and the minimalist. *Georgetown Law Journal, 89*, 2297–2350.

Gentner, D. (1983). Structure-mapping: A theoretical framework. *Cognitive Science, 7*, 155–170.

Gentner, D. (1989). The mechanisms of analogical reasoning. In S. Vosniadou & A. Ortony (Eds.), *Similarity and Analogical Reasoning.* London: Cambridge University Press.

Gentner, D. (1998). Analogy. In W. Bechtel and G. Graham (Eds.), *Companion to Cognitive Science.* Malden, MA: Blackwell.

Gentner, D., & Kurtz, K. (2006). Relations, objects, and the composition of analogies. *Cognitive Science, 30*, 609–642.

Gentner, D., & Kurtz, K. (2007). Relational categories. In W. Ahn, R. L. Goldstone, B. C. Love, A. B. Markman, & P. Wolff (Eds.), *Categorization Inside and Outside the Laboratory: Essays in Honor of Douglas L. Medin.* Washington, DC: American Psychological Association.

Gentner, D., & Loewenstein, J. (2002). Relational language and relational thought. In E. Amsel & J. P. Byrnes (Eds.), *Language, Literacy, and Cognitive Development: The Development and Consequences of Symbolic Communication.* Mahwah, NJ: Erlbaum.

Gentner, D., & Markman, A. B. (1994). Structural alignment in comparison: No difference without similarity. *Psychological Science, 5*, 152–158.

Gentner, D., Rattermann, M. J., & Forbus, K. D. (1993). The roles of similarity in transfer: Separating retrievability from inferential soundness. *Cognitive Psychology, 25*, 524–575.

George, T. E. (1998). Developing a positive theory of decisionmaking on the U.S. Courts of Appeals. *Ohio State Law Journal, 58*, 1635.

George, T. E. (1999). The dynamics and determinants of the decision to grant en banc review. *Washington University Law Review, 74,* 1635.

George, T. E., & Yooh, A. H. (n.d.). Chief judges: The limits of attitudinal theory and possible paradox of managerial judging. Available at Social Science Research Network: http://ssrn.com/abstract=1001247.

George, A. (1980). *Presidential Decisionmaking in Foreign Policy: The Effective Use of Information and Advice.* Boulder, CO: Westview Press.

George, T. E. (2001). Court fixing. *Arizona Law Review, 43,* 9–62.

George, T. E., & Epstein, L. (1992). On the nature of Supreme Court decision making. *American Political Science Review 86,* 323–337.

Gerber, S. D., & Park, K. (1997). The quixotic search for consensus on the U.S. Supreme Court: A cross-judicial empirical analysis of the Rehnquist Court justices. *American Political Science Review, 91,* 390–408.

Gey, S. G., & Rossi, J. (2005). Empirical measures of judicial performance: An introduction to the symposium. *Florida State University Law Review, 32,* 1001–1014.

Gibson, J. L. (1980). Environmental constraints on the behavior of judges: A representational model of judicial decision making. *Law and Society Review, 14,* 343–370.

Gibson, J. L. (1991). Decision making in appellate courts. In J. B. Gates & C. A. Johnson (Eds.), *The American Courts: A Critical Assessment.* Washington, DC: CQ Press.

Gibson, J. L. (2006). *The Legitimacy of the United States Supreme Court in a Polarized Polity.* Working paper.

Gick, M. L., & Holyoak, K. J. (1980). Analogical problem solving. *Cognitive Psychology, 12,* 306–355.

Gick, M. L., & Holyoak, K. J. (1983). Schema induction and analogical transfer. *Cognitive Psychology, 15,* 1–38.

Gigerenzer, G. (1993). The superego, the ego, and the id in statistical reasoning. In G. Keren & C. Lewis (Eds.), *A Handbook for Data Analysis in the Behavioral Sciences: Methodological issues.* Hillsdale, NJ: Erlbaum.

Gigerenzer, G. (2000). *Adaptive Thinking: Rationality in the Real World.* New York: Oxford University Press.

Gigerenzer, G. (2006). Heuristics. In G. Gigerenzer & C. Engel (Eds.), *Heuristics and the Law.* Cambridge, MA: The MIT Press.

Gigerenzer, G., & Selten, R. (Eds.). (2001). *Bounded Rationality: The Adaptive Toolbox.* Cambridge, MA: MIT Press.

Gillman, H. (1993). *The Constitution Besieged.* Durham, NC: Duke University Press.

Gillman, H. (1997). Placing judicial motives in context: A response to Lee Epstein and Jack Knight. *Law and Courts, 7* (Spring), 10–13.

Gillman, H. (1999). The Court as an idea. In C. W. Clayton & H. Gillman (Eds.), *Supreme Court Decision-Making.* Chicago: University of Chicago Press.

Gillman, H. (2001). What's law got to do with it? Judicial behavioralists test the "legal model" of judicial decision making. *Law & Social Inquiry, 26,* 465–504.

Gilovich, T. (1981). Seeing the past in the present: The effect of associations to familiar events on judgments and decisions. *Journal of Personality and Social Psychology, 40,* 797–808.

Gilovich, T., Griffin, D. W., & Kahneman, D. (Eds.). (2002). *Heuristics and Biases: The Psychology of Intuitive Judgment.* Cambridge, UK: Cambridge University Press.

Ginossar, Z., & Trope, Y. (1987). Problem solving in judgment under uncertainty. *Journal of Personality and Social Psychology, 52,* 464–474.

Glaser, R., & Chi, M. T. H. (1998). Overview. In M. T. H. Chi, R. Glaser, & M. J. Farr (Eds.), *The Nature of Expertise*. Hillsdale, NJ: Erlbaum.

Glöckner, A. (2007, August). *Solving complex legal cases using the intuitive system*. Paper presented at the Subjective Probability, Utility, and Decision Making Conference, Warsaw, Poland.

Glöckner, A., Betsch, T., & Schindler, N. (n.d.). *Construction of probabilistic inferences by constraint satisfaction*. Unpublished manuscript.

Goffman, E. (1959). *The Presentation of Self in Everyday Life*. New York: Doubleday.

Goldberg, L. R., & Werts, C. E. (1966). The reliability of clinicians' judgments: A multitrait-multimethod approach. *Journal of Clinical Psychology, 30,* 199–206.

Goldberg, S. (2005). Federal judges and the Heisman trophy. *Florida State University Law Review, 32,* 1237–1244.

Golde, R. A. (1969). *Can You Be Sure of Your Experts?* New York: Award Books.

Golding, M. P. (1963). Principled decision-making and the Supreme Court. *Columbia Law Review, 63,* 35–58.

Gollwitzer, P. M., & Bargh, J. A. (2005) Automaticity in goal pursuit. In A. J. Elliot & C. S. Dweck (Eds.), *Handbook of Competence and Perception*. New York: Guilford Press.

Graber, M. A. (2006). *Dred Scott and the Problem of Constitutional Evil*. New York: Cambridge University Press.

Graber, M. L., Franklin, N., & Gordon, R. (2005). Diagnostic error in internal medicine. *Archives of Internal Medicine, 165,* 1493–1499.

Granberg, D., & Bartels, B. (2005). On being a lone dissenter. *Journal of Applied Social Psychology, 35,* 1849–1858.

Greenawalt, K. (1978). The enduring significance of neutral principles. *Columbia Law Review, 78,* 982–1021.

Greenburg, J. C. (2007). *Supreme Conflict: The Inside Story of the Struggle for Control of the United States Supreme Court*. New York: Penguin Press.

Greenhouse, L. (2002, April 18). U.S. joins inmate in prison discipline case. *New York Times,* p. A23.

Greenhouse, L. (2004, June 2). Teenager's murder conviction is reinstated after challenge. *New York Times,* p. A17.

Greenhouse, L. (2005). *Becoming Justice Blackmun: Harry Blackmun's Supreme Court Journey*. New York: Times Books.

Griswold v. Connecticut, 381 U.S. 479 (1965).

Groopman, J. (2007). *How Doctors Think*. New York: Houghton Mifflin.

Groscup, J. L. (2004). Judicial decision making about expert testimony in the aftermath of Daubert and Kumho. *Journal of Forensic Psychology Practice, 4*(2), 57–66.

Gruenfeld, D. H. (1995). Status, ideology, and integrative complexity on the U.S. Supreme Court: Rethinking the politics of political decision making. *Journal of Personality and Social Psychology, 68,* 5–20.

Grutter v. Bollinger, 539 U.S. 306 (2003).

Gruenfeld, D., & Hollingshead, A. B. (1993). Sociocognition in work groups: The evolution of integrative complexity and its relation to task performance. *Small Groups Research, 24,* 383–405.

Gruenfeld, D. H., & Preston, J. (2000). Upending the status quo: Cognitive complexity in Supreme Court justices who overturn legal precedent. *Personality and Social Psychology Bulletin, 26,* 1013–1022.

Gryski, G. S., Main, E. C., & Dixon, W. J. (1986). Models of high court decision making in sex discrimination cases. *Journal of Politics, 48*(1), 143–155.

Gulati, M., & Choi, S. J. (2005). Which judges write their opinions (and should we care?). *Florida State University Law Review, 32,* 1077–1122.

Gulati, M., & Choi, S. J. (2007). Ranking judges according to citation bias. *Notre Dame Law Review, 82,* 1279–1309.

Gulati, M., & Sanchez, V. (2002). Giants in a world of pygmies? Testing the superstar hypothesis with judicial opinions in casebooks. *Iowa Law Review, 87,* 1141.

Guthrie, C., & George, T. E. (2005). The futility of appeal: Disciplinary insights into the affirmance effect on the United States Courts of Appeals. *Florida State University Law Review, 32,* 357.

Guthrie, C., Rachlinski, J. J., & Wistrich, A. J. (2001). Inside the judicial mind. *Cornell Law Review, 86,* 777–830.

Guthrie, C., Rachlinski, J. J., & Wistrich, A. J. (2002). Judging by heuristic: Cognitive illusions in judicial decision making. *Judicature, 86,* 44.

Guthrie, C., Rachlinski, J. J., & Wistrich, A. J. (2007a). Blinking on the bench: How judges decide cases. *Cornell Law Review, 93,* 1.

Guthrie, C., Rachlinski, J. J., & Wistrich, A. J. (2007b). Inside the bankruptcy judge's mind. *Boston University Law Review, 86,* 1227.

Guthrie, C., Rachlinski, J. J., & Wistrich, A. J. (2009). The "hidden judiciary:" An empirical examination of executive branch justice. *Duke Law Journal, 58,* 1477–1530. Hägerström, A. (1953). *Inquiries into the Nature of Law and Morals* (C. D. Broad, Trans.). Stockholm: Almquist & Wiksell.

Hagle, T. M. (1993). Freshman effects for supreme court justices. *American Journal of Political Science 37,* 1142–1157.

Hall v. Brooklands Auto Racing Club, K.B. 205 (1933).

Hall v. Brooklands Auto-Racing Club, 1 KB 205 (1933).

Hall, M. G. (1992). Electoral politics and strategic voting in state supreme courts. *Journal of Politics, 54,* 427–446.

Hall, M. G. (1995). Justices as representatives: Elections and judicial politics in the American states. *American Politics Quarterly, 23,* 485–503.

Hall, R. L. (1996). *Participation in Congress.* New Haven, CT: Yale University Press.

Hamdan v. Rumsfeld, 126 S.Ct. 2749 (2006).

Hammond K. R. (1996). *Human Judgement and Social Policy: Irreducible Uncertainty, Inevitable Error and Unavoidable Injustice.* Oxford: Oxford University Press.

Hammond, K. R. (2000a). Coherence and correspondence theories in judgment and decision-making. In T. Connolly, H. R. Arkes, & K. R. Hammond (Eds.), *Judgment and Decision Making: An Interdisciplinary Reader.* Cambridge, UK: Cambridge University Press.

Hammond, K. R. (2000b). *Judgments Under Stress.* Oxford: Oxford University Press.

Hammond, T. H., Bonneau, C. W, & Sheehan, R. S. (2005). *Strategic Behavior and Policy Choice on the U.S. Supreme Court.* Stanford, CA: Stanford University Press.

Hand, L. (1930). Sources of tolerance. *University of Pennsylvania Law Review, 79,* 1.

Hansford, T. G., & Spriggs, J. F., II. (2006). *The Politics of Precedent on the U.S. Supreme Court.* Princeton, NJ: Princeton University Press.

Hanson, J., & Yosifon, D. (2004). The situational character: A critical realist perspective on the human animal. *Georgetown Law Journal, 93,* 1–177.

Hare, A. P., Borgatta, E. F., & Bales, R. F. (Eds.) (1965). *Small Groups: Studies in Social Interaction,* Revised Edition. New York: Alfred A. Knopf.

Harman, G., & Kulkarni, S. R. (2006). The problem of induction. *Philosophy and Phenomenological Research, 72,* 559–575.

Hart, H. L. A. (1961). *The Concept of Law.* Oxford: Clarendon Press.

Haslett, D. W. (1987). What is wrong with reflective equilibria? *Philosophical Quarterly, 37,* 305.

Hastie, R. (2001). Problems for judgment and decision making. *Annual Review of Psychology, 52,* 653.

Hastie, R., Schkade, D. A., & Payne, J. W. (1999). Juror judgments in civil cases: Effects of plaintiff's requests and plaintiff's identity on punitive damage awards. *Law & Human Behavior, 23,* 445.

Hausegger, L., & Baum, L. (1999). Inviting congressional action: A study of Supreme Court motivations in statutory interpretation. *American Journal of Political Science, 43,*162–185.

Hausegger, L., & Haynie, S. (2003). Judicial decisionmaking and the use of panels in the Canadian Supreme Court and the South African Appellate Division. *Law & Society Review, 37,* 635–657.

Haynie, S. L. (1992). Leadership and consensus on the U.S. Supreme Court. *Journal of Politics, 54,* 1158–1169.

Heath, C., Larrick, R. P., & Klayman, J. (1998). Cognitive repairs: How organizational practices can compensate for individual shortcomings. *Research in Organizational Behavior, 20,* 1–37.

Heider, F. (1946). Attitudes and cognitive organization. *Journal of Psychology, 21,* 107–111.

Heider, F. (1958). *The Psychology of Interpersonal Relations.* New York: Wiley.

Helmke, G. (2005). *Courts under Constraints: Judges, Generals, and Presidents in Argentina.* New York: Cambridge University Press.

Henderson, L. (1987). Legality and empathy. *Michigan Law Review, 85,* 1574.

Hersch, J., and Viscusi, W. K. (2004). Punitive damages: How judges and juries perform. *Journal of Legal Studies, 33,* 1.

Hettinger, V. A., Lindquist, S. A., & Martinek, W. L. (2003). Acclimation effects on the United States Courts of Appeals. *Social Science Quarterly, 84,* 792–810.

Hettinger, V. A., Lindquist, S. A., & Martinek, W. L. (2006). *Judging on a Collegial Court: Influences on Federal Appellate Decision Making.* Charlottesville: University of Virginia Press.

Higgins, R. W., & Rubin, P. H. (1980). Judicial discretion. *Journal of Legal Studies, 9,* 129–138.

Hinckley, B. (1979). Twenty-one variables beyond the size of winning coalitions. *Journal of Politics, 41,*192–212.

Hirsch, H. N. (1981). *The Enigma of Felix Frankfurter.* New York: Basic Books.

Ho, D. E., & Quinn, K. M. (2007). Assessing political positions of media. Stanford Law and Economics Olin Working Paper No. 343.

Hoffman, P., Slovic, P., & Rorer, L. (1968). An analysis of variance model for the assessment of configural cue utilization in clinical judgment. *Psychological Bulletin, 69,* 338–349.

Hofstadter, D. R., & Mitchell, M. (1994). An overview of the copycat project. In K. J. Holyoak & J. A. Barnden (Eds.), *Advances in Connectionist and Neural Computation Theory: Vol. 2. Analogical Connections.* Norwood, NJ: Ablex.

Hollander, E. P. (1960). Competence and conformity in the acceptance of influence. *Journal of Abnormal and Social Psychology, 61,* 365–369.

Holmes, O. W. (1881). *The Common Law*. Boston: Little Brown.

Holmes, O. W. (1897). The path of the law. *Harvard Law Review, 10,* 457.

Holyoak, K. J. (1991). Symbolic connectionism: Toward third generation theories of expertise. In K. A. Ericsson & J. Smith (Eds.), *Toward a General Theory of Expertise: Prospects and Limits*. New York: Cambridge University Press.

Holyoak, K. J. (2005). Analogy. In K. J. Holyoak & R. G. Morison (Eds.), *The Cambridge Handbook of Thinking and Reasoning*. Cambridge, UK: Cambridge University Press.

Holyoak, K. J., & Koh, K. (1987). Surface and structural similarity in analogical transfer. *Memory & Cognition, 15,* 332–340.

Holyoak, K. J., & Simon, D. (1999). Bidirectional reasoning in decision making by constraint satisfaction. *Journal of Experimental Psychology: General, 128,* 3–31.

Holyoak, K. J., & Thagard, P. (1989). Analogical mapping by constraint satisfaction. *Cognitive Science: A Multidisciplinary Journal, 13,* 295–355.

Holyoak, K. J., & Thagard, P. (1995). *Mental Leaps: Analogy in Creative Thought*. Cambridge MA: MIT Press.

Hope v. Pelzer, 122 S.Ct. 2508 (2002).

Horn, J., & Masunaga, H. (2006). A merging theory of expertise and intelligence. In K. A. Ericsson, N. Charness, P. J. Feltovich, & R. R. Hoffman (Eds.), *The Cambridge Handbook of Expertise and Expert Performance*. New York: Cambridge University Press.

Howard, J. W., Jr. (1981). *Courts of Appeals in the Federal Judicial System: A Study of the Second, Fifth, and District of Columbia Circuits*. Princeton: Princeton University Press.

Howard, R. M. and J. A. Segal. 2002. An original look at originalism. *Law & Society Review, 36*(1), 113–138.

Hsee, C. K. (1996). Elastic justification: How unjustifiable factors influence judgments. *Organizational Behavior and Human Decision Processes, 66,* 122–129.

Huber, G. A., & Gordon, S. C. (2004). Accountability and coercion: Is justice blind when it runs for office? *American Journal of Political Science, 48,* 247.

Hudson v. McMillian, 503 U.S. 1 (1992).

Hughes, H. D. (1917). An interesting corn seed experiment. *The Iowa Agriculturalist, 17,* 424–425.

Hummel, J. E., & Holyoak, K. J. (2003). A symbolic-connectionist theory of relational inference and generalization. *Psychological Review, 110,* 220–264.

Hunter, D. (2001). Reason is too large: Analogy and precedent in law. *Emory Law Journal, 50,* 1197–1264.

Hurd, H. M. (1991). Challenging authority. *Yale Law Journal, 100,* 1611–1677

Hurd, H. M. (1992). Justifiably punishing the justified. *Michigan Law Review, 90,* 203.

Hurd, H. M. (1999). *Moral Combat*. Cambridge, UK: Cambridge University Press.

Hurwitz, M.S., & Stefko, J.V. (2004). Acclination and attitudes: "Newcomer" justices and precedent conformance on the Supreme Court. *Political Research Quarterly, 57,* 121–129

Hutcheson, J. C., Jr. (1929). The judgment intuitive: The role of the "hunch" in judicial decision. *Cornell Law Quarterly, 14,* 274–307.

In re Code of Judicial Conduct, 643 So. 2d 1037, (Fla. 1994).

Isikoff, M. (2006, April 3). Detainees' rights: Scalia speaks his mind. *Newsweek, 147*(14), 6.

Jacavone, J., & Dostal, M. (1992). A descriptive study of nursing judgment in assessment and management of cardiac pain. *Advances in Nursing Science, 15,* 54–63.

Jacob, H. (1983). Trial courts in the United States: The travails of explanation. *Law and Society Review, 17,* 407–423.

Janis, I. L. (1982). *Groupthink* (2nd ed.). Boston: Houghton Mifflin.

Johnson, T. R. (2004). *Oral Arguments and Decision Making on the United States Supreme Court.* Albany: State University of New York Press.

Johnson, T. R., Spriggs, J. F., II, & Wahlbeck, P. F. (2007). Supreme Court oral advocacy: Does it affect the justices' decisions? *Washington University Law Review, 85,* 457.

Jost, J. T., Glaser, J., Kruglanski, A. W., & Sulloway, F. J. (2003). Political conservatism as motivated social cognition. *Psychological Bulletin, 129,* 339–375.

Judicial Council of California. (2007). *The Strategic Plan for California's Judicial Branch 2006–2012.* San Francisco: Judicial Council of California, Administrative Office of the Courts.

Kahneman, D. (1991). Judgment and decision making: A personal view. *Psychological Science, 2,* 142–145.

Kahneman, D. (1997). New challenges to the rationality assumption. *Legal Theory, 3,* 105.

Kahneman, D., Slovic, P., & Tversky, A. (Eds.). (1982). *Judgment Under Uncertainty: Heuristics and Biases.* New York: Cambridge University Press.

Kahneman, D., & Tversky, A. (1979) Prospect theory: An analysis of decision under risk. *Econometrica, 47,* 263–291.

Kahneman, D., & Tversky, A. (1981). The framing of decisions and the psychology of choice. *Science, 211,* 453–458

Kahneman, D., & Tversky, A. (1984). Choices, values, and frames. *American psychologist, 39,* 341–350.

Kahneman, D., & Tversky, A. (Eds.). (2000). *Choices, Values, and Frames.* New York: Cambridge University Press.

Kalman, L. (1986). *Legal Realism at Yale, 1927–60.* Chapel Hill: University of North Carolina Press.

Kalven, H,. & Zeisel, H. (1966). *The American Jury.* Boston: Little, Brown.

Kansas v. Colorado, 121 S.Ct. 2023 (2001).

Kassin, S. M., Meissner, C. A., & Norwick, R. J.(2005). "I'd know a false confession if I saw one": A comparative study of college students and police investigators. *Law and Human Behavior, 29,* 211–227.

Kennedy, D. (1986). Freedom and constraint in adjudication: A critical phenomenology. *Journal of Legal Education, 36,* 518–547

Kerlinger, F. N. (1967). Social attitudes and their criterial referents: A structural theory. *Psychological Review, 74,* 110–122.

Kerr, N. & Tindale, R. S. (2004). Group performance and decision making. *Annual Review of Psychology, 55,* 623.

Kerr, N. L., Atkin, R. S., Stasser, G., Meek, D., Holt, R. W., & Davis, J. H. (1976). Guilt beyond a reasonable doubt: Effects of concept definition and assigned decision rule on judgments of mock jurors. *Journal of Personality and Social Psychology, 34,* 282–294.

Kida, T. (1980). An investigation into auditors' continuity and related qualification judgments. *Journal of Accounting Research, 8,* 506–523.

Kim, N. S., & Ahn, W. (2002). Clinical psychologists' theory-based representations of mental disorders predict their diagnostic reasoning and memory. *Journal of Experimental Psychological: General, 131,* 451–476.

King, G., Keohane, R. O., & Verba, S. (1994). *Designing Social Inquiry: Scientific Inference in Qualitative Research.* Princeton: Princeton University Press.

Kintsch, W. (1988). The role of knowledge in discourse comprehension: A construction-integration model. *Psychological Review, 95,* 163–182.

Kirkpatrick, S. A. (1976). Introduction to the special issue on small group theory. *American Behavioral Scientist, 20,* 5–9.

Kitcher, P. (1993). *The Advancement of Science.* Oxford: Oxford University Press.

Klayman, J. (1995). Varieties of confirmation bias. *The Psychology of Learning and Motivation, 32,* 385–418.

Klein, D. E. (2002). *Making Law in the United States Courts of Appeals.* New York: Cambridge University Press.

Klein, D. E. (2005). Unspoken questions in the Rule 32.1 debate: Precedent and psychology in judging. *Washington & Lee Law Review, 62,* 1709.

Klein, D. E. & Morrisroe, D. (1999). The prestige and influence of individual judges on the U.S. Courts of Appeals. *Journal of Legal Studies, 28,* 371–391.

Klein, G. A., Orasanu, J., Calderwood, R., & Zsambok, C. E. (1993). *Decision Making in Action: Models and Methods.* Norwood, NJ: Ablex Publishing Corp.

Knetch, J. C. (2000). The endowment effect and evidence of irreversible indifference curves. In D. Kahneman and A. Tversky (Eds.), *Choices Values and Frames.* New York: Cambridge University Press.

Koehler, D. J., Brenner, L., & Griffin, D. (2002). The calibration of expert judgment: Heuristics and biases beyond the laboratory. In T. Gilovich, D. Griffin, & D. Kahneman (Eds.), *Heuristics and Biases: The Psychology of Intuitive Judgment.* New York: Cambridge University Press.

Kolata, G., & Peterson, I. (2001, July 21). New Jersey is trying new way for witnesses to say, "It's Him." *New York Times,* p. A1.

Konecni, V. J., & Ebbesen, E. B. (1986). Courtroom testimony by psychologists on eyewitness identification issues: Critical notes and reflections. *Law and Human Behavior, 10,* 117–126.

Kornhauser, L. A., & Sager, L. G. (1993).The one and the many: Adjudication in collegial courts. *California Law Review, 81,* 1–59.

Kourlis, R. L., & Singer, J. M. (2007). Using judicial performance evaluations to promote judicial accountability. *Judicature, 90,* 200–207.

Kovera, M. B., & McAuliff, B. D. (2000). The effects of peer review and evidence quality on judge evaluations of psychological evidence: Are judges effective gatekeepers? *Journal of Applied Psychology, 85,* 574.

Kozhevnikov, M. (2007). Cognitive styles in the context of modern psychology: Toward an integrated framework of cognitive style. *Psychological Bulletin, 133,* 464–481.

Kozinski, A. (1993). What I ate for breakfast and other mysteries of judicial decision making. *Loyola Los Angeles Law Review, 26,* 993.

Kritzer, H. M., & Richards, M. J. (2003). Jurisprudential regimes and Supreme Court decisionmaking: The Lemon regime and Establishment Clause cases. *Law & Society Review, 37,* 827–840.

Kritzer, H. M., & Richards, M. J. (2005). The influence of law in the Supreme Court's search-and-seizure jurisprudence. *American Politics Research, 33,* 33–55.

Krueger, J. I., & Funder, D. C. (2004). Toward a balanced social psychology: Causes, consequences, and cures for the problem-seeking approach to social behavior and cognition. *Behavioral and Brain Sciences, 27,* 313–376.

Kruglanski, A. W. (1996). Motivated social cognition: Principles of the interface. In E. T. Higgins & A. W. Kruglanski (Eds.), *Social Psychology: Handbook of Basic Principles*. New York: Guilford Press.

Kruglanski, A. W., & Webster, D. M. (1996). Motivated closing of the mind: "Seizing" and "freezing." *Psychological Review, 103,* 263–283.

Kruglanski, A. W., Shah, J. Y., Fishbach, A., Friedman, R., Chun, W. Y., & Sleeth-Keppler, D. (2002). A theory of goal systems. *Advances in Experimental Social Psychology, 34,* 331.

Kulik, C. T., Perry, E. L., & Pepper, M. B. (2003). Here comes the judge: The influence of judge personal characteristics on federal sexual harassment case outcomes. *Law and Human Behavior, 27,* 69–97.

Kunda, Z. (1990). The case for motivated reasoning. *Psychological Bulletin, 108,* 480–498.

Landeo, C. M. (n.d.). *Tort reform and disputes under endogenous beliefs.* Unpublished manuscript.

Landes, W. M., & Posner, R. A. (1975). The independent judiciary in an interest-group perspective. *Journal of Law and Economics, 18,* 875–901.

Landes, W. M., & Posner, R. A. (1979). Adjudication as a public good. *Journal of Legal Studies, 8,* 235–284.

Landsman, S., & Rakos, R. F. (1994). A preliminary inquiry into the effect of potentially biasing information on judges and jurors in civil litigation. *Behavioral Sciences and the Law, 12,* 113.

Langer, L. (2002). *Judicial Review in State Supreme Courts: A Comparative Study.* Albany: State University of New York Press.

Larrick, R. P. (2004). Debiasing. In D. J. Koehler & N. Harvey (Eds.), *Blackwell Handbook on Judgment and Decision Making.* Malden, MA: Blackwell Publishing.

Lasky, M. (1965). A return to the observatory below the bench. *Southwestern Law Journal, 19,* 679.

Law, D. S. (2005). Strategic judicial lawmaking: Ideology, publication, and asylum law in the ninth circuit. *University of Cincinnati Law Review, 73,* 817–866.

Lawrence, J. A. (1988). Expertise on the bench: Modeling magistrates' judicial decision-making. In M. T. H. Chi, R. Glaser, & M. J. Farr (Eds.), *The Nature of Expertise*. Hillsdale, NJ: Erlbaum.

Lazarus, E. P. (1998). *Closed Chambers.* New York: Times Books.

Lazarus, E. P. (2000, July 9). It's all about O'Connor. *Los Angeles Times*, p. 2.

Leary, M. R. (1996). *Self Presentation: Impression Management and Interpersonal Behavior.* Boulder, CO: Westview Press.

Leblanc, V. R., Brooks, L. R., & Norman, G. R. (2002, October Supplement). Believing is seeing: The influence of a diagnostic hypothesis on the interpretation of clinical features. *Academic Medicine, 77*(10).

Lehman, D. R., Lempert, R. O., & Nisbett, R. E. (1988). The effects of graduate training on reasoning: Formal discipline and thinking about everyday-life events. *American Psychologist, 43,* 431–442.

Leiter, B. (1997). Rethinking legal realism: Toward a naturalized jurisprudence. *Texas Law Review, 76,* 267–315

Leiter, B. (2004). American legal realism. In M. P. Golding & W. A. Edmundson (Eds.), *The Blackwell Guide to the Philosophy of Law and Legal Theory.* Oxford: Blackwell.

Lerner, J. S., & Tetlock, P. E. (1999). Accounting for the effects of accountability. *Psychological Bulletin, 125,* 255–275.

Lerner, J. S., Goldberg, J. H., & Tetlock, P. E. (1998). Sober second thought: The effects of accountability, anger, and authoritarianism on attributions of responsibility. *Personality and Social Psychology Bulletin, 24,* 563–574.

Leuchtenburg, W. E. (1995). *The Supreme Court Reborn: The Constitutional Revolution in the Age of Roosevelt.* New York: Oxford University Press.

Levi, E. (1948). *An Introduction to Legal Reasoning.* Chicago: University of Chicago Press.

Levine, J. M., & Moreland, R. L. (1994). Group socialization: Theory and research. In W. Stroebe & M. Hewstone (Eds.), *European Review of Social Psychology.* Chichester: Wiley.

Lewin, K. (1935). *A Dynamic Theory of Personality.* New York: McGraw Hill.

Lewis, A. (1987, September 27). Abroad at home: Question of judgment. *New York Times,* p. D23.

Liberato, L., & Rutter, K. (2003). Reasons for reversal in the texas courts of appeals. *South Texas Law Review, 44,* 431.

Lichtenstein, S., Fischhoff, B., & Phillips, L. D. (1982). Calibration of probabilities: The state of the art to 1980. In D. Kahneman, P. Slovic, & A. Tversky (Eds.), *Judgment Under Uncertainty: Heuristics and Biases.* Cambridge, UK: Cambridge University Press.

Liebman, J. S. (2000). The overproduction of death. *Columbia Law Review, 100,* 2030.

Linder, D. O. (1985). How judges judge: A study of disagreement on the United States Court of Appeals for the Eighth Circuit. *Arkansas Law Review, 38,* 479–560.

Lindquist, S., & Klein, D. (2006). The influence of jurisprudential considerations on Supreme Court decisionmaking: A study of conflict cases. *Law and Society Review, 40,* 135–161.

Lithwick, D. (2004). A high court of one. In N. Devins & D. M. Douglas (Eds.), *A Year at the Supreme Court.* Durham, NC: Duke University Press

Llewellyn, K. N. (1930). *The Bramble Bush: Law and its Study.* New York: Columbia Law School.

Llewellyn, K. N. (1950). Remarks on the theory of appellate decision and the rules or canons about how statutes are to be construed. *Vanderbilt Law Review, 3,* 395–.

Llewellyn, K. N. (1960). *The Common Law Tradition: Deciding Appeals.* Boston: Little, Brown.

Lodge, M., & Taber, C. (2000). Three steps toward a theory of motivated political reasoning. In A. Lupia, M. D. McCubbins, & S. L. Popkin (Eds.), *Elements of Reason: Cognition, Choice, and the Bounds of Rationality.* New York: Cambridge University Press.

Loewenstein, G., & Elster, J. (Eds.). (1992). *Choice Over Time.* New York: Russell Sage Foundation.

Loewenstein, J., Thompson, L., & Gentner, D. (1999). Analogical encoding facilitates knowledge transfer in negotiation. *Psychonomic Bulletin & Review, 6*(4), 586–597.

Lord, C. G., Ross, L., & Lepper, M. (1979). Biased assimilation and attitude polarization: The effects of prior theories on subsequently considered evidence. *Journal of Personality & Social Psychology, 37,* 2098.

Louis, M. R. (1980). Surprise and sense making: What newcomers experience in entering unfamiliar organizational settings. *Administrative Science Quarterly, 25,* 226–251.

Lundberg, C. G. (2004). Modeling and predicting emerging inference-based decisions in complex and ambiguous legal settings. *European Journal of Operational Research, 153*, 417–432.

Lundberg, C. G. (2007). Models of emerging contexts in risky and complex decision settings. *European Journal of Operational Research, 177*, 1363–1374.

Lykken, D. T. (1979). The detection of deception. *Psychological Bulletin, 80*, 47–53.

MacCormick, N. (2005). *Rhetoric and the Rule of Law: A Theory of Legal Reasoning.* Oxford: Oxford University Press.

MacCoun, R. (1998). Biases in the interpretation and use of research results. *Annual Review of Psychology, 49*, 259–287.

MacCoun, R. J. (2005). Voice, control, and belonging: The double-edged sword of procedural fairness. *Annual Review of Law and Social Science, 1*, 171–201.

MacCoun, R. J., & Tyler, T. R. (1988). The basis of citizens' perceptions of the criminal jury: Procedural fairness, accuracy, and efficiency. *Law and Human Behavior, 12*, 333–352.

Macey, J. R. (1994). Judicial preferences, public choice, and the rules of procedure. *Journal of Legal Studies, 23*, 627.

Maltzman, F., & Wahlbeck, P. J. (1996). May it please the Chief? Opinion assignments in the Rehnquist Court. *American Journal of Political Science, 40*, 421–443.

Maltzman, F., Spriggs, J. F., II, & Wahlbeck, P. J. (2000). *Crafting Law on the Supreme Court: The Collegial Game.* New York: Cambridge University Press.

Mandler, J. M., & Orlich, F. (1993). Analogical transfer: The roles of schema abstraction and awareness. *Bulletin of the Psychonomic Society, 31*, 485–487.

Manning, J. (2003). The absurdity doctrine. *Harvard Law Review, 116*, 2387–2486

Markman, A. B., & Gentner, D. (1993). Structural alignment during similarity comparisons. *Cognitive Psychology, 25*, 431–467.

Martin, A. D., & Quinn, K. M. (2002). Dynamic ideal point estimation via Markov chain Monte Carlo for the U.S. Supreme Court, 1953–1999. *Political Analysis, 10*, 134.

Martin, A. D., Quinn, K. M., & Epstein, L. (2005). The median justice on the United States Supreme Court. *North Carolina Law Review, 83*, 1275.

Martinek, W. L. (2006). *Small group theory and the United States Courts of Appeals.* Paper presented at the annual meeting of the Midwest Political Science Association.

Mather, M., Shafir, E.; & Johnson, M. K. (2000). Misremembrance of options past: Source monitoring and choice. *Psychological Science, 11*, 132.

Mauro, T. (2005). Fluent in tea leaves. *American Lawyer, 27*(5), 75–76.

Maveety, N. (1996). *Justice Sandra Day O'Connor: Strategist on the Supreme Court.* Lanham, MD: Rowman & Littlefield.

Maveety, N. (2003). The study of judicial behavior and the discipline of political science. In N. Maveety (Ed.), *The Pioneers of Judicial Behavior.* Ann Arbor: University of Michigan Press.

Mayhew, D. R. (1974). *Congress: The Electoral Connection.* New Haven, CT: Yale University Press.

McAtee, A., & McGuire, K. T. (2007). Lawyers, justices, and issue salience: When and how do legal arguments affect the U.S. Supreme Court? *Law & Society Review, 41*, 259–278.

McCarty, N., Poole, K. T., & Rosenthal, H. (2006). *Polarized America: The Dance of Ideology and Unequal Riches.* Cambridge, MA: MIT Press.

McClelland, J. L., & Rumelhart, D. E. (1981). An interactive activation model of context effects in letter perception: I. An account of basic findings. *Psychological Review, 88,* 375–407.

McGuire, K. T. (1996, November). *Explaining executive success in the United States Supreme Court.* Paper presented at the conference on Scientific Study of Judicial Politics, St. Louis.

McGuire, K. T., & Palmer, B. (1995). Issue fluidity on the United States Supreme Court. *American Political Science Review, 89,* 691–702.

McGuire, K. T., & Palmer, B. (1996). Issues, agendas, and decision making on the Supreme Court. *American Political Science Review, 90,* 853–65.

McNicol, D. (2004) *A Primer of Signal Detection Theory.* (2nd ed.). London: Routledge.

Medin, D. L., Goldstone, R. L., & Gentner, D. (1990). Similarity involving attributes and relations: Judgments of similarity and difference are not inverses. *Psychological Science, 1,* 64–69.

Mehrabian, A. (1996). Relations among political attitudes, personality, and psychopathology assessed with new measures of libertarianism and conservatism. *Basic and Applied Social Psychology, 18,* 469–491.

Merida, K., & Fletcher, M. (2007). *Supreme Discomfort: The Divided Soul of Clarence Thomas.* New York: Doubleday.

Merrill, T. W. (2003). The making of the second Rehnquist Court. *St. Louis University Law Journal, 47,* 569.

Messier, W. F. (1983). The effect of experience and firm type on materiality/disclosure judgments. *Journal of Accounting Research, 21,* 611–618.

Miceli, T. J., & Cosgel, M. M. (1994). Reputation and judicial decision-making. *Journal of Economic Behavior and Organization, 23,* 31–51.

Michael H. v. Gerald D., 491 U.S. 110 (1989).

Miles, T. J., & Sunstein, C. R. (2006). Do judges make regulatory policy? An empirical investigation of Chevron. *University of Chicago Law Review, 73,* 823–881.

Milgram, S. (1974). *Obedience to Authority.* New York: Harper & Row.

Miller, G. P. (2004). Bad judges. *Texas Law Review, 83,* 431.

Minow, M. L., & Spelman, E. V. (1989). Passion for justice. *Cardozo Law Review, 10,* 37.

Minow, M. L., & Spelman, E. V. (1990). In context. *Southern California Law Review, 63,* 1597–1653.

Mireles v. Waco, 502 U.S. 9, 11-12 (1991).

Mishler, W., & Sheehan, R. S. (1996). Public opinion, the attitudinal model, and Supreme Court decision making. *Journal of Politics, 58,* 169.

Mitchell, G. (2002a). Taking behaviorism too seriously? The unwarranted pessimism of the new behavioral analysis of law. *William and Mary Law Review, 43,* 1907–2021.

Mitchell, G. (2002b).Why law and economics' perfect rationality should not be traded for behavioral law and economics' equal incompetence. *Georgetown Law Journal, 9,* 67–167.

Mitchell, G. (2003a). Tendencies versus boundaries: Levels of generality in behavioral law and economics. *Vanderbilt Law Review, 56,* 1781–1812.

Mitchell, G. (2003b). Mapping evidence law. *Michigan State Law Review, 2003,* 1065–1148.

Mitchell, M. L., & Jolley, J. M. (2007). *Research Design Explained* (6th ed.). Belmont, CA: Wadsworth/Thompson Learning.

Molot, J. T. (1998). How changes in the legal profession reflect changes in civil procedure. *Virginia Law Review, 84,* 955.

Molot, J. T. (2004). Principled minimalism: Restriking the balance between judicial minimalism and neutral principles. *Virginia Law Review, 90,* 1753–1847.

Monahan, J., & Silver, E. (2003). Judicial decision thresholds for violence risk management. *International Journal of Forensic Mental Health, 2*(1), 1–6.

Montagu, B. (ed.). (1850). *The Works of Francis Bacon, Lord Chancellor of England.* London: A. Hart.

Moors, A., & De Houwer, J. (2006). Automaticity: A theoretical and conceptual analysis. *Psychological Bulletin, 132,* 297–326.

Morehead, T. (1998). Small groups. In D. T Gilbert & G. Lindzey (Eds.), *The Handbook of Social Psychology.* New York: McGraw Hill.

Moscovici, S. (1980). Toward a Theory of Conversational Behavior. In L. Berkowitz (Ed.), *Advances in Experimental Social Psychology* (vol. 13). New York: Academic Press.

Moscovici, S., & Zavalloni, M. (1969). The group as a polarizer of attitudes. *Journal of Personality and Social Psychology, 12,* 125–135.

Moseley v. V Secret Catalogue, Inc, 537 U.S. 418 (2003).

Mosier, K. L. (1997). Myths of expert decision making and automated decision aids. In C. Zsambok & G. Klein, (Eds.), *Naturalistic Decision Making.* Hillsdale, NJ: Erlbaum.

Mott, R. L. (1948). Measurement of judicial personnel. *New York University Law Quarterly Review, 23,* 262.

Murphy, A. H., & Winkler, R. L. (1977). Can weather forecasters formulate reliable forecasts of precipitation and temperature? *National Weather Digest, 2,* 2–9.

Murphy, B. A. (2003). *Wild Bill: The Legend and Life of William O. Douglas.* New York: Random House.

Murphy, W. (1964). *Elements of Judicial Strategy.* Chicago: University of Chicago Press.

Murphy, W. F. (1966). Courts as small groups. *Harvard Law Review, 79,* 1565–1572.

Mustard, D. B. (2001). Racial, ethnic, and gender disparities in sentencing: Evidence from the U.S. federal courts. *Journal of Law and Economics, 44,* 285.

Nadeau, J. P. (2000). What it means to be a judge. *Judges' Journal, 39,* 34.

Nagel, R. F. (1994). *Judicial Power and American Character: Censoring Ourselves in an Anxious Age.* New York: Oxford University Press.

Nagel, R. F. (2006, April 17). Bowing to precedent. *The Weekly Standard,* p. 24.

Nelson, T. E., and Kinder, D. R. (1996). Issue framing and group centerism in American public opinion. *Journal of Politics, 58*(4), 1055–1078.

Nelson, T. E., Oxley, Z. M., & Clawson, R A. (1997). Toward a psychology of framing effects. *Political Behavior, 19,* 221–246.

Nelson, T. E., Maruska, S., & Braman, E. (2002). *What is the issue? Legal and media constructions and political attitudes.* Paper presented at the Annual Conference of the American Political Science Association.

Nickerson, R. S. (1998). Confirmation bias: A ubiquitous phenomenon in many guises. *Review of General Psychology, 2,* 175–220.

Nisbett, R. E., & Wilson, T. D. (1977). The halo effect: Evidence for unconscious alteration of judgments. *Journal of Personality and Social Psychology, 35,* 250–256.

Norton, M. R. (2003). Texts and manuscripts of the Old Testament. In F. F. Bruce, J. I. Packer, P. Comfort, & C. F. H. Henry (Eds.), *The Origin of the Bible.* Wheaton, IL: Tyndale House Publishers.

Novick, L. (1988). Analogical transfer, problem similarity, and expertise. *Journal of Experimental Psychology: Learning, Memory and Cognition, 14,* 510–520.

Nunnally, J. C. (1967). *Psychometric Theory.* New York: McGraw-Hill Book Company.

O'Brien, D. M. (2005). A diminished plenary docket. *Judicature, 89,* 134–137, 182.

Oklahoma Tax Commission v. Jefferson Lines, Inc., 514 U.S. 175 (1995).

Oliphant, H. (1928). A return to stare decisis. *American Bar Association Journal, 14,* 159–163.

Olivecrona, K. (1971). *Law as Fact* (2nd ed.). London: Stevens & Sons.

Olowofoyeku, A. (1993). *Suing Judges: A Study of Judicial Immunity.* New York: Oxford University Press.

Operario, D., & Fiske, S. T. (1999). Social cognition permeates social psychology: Motivated mental processes guide the study of human social behavior. *Asian Journal of Social Psychology, 2,* 63–78.

O'Sullivan, M., & Ekman, P. (2005). The wizards of deception detection. In P. A. Granhag & L. Strömwell (Eds.), *The Detection of Deception in Forensic Contexts.* Cambridge, UK: Cambridge University Press.

Otis, L., & Reiter, E. H. (2006). Mediation by judges: A new phenomenon in the transformation of justice. *Pepperdine Dispute Resolution Law Journal, 6,* 351.

Parness, J. A. (2006). Improving judicial settlement conferences. *U.C. Davis Law Review, 39,* 1891.

Payne, J. L., & Woshinsky, O. H. (1972). Incentives for political participation. *World Politics, 24,* 518–546.

Pennington, N., & Hastie, R. (1986). Evidence evaluation in complex decision making. *Journal of Personality and Social Psychology, 51,* 242.

Pennington, N., & Hastie, R. (1988). Explanation-based decision making: Effects of memory structure on judgment. *Journal of Experimental Psychology: Learning, Memory, & Cognition, 14,* 521.

Pennington, N., & Hastie, R. (1992). Explaining the evidence: Tests of the story model for juror decision making. *Journal of Personality and Social Psychology, 62,* 189.

Pennington, N., & Hastie, R. (1993). The story model for juror decision making. In R. Hastie (Ed.), *Inside the Juror: The Psychology of Juror Decision Making.* New York: Cambridge University Press.

Perry, H. W., Jr. (1991). *Deciding to Decide: Agenda Setting in the United States Supreme Court.* Cambridge, MA: Harvard University Press.

Peters, C. J. (2000). Assessing the new judicial minimalism. *Columbia Law Review, 100,* 1454–1537.

Petty, R. E., & Cacioppo, J. T. (1986). *Communication and Persuasion: Central and Peripheral Routes of Attitude Change.* New York, NY: Springer-Verlag.

Petty, R. E., & Wegener, D. T. (1993). Flexible correction processes in social judgment: Correcting for context induced contrast. *Journal of Experimental Social Psychology, 29,* 137–165.

Pfennig v. The Queen, 182 CLR 461 at 487–488 (1995).

Phelps, R. H. (1977). *Expert Livestock Judgment: A Descriptive Analysis of the Development of Expertise.* Unpublished doctoral dissertation, Kansas State University, Manhattan.

Phelps, R. H., & Shanteau, J. (1978). Livestock judges: How much information can an expert use? *Organizational Behavior and Human Performance, 21,* 209–219.

Philips, S. U. (1998). *Ideology in the Language of Judges: How Judges Practice Law, Politics, and Courtroom Control.* New York: Oxford University Press.

Phillips, F. (2002). The distortion of criteria after decision-making. *Organizational Behavior and Human Decision Processes, 88,* 769–784.

Pines, J. M. (2005). Profiles in patient safety: Confirmation bias in emergency medicine. *Academic Emergency Medicine, 13,* 90–94.

Pittman, T. S. (1998). Motivation. In D. T. Gilbert, S. T. Fiske, & G. Lindzey (Eds.), *The Handbook of Social Psychology* (4th ed.). Boston: McGraw-Hill.

Planned Parenthood v. Casey, 505 U.S. 833 (1992).

Plato. (2006). *The Republic* (R. E. Allen, Trans.). New Haven, CT: Yale University Press.

Plous, S. (1993). *The Psychology of Judgment and Decision Making.* New York: McGraw-Hill.

Plous, S., & Williams, T. (1995). Racial stereotypes from the days of american slavery: A continuing legacy. *Journal of Applied Social Psychology, 25,* 796–817.

Pollock, P. H., III, Lilie, S.A., & Vittes, M. E. (1993). Hard issues, core values, and vertical constraint: The case of nuclear power. *British Journal of Political Science, 23,* 29–50.

Posner, R. A. (1992). Legal reasoning from the top down and from the bottom up: The question of unenumerated constitutional rights. *University of Chicago Law Review, 59,* 433–50.

Posner, R. A. (1993). What do judges and justices maximize? (The same thing everybody else does). *Supreme Court Economic Review, 3,* 1.

Posner, R. A. (1995a). Judges' writing styles (and do they matter?). *University of Chicago Law Review, 62,* 1421–1436.

Posner, R. A. (1995b). *Overcoming Law.* Cambridge, MA: Harvard University Press.

Posner, R. A. (1999). *The Problematics of Moral and Legal Theory.* Cambridge, MA: Harvard University Press.

Posner, R. A. (2005). Foreword: A political court. *Harvard Law Review, 119,* 31–102.

Posner, R. A. (2006). Reasoning by analogy. *Cornell Law Review, 91,* 761–774.

Posner, R. A. (2008). *How Judges Think.* Cambridge, MA: Harvard University Press.

Postema, G. M. (1982). Coordination and convention at the foundation of law. *Journal of Legal Studies, 11,* 165.

Pritchett, C. H. (1948). *The Roosevelt Court: A Study in Judicial Politics and Values, 1937–1947.* New York: Macmillan Company.

Pritchett, C. H. (1954). *Civil Liberties and the Vinson Court.* Chicago: University of Chicago Press.

Pritchett, C. H. (1969). The development of judicial research. In J. B. Grossman and J. Tanenhaus (Eds.), *Frontiers of Judicial Research.* New York: John Wiley and Sons.

Pruitt, C. R., & Wilson, J. Q. (1983). A longitudinal study of the effect of race on sentencing. *Law & Society Review, 17,* 613–636.

Pyszczynski, T., & Greenberg, J. (1987). Toward and integration of cognitive and motivational perspectives on social inference: A biased hypothesis-testing model. In L. Berkowitz (Ed.), *Advances in Experimental Social Psychology* (vol. 20). New York: Academic Press.

Rachlinski, J. J. (1998). A positive psychological theory of judging in hindsight. *University of Chicago Law Review, 65,* 571.

Rachlinski, J. J. (2006). Bottom-up and top-down decisionmaking. *University of Chicago Law Review, 73,* 933.

Rachlinski, J. J., Guthrie, C., & Wistrich, A. J. (2006). Inside the bankruptcy judge's mind. *Boston University Law Review, 86,* 1227.

Rachlinski, J. J., Johnson, S. L., Wistrich, A. J., & Guthrie, C. (2009). Does unconscious racial bias affect trial judges? *Notre Dame Law Review, 84*(3), 1195–1246.

Radin, M. (1925). The theory of judicial decision: Or how judges think. *American Bar Association Journal, 11,* 357–362.

Rahdert, M. C. (2007). Comparative constitutional advocacy. *American University Law Review, 56,* 553.

Randazzo, K. A., Waterman, R. W., & Fine, J. A. (2006). Checking the federal courts: The impact of congressional statutes on judicial behavior. *Journal of Politics, 68*(4), 1006–1017.

Raskin, D. C., & Podlesny, J. A. (1979). Truth and deception: A reply to Lykken. *Psychological Bulletin, 86,* 54–59.

Ratterman, M. J., & Gentner, D. (1998). More evidence for a relational shift in the development of analogy: Children's performance on a causal-mapping task. *Cognitive Development, 13,* 453–478.

Ratzlaf v. United States, 510 U.S. 135 (1994).

Rawls, J. (1971). *A Theory of Justice.* Cambridge, MA: Belknap Press.

Raz, J. (1979). *The Authority of Law: Essays on Law and Morality.* Oxford: Clarendon Press.

Raz, J. (1986). *The Morality of Freedom.* Oxford: Oxford University Press.

Raz, J. (1994). *Ethics in the Public Domain.* Oxford: Oxford University Press.

Read, S. J., & Marcus-Newhall, A. (1993). Explanatory coherence in social explanations: A parallel distributed processing account. *Journal of Personality and Social Psychology, 65,* 429.

Read, S. J., & Miller, L. C. (1998). On the dynamic construction of meaning: An interactive activation and competition model of social perception. In S. J. Read & L. C. Miller (Eds.), *Connectionist Models of Social Reasoning and Social Behavior.* Mahwah, NJ: Lawrence Erlbaum.

Read, S. J., Vanman, E. J., & Miller, L. C. (1997). Connectionism, parallel constraint satisfaction processes, and Gestalt principles: (Re)introducing cognitive dynamics to social psychology. *Personality and Social Psychology Review, 1,* 26–53.

Redding, R. E., & Reppucci, N. D. (1999). Effects of lawyers' socio-political attitudes on their judgments of social science in legal decision making. *Law and Human Behavior, 23,* 31.

Redelmeier, D. A. (2005). The cognitive psychology of missed diagnoses. *Annals of Internal Medicine, 142,* 115–120.

Reed, J. W. (2005). They're playing a tango. *Michigan Bar Journal, 84,* 18.

Reeve, J. (2005). *Understanding Motivation and Emotion.* New York: John Wiley & Sons.

Resnik., J. (1982). Managerial judges. *Harvard Law Review, 96,* 374.

Resnik, J. (2002). Mediating preferences: Litigant preferences for process and judicial preferences for settlement. *Journal of Dispute Resolution, 2002,* 155.

Richards, M. J., & Kritzer, H. M. (2002). Jurisprudential regimes in Supreme Court decision making. *American Political Science Review, 96,* 305–320.

Rickard, A. (1998). *Juror Judgment and Decision Making: Prior Convictions Evidence, Instructions to Disregard and Different Standards of Proof.* Unpublished honors thesis, School of Psychology, University of Queensland.

Ridgeway, C. L. (1978). Conformity, group-oriented motivation, and status attainment in small groups. *Social Psychology, 41,* 175–188.

Ridgeway, C. L., & Berger, J. (1986). Expectations, legitimation, and dominance behavior in task groups. *American Sociological Review, 51,* 603–617.

Ridgeway, C. L., Johnson, C., & Diekema, D. (1994). External status, legitimacy, and compliance in male and female groups. *Social Forces, 72,* 1051–1077.

Ringhand, L. A. (2007). Judicial activism: An empirical examination of voting behavior on the Rehnquist natural court. *Constitutional Commentary, 24*, 43–102.

Robbennolt, J. K. (2002). Determining punitive damages: Empirical insights and implications for reform. *Buffalo Law Review, 50,* 103.

Robbennolt, J. K. (2005). Evaluating juries by comparison to judges: A benchmark for judging? *Florida State University Law Review, 32*(2), 469–509.

Robbennolt, J. K., Darley, J. M., & MacCoun, R. J. (2003). Symbolism and incommensurability in civil sanctioning: Decision makers as goal managers. *Brooklyn Law Review, 68,* 1121.

Roberts, J. G., Jr. (2005). Oral advocacy and the re-emergence of a Supreme Court bar. *Journal of Supreme Court History, 30*(1), 68–81.

Robinson, P. H., & Spellman, B. A. (2005). Sentencing decisions: Matching the decisionmaker to the decision nature. *Columbia Law Review, 105,* 1124–1161.

Roe v. Wade, 410 U.S. 113 (1973).

Rogers v. Tennessee, 532 U.S. 451 (2001).

Rohde, D. W. (1972). Policy goals and opinion coalitions in the Supreme Court. *Midwest Journal of Political Science, 16,* 208–224.

Rohde, D. W., & Spaeth, H. J. (1976). *Supreme Court Decision Making.* San Francisco: W.H. Freeman.

Rombeck, T. (2002, October 30). Justice takes time for Q and A. *Lawrence Journal-World,* p. 5B.

Rosen, J. (2007a). *The Supreme Court: The Personalities and Rivalries that Defined America.* New York: Times Books.

Rosen, J. (2007b, June 18). Supreme leader. *The New Republic,* p. 16.

Rosenberg, M. (1966). The qualities of justice—Are they strainable? *Texas Law Review, 44,* 1063.

Rosenberg, M. J., & Abelson, R. P. (1960). An analysis of cognitive balancing. In M. J. Rosenberg, C. I. Hovland, W. J. McGuire, R. P. Abelson, & J. W. Brehm (Eds.), *Attitude Organization and Change: An Analysis of Consistency Among Attitude Components.* New Haven, CT: Yale University Press.

Ross, A. (1958). *On Law and Justice.* Berkeley, CA: University of California Press.

Ross, L., & Nisbett, R. E. (1991). *The Person and the Situation: Perspectives of Social Psychology.* New York: McGraw-Hill.

Rowland, C. K., & Carp, R. A. (1996). *Politics and Judgment in Federal District Courts.* Lawrence: University Press of Kansas.

Rozin, P., & Royzman, E. B. (2001). Negativity bias, negativity dominance, and contagion. *Personality and Social Psychology Review, 5,* 296–320.

Rubin, E. (1997). Law and the methodology of law. *Wisconsin Law Review, 1997,* 521.

Ruger, T. W., Kim, P. T., Martin, A. D., & Quinn, K. M. (2004). The Supreme Court Forecasting Project: Legal and political-science approaches to Supreme Court decision making. *Columbia Law Review, 104,* 1150–1209.

Rumble, W. E. (1968). *American Legal Realism: Skepticism, Reform, and the Judicial Process.* Ithaca, NY: Cornell University Press.

Ryder, P., Pike, R., & Dalgleish, L. (1974). What is the signal in signal detection? *Perception and Psychophysics, 15,* 479–482.

Saks, M. J., & Kidd, R. F. (1980). Human information processing and adjudication: Trial by heuristics. *Law & Society Review, 15,* 123–160.

Sala, B. R., & Spriggs, J. F., II. (2004). Designing tests of the Supreme Court and the separation of powers. *Political Research Quarterly, 57,* 197–208.

Salthouse, T. A. (2005). Effects of aging on reasoning. In K. J. Holyoak & R. G. Morrison (Eds.), *The Cambridge Handbook of Thinking and Reasoning*. New York: Cambridge University Press.

Sampson, K. M., (Ed.). (2004). *Handbook for Judges: An Anthology of Inspirational and Educational Readings*. Chicago: American Judicature Society.

Sapiro, V. (1983). *The Political Integration of Women: Roles, Socialization, and Politics*. Urbana: University of Illinois Press.

Sarat, A. (1977). Judging in trial courts: An exploratory study. *Journal of Politics, 39*, 368–398.

Scalia, A. (1994). The dissenting opinion. *Journal of Supreme Court History, 1994*, 33–44.

Schaefer, W. V. (1960). Good judges, better judges, best judges. *American Judicature Society, 44*, 22.

Schaff, P. (1954). *The Life and Labors of St. Augustine* (T. C. Porter, Trans.). New York: J.C. Riker.

Schanzenbach, M. M., & Tiller, E. H. (2006). Strategic judging under the U.S. sentencing guidelines: Positive political theory and evidence. *Journal of Law, Economics, & Organization, 23*, 24–56.

Schauer, F. (1987). Precedent. *Stanford Law Review, 39*, 571–605.

Schauer, F. (1988a). Formalism. *Yale Law Journal, 97*, 509–548.

Schauer, F. (1988b). Judging in the corner of the law. *Southern California Law Review, 61*, 1717–1733.

Schauer, F. (1991). *Playing By the Rules: A Philosophical Examination of Rule-Based Decision-Making in Law and in Life*. Oxford: Clarendon Press.

Schauer, F. (1992). The practice and problems of plain meaning. *Vanderbilt Law Review, 45*, 715–741

Schauer, F. (2000). Incentives, reputation, and the inglorious determinants of judicial behavior. *University of Cincinnati Law Review, 68*, 615–636.

Schauer, F. (2008). Why precedent in law (and elsewhere) is not totally (or even substantially) about analogy. *Perspectives on Psychological Science, 3*, 454–460.

Schauer, F. (2009). *Thinking Like a Lawyer: A New Introduction to Legal Reasoning*. Cambridge: Harvard University Press.

Schauer, F. (2003). *Profiles, Probabilities, and Stereotypes*. Cambridge, MA: Harvard University Press.

Schauer, F. (2004a). The generality of law. *West Virginia Law Review, 107*, 217–238

Schauer, F. (2004b). Judicial supremacy and the modest constitution. *California Law Review, 92*, 1045–1067

Schauer, F. (2004c). The limited domain of the law. *Virginia Law Review, 90*, 1909–1956

Schauer, F. (2006a). Do cases make bad law? *University of Chicago Law Review, 73*, 883–918.

Schauer, F. (2006b). On the supposed jury-dependence of evidence law. *University of Pennsylvania Law Review, 155*, 165–202.

Scheb, J. M., II, & Lyons, W. (2001). Judicial behavior and public opinion: Popular expectations regarding the factors that influence Supreme Court decisions. *Political Behavior, 23*, 181–194.

Schick, M. (1970). *Learned Hand's Court*. Baltimore: John Hopkins Press.

Schlag, P. (1985). Rules and Standards. *University of California Law Review, 33*, 379–430.

Schlenker, B. R., & Pontari, B. A. (2000). The strategic control of information: Impression management and self-presentation in daily life. In A. Tesser,

R. B. Felson, & J. M. Sulls (Eds.), *Psychological Perspectives on Self and Identity.* Washington, D.C.: American Psychological Association.

Schroeder, T. (1918). Psychologic study of judicial opinions. *California Law Review, 6,* 89–113.

Schubert, G. (1962). Policy without law: An extension of the certiorari game. *Stanford Law Review, 14,* 284–327.

Schubert, G. (1964). The power of organized minorities in a small group. *Administrative Science Quarterly, 9,* 133–153.

Schubert, G. (1965). *The Judicial Mind: Attitudes and Ideologies of Supreme Court Justices 1946–1963.* Evanston, IL: Northwestern University Press.

Schuette, R. A., and Fazio, R. H. (1995). Attitude accessibility and motivation as determinants of biased processing: A test of the MODE model. *Personality and Social Psychology Bulletin, 21,* 704–710.

Schwartz, S., & Griffin, T. (1986). *Medical Thinking: The Psychology of Medical Judgment and Decision Making.* New York: Springer-Verlag.

Sears, D. O. (1986). College sophomores in the laboratory: Influences of a narrow data base on social psychology's view of human nature. *Journal of Personality and Social Psychology, 51,* 515–530.

Sears, D. O., Huddy, L., & Jervis, R. (Eds.). (2003). *Oxford Handbook of Political Psychology.* New York: Oxford University Press.

Segal, J. A. (1984). Predicting Supreme Court cases probabilistically: The search and seizure cases. *American Political Science Review, 78,* 891–900.

Segal, J. A. (1986). Supreme Court justices as human decision makers: An individual-level analysis of the search and seizure cases. *Journal of Politics, 48,* 938–955.

Segal, J. A. (1997). Separation-of-powers games in the positive theory of law and courts. *American Political Science Review, 91,* 28–44.

Segal, J. A., & A. D. Cover. (1989). Ideological values and the votes of U.S. Supreme Court justices. *American Political Science Review 83,* 557–565.

Segal, J. A., & Spaeth, H. J. (1993). *The Supreme Court and the Attitudinal Model.* New York: Cambridge University Press.

Segal, J. A., & Spaeth, H. J. (1994). The authors respond. *Law and Courts, 4,* 10–12.

Segal, J. A., & Spaeth, H. J. (1996). The influence of stare decisis on the votes of United States Supreme Court justices. *American Journal of Political Science, 40,* 971–1003.

Segal, J. A., & Spaeth, H. J. (2002). *The Supreme Court and the Attitudinal Model Revisited.* New York: Cambridge University Press.

Shah, J. Y. (2005). The automatic pursuit and management of goals. *Current Directions in Psychological Science, 14,* 10–13.

Shah, J. Y., & Kruglanski, A. W. (2000). The structure and substance of intrinsic motivation. In C. Sansone & J. M. Karackiewicz (Eds.), *Intrinsic and Extrinsic Motivation: The Search for Optimal Motivation and Performance.* San Diego: Academic Press.

Shanteau, J. (1992a). Competence in experts: The role of task characteristics. *Organizational Behavior and Human Decision Processes, 53,* 252–266.

Shanteau, J. (1992b). How much information does an expert use? Is it relevant? *Acta Psychologica, 81,* 75–86.

Shapiro, S. (1998). The difference that rules make. In B. Bix (Ed.), *Analyzing Law: New Essays in Legal Theory.* Oxford: Clarendon Press.

Shapiro, S. (2007). *The "Hart-Dworkin" Debate: A Short Guide for the Perplexed*. University of Michigan Public Law Working Paper No. 77.

Sherif, M. (1936). *The Psychology of Social Norms*. New York: Harper and Row.

Sherry, S. (2003). Judges of character. *Wake Forest Law Review, 38*, 793–812.

Sherry, S. (2005). Politics and judgment. *Missouri Law Review, 70*, 973–987.

Sherry, S. (2006). Logic without experience: The problem of federal appellate courts. *Notre Dame Law Review, 82*, 97–154.

Sherry, S. (2007). Democracy and the death of knowledge. *University of Cincinnati Law Review, 75*, 1053–1069.

Sherwin, E. (1999). A defense of analogical reasoning in law. *University of Chicago Law Review, 66*, 1179–1197.

Shoemaker, P. J. H. (1982). The expected utility model: Its variants, purposes, evidence, and limitations. *Journal of Economic Literature, 20*, 529.

Shullman, S. L. (2004). The illusion of devil's advocacy: How the justices of the Supreme Court foreshadow their decisions during oral argument. *Journal of Appellate Practice and Process, 6*, 271–293.

Simon, D. (1998). A psychological model of judicial decision making. *Rutgers Law Journal, 30*, 1–142.

Simon, D. (2002). Freedom and constraint in adjudication: A look through the lens of cognitive psychology. *Brooklyn Law Review, 67*, 1097–1139.

Simon, D. (2004). A third view of the black box: Cognitive coherence in legal decision making. *University of Chicago Law Review, 71*, 511–586.

Simon, D., & Holyoak, K. J. (2002). Structural dynamics of cognition: From consistency theories to constraint satisfaction. *Personality and Social Psychology Review, 6*, 283–294.

Simon, D., Krawczyk, D. C., & Holyoak, K. J. (2004a). Construction of preferences by constraint satisfaction. *Psychological Science, 15*, 331–336.

Simon, D., Krawczyk, D. C., Bleicher, A., & Holyoak, K. J. (2008). The transience of constructed preferences. *Journal of Behavioral Decision Making, 21*, 1–14.

Simon, D., Pham, L. B., Le, Q. A., & Holyoak, K. J. (2001). The emergence of coherence over the course of decision making. *Journal of Experimental Psychology: Learning, Memory, & Cognition, 27*, 1250–1260.

Simon, D., Snow, C. J., & Read, S. J. (2004b). The redux of cognitive consistency theories: Evidence judgments by constraint satisfaction. *Journal of Personality and Social Psychology, 86*, 814–837.

Simon, J. F. (1980). *Independent Journey: The Life of William O. Douglas*. New York: Harper & Row.

Simon, R., & Mahan, L. (1971). Quantifying burdens of proof: A view from the bench, the jury, and the classroom. *Law and Society Review, 5*(3), 319–330.

Simonson, I., & Staw, B. M. (1992). Deescalation strategies: A comparison of techniques for reducing commitment to losing courses of action. *Journal of Applied Psychology, 77*, 419–426.

Sisk, G. C., & Heise, M. (2005). Judges and ideology: Public and academic debates about statistical measures. *Northwestern University Law Review, 99*, 743–803.

Slotnick, E. E. (1979). Judicial career patterns and majority opinion assignment on the Supreme Court. *Journal of Politics, 41*, 640–648.

Slovic, P. (1969). Analyzing the expert judge: A descriptive study of a stockbroker's decision processes. *Journal of Applied Psychology, 53*, 255–263.

Smith, J. L. (2005). Patterns and consequences of judicial reversals: Theoretical considerations and data from a district court. *Justice System Journal, 27,* 28.

Snow, R. E., Kyllonen, P. C., & Marshalek, B. (1984). The topography of ability and learning correlations. In R. J. Sternberg (Ed.), *Advances in the Psychology of Human Intelligence* (vol. 2). Hillsdale, NJ: Erlbaum.

Snyder, E. C. (1958). The Supreme Court as a small group. *Social Forces, 36,* 232–238.

Solan, L., Rosenblatt, T., & Osherson, D. (2008). False consensus bias in contract interpretation. *Columbia Law Review, 108,* 1268.

Solum, L. B. (1988). The virtues and vices of a judge: An Aristotelian guide to judicial selection. *Southern California Law Review, 61,* 1735–1756.

Solum, L. B. (2003). Virtue jurisprudence: A virtue-centered theory of judging. *Metaphilosophy, 34,* 178–213.

Solum, L. B. (2005a). A tournament of virtue. *Florida State University Law Review, 32,* 1365–1400.

Solum, L. B. (2005b). Judicial selection: Ideology versus character. *Cardozo Law Review, 26,* 659–689.

Songer, D. R. & Haire, S. (1992). Integrating alternative approaches to the study of judicial voting: Obscenity cases in the U.S. Courts of Appeals. *American Journal of Political Science, 36*(4), 963–982.

Spaeth, H. J. (1964). The judicial restraint of Mr. Justice Frankfuter—Myth or reality? *Midwest Journal of Political Science 8*(1), 22–38.

Spaeth, H. J. (1979). *Supreme Court Policy Making: Explanation and Prediction.* San Francisco: W. H. Freeman.

Spaeth, H. J., and Segal, J. A. (1996). The influence of stare decisis on the votes of United States Supreme Court justices. *American Journal of Political Science, 40,* 971–1003.

Spaeth, H. J., & Segal, J. A. (1999). *Majority Rule or Minority Will: Adherence to Precedent on the U.S. Supreme Court.* New York: Cambridge University Press.

Spellman, B. A. (2004). Reflections of a recovering lawyer: How becoming a cognitive psychologist—and (in particular) studying analogical and causal reasoning—changed my views about the field of psychology and law. *Chicago-Kent Law Review, 79,* 1187–1214.

Spellman, B. A. (2007). On the supposed expertise of judges in evaluating evidence. *University of Pennsylvania Law Review PENNumbra, 156,* 1–9.

Spellman, B. A., & Holyoak, K. J. (1992). If Saddam is Hitler then who is George Bush? Analogical mapping between systems of social roles. *Journal of Personality and Social Psychology, 62,* 913–933.

Spellman, B. A., & Holyoak, K. (1996). Pragmatics in analogical mapping. *Cognitive Psychology, 31,* 307–346

Spiller, P. T., & Tiller, E. H. (1996). Invitations to override: Congressional reversals of Supreme Court decisions. *International Review of Law and Economics, 16,* 503–521.

Stangor, C. (2004).*Social Groups in Action and Interaction.* New York: Psychology Press.

Stainslaw, H., & Todorov, N. (1999). Calculation of signal detection theory measures. *Behaviour Research Methods, Instruments, and Computers, 31,* 137–149.

Stanovich, K. E. (1999). *Who is Rational? Individual Differences in Reasoning.* Mahwah, NJ: Lawrence Erlbaum Associates.

Starr, K. W. (2002). *First Among Equals: The Supreme Court in American Life*. New York: Warner Books.

Staudt, N., Friedman, B., & Epstein, L. (2008). On the role of ideological homogeneity in generating consequential decisions. *University of Pennsylvania Journal of Constitutional Law, 10*, 361.

Steblay, N., Dysart, J., Fulero, S., & Lindsay, R. C. L. (2001). Eyewitness accuracy rates in sequential and simultaneous lineup presentations: A meta-analytic comparison. *Law & Human Behavior, 25*, 459.

Stein, A. (2005). *Foundations of Evidence Law*. Oxford: Oxford University Press.

Stein, E. (1996). *Without Good Reason: The Rationality Debate in Philosophy and Cognitive Science*. Oxford: Clarendon Press.

Sternberg, R. J. (1999). The theory of successful intelligence. *Review of General Psychology, 3*, 292–316.

Stewart, T. R., Roebber, P. J., & Bosart, L. F. (1997). The importance of the task in analyzing expert judgment. *Organizational Behavior and Human Decision Processes, 69*, 205–219.

Stith, K. (2008). The arc of the pendulum: Judges, prosecutors, and the exercise of discretion. *Yale Law Journal, 117*, 1420.

Stone Sweet, A. (2002). Path dependence, precedent, and judicial power. In I. Shapiro & A. Stone Sweet (Eds.), *On Law Politics and Judicialization*. New York: Oxford University Press.

Suedfeld, P. (2000). Cognitive styles: Personality. In A. E. Kazdin (Ed.), *Encyclopedia of Psychology* (Vol. 2, pp. 166–169). Washington, DC and New York: American Psychological Association and Oxford University Press.

Suedfeld, P., & Tetlock, P. E. (2001). Individual differences in information processing. In A. Tesser & N. Schwarz (Eds.), *Blackwell International Handbook of Social Psychology* (pp. 284–304). Boston, MA: Blackwell Publishers.

Sullivan, K. M. (1992). The Supreme Court 1991 Term: The Justice of Rules and Standards. *Harvard Law Review, 106*, 22–123.

Sunstein, C. R. (1993). On analogy in legal reasoning. *Harvard Law Review, 106*, 741–789.

Sunstein, C. R. (1996). On the expressive function of law. *University of Pennsylvania Law Review, 144*, 2021.

Sunstein, C. R. (1996). *Legal Reasoning and Political Conflict*. New York: Oxford University Press.

Sunstein, C. R. (1999). *One Case at a Time: Judicial Minimalism on the Supreme Court*. Cambridge, MA; Harvard University Press.

Sunstein, C. R. (2000). Deliberative trouble? Why groups go to extremes. *Yale Law Journal, 110*, 71–119.

Sunstein, C. R. (2003). *Why Societies Need Dissent*. Cambridge: Harvard University Press.

Sunstein, C. R. (2005). *Radicals in Robes: Why Extreme Right-Wing Courts Are Wrong for America*. Cambridge, MA: Basic Books.

Sunstein, C. R. (2007). If people would be outraged by their ruling, should judges care? *Stanford Law Review, 60*, 155–212.

Sunstein, C. R., Hastie, R., Payne, J. W., Schkade, D. A., & Viscusi, W. K. (2002). *Punitive Damages: How Juries Decide*. Chicago: University of Chicago Press.

Sunstein, C. R., Schkade, D., Ellman, L. M., & Sawicki, A. (2006). *Are Judges Political: An Empirical Analysis of the Federal Judiciary*. Washington, DC: Brookings Institution Press.

Sunstein, C., & Ullman-Margalit, E. (1999). Second-order decisions. *Ethics, 110,* 5–26

Symposium. (2002). Expedited appeals in selected state appellate courts. *Journal of Appellate Practice and Process, 4,* 191–302.

Symposium. (2005). The behavioral analysis of legal institutions: possibilities, limitations, and new directions. *Florida State Law Review, 32,* 315.

Taber, C., & Lodge, M. (2006). Motivated skepticism in political information processing. *American Journal of Political Science, 50,* 755–769.

Taha, A. (2004). Publish or Paris? Evidence of how judges allocate their time. *American Law and Economics Review, 6,* 1.

Tajfel, H., & Turner, J. (1985). The social identity theory of intergroup behavior. In S. Worchel and W. Austin (Eds.), *Psychology of Intergroup Relations.* Chicago: Nelson-Hall.

Tate, C. N. (1981). Personal attribute models of the voting behavior of U.S. Supreme Court justices: Liberalism in civil liberties and economic decisions, 1946–1978. *American Political Science Review, 75,* 355–367.

Taylor, S. (2005, September 12). The Roberts court will decide. *Legal Times,* pp. 60–61.

Tetlock, P. E. (1983a). Cognitive styles and political ideology. *Journal of Personality and Social Psychology, 45,* 118–126.

Tetlock, P. E. (1983b). Accountability and the complexity of thought. *Journal of Personality and Social Psychology, 45,* 74–83.

Tetlock, P. E. (1985). Accountability: A social check on the fundamental attribution error. *Social Psychology Quarterly, 48,* 227–236.

Tetlock, P. E. (1986). A value pluralism model of ideological reasoning. *Journal of Personality and Social Psychology, 50*(4), 819–27.

Tetlock, P. E. (2000). Cognitive biases and organizational correctives: Do both disease and cure depend on the politics of the beholder? *Administrative Science Quarterly, 45,* 293.

Tetlock, P. E. (2002). Social functionalist frameworks for judgment and choice: Intuitive politicians, theologians, and prosecutors. *Psychological Review, 109,* 451.

Tetlock, P. E. (2005). *Expert Political Judgment: How Good is It? How Can We Know?* Princeton, NJ: Princeton University Press.

Tetlock, P. E., Bernzweig, J., & Gallant, J. L. (1985). Supreme Court decision making: Cognitive style as a predictor of ideological consistency of voting. *Journal of Personality and Social Psychology, 48,* 1227–1239.

Tetlock, P. E., & Mitchell, P. G. (1993). Liberal and conservative approaches to justice: Conflicting psychological portraits. In B. Mellers & J. Baron (Eds.), *Psychological Perspectives on Justice.* Cambridge, UK: Cambridge University Press.

Tetlock, P.E., & Mitchell, G. (Forthcoming). Implicit Bias and Accountability Systems: What Must Organizations Do to Prevent Discrimination? *Research in Organizational Behavior, 28.*

Tetlock, P. E., Skitka, L., & Boettger, R. (1989). Social and cognitive strategies for coping with accountability conformity, complexity, and bolstering. *Journal of Personality and Social Psychology, 57,* 632–640.

Thagard, P. (1989). Explanatory coherence. *Behavioral and Brain Sciences, 12,* 435.

Thagard, P. (1992). *Conceptual Revolutions.* Princeton: Princeton University Press.

Thagard, P. (2000). *Coherence in Thought and Action.* Cambridge, MA: MIT Press.

Thagard, P. (2006). *Hot Thought.* Cambridge, MA: MIT Press.

Thagard, P., & Kunda, Z. (1998). Making sense of people: Coherence mechanisms. In S. J. Read & L. C. Miller (Eds.), *Connectionist Models of Social Reasoning and Social Behavior*. Hillsdale, NJ: Lawrence Erlbaum.

Thagard, P., & Millgram, E. (1995). Inference to the best plan: A coherence theory of decision. In A. Ram & D. B. Leake (Eds.), *Goal-Driven Learning*. Cambridge, MA: Bradford Books.

Thaler, R. H. (1991). *Quasi Rational Economics*. New York: Russell Sage.

Thompson, W. C., Cowan, C. L., Ellsworth, P. C., & Harrington, J. C. (1984). Death penalty attitudes and conviction proneness: The translation of attitudes into verdicts. *Law and Human Behavior, 8*, 95–113.

Tindale, R. S., Meisenhelder, H. M., Dykema-Engblade, A. A., & Hogg, M.A. Shared cognition in small groups. In M. A. Hogg & R. S. Tindale (Eds.), *Blackwell Handbook of Social Psychology: Group Processes*. Malden, MA: Wiley-Blackwell.

Time Magazine. (1975, November 24). The Court's uncompromising libertarian, p. 69.

Tinsdale, R. S., Meisenhelder, H. M., Dykema-Engblade, A. A., & Hogg, M. A. (2000). Shared cognition in small groups. In M. A. Hogg & R. S. Tinsdale, (Eds.), *Blackwell Handbook on Psychology: Group Practices*. Malden, MA: Blackwell.

Toobin, J. (2007). *The Nine: Inside the Secret World of the Supreme Court*. New York: Doubleday.

Toward "Active Liberty": A Supreme Court Justice Offers a View from the Top. (2006, Spring). *Harvard Law Bulletin, 57*(14), 17.

Trumbo, D., Adams, C., Milner, M., & Schipper, L. (1962). Reliability and accuracy in the inspection of hard red winter wheat. *Cereal Science Today, 7*, 62–71.

Tushnet, M. (1992). Thurgood Marshall and the brethren. *Georgetown Law Journal, 80*, 2109–2130.

Tushnet, M. (2005). *A Court Divided: The Rehnquist Court and the Future of Constitutional Law*. New York: Norton.

Tversky, A., & Kahneman, D. (1974). Judgment under uncertainty: Heuristics and biases. *Science, 185*, 1124–1131.

Tversky, A., & Kahneman, D. (1982). Availability: A heuristic for judging frequency and probability. In D. Kahneman, P. Slovic, & A. Tversky (Eds.), *Judgment under Uncertainty: Heuristics and Biases*. Cambridge, UK: Cambridge University Press.

Twining, W. (1973). *Karl Llewellyn and the Realist Tradition*. London: Weidenfeld & Nicolson.

Tyler, T. R., & Huo, Y. J. (2002). *Trust in the Law*. New York: Russell Sage Foundation.

Tyler, T. R., & Mitchell, G. (1994). Legitimacy and empowerment of discretionary legal authority: The United States Supreme Court and abortion rights. *Duke Law Journal, 43*, 703–815.

Ulman, J. N. (1933). *A Judge Takes the Stand*. New York: Alfred A. Knopf.

Ulmer, S. S. (1971). *Courts as Small and Not So Small Groups*. New York: Basic Books.

Unah, I., & Hancock, A. M. (2006). U.S. Supreme Court decision making, case salience, and the attitudinal model. *Law & Policy, 28*, 295–320.

United States v. Locke, 471 U.S. 84 (1985).

United States v. Terry, 392 U.S. 1 (1968).

Vanberg, G. (2005). *The Politics of Constitutional Review in Germany*. New York: Cambridge University Press.

References 333

Vandevelde, K. J. (1996). *Thinking Like a Lawyer: An Introduction to Legal Reasoning.* Boulder, CO: Westview Press.

Vermeule, A. (2006). *Judging Under Uncertainty: An Institutional Theory of Legal Interpretation.* Cambridge, MA: Harvard University Press.

Vickers, A. L. (2005). Daubert, critique, and interpretation: What empirical studies tell us about the application of Daubert. *University of San Francisco Law Review, 40,* 109–147.

Volokh, A. (1997). N guilty men. *University of Pennsylvania Law Review, 146*(1), 173–216.

von Neumann, J., & Morgenstern, O. (1944). *Theory of Games and Economic Behavior.* Princeton, NJ: Princeton University Press.

Wachovia Bank, N. A. v. Schmidt, 126 S.Ct. 941 (2006).

Wahrman, R., & Pugh, M. D. (1972). Competence and conformity: Another look at Hollander's study. *Sociometry, 35,* 376–386.

Waldron, J. (2007). Temperamental justice. *The New York Review of Books, 54*(8), 15–17.

Walker, L., & Monahan, J. (2007). Sampling evidence at the crossroads. *Southern California Law Review, 80,* 969.

Walker, T. G. (1973). Behavioral tendencies in the three-judge district court. *American Journal of Political Science, 17,* 407–413.

Walker, T. G. (1974). The decision-making superiority of groups: A research note. *Small Group Research, 5,* 121–128.

Walker, T. G. (1976). Leader selection and behavior in small political groups. *Small Group Research, 7,* 363–368.

Wallsten, T. (1981). Physician and medical student bias in evaluating diagnostic information. *Medical Decision Making, 1,* 145–164.

Wambaugh, E. (1894). *The Study of Cases* (2nd ed.). Boston: Little, Brown.

Ward, A., and Weiden, D. L. (2006). *Sorcerers' Apprentices: 100 years of Law Clerks at the United States Supreme Court.* New York: New York University Press.

Ware, S. J. (1999). Money, politics, and judicial decisions: A case study of arbitration law in Alabama. *Journal of Law and Politics, 15,* 645.

Washington v. Glucksberg, 521 U.S. 702 (1997).

Wasserstrom, R. (1961). *The Judicial Decision: Toward a Theory of Legal Justification.* Stanford, CA: Stanford University Press.

Wazereud-Din v. Goodwill Homes and Mission, Inc., 737 A.2d 683 (N.J. Super. A.D., 1999).

Weber, H. J. (1979). The perfect judge. *Court Review, 17,* 11.

Wegener, D. T., & Petty, R.E. (1995). Flexible correction processes in social judgment: The role of naïve theories in corrections for perceived bias. *Journal of Personality and Social Psychology 68,* 36–51.

Weinreb, L. (2005). *Legal Reason: The Use of Analogy in Legal Argument.* New York: Cambridge University Press.

Wells, G. L. (1992). Naked statistical evidence of liability: Is subjective probability enough? *Journal of Personality and Social Psychology, 62,* 739.

WERL (Workshop on Empirical Research in the Law). (2004). On tournaments for appointing great justices to the U.S. Supreme Court. *Southern California Law Review, 78,* 157–79.

Wertheimer, W. (1923/1938). Laws in organization of perceptual forms. In W. D. Ellis (Ed.), *A Source Book of Gestalt Psychology.* London: Routledge & Kegan Paul.

West, A., Desdevises, Y., Fenet, A., Gaurier, D., & Heussaff, M. (1992). *The French Legal System*. London: Fourmat Publishing.

Whittington, K. E. (2000.) Once more unto the breach: Post-behavioralist approaches to judicial politics. *Law & Social Inquiry, 25,* 601–634.

Wickard v. Filburn, 317 U.S. 111 (1942).

Wilkerson, J. D. (1990). Reelection and representation in conflict: The case of agenda manipulation. *Legislative Studies Quarterly, 15,* 263–282.

Williams, F. V., III. (2007). Reinventing the courts: The frontiers of judicial activism in the state courts. *Campbell Law Review, 29,* 591.

Wilson, T. D., & Brekke, N. (1994). Mental contamination and mental correction: Unwanted influences on judgments and evaluations. *Psychological Bulletin, 116,* 117–142.

Windschitl, P. D., & Wells, G. L. (1996). Base rates do not constrain nonprobability judgments. *Behavioral & Brain Sciences, 19,* 40.

Winter, D. G. (2002). Motivation and political leadership. In L. O. Valenty & O. Feldman (Eds.), *Political Leadership for the New Century: Personality and Behavior among American Leaders*. Westport, CT: Praeger.

Winter, D. G. (2003a). Measuring the motives of political actors at a distance. In J. M. Post (Ed.), *The Psychological Assessment of Political Leaders*. Ann Arbor: University of Michigan Press.

Winter, D. G. (2003b). Personality and political behavior. In D. O. Sears, L. Huddy, & R. Jervis (Eds.), *Oxford Handbook of Political Psychology*. New York: Oxford University Press.

Wissler, R. L., Hart, A. J., & Saks, M. J. (1999). Decisionmaking about general damages: A comparison of jurors, judges, and lawyers. *Michigan Law Review, 98,* 751.

Wistrich, A. J., Guthrie, C., & Rachlinski, J. J. (2005). Can judges ignore inadmissible information? The difficulty of deliberately disregarding. *University of Pensylvania Law Review, 153,* 1251.

Wold, J. T. (1978). Going through the motions: The monotony of appellate court cecisionmaking. *Judicature, 62,* 58–65.

Wood, S. L. Keith, L. C., Lanier, D. N., & Ogundele, A. (1998). "Acclimation effects" for Supreme Court justices: A cross-validation, 1888–1940. *American Journal of Political Science, 42,* 690–697.

Wright, D. B., & Hall, M. (2006). How a "reasonable doubt" instruction affects decisions of guilt. *Basic and Applied Social Psychology, 29*(1), 85–92.

Wrightsman, L. S. (1999). *Judicial Decision Making: Is Psychology Relevant?* New York: Kluwer Academic.

Wrightsman, L. S. (2006). *The Psychology of the Supreme Court*. New York: Oxford University Press.

Wrightsman, L. S. (2008). *Oral Arguments Before the Supreme Court: An Empirical Approach*. New York: Oxford University Press.

Yarborough v. Alvarado, 124 S.Ct. 2140 (2004).

Yates, J. F. (1990). *Judgment and Decision Making*. Englewood Cliffs, NJ: Prentice-Hall.

Yuille, J. C., & Cutshall, J. L. (1986). A case study of eyewitness memory of a crime. *Journal of Applied Psychology, 71,* 291–301.

Index

Note: The letter "n" following locators refers to notes.